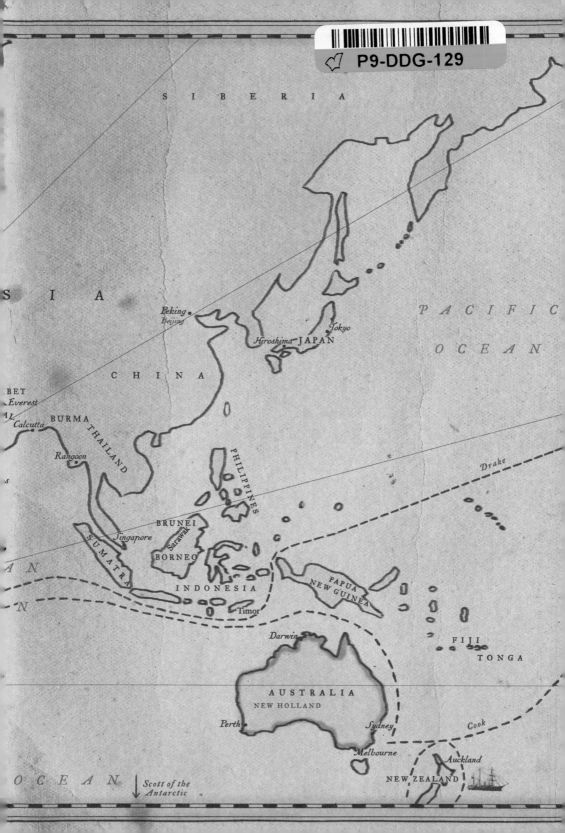

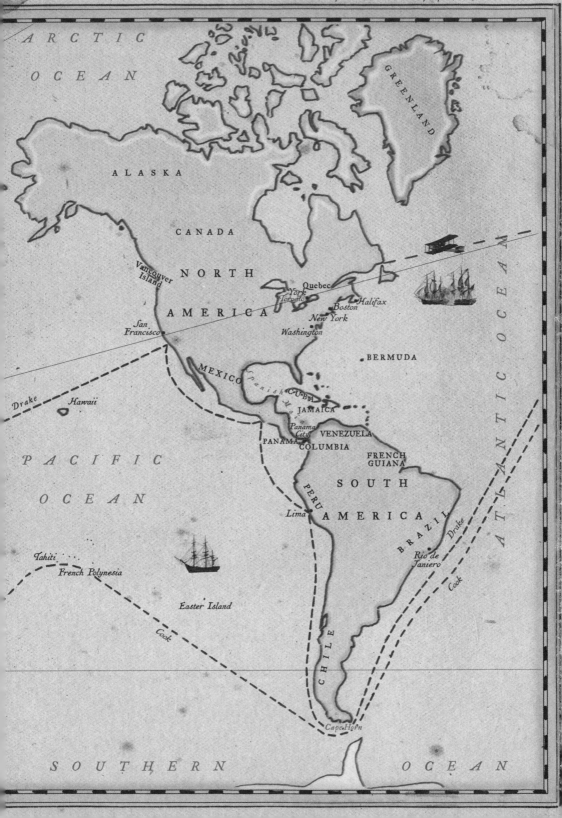

ARCTIC OCEAN

GREENLAND

ALASKA

CANADA

NORTH

Vancouver
Island

AMERICA

Quebec
York
Toronto
San
Francisco

Boston
New York
Washington

Halifax

BERMUDA

MEXICO

Spanish M.

CUBA

JAMAICA

Drake

Hawaii

Panama
City
PANAMA

VENEZUELA

COLUMBIA

FRENCH
GUIANA

PACIFIC

SOUTH

OCEAN

PERU

AMERICA

BRAZIL

Lima

ATLANTIC OCEAN

Drake

Tahiti

Rio de
Janiero

French Polynesia

Cook

Easter Island

Cook

CHILE

Cape Horn

SOUTHERN   OCEAN

About the Authors

Born in London, Conn Iggulden read English at London University and worked as a teacher for seven years before becoming a full-time writer. He is the author of the bestselling Emperor series and Conqueror series and co-author of *The Dangerous Book for Boys*. Conn lives in Hertfordshire with his wife and their children. Visit his website at www.conniggulden.com.

David Iggulden served as a deck officer in the Merchant Navy and a private in the Army Reserves, before reading Journalism and English at Charles Sturt University, Australia. He has since worked as a journalist, press officer and projects manager, and published several non-fiction books. He has been part of many international adventures, including In The Footsteps of Scott Expedition, the First Fleet Re-enactment and the 2000 Olympic Games. David lives in the Blue Mountains, Australia.

The illustrations in *The Dangerous Book of Heroes* were done by Graeme Neil Reid. To see more of his work go to www.gnreid.co.uk.

BY CONN AND HAL IGGULDEN

The Dangerous Book for Boys
The Pocket Dangerous Book for Boys: Things to Do
The Pocket Dangerous Book for Boys: Things to Know
The Pocket Dangerous Book for Boys: Facts, Figures and Fun
The Pocket Dangerous Book for Boys: Wonders of the World
The Dangerous Book for Boys Yearbook

BY CONN IGGULDEN:

The Emperor series

The Gates of Rome
The Death of Kings
The Field of Swords
The Gods of War

The Conqueror series

Wolf of the Plains
Lords of the Bow
Bones of the Hills

Blackwater

The DANGEROUS Book of

HEROES

HarperCollins*Publishers*

HarperCollins*Publishers*
77–85 Fulham Palace Road,
Hammersmith, London W6 8JB

www.harpercollins.co.uk

Published by HarperCollins*Publishers* 2009
1

A catalogue record for this book
is available from the British Library

ISBN: 978 0 00 726092 8

Printed and bound in Great Britain by
Clays Ltd, St Ives plc

Mixed Sources
Product group from well-managed
forests and other controlled sources
www.fsc.org Cert no. SW-COC-1806
FSC © 1996 Forest Stewardship Council

'People who lose their history, lose their soul.'
– Australian Aboriginal saying

In memory of John Hall and John Hunt,
who in their different ways, lived life to the full.

Contents

Introduction

There is a moment in some lives when the world grows still and a decision must be made. Robert Clive knew it when the Indian sun rose and he saw the huge army he had to defeat at Plassey, camped within shouting distance. Lisa Potts knew it when she decided to go outside one more time to rescue children from a machete-wielding maniac. At such moments, *there is no one to save you*. The decision is yours alone.

The heroes in this book are from a variety of centuries. They are British and Empire and Commonwealth first and last. That constriction was no hardship, as it left a gold-bearing seam of hundreds of wonderful, inspiring lives. When we were boys, we thought Hillary and Tenzing *were* British – certainly our father saw no distinction to be made when he talked of them conquering Everest.

We have not gone too far back into history – so no Boadicea, though Hereward the Wake and the Magna Carta barons are in. We've avoided the stories of monarchs, saints and scientists. Once started, those would easily fill a book to the exclusion of all else. Politicians too have not made the cut, with the exception of men like Wellington, Churchill and Cochrane, who deserve their place for other reasons. There must be an element of choice in compiling such a book. No collection of heroes can be utterly definitive and there will always be too little space for every great tale. Courage is perhaps the first requirement for inclusion here. Courage, determination and some dash.

Some of the heroes in this book are more rogue than angel – and one or two are absolute devils. Yet in their brief existence they showed what can be done with a life, one single span of decades in the light. We have not judged them by modern standards. They would have scorned such a judgement.

When you tire of humanity's flaws, perhaps you will read a few chapters and be reminded that we can also be inspiring. Fortune played its part, of course, but there was always that moment when the world fell still and the searchlights of Colditz drifted silently across the yard. They did not falter then – and their lives should be known to all.

– Conn and David Iggulden

'And I tell you, if you have the desire for knowledge and the power to give it physical expression, go out and explore. If you are a brave man you will do nothing: if you are fearful you may do much, for none but cowards have need to prove their bravery. Some will tell you that you are mad, and nearly all will say: "What is the use?" For we are a nation of shopkeepers, and no shopkeeper will look at research which does not promise him a financial return within a year. And so you will sledge nearly alone, but those with whom you sledge will not be shopkeepers: that is worth a good deal.'

The Worst Journey in the World,
Apsley Cherry-Garrard, 1922

Sir Ranulph Fiennes

Through obsession, daring and sheer talent, the men and women in this book often achieved extraordinary things. They saved India, escaped from Colditz, climbed Everest and even defeated Napoleon. There is a reason for including such lives that goes beyond a collection of 'ripping yarns from history'. In this day and age, it is all too easy to become mired in paying the mortgage, being promoted, filling the hours with hobbies and anything else we can find. There is a place for such things, of course – we cannot all climb Everest.

When disaster strikes, each of us is capable of courage and quiet dignity. Yet somehow, it is harder to do so without these stories and others like them. Men and women alike take strength from the courage of Edith Cavell or the insane recklessness of James Wolfe, Charles Napier or, indeed, Ranulph Fiennes. Put simply, their lives help us to endure the hard times. As Prince Charles once said: 'My admiration for Ranulph Fiennes is unbounded and thank God he exists. The world would be a far duller place without him.'

Ranulph Twisleton-Wykeham-Fiennes was born in Windsor on 7 March 1944. His father commanded the Royal Scots Greys Regiment in World War II and died without seeing his son. In fact, Ranulph Fiennes's first claim to fame was being the youngest posthumous baronet in existence.

His first years were spent in South Africa, in idyllic surroundings. He ran around with a gang of local lads, sometimes carrying bamboo spears. They took it in turns to throw them at each other, protected by a dustbin lid.

In 1952, Fiennes was sent as a boarder to Western Province Preparatory School. When he won the Divinity prize, he was so pleased he decided briefly to become a priest. That dream fell in pieces when he was taken to see a film on the ascent of Mount Everest in 1953. Given the man he became, it is not fanciful to suggest that the film shaped his life.

The following year, his mother took the family home to England, drab and grey to a boy who had known the suns of South Africa. She rented a small cottage and he was sent to board at Sandroyd School near Salisbury. After a miserable start, he grew to love his time there, though mathematics was always a particular challenge. He found that his classmates would listen to stories based in South Africa and he charged them squares of chocolate to hear them. He formed a gang named the Acnuleps (Latin for 'cave' spelled backwards) who signed their rules in blood, as boys tend to do. They went on to fight another gang, which led to the leaders being caned and the gangs disbanded.

After prep school, Fiennes went to Eton, where he was bullied and made thoroughly miserable. It is interesting to consider the old myth that the British Empire was won on the playing fields of Eton. The implication is of fair play and teamwork, but there may be an underlying truth. Boys' private schools can be hellish places, but those who survive them are rarely worried by any other difficulty in later life.

At Eton, Fiennes made the boxing team and learned to love history. He was thrilled at news of Edmund Hillary's expedition to the South Pole. At 16, he was diagnosed with rheumatic fever and told to rest for six months. He spent part of that golden spring and summer learning to make explosives in a gardener's shed at home.

Back at school, he moved up to light-heavyweight boxing and he and a friend began to climb the school buildings at night, despite the threat of expulsion for anyone caught. One night they successfully left a toilet seat and a dustbin lid on the summit of the school hall, but on another occasion they were discovered sitting on a roof. Fiennes got away without being caught, but his friend was found and questioned by the headmaster. As it turned out, the Head had been a keen climber in his youth and was more interested in their methods than in punishment.

After Eton, Fiennes joined the Royal Scots Greys tank regiment in 1963. He trained in Germany on 70-ton Centurions. At six foot two, he had grown to the point where he could box in the heavyweight division. He also joined the cross-country running team, the ski team and formed a canoe club. Under his supervision, the men would regularly paddle a hundred miles a day. To Scots, his name was pronounced 'Feens' and they described it as 'Mr Feens's Concentration Camp'.

From the Scots Greys, he applied to join the SAS. To prepare, he trained alone in the Brecon Beacons and took a parachuting course. The highest peak in the Brecons is Pen-y-Fan, and one part of the training was to run up and down it three times in eight hours. Another unusual part of SAS training was planning and carrying out a bank raid in Hereford. To his great embarrassment, he managed to leave the plans in an Italian restaurant. They were handed to the police and the plans reported in newspapers around the country. Despite that incident, Fiennes passed the famously harsh training and specialised in demolitions.

His career with the SAS came to an abrupt end in 1966. A friend of his told him about a film set in Castle Combe, Wiltshire. 20th Century Fox were about to begin shooting *Dr Dolittle* and had built sets and a twenty-foot-high concrete dam in the area, ruining the peace of an ancient English village. Fiennes agreed to help destroy the dam and also to tip off an ex-SAS man named Gareth Jones who had become a journalist. Instead, Gareth Jones told the *Daily Mirror* and they called the police. With explosives and detonators, Fiennes went in darkness to Castle Combe, unaware that police cars were waiting for him. His own car was an ancient and unreliable Jaguar, which he parked nearby and then walked in across the fields.

Unseen, he and two friends laid explosive charges as well as petrol flares on timers to lure away the film company's security men. As they lit the fuses, the night was shattered by police with dogs. The dam was destroyed in the explosion that followed, but the trap had been sprung.

Interestingly, Fiennes had been trained to avoid exactly this sort of capture. He submerged himself in the river and made his way in darkness back to his waiting car. However, it wouldn't start without a tow, so he was stuck. Things were not looking good for the escape when a police car came up and parked next to it. Trying to brazen it out, Fiennes asked the policemen if they would help him start his car. He was arrested.

For his efforts that night, Fiennes was expelled from the SAS and demoted from captain to second lieutenant. He rejoined the Scots Greys and became engaged to his childhood sweetheart, Virginia 'Ginny' Pepper, before travelling with his regiment to Oman in Arabia. He took part in active fighting there and won the Sultan's Medal for bravery. At the same time, he was looking ahead to a life after the army, hoping to make his later career with exploration and record-breaking. On leave, he made preparations for an expedition to follow the Nile from the mouth, near Alexandria, to the source, 2,000 miles south. He assembled a group of like-minded adventurers and used Land Rovers and hovercrafts to reach the source successfully, following in the footsteps of earlier adventurers like Richard Francis Burton. The Nile trip would be the first of many such expeditions.

After his tour in the army ended, he needed to earn money and a chance came with an advance to write a book on the Nile expedition. Fiennes wrote it in six weeks, while his fiancée researched the history. It was his first experience of publishing. His plan was to make a living through expeditions and writing about them. However, his drive to travel and explore meant he and Ginny separated for a time, as he did not seem ready to marry.

Alone again, Fiennes joined 'R' Squadron of the Territorial Army, who acted as reinforcements for the SAS in time of war. The physical tests were the same as for the SAS and he passed the gruelling ordeal. At the same time, he set about assembling a team for an expedition to Norway. The plan was to freefall and parachute from a small Cessna plane onto Europe's highest glacier. The *Sunday Times* referred to it as 'The World's Toughest Jump' and paid to cover the event.

Fiennes was first out of the plane and quickly reached terminal velocity of 120 mph before pulling his ripcord and making a safe

landing in the drop zone. The rest of
the team came down in two runs, and
from a safe base, they began to climb
and survey the area. A storm came in
and almost killed them, but they survived
to get down. His career as a renowned explorer had begun in earnest.
Ten days after his return to England, he married Ginny.

In the early 1970s, he was asked to audition for the part of James
Bond. Producer Cubby Broccoli said he had a face and hands like a
farmer and chose Roger Moore instead. It's interesting to speculate how
different the films would have been with Fiennes as the hero. Instead,
he took part in unmapped river expeditions across British Columbia,
where he survived rapids and moose stew. The BBC accompanied him
to make a documentary, which was better paid than finding sponsors,
but he was unhappy with the final programmes, as they portrayed
him as both cruel and incompetent. Yet the audiences were eight
million for each episode, and he actually found sponsors easier to find
afterwards.

To supplement his income, Fiennes began to give lectures. He wrote
about the Canadian experience and for years planned what would
become one of his most famous exploits, the attempt to circumnavigate
the world around both poles. The 'Transglobe Expedition' of 52,000
miles would last from 1979 to 1982 and lead to Fiennes and Charlie
Burton being the first men to reach both poles overland.

In most lives, that single achievement would have been enough to
make him what the *Guinness Book of Records* once called 'the greatest
living explorer'. Yet other, more astonishing events were still to come.
Fiennes continued to write, uniquely qualified to produce a biography
of Robert Falcon Scott's tragic race to the South Pole. His life had
brought him fame and he travelled around the world to give lectures.
He took a job for a time with Occidental Petroleum, an echo of Douglas
Bader's post-war occupation, but it was always with an eye to planning
the next great expedition.

In 1992, he discovered the lost city of Ubar in Oman, previously
believed to be a myth. He went on to make the first unsupported crossing

of the Antarctic continent on foot. He endured heat and cold and continued to demonstrate what a human being can do in extremes.

In 2000, he was involved in a solo, unsupported attempt to walk to the North Pole. Disaster struck when his sledge fell through the ice and he suffered frostbite in his fingers trying to pull it out. He had known this danger before and found that windmilling his arms restored circulation, but on that occasion it didn't work. His fingertips had frozen solid. The attempt had to be abandoned and by the time he came home, the first joints of all the fingers on his left hand had died. Amputation was the only answer, but his surgeon wanted to wait for five months to allow as much skin as possible to recover. Fiennes found the pain of jarring the fingertips excruciating and decided to cut them off in his toolshed. His first attempt with a hacksaw was too slow and agonising, so he used a Black & Decker fretsaw. Strangely enough, Black & Decker have yet to use this in their advertising. He also lost a toe to frostbite; it came off in the bath and he put it on the side and forgot about it until his wife found it still lying there.

In 2003, Fiennes had a heart attack and endured a double bypass operation. Months later, he wanted to raise money for the British Heart Foundation and planned a series of seven marathons in seven days on seven continents. At the time, he asked his doctors whether such activity would put too much strain on his heart. They replied that they had no idea – no one had ever tried such a thing before. In November of that year, he completed all seven with his running partner, Mike Stroud.

In 2005, he came to within a thousand feet of the peak of Everest. He tried again in 2008, aged 64, but bad weather and exhaustion overcame him.

One of the strangest things about him is that despite the similarities to other heroes in this book, Fiennes is always understated, softly spoken and modest about his achievements. He is certainly a man driven to push himself to extraordinary lengths, to such a degree that he becomes not so much an inspiration as a force of nature. His attitudes to trials and hardship are a pleasant antidote to some of the touchy-feely aspects of modern society. In short, he is not the sort of man for whom the 'compensation culture' caters. We do need such men, if only to highlight the silliness of some of the other sort.

Recommended
Living Dangerously and *Mad, Bad and Dangerous to Know* by Ranulph Fiennes.

Robert Clive

It is only when we look back on history that it seems inevitable. How could the Greek nations *not* triumph over Persia? How could the survival of Rome ever have been in doubt against Hannibal? Yet at the time, those involved could not have had our confidence. The future would have been a distant blur of hope and prayers, with only courage, strength and sharp wits to save it.

At times, a key battle made the difference, as at Marathon, Hastings or Waterloo. In other eras, a small number might wrench an entire people onto a new course, as when King Charles I was executed and Cromwell brought democracy to England. These too could have failed. History is written in water as it happens, then paper, then at last, stone.

In the centuries behind our own, there are also single lives that have changed the history of the world. It can be a choice on a single day, or even a pistol that misfired. The life of Robert Clive was one of those. Without him, Britain would have lost India to the French and there would have been no Empire. Without the wealth of India, there may well have been no Industrial Revolution – and without that, the world would be a very different place today.

Robert Clive was born in 1725 in Shropshire, the eldest of thirteen children. He was an unruly youth, well known to the people of Market Drayton, where he gathered a group of schoolmates and terrorised the town, blocking drains and demanding money from shopkeepers if they did not want their windows smashed. The moment he was 18, he was put aboard a ship bound for India to be a clerk for the British East India Company. His family and neighbours were pleased to be rid of him.

The British East India Company (also known as John Company) was a private entity that existed to trade in the subcontinent. As far back as 1668, Charles II had given them Bombay on the west coast, once part of the dowry of his Portuguese wife, Catherine of Braganza. The Company maintained their own army and made alliances with Indian princes without the interference of the British government. Like the Portuguese and Dutch before them, the French also had a trading company in India, though it was far less influential.

When Clive arrived in Madras on the south-east coast, the surrounding country was relatively quiet. In theory, it was a perfect place to send a difficult and impatient young Englishman. However, Clive hated his new work, finding it dull and oppressive. He was given to fits of depression and at the age of 19, in 1744, he decided to end it all. He took a pistol from his locker, held it to his forehead and pulled the trigger. It misfired. Shaken, but still determined, Clive pulled the trigger once more. For the second time, it misfired and he stood staring at it. Another clerk happened by at that moment. Clive handed him the gun and said: 'Fire it out of the window, would you?' The clerk aimed and the pistol fired perfectly, the shot echoing across the garden.

Clive wondered if he had been spared for a reason, saying: 'I feel that I am reserved for some end or other.' He was right: his life would alter the future of India.

In Europe, war had broken out between France and Britain over the Austrian succession. It was inevitable that the mercantile interests of those two countries would also come into conflict, though the British did not appear to consider the danger in India until the French attacked. In 1744, Joseph Dupleix, governor of French settlements in India, decided the time was right to force the British out of the subcontinent once and for all.

After hostilities had simmered for two years, the first major attack on a British settlement was by Bertrand de la Bourdonnais, the French governor of Mauritius, in September 1746. As well as landing an army, French ships bombarded Madras for three days in September 1746. Taken by surprise, the British surrendered and began negotiations to pay a ransom for the settlement. However, Dupleix wanted power rather than wealth, so he refused to ratify the agreement. Instead, he had the English governor, Nicholas Morse, dragged through the local bazaars in chains. Morse and other officers were then taken to Pondicherry, a French stronghold. After seeing this, Clive abandoned his counting house with another clerk named Edmund Maskelyne and escaped to Fort St David, some twenty miles away. There, he accepted a commission in the Company army as an ensign.

At Fort St David, an incident occurred that established Clive's reputation for reckless daring. He played cards in the evenings with other Company men, one of whom was a well-known bully and duellist. Clive lost several hands to the man and became convinced he was being cheated. Clive stood up and snapped, 'You have cheated, sir, and I'm damned if I'll pay you!' His accusation could only be answered by a duel and pistols were brought. The two men faced each other and Clive fired first, missing. The man could have fired at him, but instead he put his pistol to Clive's head, saying: 'Withdraw or I fire.' Without hesitation, Clive replied: 'Fire and be damned. I say you cheated and say so still. I'll never pay you.' The man was staggered by this display of wild courage. He threw down the pistol and walked away. This story became famous across India.

As well as direct conflict, French and British forces enlisted local princes to their cause, aiming to have their choices installed in key positions, such as the Nawab of the Carnatic coast. Treaties and alliances were made, then broken. Though a large British force arrived in 1748 and laid siege to Pondicherry, the attack was poorly led and ended in near disaster. One of the very few men who distinguished himself there was Clive.

Nearby, the Carnatic capital city of Arcot was given into the hands of Murzafa Jung, who supported the French. Another prince declared Dupleix 'Nawab of southern India'. Deals were struck and allies betrayed or assassinated, with Dupleix coming out well ahead in the diplomatic game. For a time, the future of the British in India looked as if it might go the way of the Dutch and Portuguese, leaving the French in complete political control of the subcontinent.

In 1750, after a time running the civilian commissariat for the Company and making a small fortune, Clive re-enlisted as captain.

He had never seen a full battle, though Major Stringer Lawrence had noted Clive during an earlier attack on Devi Kotal, where Clive was one of three survivors out of thirty. Lawrence described Clive as 'a man of unprecedented resolution ... he behaved in courage and judgement much beyond what could have been expected from his years.'

When Clive came up with a plan to take Arcot back from French control, his superiors agreed to let him try. He set off with eight officers, 200 British and 600 sepoys, or native soldiers. At Conjeveram, he learned that the Arcot garrison was a thousand strong. He sent back for

— 11 —

two eighteen-pounder guns, but then with typical brashness, pushed on without them. Incredibly, he arrived at Arcot in the midst of a violent tropical storm that terrified and paralysed the Indian garrison. Clive and his men strode up to the gates regardless. Seeing this, the garrison became convinced that the British forces were under supernatural protection. They abandoned Arcot and Clive took possession of a fortress city of 100,000 inhabitants without a single shot being fired.

When Dupleix heard about this daring snatch of a city, he detached 10,000 men from the siege of Trichinopoly with orders to take Arcot back for France. They assaulted the position for fifty days. Clive's men responded neither to bribes nor to threats and his native soldiers were impressed by his fortitude and courage. When food was running out inside the fortress, they offered to consume only rice-water so that he and the British soldiers would live longer.

The attacks built to a climax on the fiftieth day, when an assault was mounted with armoured elephants. At that point, Clive found an unexpected ally in a local Mahratta chief, Morari Rao. Morari Rao had been impressed by the bravery and discipline of the defenders as he viewed them from hills around the city. With the help of the Mahrattas, that final attack was smashed. Clive's soldiers shot at the elephants and stampeded them through the enemy. The Franco-Indian forces abandoned the siege, leaving Clive triumphant and his fame assured. After Arcot, he was known to Indian forces as 'Sabat Jung', or 'Daring in War'. Prime Minister Pitt the Elder described him as a 'heaven-born general' and in later years, when 1,500 British administered an Indian nation of 300 million, they took it as a name for themselves: 'the heaven-born'.

Clive waited four days to be relieved, then sallied out after the retreating enemy. At Arni, he fought his first set-piece battle with only 300 men. They destroyed a French and Indian force, capturing 700 French sepoys, whom Clive promptly enrolled in his own force. With Major Lawrence, he went on to a series of stunning victories against French-held fortresses. Clive had found his calling.

In 1753, his health deteriorated in fevers, and his sporadic bouts of depression became worse. His time running the Company commissariat had brought in a personal fortune of £50,000, a huge sum. Financially secure for the first time in his life, he married Margaret Maskelyne, the sister of the clerk with whom he had escaped Madras seven years before.

On leave, Clive came back to England a famous and wealthy man, which must have surprised those who remembered him. He paid his father's debts and rebuilt his family home. He had come a long way from the young fool who dangled from the roof of St Mary's church in Market Drayton, pretending to be a gargoyle.

Clive spent most of the £50,000 in just eighteen months, some of it in an unsuccessful attempt to enter Parliament. Running low on money again, he signed up with the Company to return to India. He and his wife sailed back in 1756, leaving two infant sons to be cared for by relatives.

By 1756, Dupleix had fallen from favour and was recalled to France without a pension, where he later died in poverty. In comparison, Clive's star was still on the rise. He returned with the rank of lieutenant colonel in the Company army and became governor of Fort St David. Rather than sit idle, one of his first actions was to burn out a nest of pirates with Admiral Watson. That action won both men £5,000 in prize money and loot. Clive was solvent once more.

Meanwhile, India was still in turmoil. In June 1756, the Nawab of Bengal, Suraj-ud-Daula, attacked the British colony at Calcutta when it was fortified against him. There were only 280 badly armed defenders, seventy of whom were ill. Against them was an army of 50,000, which included French mercenaries and cannon. Though the British force fought valiantly, they were overwhelmed when a Dutch sergeant opened a gate to the besiegers. Calcutta fell.

At eight o'clock that night, 145 British men and one woman were pressed into a room only eighteen feet by fourteen. In the intense heat, they were crowded so tightly that even when a man died, he remained upright in the press. Some slashed their wrists to drink blood and others sucked sweat from their shirts. Without water, more than a hundred perished before dawn, leaving only twenty-three survivors. It has been known ever after as the Black Hole of Calcutta. Suraj-ud-Daula is recorded as saying 'A pair of slippers is all that is needed to govern the English.' It would fall to Clive to avenge the British dead.

When the terrible news reached Madras in August, Clive immediately prepared an expedition to retake Calcutta. Under his command, 900 British troops joined the British fleet under Admiral Watson. Storms delayed the ships, but they reached the coast of Bengal in January 1757 and fought their way past local forts upriver to Calcutta.

One odd victory at Budge-Budge fort came when a sailor named Strahan climbed into a hole made by the British ships in the small hours of the morning. Completely inebriated, he fired his pistol and flourished his sword at the astonished defenders, roaring that the place was his. Strahan's friends heard his cry and followed him in through the breach. Four of them took wounds in the struggle, but by dawn, the fort was indeed theirs. Strahan was later reprimanded for drunkenness by the admiral. As he was marched out of the admiral's presence, he remarked, 'If I am flogged for this action, I will never take another fort by myself as long as I live.'

Clive's army retook Calcutta with little difficulty. The British warship fired rounds into the city and the occupying garrison fled after only a brief response.

Suraj-ud-Daula responded by marching on Calcutta with his main army of 18,000 cavalry, 22,000 infantry, fifty elephants and forty field guns. Clive had only 470 men of the 39th Regiment, 800 sepoys, 600 sailors and just seven guns. With those, Clive moved to attack. The first contact took place in a white dawn mist that left them all blind. Clive's men encountered the Nawab's own bodyguard and they fought savagely as the mists began to lift. As soon as they were visible, Clive's force came under heavy fire and he and his men fought a running battle before withdrawing. His losses were heavy: 57 killed and 134 wounded. He would discover later that the Nawab's force had lost more than a thousand killed and wounded in that brief skirmish. Clive's men may have been vastly outnumbered, but they were also the best in India. Even against overwhelming numbers, they could hold formation, manoeuvre and pour death and destruction into their enemies. They never broke and ran. The 39th Regiment later took 'Primus In Indis', or 'first in India', as their motto.

Suraj-ud-Daula's confidence was severely shaken. He signed a peace treaty in February 1757, agreeing to all British demands, but continued to plot for their destruction. In the days that followed, Clive proved the Machiavellian master of a complex game of letters, spies, double agents, broken treaties, bribery and threats. Through Clive's machinations, 2,000 of the Nawab of Bengal's men went over to the British and the Nawab was confused by a forged dispatch he was allowed to capture. He swore again to exterminate the British. Yet he and Clive continued to exchange letters of mutual support and duplicity. Clive informed Suraj-ud-Daula that half the British force had marched back to Calcutta, while he actually prepared for another battle. He also forged Admiral Watson's signature on a false treaty designed to lull Suraj-ud-Daula into complacency. Clive had never been a man to give up the least advantage to his enemies. He was not a great believer in playing by the 'rules' of war. Instead, he played to win – ruthlessly and without regard for his own life or those around him.

Eventually, the complex manoeuvres, lies and tricks brought the two opposing forces together. The village where the battle took place was called Palasi, known to the British as Plassey.

As well as around 50,000 infantry and cavalry, Suraj-ud-Daula had amassed 53 field guns, this time commanded by expert French gunners. Clive had no cavalry. He still had 600 of the 39th, as well as 2,100 sepoys and another hundred Anglo-Indians of mixed blood. Accompanying them were just ten field guns and two small howitzers. He hoped to see the defection of more of Suraj-ud-Daula's forces to even the odds and had secretly approached the Nawab's own uncle, Mir Jaffa. Mir Jaffa had sent a positive reply, sewn into a silk slipper. The stakes could not have been higher. Clive knew very well that if he lost at Plassey, the entire future of the British in Bengal, perhaps the whole of India, would be affected.

On the hot and humid morning of 23 June 1757, Clive climbed on a roof to observe the enemy. The ground was wreathed in mist and he could smell the cooking fires of the Nawab's huge force, camped within calling distance. He moved his men out from the village in battle order, and the French gunners opened fire immediately. Clive's men ran for cover behind mud banks, but forty were killed or wounded in that first attack. However, they were then effectively immune to the French guns while their own cannon tore bloody strips through the enemy army. The Nawab's artillery commander was killed by a British cannonball and without his leadership, his men lost their nerve and ceased firing. Suraj-ud-Daula fought on for a time, but his army was beginning to waver under the cannon fire as he sent desperate messages to his commanders. Unaware of the deal Clive had struck with his uncle, Suraj-ud-Daula pleaded with Mir Jaffa to save his honour and his life. Mir Jaffa promised he would, but then sent a messenger to Clive, promising support.

Clive's guns pounded the forces of Suraj-ud-Daula until midday, when a downpour of rain began. The British force protected their ammunition with tarpaulins, but the enemy failed to take similar precautions and their guns became useless. Effectively disarmed, Suraj-ud-Daula's men began a desperate retreat at three that afternoon. Clive was delighted and ordered his entire force into the attack.

Mir Jaffa's wing of 16,000 tried to join the approaching British line, but was fired upon by Clive's sepoys, who knew nothing of the secret plans. Unable to join Clive, Mir Jaffa withdrew his men from the battle and waited it out. In the face of British fire, Siraj-ud-Daula climbed onto a camel and deserted the field. He did not stop riding until he was back home at Murshidabad and was later murdered by his own people.

After their commander had deserted them, it took only two more hours to rout the rest of the Nawab's army.

As there was very little hand-to-hand fighting, Clive's losses were just twenty British, fourteen sepoys and thirty-six wounded. The Nawab's army lost around 500 killed or wounded. However, Clive had captured all the enemy cannon, routed an immense force and broken the last chance for French dominance in India. That single battle was won as much by Clive's deals and chicanery as martial skill, but it is one of those rare moments, like Marathon, Hastings and Waterloo, where the future of the entire world hung on a single day and a single man.

Clive established Mir Jaffa as Nawab of Bengal and accepted 'gifts' in return that eventually led to him being the subject of a parliamentary inquiry in Britain. He said of this part of his life: 'A great prince was dependent on my pleasure ... I walked through vaults which were thrown open to me alone, piled on either hand with gold and jewels! By God, Mr Chairman, at this moment I stand astonished at my own moderation!'

He did use some of his wealth to form a pension fund for disabled officers and also to have another run at political office. On that occasion, he was successful and became Member of Parliament for Shrewsbury. In 1762, he was made Baron Clive. As a man who made enemies *far* more easily than friends, it was quite an achievement.

He had long been subject to depression and the exact manner of his death is still disputed. He died on his own and whether it was a heart attack, a deliberate overdose, or one of the more scandalous rumours, like cutting his own throat, can never be known. He was 49 years old. His body was buried in haste by his family, almost before the ill-wishers could begin dissecting his memory.

He is remembered today as the man who saved British India and as victor against the most overwhelming odds ever faced in battle. Plassey is his victory and India his headstone.

Recommended
Clive: The Life and Death of a British Emperor by Robert Harvey.
The Honourable Company: A History of the English East India Company by John Keay.

Dr Bruce Hunt

Singapore was burning.

Greasy black smoke from bombed and shelled oil tanks outside the city drifted above the low rooftops. Smoke from the city itself, from burned-out buildings, markets and docks, rose to join the murk and create a canopy of stifling heat. From RAF Changi in the east of the island, from Kallang airport, from the Royal Naval base in the north, from Fort Canning and from the nearby oil islands, more smoke spiralled into the heavy tropic air, telling the story of one of the worst ever defeats of British arms.

Prime Minister Churchill had given an order to fight on against the invading Japanese, but on 15 February 1942, Lieutenant General Percival surrendered unconditionally to Lieutenant General Yamashita. Some 85,000 Australian, British, Indian and other forces were ordered to lay down their weapons to a Japanese force of about 30,000. In the following month, Japanese soldiers beheaded prisoners of war in front of the cricket pavilion on the Padang, raped nurses in the hospitals, bayoneted patients in their beds, and murdered 5,000 to 50,000 Chinese Singaporeans. No one will ever know the exact figure, because the Japanese destroyed the records when they were defeated three and a half years later.

Caught in this disaster was Major Bruce Atlee Hunt, volunteer doctor of the Australian Army Medical Corps. It wasn't his first taste of war but, comparing that tropical experience with his time on the Western Front in the 1914–18 war, he must have been bemused by the speed and the scale of the debacle.

From an immigrant family from Hayes in Middlesex, Bruce Hunt was born in Melbourne on 23 February 1899. One day after his eighteenth birthday in 1917, he joined the Australian Army. There was no conscription in Australia; it was volunteers only, so he volunteered.

Hunt trained as a gunner in the 8th Field Artillery Battery and found himself in the mud of Belgium and France. He was made sergeant in early 1918, in charge of a horse-drawn eighteen-pound field gun team. That spring the battery was involved in the defence of Amiens, playing its part in stopping the last German advance of the war. In August 1918 the Hundred Days Battle began, when the Anzacs, British and Canadians broke through the German trenches. Attacking in battle after battle, from France into Belgium, by November they'd pushed the German armies back to Mons, where it had all begun in 1914. Sergeant Hunt's gun team moved north and east in that last great advance, defeating Germany and ending the war.

That victory became a defining time in Bruce's life for another reason. He caught the influenza which swept the world in 1919, killing 20 million people, more than had died in the four years of world war. He was in hospital in Kent for almost a year, where the care of an English doctor saved his life and inspired him to become a doctor himself. After demobilisation from the army, Bruce remained in Britain until 1920 to complete a University of London pre-medical course.

On his return home, he completed his degree in medicine and surgery and followed with his doctorate in medicine. He married Maedhail Harper in 1927. Maedhail suffered from diabetes, so Bruce specialised in the treatment of diabetes, as well as of heart and lung diseases. They sailed to Britain in 1928 for further experience, where Hunt was admitted as a Member of the Royal College of Physicians.

Maedhail and Bruce had two children before world war again intruded. In 1939, he joined the Royal Australian Air Force Reserve as a doctor, but in 1941 transferred to the Army Medical Corps and was promoted to major. Hunt was sent to the defence of Singapore, in reality the defence of Australia. He was 42 years old.

After the fall of Singapore and imprisonment in Changi prison, Major Hunt volunteered in April 1943 to go north with F-force to the Siam–Burma railway. Building of this railway had begun in June 1942 with successive 'forces' of Australian, British and Dutch prisoners of war. The Japanese told F-force it was going to a Red Cross convalescent camp. Hunt told them: 'You will encounter diseases you have never heard of and I fear for the future.'

The new railway would link the existing line at Ban Pong in Siam (Thailand) with the line in Burma. The route passed over the mountains by the valley of the River Kwai Noi, crossing the border at Three Pagodas Pass. Thus Singapore, Hanoi and even Korea would be joined to Rangoon by rail, providing a supply route to the Japanese army in Burma for the invasion of India. The existing sea route through the China Sea and the Indian Ocean was severely disrupted by British submarines operating from Ceylon and West Australia.

The 258-mile railway had been surveyed twice before by British engineers. Each time the proposal had been rejected because of the dangers. The Siamese called one stretch 'Death Valley'. Under Japanese engineers the whole route became known as the Death Railway.

F-force comprised 3,666 Australians and 3,334 British, under overall command of Lieutenant Colonel 'Taffy' Harris. From the terminus at Ban Pong, the men marched for 186 miles to a camp at Konkoita, a fortnight carrying Japanese stores and their own meagre possessions. There, they were quartered next to Asian workers forced to work on the railway as slave labour. To the prisoners' malaria, dengue fever, running sores, tropical ulcers and other jungle fevers was soon added cholera. It was not long before some thirty men were dying every night.

F-force was distributed among five work camps to construct the railway on either side of the border at Three Pagodas Pass. That stretch of the railway was the most isolated and had the worst conditions. When the senior doctor fell ill, Bruce Hunt became Senior Medical Officer.

The camps were in low, tumbled mountains of greens and misty blues. The River Kwai Noi, swift and brown in the valley below, looped from Burma down to the sea. The jungle was not dank and dark green like Malayan jungle, but a drier scrub, a jungle of thin trees, thickets of dense brush and thorny bamboo that ripped open the prisoners' arms and legs. In the wet monsoon the red earth turned to thick, sucking mud, and the dirt roads were often impassable. There was nowhere to escape to and no contact with anyone. There was only gasping heat, monsoon rains, and the sweating Japanese and Korean guards.

Every morning before sunrise, the prisoners of war were paraded for work details. These invariably included sick men forced from the hospital huts by the guards, and so would begin a desperate argument between Hunt and the Japanese as he tried to shield his patients. Well-built, tall, with hairy shoulders and the strength of a bull, he protected the sick and wounded by his sheer presence. Sometimes only a few of the sick were forced to work on the railway; at other times all the patients had to go, whether they were supported or carried, or even on stretchers. A sick man on a stretcher could still hold a spike while another POW swung the hammer. For his stubborn resistance, Bruce was often beaten by the guards.

He wrote about one beating: 'At the time scheduled for the parade, I fell in the thirty-seven men in two batches [malaria and infected feet]. Major Wild [British army interpreter] and I stood in front of them. The corporal approached with a large bamboo in his hand and spoke menacingly to Major Wild, who answered in a placatory fashion. The corporal's only reply was to hit Major Wild in the face. Another guard followed suit and as Major Wild staggered back the corporal thrust at the Major's genitalia with his bamboo. I was left standing before the patients and was immediately set upon by three guards. One tripped me while two others pushed me to the ground. The three men set about me with bamboos, causing extensive bruising of the skull, hands and arms, and a fractured left five metacarpal bone. After I was disposed of, the corporal then made the majority of the 27 foot-sufferers march with the rest of the troops.' Bruce added: 'Most of these men, including an Australian chaplain, died during succeeding weeks, largely as a result of this calculated brutality.'

There were few medicines available and the era of antibiotics such as penicillin came after the war. Bruce and the other doctors were forced to improvise. Petrol cans and fuel lines stolen from abandoned lorries were transformed into stills to produce saline solution from cooking salt and boiled water. Beer bottles or paraffin tins and stethoscope tubes became the saline dispensers, while bamboo thorns were used as needles for intravenous drips. Water containers, crutches, artificial legs, beds, hospitals, instrument containers, even bedpans, were fashioned from the hollow bamboo. A Japanese bicycle was used as a centrifuge to produce blood plasma from prisoners' donations. Nevertheless, life-saving amputations still had to be carried out without anaesthetic and using a wooden saw. Often there wasn't even an aspirin.

Bruce Hunt visited all the camps of F-force, British as well as Australian. He organised cholera isolation huts, inoculated when vaccine was available, provided treatment, and spoke to the prisoners privately and in camp addresses. When they grew slack in their hygiene he called them 'a pack of bastards!' and they cheered him. Englishman Bill Holtham remembers the tall Aussie doctor sitting with dispirited soldiers. 'Bruce Hunt would plead with those who'd given up to eat their meagre rice rations. "Remember your wife, remember your children back home," he'd say to them. Sometimes, if that didn't work, he'd punch them, hard. That often worked.'

Another doctor, Glyn White, wrote: 'He repeatedly and fearlessly approached the Japanese army authorities in attempts to obtain some alleviation of the conditions of the sick.' Sometimes, he was even listened to. Lieutenant Wakabyashi was one of the very few camp commanders who did listen. At Bruce's urging, a hospital camp was built at Tanbaya and here Bruce Hunt moved 1,900 patients, six doctors and ten assistants.

Usually, however, his arguments fell on deaf ears. 'He stood up to the Japanese on our behalf time and again, knowing he would be punished for it,' recalled one Australian.

'Once, they crushed his hand because he protested about his men being put into huts that cholera patients had been in.'

Syd Marshall said: 'When it would mean likely death for a man to leave the hut called a hospital, Bruce Hunt just said no and awaited his punishment, day by day.' 'He stood like an avenging angel between the Nips and us when we were sick,' said another. 'Later he made light of it, but we know what we saw.' Over time, every finger in both of Hunt's hands was broken by the Japanese.

When cholera struck, Hunt played upon Japanese fear of the disease and their fear of the 'loss of face' that would result from slower work when their POW and Asian slaves died. Using these arguments, he wheedled vaccines from the Japanese. He'd wait for the POWs in the dark on their return from work, attend to their wounds, dress their injuries and ensure they sterilised their mess gear before drawing their water and rice rations. Bruce had always enjoyed gambling and he was ready to sit down for a game of cards with anyone. He'd wager extra cleaning duties and hospital and repair details.

The main killers along the Death Railway were cholera, beriberi, pellagra, dysentery, malaria, pneumonia, enteritis, tropical ulcers – and malnutrition, brutality, torture and murder by the Japanese and Korean guards.

Bruce was told by a camp commander: 'You are not our equals; you are our inferiors ... Some Japanese will die in the making of this railway. POWs will also die. You have spoken of the Geneva Convention and humanity. In present circumstances these things do not apply.'

One can argue that war is illogical, nonsensical, and therefore to apply rules to how it is fought is equally illogical. Yet surely any law introduced to reduce the barbarity and cruelty of war is worthwhile. That the Japanese destroyed most of the incriminatory records when they realised they would be defeated confirms their knowledge of their guilt.

The Japanese army also referred to its own Bushido Code to explain its brutality, torture and murder of prisoners of war, a code in which a Japanese soldier should commit ritual suicide rather than surrender. Any soldier who does not is dishonoured and thus all prisoners of war are viewed as men without honour, the lowest of the low. However, when Emperor Hirohito surrendered Japan on 15 August 1945, he absolved his soldiers, sailors, airmen and himself from the obligation of ritual suicide. You can't have it both ways.

As well as the 61,811 prisoners of war building the Death Railway, there were also 300,000 civilian labourers from the invaded countries. Voluntary recruitment of Chinese, Tamils, Malays, Burmese and Indians was tried but with little success, so they were captured and forced to work alongside the servicemen. Siam was an ally of Japan and so few Siamese were used. Similarly, no French were on the railway, as they were nominal allies of Japan. Bletchley Park intelligence revealed that France had agreed to the Japanese invasion of French-controlled Vietnam, Cambodia and Laos, and the French there were well treated.

The conditions for Asian labourers were just as bad. I-force and K-force were created by the POWs to provide medical help to the Asian camps but, without military discipline and hygiene, their effectiveness was greatly reduced.

The POWs kept notes of mistreatment and deaths, hiding the records in graves for recovery after the war. According to the Hellfire Pass Memorial in Thailand, 12,399 POWs died building the Death Railway, while the death toll of Asian labourers is somewhere between 70,000 and 90,000.

Against cholera, there was little doctors could do when there was no vaccine, although many lives were saved by massive saline transfusions to counter the dehydration. The beer bottle, stethoscope and bamboo drips came into their own. Yet almost half of F-force deaths were from cholera. The dead were burned to help prevent the spread of the disease.

One POW remembers: 'The jungle itself had a primitive force and the sense it created of closing in was overawing, if not actually demoralising. The never-ending downpour, the filthy mud, the whole gamut of disease and the grossly inadequate rations all eroded the will to get things done, but not with Bruce. If he felt these influences they never showed – and he got things done.'

Hunt regularly left camp, a haversack across his naked shoulders, foraging for medicines and food from nearby villages, from the jungle, from the Japanese themselves. On his return, he would hide his pickings, report to the Japanese commander and, usually, be beaten for leaving camp. With his medics and volunteers he reduced the death rate from disease and injury, yet in F-force, working in the worst conditions, 45 per cent still died – 1,060 Australians and 2,036 British. Dr Hunt thought the comparatively poor childhood diet of the British soldier was the major cause of their higher death rate.

Suffering himself from beriberi, a disease caused by vitamin deficiency from the appalling food, Bruce carried out operations while lying in his sickbed. Eventually he succumbed completely and, in November 1943, was bedridden with acute cardiac distress. By then, however, the railway had been completed.

The pressure on the POW and Asian labourers was over. No more cries of 'Speedo! Speedo!' from the guards as they beat prisoners with bamboo clubs and kicked them with their boots. The struggle of eighteen-hour workdays was at last ended, but for every railway sleeper laid, a man had died.

Lieutenant Norman Couch reckoned that Bruce Hunt saved hundreds, perhaps a thousand, Australian and British lives on the railway. 'He was the dominant figure, the driving force, the metaphorical star to which men in peril looked for guidance ... Major Hunt's Burma Line leadership success stemmed from his personal attributes which made him a giant among all men in that soul-destroying environment.' When someone in camp said 'The major's back' no one needed to ask which major.

The whole horror finally ended in August 1945, when Japan surrendered after the dropping of the hydrogen bombs on Hiroshima and Nagasaki. Without that sudden surrender, half a million or more Allied soldiers, sailors and airmen would have died in the liberation of South East Asia, as well as the million or more Japanese who would have died defending Japan.

The emotion of that 1945 August was recalled by POW Fred Seiker: 'I remember the feeling of triumph that swept over me. I had done it! I had outlived all attempts by Hirohito and his murdering freaks to kill me. But, above all else, I could say "no" again to anything and anyone. It is called democracy and freedom. Believe me, it is worth fighting for. The present and the generations to come around our world must be made aware of this so they can guard their birthrights with all their might.'

As for the Death Railway, the section across the border through Three Pagodas Pass was dismantled by Britain in 1947. A dam covers much of the northern Thailand route, so that now only eighty-one miles remain from Ban Pong to Nam Tok. It can never be reconnected. In 1996, however, a Japanese company proposed rebuilding as much as possible and marketing it as a tourist attraction...

In Japan, former members of the two railway regiments involved continue to regard the railway as a triumph and celebrate it each year. It is difficult to understand why, from any viewpoint. As an engineering achievement it was poor. In the original Japanese survey, the section built from Burma would have missed alignment with the section built from Siam by more than half a mile. One bamboo bridge, nicknamed by POWs 'the Pack of Cards', collapsed three times before an alternative route was built.

Of course, some credit for this must go to the POWs, who carried out subtle and discreet sabotage. During the railway's operation, derailments were common, bridges and trestles collapsed, embankments were washed away and constant maintenance was required to keep the line open. Instead of the planned 3,000 tons per day, the railway could carry only 1,000 tons, and the section in Thailand had to be virtually rebuilt in the 1950s to meet Thai Railway standards.

As a human achievement it was a disaster. In addition to the 100,000 and more Asians and POWs killed, the Japanese lost 1,000 of their own. If Australian or British regiments lost 1,000 men constructing 250 miles of railway there would be courts martial, not annual celebrations.

Without the doctors, qualified assistants and unqualified volunteers, there would have been many more deaths. Alex Kelly of the RAAF wrote: 'All our doctors were good ... Bruce Hunt had as much form as any other doctor, probably more so because the heat was on much harder on his force than it was down in the railway cutting ... Bruce had all that to go through to fill working parties, to stand over the Japs, to get better conditions, all that sort of thing.' In his tribute Lieutenant Kelsey wrote: 'To this camp God sent Bruce Hunt with two junior medical officers [Captains John Taylor and Frank Cahill] ... I think of Bruce every day of my life.'

Like most POWs, Hunt took many years to recover from the Death Railway – if he ever did. Recurring nightmares are one of the features of the survivors' lives and Bruce suffered those for years, as well as malaria and permanent heart damage. He had left Maedhail in 1941 weighing fourteen stone; he returned to her in 1945 weighing seven stone. It was a common story for most POWs from the Death Railway. Bruce received a citation for 'Highly meritorious service as a Prisoner of War'. Quieter and grey-haired, with scars upon his head, he returned to medicine in Western Australia.

He was awarded the MBE and in 1951, during further medical studies in London, was elected a Fellow of the Royal College of Physicians. Later, he became president of the Western Australian branch of the British Medical Association and was a constant support to Western Australian ex-POWs. In Australian newspapers, Hunt was often referred to as 'the fiery doctor from the West'. No doubt the Japanese had another name for him. He died in October 1964, aged 65.

His understated appraisal of the horror of the Death Railway, originally broadcast on Singapore Radio in 1945, is displayed in the Hellfire Pass Memorial. He said: 'In a reasonably varied experience of two wars, I have on many occasions seen men tried up to and beyond the limits of reasonable human endurance. I would say that F-force was of all these occasions the most searching test of fundamental character and guts that I have ever known. That so many men – British and Australian – came through this test with their heads high and their records unblemished is something of which we of the British race may be not unreasonably proud.'

Recommended
The Knights of Bushido by Lord Russell of Liverpool.
The Burma–Siam Railway: The Secret Diary of Dr Robert Hardie by Robert Hardie.
The Colonel of Tamarkan: Philip Toosey and the Bridge on the River Kwai by Julie Summers.
Heroes of F Force by Don Wall.
Thailand–Burma Railway Museum, Kanchanaburi, Thailand.
The Australian War Memorial, Canberra, Australia.
The Imperial War Museum, London.

Hereward the Wake
and the Rebels of Britain

In a time when the Romano-Britons and Anglo-Saxons of England were disinherited and suppressed by the Norsemen or Vikings from Normandy, outlaw Hereward the Wake's resistance in the Fens of Anglia became a national symbol of liberty and freedom.

When King Harold was defeated at the Battle of Hastings in October 1066 by William of Normandy, Hereward was abroad in Flanders. That absence possibly saved his life, for Harold would have used Hereward at Hastings. Even then, he was known as a fearsome wielder of the Saxon broadsword and the axe.

Little is known about Hereward's early life. The ballads say he was banished by his father from his home at Bourne, in Lincolnshire, because of high spirits and fighting. His parents were perhaps Leofric and Lady Godiva of Coventry. In the years after 1062, Hereward wandered through Northumbria, Cornwall and Ireland before reaching Flanders, where he married the comely Turfrida.

He is mentioned by name in Flemish histories and the battles in the ballads did take place. What is also true is that after Hastings, Hereward returned home to find his father dead, his brother beheaded and his lands seized by the Normans.

The Domesday Books list Hereward as a Lincolnshire landowner in 1066. He held a small estate of fifty acres north of Bourne, and was tenant of four separate lands held by Peterborough and Crowland abbeys. He was a man of status in Harold's England and was probably a thane, a lower order of Saxon nobleman.

Disinherited and discontented, Hereward the Wake resisted the disaster of the Norman conquest. He slew at least one Norman usurper, the brother-in-law of William de Warenne, and became the focus of other rebellious Englishmen in Lincolnshire and Cambridgeshire. He was also a friend of the abbot and monks of Peterborough Abbey. However, it was the arrival of a Danish fleet in the spring of 1070 which lit the fuse of Hereward's revolt.

The new King of England, by then calling himself William the Conqueror, descended from the Vikings of Denmark. Part of his claim to the English throne came through the wife of Anglo-Danish King Canute (1016–35), so a treaty with the Danes for their fleet to winter in warmer England was not surprising – though the English hoped that King Sweyn II of Denmark had plans of his own for England. The Danes also had no love for their Norman cousins with their French manners and habits.

Encouraged by Sweyn, the arrival of the Danish ships in the River Humber roused the English to revolt. William responded with speed and harshness, crushing one uprising after another. North of the Humber, the Normans laid England to waste, burning hamlets and villages, sacking churches and halls, even burning the food stores so that famine followed that winter. It's remembered as the Harrowing of the North. Quickly and brutally the rebellions were suppressed – except in the Fens.

In 1070, the bay called the Wash brought the North Sea much further into England than it does now – west to Peterborough, south to Cambridge and east to Thetford Forest, deep into the counties of Lincolnshire, Cambridgeshire and Norfolk. There were 2,000 square miles of deep-water channels, shallow ditches, low-lying islands, marshes and rich wetlands. Treacherous with quicksand, the few sodden paths disappeared beneath seeping tides and sudden sea surges; horses and riders simply vanished in the Fens. At night, through the mists, the 'Fen Nightingale' could be heard, the eerie croaking of wetland frogs.

When Danish ships reached the River Ouse in the north of the Fens, the people rose in rebellion. At the same time, high rents, taxes and excommunications by Turold, the new Norman Abbot of Peterborough, caused a revolt by the abbey's tenants. Hereward led this revolt and joined the Danes and the Fen people. They based themselves on the almost inaccessible Isle of Ely, one of the strange islands deep in the Fens. Ely monastery became his stronghold, one of the most isolated places in Britain.

In 1070, Hereward led an attack on Peterborough Abbey. The outlaws and the Danes sailed their small ships to Peterborough, overran the monks and took the town and the monastery. The monks' houses were burned and the abbey sacked. When Abbot Turold approached with 160 soldiers – effectively a small army in those days – the outlaws withdrew in their ships to Ely.

The Anglo-Saxon Chronicle of 1071 records that 'Hereward and his crew … went away with so many treasures as no man may tell another, saying that they did it from love of the monastery.' Monk Hugh Candidus in his history of the abbey also wrote that this was the reason for the raid. Another account says that the monks called on Hereward to stop Abbot Turold from stealing the treasures of the abbey himself. That would certainly account for the token resistance of the monks.

Meanwhile, King William and King Sweyn made peace and the Danes abandoned Ely to return to Denmark with most of the abbey treasure. Hereward fought on in the Fenlands against the hated Normans. Soon, his was the only major resistance in the whole of England and his fame grew.

On the other side of the kingdom a smaller rebellion did continue. The Welsh Marches – borderlands between England and Wales – was a bandit country of rock, hills and dense forests, in which Edric the Wild led a band of English outlaws. As this revolt was gradually crushed by the Norman barons, one of the outlaws, Godfrew, escaped from the Marches, crossed England and joined the uprising in the Fens.

Other disaffected English joined Hereward in Ely, including Morcar, Earl of Northumbria, and even the English Bishop of Durham, Aethelwine. For a year, the revolt in the Fens continued, the outlaws carrying out raids on wealthy Normans, much like the ballads of Robin Hood 150 years later. Hereward became a hero to the downtrodden Saxons, many of whom were virtually slaves to the Normans. The liberties and land ownership of the Saxon freeman system had been replaced by the feudal system imposed from Europe.

Norman attempts to reach the Isle of Ely and defeat the rebels failed. Fighting in the Fens was difficult and the outlaws lured Norman soldiers and horsemen to their deaths in the marshes and quicksand. Finally, in the summer of 1071, King William himself led a small army to the Fens, established camp at Cambridge and attacked Ely.

He first built a floating wooden causeway across the wetlands to Hereward's stronghold. As the Norman soldiers advanced along the swaying planks, they were attacked by Hereward and his men. First came the arrows out of the mist, then the English outlaws themselves leapt onto the causeway. Lightly clad in woollen shirts, leather jerkins and soft hide shoes, the outlaws overwhelmed the cumbersome armoured soldiers. Many Normans drowned in the Fens and, according to the ballads, many were slain by Hereward's own sword, the mighty 'Brain Biter'. The causeway was destroyed.

The ballads report that William also tried witchcraft to frighten the English, but Hereward set fire to the dry summer reeds and grasses growing above the waters. The flames and choking smoke drove William's men back.

William then laid siege to Ely until a traitor, possibly a monk from the monastery, guided the Normans through the marshes and William's soldiers at last reached the isle. It was quickly over. Morcar, Aethelwine and many more surrendered 'and the king took their ships, weapons, and treasures, and all the men, and did with them what he would.' Which was death for the leaders, imprisonment for some, while others were freed with their hands cut off or their eyes put out.

Hereward the Wake escaped that fate. With loyal and faithful followers 'he led them out valiantly' from the Isle of Ely to again elude the Normans. His passage through the marshes with his companions is confirmed by several chronicles of the time. The failure of William to slay or even capture Hereward only added to the legends.

What happened to Hereward after his dramatic escape is not certain. The historical records and romantic ballads both state he survived, most saying he died in his bed and was buried at Crowland in Lincolnshire. One Norman account says he was murdered in 1073 by jealous knights, but not before he had slain fifteen with Brain Biter. Every account agrees that he was pardoned and reconciled with King William, which is supported by entries in the Domesday Book. The 1086 records state that Hereward conferred the title for much of his land on Oger the Breton, who also held the manor of Bourne. This suggests that Hereward survived and was pardoned, or his lands would not have been his to pass on. There was a tradition of forgiving worthy and respected foes.

Possibly as a result of Hereward's revolt, soon there were Norman plans for the Fens. A sixty-mile earthwork was constructed across the Wash as a barrier against the North Sea and enemy ships, but it was another 650 years before most of the Fens were drained. In the 1200s there still remained deep in the Fens the ruins of a wooden fortress known as Hereward the Wake's Castle.

There are two explanations of why Hereward was called 'the Wake'. The earliest again connects Hereward with the manor of Bourne which, after Oger's death, was held by a family named Wake. The ballads say that Hereward's family held Bourne earlier and so we have Hereward the Wake. A later explanation from the mid-1200s suggests that 'the Wake' means 'the watchful one'.

Hereward was also called the 'Last of the English' because he led the last English resistance against the Norman invasion. In another way he is the 'First of the British', for he led the first resistance against the European feudal system and loss of liberty. A century later, in King John's reign of 1199–1216, even the barons and nobles were sick of the excesses and abuses of their Norman king. The barons began their own revolt against John, the second resistance against the feudal system.

One baron, Fulke Fitz Warrin of Herefordshire, was dispossessed of his lands and property and outlawed by King John. As Hereward had taken to the Fens, so Fitz Warrin took refuge in the Welsh Marches, waging rebellion while living off the king's deer. Fitz Warrin was joined by other outlaws and victims of the king's oppression, including his brother John, an immensely tall man. John became the lieutenant of the band.

It's possible that Fulke Fitz Warrin's outlaw days are the origin of the legends of Robin Hood. The first written record of Robin Hood is by the Welsh Marches poet William Langland in 1370, while one of the earliest tales is that Robin was the outlawed Earl of Huntingdon, Robert Fitzooth. There are many similarities between the Robin Hood ballads, the exploits of Hereward the Wake and the exploits of Fulke Fitz Warrin. There is a Huntingdon in Herefordshire and there is also a Huntingdon in the Fens, not far from Nottingham. Fulke Fitz Warrin eventually regained his lands and was one of the barons who supported King John's signing of Magna Carta in 1215.

With Hereward begins the long and dramatic British tradition of rebellion against loss of liberties and the fight for freedom against oppressive governments and their laws. In fiction there is Robin Hood, Ivanhoe, Black Arrow; in fact there is Hereward the Wake, Fulke Fitz Warrin, David Llewyllen and Rob Roy. In effect, it is the beginning of the struggle for the modern rights of man.

Recommended
The Anglo-Saxon Chronicle.
The Domesday Book.
Hereward the Wake by Charles Kingsley.
The Chronicle of Hugh Candidus, a Monk of Peterborough edited by W.T. Mellows.
'*Hereward the Outlaw*' by John Hayward.
'*Hereward "the Wake" and the Barony of Bourne: a Reassessment of Fenland Legend*' by D.R. Roffe.

Captain Sir Richard Francis Burton

<hr />

Richard Francis Burton was born in 1821. Victoria came to the throne in 1837, when he was just 16, so he was in some ways the archetypal Victorian scholar-adventurer. In his life, he was a soldier, a spy, a tinker, a surveyor, a doctor, an explorer, a naturalist and a superb fencer. As an undercover agent, he was instrumental in provinces of India coming under British control, playing what Kipling called 'The Great Game' with skill and ruthlessness. In recent times, Burton was one of the inspirations of Harry Flashman in the books by George MacDonald Fraser.

Burton spoke at least twenty-five languages, some of them with such fluency that he could pass as a native, as when he disguised himself as an Afghan and travelled to see Mecca. He spent his life in search of mystic and secret truths, at one point claiming with great pride that he had broken all ten commandments. In that at least, he was not the classic Victorian adventurer at all. Like Clive before him, Burton always went his own way. When he was asked by a preacher how he felt when he killed a man, he replied: 'Quite jolly, how about you?'

At various points in his life, he investigated Catholicism, Tantrism, a Hindu snake cult, Jewish Kabbalah, astrology, Sikhism and Islamic Sufism. He was convinced that women enjoy sexual activity as much as men, a very unfashionable idea in Victorian England. He enjoyed port, opium, cannabis and khat, which has a priapic effect. He was six feet tall, very dark and devilishly handsome, with a scar from a Somali spear wound on his cheek that seemed only to add to his allure. In short, he was a romantic and a devil, a dangerous man in every sense.

After Richard was born, his parents moved to France in an attempt to ease his father's asthma. Two more children were born to them there: Maria and Edward. Richard showed a remarkable facility for languages from an early age, beginning Latin at the age of three and Greek the following year.

The two boys were also taught arms as soon as they could hold a sword. They thrived on rough play, and around the age of five, knocked their nurse down and trampled her with their boots. They fought with French boys and were constantly beaten by their father, but to little effect. Their tutor took all three children to see the execution by guillotine of a young French woman. This did not produce nightmares, however, and the children later acted out the scene with relish.

At the age of nine, Richard used his father's gun to shoot out the windows of the local church. He lied, stole from shops and made obscene remarks to French girls. His appalled father realised that France was not producing the young gentlemen he had wanted, so he packed up and took the family back to England.

At home, Burton made new enemies at school, until at one point he had thirty-two fights to complete. In frustration, the senior Burton decided to take his family back to France. They settled at Blois, where the children were taught by a Mr Du Pré and a small staff. They learned French, Latin, Greek, dancing – and best of all, fencing. Both boys excelled with foils and swords.

It was perhaps their father's restless spirit that would infect Richard with the desire for constant movement. From Blois they went to Italy, where Richard learned the violin until his master said that while the other pupils were beasts, Richard was an 'archbeast'. In reply, Richard broke the instrument over the master's head.

The family moved on to Siena, then Naples, where the boys learned pistol shooting, cockfighting and heavy drinking. Cholera swept Naples, and out of ghoulish curiosity, Richard and Edward dressed as locals and helped to remove the dead to the plague pits outside the city. They also discovered prostitutes and spent all their pocket money on them.

From a young age, the brothers were determined to enter the military. Their father was equally determined they should be clergymen. To that end, he sent Richard to Oxford University and Edward to Cambridge, splitting them up for their own safety. Other tutors were engaged and it was then that Richard met Dr William Greenhill, who spoke not only Latin and Greek fluently, but Arabic as well.

Despite his delight in languages, Burton disliked Oxford intensely. He attempted to arrange a duel on his first day, only to be ignored. He said later that he felt he had fallen among grocers. He hated the food, the beer and the monotony. Annoyed by the hostility towards his dark and foreign appearance, he kept his door open, but left a red-hot poker in the fireplace to repel unwanted visitors. He became determined to have himself expelled and broke every rule he could find, but at first, the university ignored his excesses. Over the winter holidays in London, Richard and Edward met the sons of a Colonel White, from whom they heard tales of service in India and Afghanistan, where British forces had recently been defeated with great losses. Burton redoubled his efforts to be thrown out of Oxford, going to a horse race after being forbidden to attend. Called before the university authorities, Burton launched into a long speech about morality and trust and showed no remorse. He was expelled at last and left Oxford riding on a tandem-driven dog cart, blowing a coaching horn.

Richard's father was appalled and furious, but recognising the inevitable, allowed both his sons to join the East India Company army. Edward was posted to Ceylon, now known as Sri Lanka, while Richard was posted to the subcontinent itself.

Warned of the heat in India, Richard shaved his head and bought a wig as well as learning Hindustani. During the voyage, he boxed, fenced and practised his language skills. By the time he landed in India, he was almost completely fluent. He did not know it then, but he was about to begin a relationship with the subcontinent that would provide a driving force to his previously aimless life.

It did not begin well. Burton fell ill with diarrhoea and spent time in a sanitarium. He disliked the smell of curry and the lack of privacy in the company rooms. He began to learn Gujerati and Persian, ignoring the distressing presence of a crematorium next door, of which he said 'the smell of roast Hindu was most unpleasant'. He found the tiny society of five hundred Europeans stifling, though he enjoyed the brothels and bazaars. For almost two months he endured, then he was sent at last to his first posting at Baroda. He took a horse, servants, a supply of port and a bull terrier with him. He was slowly falling in love with India, in all its endless variety.

Baroda was a baking hot maze of alleys and exotic sights, with summer temperatures up to 120 °F. The lives of the inhabitants were brutal, with appalling punishments for misdeeds, such as placing a criminal's head beneath an elephant's foot to be crushed. Burton loved it, from the strange smells of incense, hashish and opium, to the courtesans, shrines, alien flowers and colourful mosques. Of the white officers, he said: 'There was not a subaltern in the 18th Regiment who did not consider himself capable of governing a million Hindus.' He took a temporary native wife whom he described as his 'walking dictionary' and found the courtesans more playful and less inhibited than their frosty counterparts in England. He threw himself into an exploration of sexual matters that would inform his writings many years later. He tried hunting and hawking in Baroda, but quickly lost the taste for it and instead kept a troupe of monkeys who ate at table with him. He won the regimental horse race, learned the Indian style of wrestling and taught his troops gymnastics to keep them agile.

In 1843, Burton took government examinations in Hindustani and passed first in his class. He was so successful in his total immersion in a Hindu snake cult that he was given the janeo, the three-ply cotton cord that showed he was a Brahmin, the highest caste. This was a unique event, unheard of before or since. In all other cases, a Hindu had to be born into that religion and only attained the highest caste after millennia of reincarnation. This honour came despite the fact that he remained a meat-eater, and is the more astonishing for it. He went on to discover Tantrism, with its philosophy, as he wrote: '... not to indulge shame or adversion to anything ... but freely to enjoy all the pleasures of the senses.'

He attended Catholic chapel, then later converted to Islam and then Sikhism, in love with the mysticism of all faiths and throwing himself into them until he found himself drawn to the next. He was not a dilettante, however. In each case, he searched and learned all he could and completed every ritual with steadfast determination and belief, yet somehow his soul wandered as much as his feet and there were always new towns to see.

In 1843, Burton became the regimental interpreter for the 18th Bombay Native Infantry and moved to Bombay, bound for Karachi to join General Charles Napier and the British forces fighting in Sindh. Napier recognised Burton's abilities and used him in a variety of diplomatic missions through 1844 and 1845. Many of the details have been lost, but Burton became indispensable, a man who could fight or talk his way out of anything. He became used to travelling in disguise and his contemporaries whispered that he had 'gone native'. In 1845, when Burton was just 24, Napier sent him to infiltrate and report on a male brothel. Burton wrote of what he saw in such grisly detail that his many enemies suggested he had taken part in the activities he witnessed. There is, however, no evidence for this, and in fact Burton was always scathing about 'Le Vice', as he called it. Napier had the brothels destroyed after reading the reports and it is worth pointing out that the famously strait-laced general lost no confidence in his agent as a result of this mission.

Away from the society of Britons in India, Burton became more and more of an outsider. He wore native clothing constantly, complete with turban and loose cotton robes. His experience of different faiths meant he could work as a spy among Muslims or Hindus with equal invisibility. He also had himself circumcised so that his disguise could not be broken even while bathing. In the Indus Valley, he found remnants of Alexander the Great's forts, as well as far more ancient ruins. He soaked it all up into his prodigious memory and delighted in fables and stories wherever he travelled for Napier. His reports were often inflammatory and he complained constantly that the English did not understand the natives. Napier, for example, tried to make punishments humane, and in doing so lost their effect on a people used to brutal rulers. Instead of cutting off a hand for stealing, the English merely imprisoned a man, who then thought them effete. Napier also issued a proclamation that he would hang anyone who killed a woman on suspicion of unfaithfulness, as was common in Sindh at that time. Burton may have had a personal reason to resent this practice as his own affair with a high-born Persian woman came to an abrupt and possibly violent end, though details are sketchy.

When Burton was not working, he endured the hottest months, wrote notes and drew everything he saw. He was always prolific and either wrote or translated more than fifty different books in his time, on subjects from the history of sword-making to works on the strange places and people he saw. He was the first white man to publish details of the Islamic Sufi sect, which Burton threw himself into with his usual ferocious enthusiasm.

In 1845, suspecting the British were about to annex the Punjab, a Sikh army crossed into British-held territory. It was a short war but hard fought, and the Sikhs were brought to the negotiating table by 1846. The Punjab came under British rule. Around this time, Burton became ill with cholera and recovered very slowly. During his sick leave, he explored the Portuguese colony at Goa. He left his regular mistress behind in Sindh and spent some time trying to get a nun out of a local convent to be his next one. In one attempt, he visited the wrong room in the night and found himself being chased by an elderly nun. He pushed her into a river as he made his escape.

In the company of English women, he found himself a man apart, almost unable to communicate or remember the strict rules of contact and flirtation. In the end, he managed to find another 'temporary wife'. By this time, Burton dressed and acted as a man of the East rather than the West and had been made very dark by the constant sun.

He continued to study Sufism, but around 1847–8 also had himself inducted into Sikhism, a 'conversion' that was never likely to last long with this firebrand of a man.

In 1848, war with the Sikhs broke out again. Burton was passed over for duties as an interpreter, a decision he later claimed was due to his report on the brothel. Ill and thin, he decided to return to Europe in 1849 after seven years in India. He made a partial recovery on the voyage, but ill health continued to plague him. He travelled to Italy and settled for a time in France, where he began further study of sword work, becoming a renowned master of the blade. In one exhibition, he disarmed a French master seven times in a row.

In the relative peace of France, Burton completed many of the manuscripts that survive today, such as *Falconry in the Valley of the Indus* and *A Complete System of Bayonet Exercise*. In Boulogne, he met the woman who would become his wife, Isabel Arundell. She was beautiful, of ancient English family and 19 years old. Perhaps surprisingly, he would remain faithful to her always. She wrote in her diary: 'Where are the men who inspired the "grandes passions" of bygone days? Is the race extinct? Is Richard the last of them?' Burton adored her, but at the same time, the world of France and England was too small for him. He was given a year's leave from the East India Company for a journey to Arabia, where he would need all the skill and knowledge he had won in India to survive. The Royal Geographical Society backed him and supplied him with funds. He set off in 1853 and once again fell into the role of a Muslim, even to the point of working as a doctor in Alexandria for a month. He travelled from Cairo to Suez, his companions growing to a large party as he met others making journeys to Medina, where the tomb of Muhammad lies. Burton was not impressed by the place, finding it 'mean and tawdry' after great expectations. He wrote notes on everything he saw and learned, from folklore and the prices of slaves to the practice of female circumcision. The discovery of such notes would have meant his death and he kept them in numbered squares that only he could reassemble.

From Medina, he travelled to Mecca itself. Burton saw the fabled black stone there, deciding to his own satisfaction that it was a meteorite. He completed the tour of the pilgrim sites and got out alive. He was due back in Bombay by 1854 and was not able to return to London in time, though he would have been lionised there for his achievement.

After Mecca, Burton became famous and his exploits were widely reported. He had a free hand in choosing other expeditions. With Company approval, he visited the fabled Ethiopian city of Harar, where he was held prisoner for ten days. Around that time, in 1855, his brother Edward was badly wounded by natives in Ceylon. Though Edward recovered for a time, he lost his health and sanity and spent his last forty years in a sanatorium in Surrey, a sad end for the less turbulent Burton brother.

Meanwhile, Richard Burton went from triumph to triumph. At that time, Africa was truly 'the dark continent', a place of mystery, strange animals and vast unknown lands. With John Speke, Burton attempted a trip into the continental interior, known as the 'Mountains of the Moon', but was badly wounded by a Somali spear. Speke was wounded in eleven places and they were lucky to survive. However, Burton was still the man of choice when the Royal Geographical Society wanted to organise an expedition to find the fabled 'inner sea' of Africa and the source of the Nile in 1856. Burton became secretly engaged to Isabel before he went with Speke to become the first white men to see Lake Tanganyika. Speke went on to find what is now known as Lake Victoria, though the journey almost killed both men. It was Burton's most celebrated exploration, though he fell out publicly with Speke afterwards. On their return to London, Burton and Speke wrote viciously about each other, each one claiming the glory for himself and ignoring the other's contribution.

In 1861, Burton married Isabel at last in a Catholic ceremony, though with his history, it is likely to have been merely expedient. He continued to explore West Africa after his marriage and became Consul in Damascus for a time. He also continued to write and in 1863 founded the Anthropological Society of London. By then an establishment figure, he was knighted by Queen Victoria in 1886.

He is perhaps best known for his translation into English of the *Kama Sutra*, an Indian sexual manual, as well as *Arabian Nights*, *The Perfumed Garden* and *Vikram and the Vampire*, a collection of Hindu stories. He died in 1890 of a heart attack and his wife had the Catholic last rites performed for him. Sadly, she then burned all his surviving notes and manuscripts, just as Byron's were burned before him. It was a truly great loss to both literature and culture. There are some men who rise above the period of their lives and the cultures in which they are born. Burton was a man of insatiable curiosity and endless wonder. His example has inspired many explorers after him, both of the world and the spirit. He and his wife are buried together in a tomb shaped like a Bedouin tent in Mortlake, near Richmond in London.

Recommended
Captain Sir Richard Francis Burton: A Biography by Edward Rice.
A Rage to Live: A Biography of Richard and Isabel Burton
by M.S. Lovell.

The Few

There were: 2,340 British, 32 Australians, 112 Canadians, 1 Jamaican, 127 New Zealanders, 3 Rhodesians and 25 South Africans. In addition, there were 9 Americans, 28 Belgians, 89 Czechoslovakians, 13 French, 145 Polish and 10 from the Republic of Ireland. They were the men and women of Royal Air Force Fighter Command and they fought the most famous air battle of them all – the Battle of Britain.

By the end of June 1940, the United Kingdom stood alone against Nazi Germany, Austria, Czechoslovakia and France. The Czechs were conscripted into Nazi forces, while Vichy French forces fought with Germany until 1943 against Britain in the Middle East, North and West Africa. French spies around the world reported to Germany and Japan until they were captured, while in South East Asia the French agreed for Japan to control French Indochina (Vietnam, Cambodia and Laos).

From Norway to the Pyrenees, all of western and central Europe was Nazi-controlled, with enemy radio interception and spy networks operating in neutral Spain and Eire. In the north, Sweden supplied the Nazis with steel and other metals. In the east, Russia, Hungary, Romania and the Balkans supplied oil, coal and food. In the south, fascist Italy joined Germany and opened two more fronts against Britain in North and East Africa. At sea, German submarines and surface raiders attacked unprotected British convoys, the escorts having been withdrawn to defend Britain against invasion.

The German victory in Europe had been so fast that no plans had been prepared for an invasion of Britain. In July, that was remedied with Hitler's War Directive 16, code-named 'Sea-Lion':

'As England, in spite of her hopeless military situation, still shows no signs of willingness to come to terms, I have decided to prepare, and if necessary to carry out, a landing operation against her. The aim of this operation is to eliminate the English Motherland.'

For a German invasion to be possible, the Royal Navy had to be pushed out of the eastern English Channel, at least temporarily. To do that, Germany needed command of the air so that its formidable and experienced bomber and dive bomber squadrons could knock out the navy. For command of the air, Royal Air Force Fighter Command first had to be destroyed.

To defeat Britain in 1940, German forces had only to take London to claim victory, just fifty to sixty miles from the Kent and Sussex coasts. As with the Norman invasion of 1066, the remainder of the country could be overrun later. There would have been resistance, of course, far stiffer than they had encountered in Europe, but an invasion was on. After all, the 1915 Gallipoli landings in the Mediterranean had been carried out successfully from ships' boats in the face of machine guns, artillery fire and barbed-wire defences, and without tanks. The Gallipoli campaign failed only because it was fought on a narrow peninsula and uphill against cliffs. No such problems would confront German troops on the broad and level battlefront of south-east England.

With German control of the air, there would have been no insurmountable problems for an invasion fleet to cross the Channel, supported by glider troops and parachutists. The Royal Navy stated that it could not prevent an invasion, because it wouldn't know the landing ports and beaches, but it would be able to stop support and supplies by sea to that invasion – as long as the RAF maintained control of the air.

The German 16th and 9th armies rehearsed for landings at ports and beaches between Folkestone and Brighton, while the 6th Army practised for landings between Weymouth and Lyme Regis. Panzer tanks were made watertight, fitted with snorkels, and rehearsed offloading some distance from a beach to proceed along the seabed and then ashore. The German navy scoured western Europe for suitable ships, barges, craft and tugs – some 2,500 – and moved them to the ports of Holland, Belgium and France. Meanwhile, under Reichsmarschall Hermann Goering, the Luftwaffe prepared for 'Eagle Attack'.

The invasion was scheduled for the week of 19 to 26 September 1940, the date by which an invasion fleet could be assembled and when the tides were favourable for a dawn landing on the Kent and Sussex beaches. Goering promised Hitler that by then Germany would command the air over the Channel and south-east England. On 1 August, Hitler signed War Directive 17 for the destruction of RAF Fighter Command, and so began the Battle of Britain. It was to be a busy three months.

RAF Fighter Command was then led by Air Chief Marshal Sir Hugh Dowding, a brilliant, determined but reserved man who knew more about aerial warfare than anyone else in Britain. It was Dowding

who had changed the peacetime RAF from wooden biplanes to metal monoplanes. As a result, the first Hawker Hurricane flew in 1935 and the first Vickers Supermarine Spitfire in 1936. It was Dowding who arranged the first demonstration of Watson-Watt's new radar, who created the radar air defence network, and who developed airborne radar for night-fighters. In 1936, he was appointed Commander-in-Chief of the newly formed Fighter Command.

His senior officer was Air Commodore Keith Park, a New Zealand air ace who had twenty-four victories in the 1914–18 war and who was the RAF's fighter expert. Together, they reorganised Fighter Command and the fighter defences of Britain for war. An Observer Corps was formed of volunteers who reported from the ground all aircraft movements over Britain. Operation rooms were created for all levels of command, from airfields like RAF Duxworth to Group Operations Headquarters at RAF Uxbridge. The airfields were converted to all-weather aerodromes – concrete runways as opposed to grass.

Dowding and Park also realised that, although the theorists correctly anticipated attack by large bomber squadrons, they were incorrect when they said there was no defence except attack by opposing bomber squadrons. There was a defence: fighter squadrons. Fortunately, they were supported in this belief by the new Minister of Defence, Sir Thomas Inskip. Dowding increased the number of fighter squadrons, aerodromes and pilot-training units, and created the vital centralised command linked to the new radar network. He pressed and argued for even more pilots and ever more aircraft, although one type, the Defiant, turned out to be a turkey.

However, Dowding was not popular in the Air Ministry. He was usually right and ruffled too many feathers. He was 'retired' in 1938, but immediately reinstated, a sequence which would happen four times. He sent a requisition to the Air Ministry for bulletproof glass for Hurricane and Spitfire cockpits; the politicians laughed at him. He told them: 'If Chicago gangsters can have bulletproof glass in their cars, I can't see any reason why my pilots cannot have the same.' He got the glass. How out of touch many politicians were with the reality of modern warfare and the role of the RAF is difficult to appreciate many years later.

During the collapse of France, despite Dowding's advice, squadron after squadron of Hurricane fighters was deployed to France and destroyed. However, Dowding refused to commit Spitfire squadrons and, eventually, any more squadrons at all. Of 261 Hurricanes sent to France only 66 returned, a destruction rate of 75 per cent. As a result, Fighter Command was reduced to almost half its strength, the loss of experienced pilots more critical than the loss of aeroplanes. If more squadrons had been sent to France, the Battle of Britain would have been lost and Britain invaded.

Behind the scenes, Prime Minister Churchill appointed Canadian Lord Beaverbrook as Minister of Aircraft Production, an inspired choice. Beaverbrook bypassed the Air Ministry, took over factories and stopped production of bombers to increase production of Spitfire and Hurricane fighters. He had them delivered directly from the factories to the squadrons, created a 'while-you-wait' repair service to which pilots flew their damaged fighters, and arranged the ferrying of aircraft across the Atlantic from Canada, which the Air Ministry had said was impossible. When the pro-Nazi American Henry Ford refused to support Britain by building Rolls-Royce Merlin engines under licence, Beaverbrook paid the rival Packard company to do so. Later in the war, this led to the building of the brilliant British-designed and -engined P-51 Mustang fighter for the US Army Air Force.

Dowding said later: 'The country owes as much to Beaverbrook for the Battle of Britain as it does to me. Without his drive behind me I could not have carried on during the Battle.'

In the spring of 1940, Dowding appointed Keith Park as Commander of 11 Group, the squadrons defending the vital south-east of England. Trafford Leigh-Mallory already commanded 12 Group, defending central England and Wales. Richard Saul commanded 13 Group, defending Scotland and northern England, while Quintin Brand commanded 10 Group, defending the west and south-west England.

So Dowding and a depleted Fighter Command entered the Battle of Britain, facing a Luftwaffe which had flown and fought successfully in Spain, Poland and western Europe. Goering's strategy was to bomb the fighter aerodromes out of action, destroy fighter aircraft on the ground by bombing and strafing, and destroy them in the air with his fighters. It was the same tactic used successfully against the Polish, Norwegian, French, Dutch and Belgian air forces.

For the attack on Britain, the Luftwaffe had operational along the Channel coast: 656 single-seat single-engine Messerschmitt 109 fighters, 168 two-seat two-engine Messerschmitt 110 fighters, 248 two-seat single-engine Junkers Stuka dive bombers, and 769 twin-engine bombers. Also on squadron strength but not operational were: 153 Messerschmitt 109 fighters, 78 Messerschmitt 110 fighters, 68 dive bombers, and 362 bombers.

In Denmark and Norway they had a further 34 Messerschmitt 110 fighters, 129 bombers to attack northern Britain, and 84 Messerschmitt 109 fighters (out of range of England but which could be brought south within range). A total of 2,749 aircraft. In addition, there were 244 reconnaissance and coastal aircraft for mine-laying and pilot recovery.

On 20 July, Fighter Command had operational: 504 single-seat single-engine fighters, Hurricanes and Spitfires in a ratio of approximately four to one. Also on squadron strength but not operational were seventy-eight Hurricanes or Spitfires. A total of 582 aircraft.

There were also twenty-seven Boulton Paul two-seat single-engine Defiant fighters. On the only time these were sent into action, 19 July, they lost two-thirds of their number without a single loss to the enemy. They were not used again. The RAF also had Bomber Command and Coastal Command, but those aircraft could not be involved in the Battle of Britain; they were not suitable.

In all aircraft, Fighter Command was outnumbered by four to one. In fighters, it was outnumbered by two to one.

Radar detection gave Fighter Command the time to deploy its squadrons to the right place at close to the right time, but rarely to the right height. The Nazi fighters invariably had the great advantage of height. Radar was vital to the battle, giving Fighter Command's fewer aircraft more time in the air, and to a certain extent redressing the imbalance of numbers, but this became a double-edged sword for the RAF pilots. It meant they flew many more hours than the German pilots, an average of six sorties or more each day. In addition, Luftwaffe aircrew knew the time they were to fly every day, whereas RAF pilots were on standby to 'scramble' from dawn to dusk (woken at about 3.30 a.m., stood down at about 8.30 p.m.). As a result, the British pilots eventually became exhausted, and exhausted pilots make fatal mistakes.

Fighter Command did have the advantage of fighting over home territory, so that most of the pilots who survived a destroyed aircraft were returned to their squadron, whereas most Luftwaffe pilots who survived became prisoners of war. However, in numbers of war-experienced pilots as well as in numbers of reserve pilots, Fighter Command was vastly outnumbered by the Luftwaffe. It was this lack of pilots and experience that brought it closest to defeat.

In early July, the Luftwaffe attacked shipping and convoys in the English Channel and North Sea, made fighter sweeps across Kent and Sussex, and probed and tempted Fighter Command in order to assess its response times and the standard of the opposition. Dowding was careful not to commit his men and aeroplanes at the beginning of the battle, so Park and Leigh-Mallory made only limited responses to the attacks on shipping. The fighter sweeps were ignored. Even so, air activity was increasing. As early as 10 July, Fighter Command flew more than 600 sorties.

By the 17th, there were daylight bombing raids on factories in England and Scotland, on southern coastal towns, ports and radar stations, as well as night bomber training flights. On the 25th – a rare sunny day in an overcast and wet July – several engagements took place protecting a convoy in the Dover Straits. Fighter Command lost seven fighters against sixteen German aircraft shot down, the heaviest casualties to that point. It was during July that Park developed the tactic of sending Hurricanes to attack enemy bombers while Spitfires attacked the protecting fighters above. By the end of the month, however, neither air force was clear about how much damage had been done to the other.

For the benefit of the German public and the occupied countries, Luftwaffe propaganda announced only half its losses and announced higher RAF losses than even its pilots claimed. Fighter Command on the other hand announced its true losses, which the Luftwaffe assumed were false figures like its own. This resulted in the Luftwaffe believing it was doing better than it was. For the British public, Fighter

Command accepted its pilots' high claims of enemy aircraft destroyed, claims which were naturally error-prone from emotion, from two or more pilots claiming the same aircraft, and from the fact that everything happened in three dimensions at 300 miles per hour.

Fighter Command lost 145 aircraft in July, the majority of which had been replaced by Beaverbrook's supply chain, but it was the loss of pilots that was the major concern. Of all aircrew lost in July, eighty were experienced flight and squadron commanders of Fighter Command, irreplaceable and vital men.

On 8 August, another convoy battle took place in the Channel over which several hundred aircraft fought. Thirty-one German aircraft were destroyed for the loss of nineteen British fighters.

Still Dowding held Fighter Command back, so that the intercepting fighters were heavily outnumbered by both German fighters and bombers. This caused some questioning, even by the pilots themselves. It must also have reduced the chances of destroying German aircraft and increased the chances of losing more British aircraft, but Dowding knew that the crisis was yet to come. It began on 12 August, coincidentally the opening of the grouse-shooting season.

Radar stations along the south-east coast were bombed, Portsmouth was hit by 150 bombers, aerodromes of 11 Group were bombed, while hundreds of Luftwaffe 109 and 110 fighters protected their bombers. RAF Biggin Hill in Kent was in the thick of it, and its close-of-day intelligence report was typical for 11 Group: 'Operational sorties: 36. Enemy casualties: 5 confirmed, 16 unconfirmed, 4 probables and damaged. All pilots safe. 1 in hospital.' The average age of the fighter pilots at Biggin Hill was several months under 21. A headline in the following day's newspapers read: 'The Battle of Britain is on.'

The 13th was Goering's 'Eagle Attack' day. The Luftwaffe flew 1,485 sorties and night-bombed cities in all four countries of the kingdom, including two aircraft factories in Belfast and Birmingham. The RAF responded with 700 sorties, shooting down 46 enemy aircraft for the loss of 13 fighters but losing a further 47 assorted aircraft on the ground. Overall it was the Luftwaffe's day. On the 14th more aerodromes, radar stations and factories were bombed.

The 15th saw the largest attack of the battle. More than 1,800 aircraft attacked Britain in five massive assaults. It included all German aircraft stationed in Norway, Denmark, Holland, Belgium and France in an all-out attempt to smash Fighter Command and bring the RAF to its knees. Hurricane and Spitfire pilots shot down 75 aircraft for the loss of 34 fighters shot down and 16 destroyed on the ground. That was the RAF's day. The Luftwaffe called it 'Black Thursday', yet the following day it continued the onslaught, flying another 1,700 sorties against Britain.

By mid-August, the Luftwaffe had lost a total of 363 aircraft and most of their pilots and crews. The RAF had lost 181 fighters shot down and 30 destroyed on the ground, a total of 211, but Fighter Command also had lost 154 pilots of which only 63 could be replaced. In addition, a further 80 per cent of squadron commanders had been lost to death, injury or exhaustion, so that by then, inexperienced commanders were leading inexperienced pilots into battle. Fighter Command was wavering.

The smiling young pilots in their white silk scarves, leather sheepskin flying jackets, blue uniforms and shaggy flying boots were becoming drawn and exhausted. During standby, they lounged on chairs in the mess or sprawled outside in deckchairs and on the grass, reading, smoking, chatting, drinking tea or coffee, waiting for the inevitable telephone call from Control to scramble once again. Some dozed under the wings of their aeroplanes; one squadron's pilots remained in their cockpits. In the few hours off-duty, they slept, went to the local pub and scrawled their names on the ceilings and walls, went to the pictures, fell in love, or made the occasional trip to London on a twenty-four-hour pass.

The ground crews, too, suffered heavy casualties and were tired, working throughout the day and night repairing, servicing, re-arming and refuelling the aeroplanes, then repairing the aerodromes. The effectiveness of the Hurricanes and Spitfires depended as much on the ground crews as the pilots. Dowding rotated his squadrons – pilots and ground crews – whenever possible; during the three months of the Battle of Britain six different squadrons flew from Biggin Hill.

Yet there were simply not enough replacement pilots and, at the end of each day, even more were required. From the Fleet Air Arm, fifty-eight pilots were transferred to Fighter Command, a few suitable bomber pilots were retrained as fighter pilots and RAF technicians who at least knew about fighters were sent to flying school.

On the other side of the Channel, Goering was fuming at his Luftwaffe's inability to destroy the RAF. His pilots, too, were frustrated. Every time they attacked, there were the Hurricanes and Spitfires, always waiting, no matter how many they shot down.

At a meeting on 19 August, Goering asked his two most experienced and successful fighter pilots what they required to defeat the RAF. Major Moelders asked for a more powerful engine for the Messerschmitt 109 to counter the Rolls-Royce Merlins, while Major Galland famously asked for an 'outfit of Spitfires for my Group'.

Goering changed tactics to twenty-four-hour attack. He relocated most of his fighters to airfields around Calais to provide even closer support for his bombers, and concentrated the assault on fighter aerodromes. He was forced to withdraw the Stuka dive bomber because of its high casualty rate. Dowding and Park countered by ordering their pilots to concentrate on the bombers, to leave the fighters alone whenever possible, and not to pursue over the English Channel. The bombers were the priority. The Battle of Britain now entered its critical period.

On the night of the 24th, during a 170-bomber raid against the Thameshaven oil tanks, a German aircraft dropped its bombs on the centre of London, apparently because of a navigational error. Already bombs had been dropped around the capital and in the suburbs as well as other British cities and ports, but never before on the centre of London. Similarly, no raids had been made against Berlin by Bomber Command, which itself was beginning strategic night bombing.

Churchill naturally assumed it was intentional and, as in May when Rotterdam was blitzed by the Luftwaffe, ordered a retaliatory raid. The target was Berlin, which Goering had boasted would never be bombed.

On the very next night, the 25th, Bomber Command sent eighty-one twin-engine bombers to Berlin. Twenty-nine reached the target and dropped their bombs on the city. Hitler was enraged. He pledged to annihilate London. He ordered Goering to commence the wholesale bombing of London and other British cities by day and night, a destruction he hoped would bring Britain to demoralised defeat. So began 'the Blitz', which Hitler called 'terror raids'. The first city to catch it badly was Liverpool, bombed four nights in succession.

On 30 August, a feint by the Luftwaffe to the Thames estuary was followed by repeated and heavy raids on aerodromes. Fighter Command destroyed forty-nine German aircraft for the loss of twenty-five fighters and ten pilots but its south-eastern airfields were a mess. A shop in the village became the operation room for Biggin Hill, yet Fighter Command still flew 1,000 sorties for the first time.

The next day the Luftwaffe struck again, bombing aerodromes and radar stations. It lost thirty-nine aircraft, but Fighter Command also lost thirty-nine fighters and thirteen pilots. Several squadrons were forced to relocate to the grass fields of private flying clubs. Dowding told Churchill: 'We are fighting for survival, and we are losing.'

To a major extent, both air forces were boxing blind, not knowing how much damage they were inflicting on the other. Fighter Command had destroyed 800 Luftwaffe aircraft, but thought that they'd destroyed more. The error didn't matter, for while the Luftwaffe continued its assaults across the Channel they had to be countered. On the other side of the coin, between 24 August and 5 September the Luftwaffe destroyed 466 RAF fighters, killed 231 pilots, damaged several radar stations and put six fighter aerodromes out of action. German Intelligence reported Fighter Command was on its knees. Yet, somehow, Hurricanes and Spitfires rose from the green fields to meet every attack.

Dowding could no longer rotate his squadrons – there weren't enough left – so resorted to A, B and C designations. 'A' squadrons were in the south-east front line commanded by Keith Park, 'B' squadrons were in the centre and west of Britain commanded by Leigh-Mallory, while 'C' were as far from the fighting as possible, training new pilots. In those appalling two weeks to 5 September, Dowding lost a quarter of his remaining fighter pilots. With the best will in the world, their replacements were rookies with only a few flying hours in their log books – often as little as ten – and under two weeks' squadron experience. Their survival in battle was numbered in just days.

There were instances of Luftwaffe pilots machine-gunning RAF pilots in parachutes. There were also isolated incidents of the machine-gunning of British civilians, as earlier machine-gunning of civilians on the continent had been common. Goering was a fighter ace from the 1914–18 war, but he was also the creator of the German secret police, the Gestapo.

In September 1940, Goering announced on radio: 'I myself have taken command of the Luftwaffe's battle for Britain.' The two air forces were now trading punches, losing as many of their own aircraft as they destroyed of the other, the Luftwaffe flying about 770 sorties a day and Fighter

Command just under 1000. On one horrific day, for the first time, Fighter Command lost more aircraft – and pilots – than it shot down.

The 7th of September began as usual with Luftwaffe attacks on aerodromes, but on this occasion it was a feint for the first mass attacks upon London. In the afternoon, 1,000 aircraft crossed the English Channel from France in a formation two miles high, flying over Cape Blanc Nez and a watching Goering below. No intelligence reports suggested such a raid was planned. The controllers expected further attacks upon their airfields and so delayed the fighters from taking off until the last moment, too late for London.

There had never been an attack on a city on that scale before, anywhere in the world. The bombings of Guernica, Warsaw and Rotterdam paled into insignificance. From 16,000 to 20,000 feet, new high-explosive bombs and incendiaries hammered the London docks and homes. There were more raids in the evening, and raids throughout the night until dawn on the 8th. At night, the bombers followed radio beams to London, although little navigation was required: the East End was burning and the glow of its fires could be seen ninety miles away. That was a day for the Luftwaffe.

They bombed London again on the night of the 8th, and a second massive daylight attack was launched on the 9th, again with almost 1,000 enemy aircraft, in two formations crossing the coast above Dover and Beachy Head. Park's 'A' Group squadrons scrambled to meet them in the air south of London. So fiercely did the Hurricane and Spitfire pilots fight they literally forced back the first formation above Canterbury – upon which the Luftwaffe dropped their bombs as they retreated – and scattered the second formation away from the docks into the south and west of London. There, Mallory's 'B' Group met them. Bombs were jettisoned anywhere as the Luftwaffe retreated. That was the RAF's day.

At the end of that momentous week, Fighter Command's aeroplane reserves reached their lowest – just eighty Hurricanes and forty-seven Spitfires.

The fifteenth of September saw the climax of the struggle. It was also the day Prime Minister Churchill chose to visit 'A' Group Operations HQ, the underground Command Centre at Uxbridge in Middlesex.

That day the German attacks on Britain came in two waves at very high altitude, 20,000 feet and higher, above radar. However, British intelligence had monitored the increased radio traffic, giving Park time to move his squadrons forward. They fought the 500 enemy aircraft all the way to London and all the way back. RAF ground crews refuelled and re-armed aircraft in a frenzy of servicing whenever and at whatever airfield the pilots landed, so that from the ground it seemed as if the skies were permanently full of aircraft. Vapour trails and smoke trails scrawled the signature of battle across the summer sky.

While the fighters of 'A' Group fought above Kent, Sussex and the coast, that was the day that Londoners – and the Luftwaffe pilots – saw 200 Hurricanes and Spitfires together above the city, Mallory's 'big-wing' from 'B' Group. All squadrons and reserves of 'A' and all squadrons of 'B' were scrambled that day.

Fighter Command shot down and destroyed sixty Nazi aircraft. It lost twenty-six fighters and thirteen pilots. Two days later Hitler postponed indefinitely the invasion of Britain. Later, he cancelled it completely. Since the end of the 1939–45 war, that 15 September is celebrated every year. It is the Royal Air Force's Battle of Britain Day.

Yet the Battle of Britain did not end then. It continued for the rest of the month and into October, gradually reducing in intensity as the Luftwaffe ran out of steam. Bletchley Park had decoded Hitler's Enigma signal of the 17th postponing the invasion, as well as further military signals authorising the dismantling of invasion air transport units.

From 7 to 30 September, Fighter Command destroyed 380 German aircraft for the loss of 178 fighters. The Luftwaffe's brief aura of invincibility was destroyed for ever. By the end of October, Goering was forced to reduce daylight attacks to mere harassing sorties and to direct his bombers to night raids against Britain. There is a limit to the losses any military force can withstand, and the Luftwaffe had reached its own. The Battle of Britain was won.

RAF Fighter Command lost 544 killed. The Luftwaffe lost 2,877: 1,176 bomber crew, 171 fighter pilots, 85 dive-bomber crew, and 1,445 missing in action, assumed killed.

In that autumn of 1940, London was bombed fifty-seven nights in succession, still a record for sustained bombing. Buckingham Palace and the Houses of Parliament were hit. The Blitz continued into 1941, culminating in a 550-bomber raid on 10 May. Fighter Command had few effective night fighters at that stage of the war – no air force did, although Dowding's developments were soon to reap benefits with Airborne Intercept radar in the Bristol Beaufighter. The defence of London and other cities meanwhile was maintained by anti-aircraft batteries.

The United Kingdom was bombed north, south, east and west by the Luftwaffe. In particular Bath, Belfast, Birkenhead, Birmingham, Bristol, Cardiff, Clydeside, Coventry, Exeter, Glasgow, Hull, Ipswich, Liverpool, London, Manchester, Middlesbrough, Norwich, Plymouth, Portsmouth, Sheffield, Southampton, Sunderland, Swansea and Wolverhampton suffered heavy damage from indiscriminate night bombing.

Winston Churchill crystallised the importance of victory in the Battle of Britain in seventeen words: 'Never in the field of human conflict was so much owed by so many to so few.'

About 75 per cent of Fighter Command pilots were commissioned officers and 25 per cent were non-commissioned sergeants, although their ranks don't matter: they flew identical aeroplanes against an enemy who operated a similar system in its air force. Some of their names are legend – Ginger Lacey, Peter Townsend, Josef Frantisek, Al Deere, Douglas Bader, Richard Hillary, Stanford Tuck, Johnnie Johnson, Pat Hughes, Sammy Allard, Sailor Malan, John Kent, J.C. Mungo-Park,

'Kill 'em' Gillam, Michael Crossley – while others are proud names on a stone memorial or a part of family history. More than 500 RAF fighter pilots were killed in their tubes of aluminium, but many more were wounded, some crippled, some disfigured terribly from burns. Those who survived continued flying, through a further four and a half years of world war. There were 791 fewer at the end of that.

The successful and the unsuccessful, the brave and the fearful, Dowding and Park, the pilots, the ground crews, the radar plotters and the observers, the controllers, Beaverbrook, those who flew all the sorties and those who flew only one: they all played their part in the victory over evil.

For if the Battle of Britain had been lost and the United Kingdom invaded, Europe would not have been liberated from Nazism. The German death camps would have multiplied, Russia would have been defeated, Japan would have conquered Asia and India and all the Commonwealth and Empire countries would have fallen to the Nazis and Japan. As Churchill warned in 1940, a new dark age would have fallen upon the world.

Bless 'em all.

Recommended
The Last Enemy by Richard Hillary.
Leader of the Few: The Authorised Biography of Air Chief Marshal the Lord Dowding by Basil Collier.
Dowding and the Battle of Britain by Robert Wright.
Duel of Eagles by Peter Townsend.
One of the Few by John Kent.
Film: *Battle of Britain*, United Artists, 1969.
The RAF Church, St Clement Danes, the Strand, London. The Battle of Britain Memorial, Runnymede, River Thames. The Royal Air Force Museum, Hendon, Middlesex. The surviving inns and pubs in Kent, Sussex and Essex with pilots' signatures and messages preserved on their ceilings and walls.

The Magna Carta Barons

Article 39: 'No *free man shall be seized or imprisoned, or stripped of his rights or possessions, or outlawed or exiled, or deprived of his standing in any other way, nor will we proceed with force against him, or send others to do so, except by the lawful judgement of his peers or by the law of the land.*'

Two of the sons of Henry II would become king after him. Richard I was the older brother. He was a famous warrior and is better known as 'the Lionheart'. He fought constantly to retake Jerusalem for Christianity and after becoming king in 1189, spent only seven months of his ten-year rule at home. In his absence, his younger brother John ruled as regent. When Richard was captured by the Holy Roman emperor, John wrote a letter offering to pay £60,000 to have Richard quietly disappear. Instead, the emperor ransomed Richard back to England for £100,000 – at that time, more than twice the annual income of the country. Their mother organised the ransom. Churches were ransacked for silver and gold and rich and poor were taxed for a quarter of everything they owned. When Richard returned home. John begged him for mercy and Richard forgave him, where any other king would have had him beheaded for treason. Richard had unfinished battles in Jerusalem and he knew there was a good chance he would die there.

In 1199, when the news came that Richard the Lionheart had been killed in a siege, John had himself crowned king of England. The one danger to his new position was the line of his older brother Geoffrey. Though Geoffrey had died, his young son Arthur had a strong claim to the throne of England. The boy was in France when John became king and was barely 12 years old, but John feared he would one day become a threat. Worse news came when the French king, Philip, decided to support Arthur and made him Duke of Normandy and Aquitaine. Those titles were John's, as they had been his father's before him. In fury, John ordered every shipyard in England to create at least one ship for a fleet. By the end of 1204, he had forty-five heavy galleys and he is sometimes credited with beginning the domination of the seas that would be the hallmark of British history for the next seven centuries.

As soon as he had the ships, John embarked an army and sailed for France. His one ally was his mother Eleanor. She doted on John and, when he was forced to return to England for a time, even organised the battles without him. She was outmatched by the French forces and found herself besieged in a castle by Philip's army and the boy Arthur.

John returned to France at great speed when he heard the news. He landed in secret and force-marched an army to save his mother. The sudden appearance of his soldiers surprised the French and they were routed. Arthur became John's prisoner, completely at his mercy. At first, John merely demanded that Arthur renounce his claim on the English throne. Arthur refused. We do not know if John killed his nephew personally or merely gave the order, but Arthur was never seen again. There are various records from the period that suggest the boy was either blinded, castrated or had his throat cut. John was already known as treacherous, cruel and spoiled. He was ever after known as a murderer.

While in France, John met a beautiful young noblewoman named Isabella. Lusting after her, he sent armed men to carry her off. He then arranged a divorce from his wife to marry the woman he had kidnapped. The French king demanded that John appear before him to answer for his crimes, but John decided it was too dangerous and stayed at home. As a result, King Philip of France declared the French possessions of the English Crown forfeit. John did not have the army to resist the decision and all the gains of his father were lost.

In 1205, John quarrelled with the Pope in Rome. At that time, England was Catholic, but John refused to acknowledge the Pope's authority in appointing archbishops. Instead, he sent armed men to drive the priests out of the country. In response, the Pope placed England under an Interdict in 1208: all religious services were forbidden, all churches closed. Not even church bells could be rung, and there were no marriages, christenings or funerals. The bishops left England together and only one stayed. John himself was excommunicated in 1209, which had serious implications for the Christian ruler of a Christian country.

Day by day, John made enemies and lost loyal supporters. When one of his lords fled the country, John had the man's wife and children imprisoned and starved to death. The King of France was building an army to invade and remove him and John had no allies to resist them. He wrote to an Islamic ruler in Spain, offering to become a Muslim and pay annual tribute if the man lent his soldiers. The Emir of Cordova refused, saying to the ambassador from John: 'Your king is unworthy to be a vassal. He is a coward and a weakling and his infamy stinks in my nostrils.' The fortunes of the English Crown had never been so low.

With an invasion expected at any moment, John decided to grovel to the Pope and allow his choice as Archbishop of Canterbury. He hoped this would mean the French king cancelled his invasion. Unable to trust even his own men, John sealed himself in Nottingham Castle and waited for the papal legate to arrive. In 1213, he travelled to Dover to meet the legate and heard alarming descriptions from him of the French army massing across the channel.

In terror, John promised to abide by anything the Pope wanted and even handed his crown to the papal legate, who handed it back as a master to a servant. John also gave the legate a bag of gold coins as tribute, but the man showed his contempt by scattering the coins with his foot. In all of England's extraordinary history, there has never been such a moment of humiliation as the one John brought about.

News of his appalling actions spread to nobles and commoners alike. Wherever John went in England, he was greeted by hostile crowds, furious with what he had done. Taxes remained cruelly high and poverty and starvation were widespread. Having lost his French possessions, the king was known as John Lackland, John Softsword, or sometimes simply John the Bastard.

John had one success when one of his lords, the Earl of Salisbury, took the English fleet and destroyed French ships waiting to carry the invasion army. The King of France could not cross without them and John was safe for a time.

However, he made the situation worse at home when he hired foreign soldiers to take revenge on his enemies in the north of England. They burned and slaughtered freely and John merely cheered them on. The Archbishop of Canterbury came north to see the king and, in an act of great courage, rebuked John for his actions, reminding him of his coronation oath, when he had sworn to protect his people. John raged at him, telling him to mind his church while leaving the king to mind the country. The archbishop faced him again and threatened to excommunicate the King of England once more. The threat was a potent one, as it had once almost led to his destruction. Reluctantly, John agreed to take council with his barons.

The barons of England did not trust him. They were led by Stephen Langton, a name once famous in British history as a founder of freedom. Rather than accept his promises and see them broken, they began to consider drawing up a charter of rights that they could make him seal in front of witnesses. His great grandfather, King Henry I, had once created such a document of rights. From it, they would write a Great Charter – in Latin, a Magna Carta.

In 1214, the barons met in secret at Bury St Edmunds. At the altar of the church, as the frozen air made plumes of their breath, they swore a holy oath to force the king to accept the charter, or begin bloody civil war. There was no mention of parliament in the document, as the idea did not yet exist, but these men were the first parliament of England. Kings had always had councillors and advisers, but before that date, without real authority.

That winter was bitterly cold and the country suffered. At Christmas, John met the Council of Barons in Worcester. Despite the driving rain and wind, men gathered around the country, ready to go to war if John refused. Even then, John tried to delay the process by offering to let the Pope decide the dispute, but the barons knew the cunning king too well. They presented their Magna Carta. He could not read, so had a scribe explain the details. As he understood the contents, he raged at them, shouting: 'You wish to take away my crown and make a slave of me!' His temper left them unmoved. One by one, the barons walked out and left him to his choice.

The barons had demanded he meet them to seal the document at Runnymede, near Windsor, the date set for 15 June 1215. As the spring turned to summer, his remaining knights left him, until in the whole of his kingdom, he commanded only seven men. His choice was stark: accept the new order, or lose his life and his kingdom.

As the 15th dawned, King John came to the meadow by the Thames, where he was met by twenty-five armed nobles and a much larger number of witnesses and retainers. Those twenty-five would offer their personal surety that the charter would be observed, but in addition, more than a hundred and forty noblemen had taken up arms and declared against the king, Fulke Fitz Warrin of the Robin Hood legends among them. They had chosen a place where John could not launch a surprise attack, even if he had been able to find supporters. He was completely in their power and all his treachery and cunning had brought him to that chill morning, with the cold and misty river running past.

John took his seat by a tented pavilion, with the flags of the barons fluttering around him. The archbishop handed him the Magna Carta, but even then John did not act. He argued long and passionately and the barons waited as the evening came, ignoring all his protests. Those twenty-five noblemen had the support of both Prince Llywelyn of Wales and Alexander II of Scotland, as well as eleven bishops, twenty abbots and the archbishops of Canterbury and Dublin. Almost without exception, every man of power in Britain supported the attempt to limit John's powers. The only commoner to offer surety with the barons was William Hardel, the Lord Mayor of London.

As servants lit the lamps, John gave up and pressed his royal seal to the Charter. In one stroke, he had given away power to elect a council of twenty-five barons. Though neither he nor they were aware of all the implications, they were laying the foundations of constitutional government, an independent judiciary and trial by jury.

There are sixty-three different parts to the astonishingly varied document. For example, it states that a widow must receive her husband's goods without delay, that only competent men can be appointed as justices and constables, and forbids court cases on the word of a single accuser.

'... and that men in our kingdom shall have and keep these liberties, rights and concessions ... for them and for their heirs, in all things and in all places for ever.'

John went on to break his oath and all the promises he had made. With another mercenary army, he laid waste to the lands of the barons, even burning down the house where he stayed each night in his royal fury. Thousands were killed by his foreign soldiers and some of the barons sent an appeal to the King of France to enter the country. The French Dauphin moved quickly and entered London just a few days after landing. It would fall to John's son Henry III to make peace with the French.

For a time after 1215, it seemed that all the work that had gone into the creation of the Great Charter had been in vain. Although it was confirmed and reissued over the following decade, it would not be until the seventeenth century that it was recognised as the foundation stone of democracy and constitutional liberty.

One famous incident remains of John's ill-favoured reign. He retreated north when he heard of the French threat, and on crossing the Wash, where Norfolk meets Lincolnshire, his baggage carts were caught by a rising tide and he lost the crown jewels as well as the money to pay his men. He rode on to Newark without them and died in 1216, alone, despised, unmissed and probably from dysentery. He is buried in Worcester Cathedral. His oldest son went on to be King Henry III, and from him, the Plantagenet, Tudor and Stuart dynasties arose, including famous monarchs like Edward I, Henry V, Henry VIII and Elizabeth I.

There are four copies of the Magna Carta still in existence, all in Latin. Two are in the British Library and the others in the cathedrals of Lincoln and Salisbury. The great charter was designed to protect the rights of nobles and commoners against the king. There were earlier charters, but this was the first to grant liberties to 'all the free men of our kingdom'. It also bore witness to the king being bound by the law, rather than above it. That is what is meant in the phrase 'the rule of law' – that all authority comes from the law itself.

From 1215 onward, rights existed in England that would travel to Ireland, Wales, Scotland, America and much of the English-speaking world. It provided the foundation of Parliament and English law, which would influence the world through the British Empire. It was also the first step in an independent judiciary, as it allowed cases to be heard away from the king's presence. Those judges became the Common Bench, while the judges who followed the king were called the King's Bench. They too would eventually become separate from the royal court.

The original charter was confirmed more than fifty times by kings from Henry III to Henry V. Though it was largely overlooked between the thirteenth and seventeenth centuries, it became prominent in the Puritan parliament after the civil war as a bulwark of democracy against dictatorship. As such, it was the basis of written law in the country and remained on the statute book until the nineteenth century, with some clauses surviving until the 1950s before being superseded by other laws. It is at least as important as the English Declaration of Rights in 1689, which allowed freedom of speech and was the condition by Parliament of the Prince of Orange taking the British throne.

The ideals of the Magna Carta form the basis of legal systems around the world, from Australia and New Zealand to America, India and Canada. In the US Declaration of Independence and its Constitution, the words of Clause 39 appear twice in direct quotation. In Europe, the system of law has its origins in ancient Rome. One stark difference between the systems remains today. Under British law, that which is not forbidden is allowed. On the continent, only that which is granted is allowed. It is a subtle but crucial distinction.

Clause 39, as quoted at the beginning of this chapter, created 'habeas corpus' – literally 'thou shalt have the body' – which is fundamental to good governance. No man can be taken from his home and imprisoned without charge in England – until very recently, with the introduction of anti-terror legislation. Although recently defeated in the House of Lords, the notion that the House of Commons could vote to imprison a subject for forty-two days without charge is a step backwards to John's times, when the monarch or nobles could take whatever they wanted and common men had no recourse to law.

In recognition of our common heritage with America, Queen Elizabeth II gave an acre at Runnymede to the US on 14 May 1965. Apart from the American embassy, it is the only piece of US soil in England. A memorial garden to John F. Kennedy is there, with views across the river to where King John sealed the Magna Carta. As Winston Churchill once said: 'When the long tally is added, it will be seen that the British nation and the English-speaking world owe far more to the vices of John than to the labours of virtuous sovereigns.'

Recommended
History of England by G.M. Trevelyan.
Magna Carta and its Influence in the World Today by Sir Ivor Jennings.
The Magna Charta Barons and Their American Descendants by Charles Browning.

Oliver Cromwell

Oliver Cromwell remains one of the most controversial figures in history – and indeed in this book. He is a hero to few, but it is no exaggeration to say he changed his country for ever and ushered in the modern age. Cometh the hour, cometh the man. He fought a civil war and executed a king – and by doing so, saved the nation from tyranny. He had no appreciable charm or desire to flatter, yet he could inspire intense loyalty. He was certainly a man of heroic imagination, able to encompass a future without slavish obedience to inherited nobility.

In Cromwell's time, kings like James I and Charles I believed they ruled by divine right, that they had been appointed by God. No royal decision could ever be questioned and no injustice challenged. The man who reversed this style of government was a fanatic both for Protestantism and England. His life would make him the champion of the common man and his efforts were the crucible out of which parliamentary democracy arose. As Churchill would say in 1947: 'Democracy is the worst form of government except all those other forms that have been tried from time to time.'

Very little is known about Cromwell's first forty years. He was born in 1599, at the end of the Elizabethan age. Though the great storms of Elizabeth and Mary had passed, it remained an age of fervent religious belief, with Catholics and Protestants often in brutal conflict.

Cromwell went to Cambridge University in 1616 and left a year later when his father died. His mother was alone with seven unmarried daughters and it is likely that Cromwell returned home to Cambridgeshire to protect them. He married Elizabeth Bourchier of a wealthy Essex family in 1620. The marriage seems to have been a happy one and produced nine children: five boys and four girls.

When James I died in 1625, his son ascended the throne as Charles I. From the first, Charles ruled as an autocrat, utterly disdaining the power of Parliament. He married a French Catholic and had obvious sympathies with Catholic countries such as Ireland and France. He created new taxes and made sweeping decisions on commercial policy. Lacking his father's intelligence and political sense, he simply could not see that the age had changed and men like Cromwell were on the rise.

In 1628, Cromwell stood for Parliament and in the same year was treated for 'Valde Melancholicus' – depression. His health was poor and it was around this time that he experienced the conversion to Puritan Protestantism that would dominate his personal and political life. In a letter, he wrote: 'If I may serve my God either by my doing or my suffering, I shall be most glad.'

Charles I resorted to 'forced loans' to support himself and imprisoned those who refused to pay. Puritans like Cromwell held up the king's lavish lifestyle as an example of everything they despised. In 1628, Cromwell took his seat in Parliament as they declared such taxation illegal. It was Parliament that voted the king's funds, so to maintain control, they attempted to make sure he could not find money anywhere else. The battle lines had been drawn.

In 1629, Charles dissolved Parliament and attempted to rule without them. Until he called them back to Westminster, they could not legally meet. He did not call them for eleven years. During that time, the king raised taxes directly from the population, which caused great resentment. Many Puritans left for America, to find new lives. The famous Mayflower had sailed in 1620, but there were many others in the years that followed.

In addition to Charles's English troubles, his attempt to reform the Scottish Church led to war. Desperate for money, the king could not raise funds on his own and was forced to return Parliament, Cromwell among them. Instead of arranging the king's money, the MPs discussed the legality of his taxes. The 'Short Parliament' lasted for only three weeks before Charles dissolved it in disgust.

By August 1640, the Scots had brought an army to Newcastle. Reluctantly, Charles was forced to recall Parliament once more. This is known as the 'Long Parliament' and once again Cromwell was present. They brokered the Treaty of London with the Scots in 1641 and one of Charles's problems ended. However, on that occasion the Members of Parliament became determined to curtail the king's power over them, even if it meant civil war.

The mood of the country was with Parliament, in part because there was still a great fear of 'Popish' Catholic plots. Money and faith were the main issues that brought about the civil war.

In 1642, Charles wrote to Cambridge University for a loan which would have made him temporarily immune to parliamentary control. Cromwell himself went north on the orders of Parliament. With two hundred men, he blocked the road so that the silver could not be moved south, then took command of Cambridge Castle.

It was the last straw for the king, and in August 1642 Charles I raised his banner in Nottingham. His loyal supporters, known as 'Royalists' or 'Cavaliers', began to flock to him, while an army of Parliamentarians assembled under the Earl of Essex, Cromwell with them. They were commonly known as 'Roundheads' after the shape of their helmets.

The armies met first at Edgehill in October, a few miles from Banbury. In numbers, they were roughly equal and the battle ended in stalemate. The king was unable to return to London and withdrew first to Reading and then to Oxford.

It is difficult now to imagine the shock wave that went through England at the outbreak of civil war. To attack the king himself was considered close to blasphemy in some quarters. Men like Cromwell had a sense of purpose, of right, of God-given destiny, that held the doubters together. He rose quickly in the ranks and in 1643 was effectively in sole command of forces in Essex, Hertfordshire, Cambridgeshire, Huntingdonshire, Suffolk and Norfolk.

His military ability has led some biographers to speculate that he must have been a soldier on the continent for some of those mysterious early years. He was certainly a man who handled authority as if he had been born to it. As Cromwell wrote in a letter to subordinates: 'Service must be done. Command you and be obeyed!' He regarded the battles as a test of Puritanism, but he was also a pragmatist. Famously, he warned his men: 'Put your trust in God, but mind to keep your powder dry.'

The Royalists won a victory at Roundaway Down in 1643, while other battles ended in stalemate. No one could have predicted the outcome of the war as the year ended, but the most important battles were still to come.

Cromwell was more than just a brave and quick-thinking military officer. He was also an able politician and, as the war went on, played a key role in parliamentary discussion. He proposed reform of the churches and the power of the bishops. He opposed the enclosure and sale of common land that was often the only means of support for the poorest families.

In February 1644, Cromwell was promoted to lieutenant general. Conscription was introduced around that time, in part to counter Highland Scottish forces coming south to support the king. The Parliamentary force became known as 'The New Model Army'.

On 2 July 1644, Cromwell commanded the left cavalry wing at Marston Moor, one of the most important battles of the English Civil War. Parliamentary forces outnumbered the Royalists, and for the first time a Royalist cavalry charge was broken in the field. The king's infantry was then slaughtered. Cromwell later denied his own part in it, giving the honour to God, who may or may not have been there. It was at Marston Moor that Prince Rupert, a grandson of James I, nicknamed Cromwell 'Ironside' for his stern demeanour.

The Battle of Naseby in 1645 was Cromwell's greatest military triumph. He commanded the cavalry at the town near Oxford and faced a roughly equal force of Royalist horse under Prince Rupert. King Charles I commanded a small reserve of infantry. Though the battle took place in June, the ground was sodden and soft in places, hampering manoeuvres. As the forces came into range of each other, Cromwell saw that a line of trees and hedges provided perfect cover for a flank attack. He sent a message to his commanding officer asking him to withdraw and, as Cromwell had hoped, the Royalist forces came forward in response. Cromwell sent a detachment of cavalry under cover of the hedges to pour musket fire into the Royalist flank. Like Marlborough and Wellington, he was a man able to read a battlefield and position his forces for maximum effect, remaining calm even under heavy fire.

The Royalist cavalry responded to the flanking attack with a sudden charge, routing some of the Parliamentary forces against them and almost carrying the day. In one of those strange events that can decide battles and even the fate of nations, the pursuing Royalists came across the enemy baggage train and stopped to loot it. For a short time, the Royalist infantry was left with just one cavalry wing. Nonetheless, they pushed the Parliamentary forces back in brutal hand-to-

hand fighting and with musket fire. From a hill, Cromwell watched coldly as men struggled and died in the mud. He held his own riders back, waiting for the remaining Royalist cavalry to charge. At the height of the battle, he saw them move.

He spurred his horse and the two forces galloped together in a great crash. The air filled with bitter musket smoke and the screams of the dying. It was a brief and bloody fight. The Royalists were quickly routed and by the time Prince Rupert brought his cavalry back, the day had been lost.

Over the following year, Cromwell commanded at many different sieges. In 1646, his army moved through Devon and Cornwall, rooting out the king's supporters. He accepted surrender whenever he could, more interested in winning quickly than crushing the enemy. The first major conflict of the civil war ended in 1646.

Parliament was triumphant, the king had survived and some regiments of the New Model Army were disbanded. For a time it looked as if Charles I might accept the limited power of a constitutional monarchy. He was held in various country houses in East Anglia and Hertfordshire and finally at Hampton Court. There, Cromwell met the king and presented parliamentary bills that would severely limit the monarch's powers. Charles prevaricated and delayed, then escaped from custody in 1647, fleeing to the Isle of Wight.

The king still had many supporters in Ireland, Scotland, Wales and the south of England. In 1648, revolts against the New Model Army broke out and the Scots gathered an army of invasion to relieve Charles.

Once more, Cromwell joined his army. He took

back Chepstow and Tenby, then starved Pembroke Castle in Wales into surrender. After that, he marched north against the Scottish army and defeated them at the Battle of Preston, in Lancashire. Denied support, the king was taken into custody once more.

Parliament tried to open negotiations with Charles I. At first, Cromwell supported the king abdicating in exchange for his life, but Charles scorned the offer. He was then sent for trial in London. At an early session, the king said: 'I would know by what power I am called hither. I would know by what authority, I mean lawful authority.' He was found guilty of high treason and Cromwell was one of those who signed his death warrant.

King Charles I was executed in London on 30 January 1649. When his head was cut off, the crowd were allowed to dip their handkerchiefs in royal blood as a souvenir. Cromwell looked down on the body and murmured: 'Cruel necessity.'

England was without a king for the first time in more than a thousand years and there were many who feared the void in power that lay before them.

Cromwell's immediate purpose was to prevent the new regime collapsing after the traumatic event. Ripples of shock spread through society and there was even a threat of foreign invasion from Scotland, France, Ireland or Spain. Not many in Parliament had thought beyond the death of the king. Mutinies occurred around England and had to be put down with force. The country was in danger of flaring up into a bloody revolution and Parliament was hard-pressed to keep the peace.

In Ireland and Scotland, support was staunch for King Charles's eldest son, also named Charles. His father had been King of England, Scotland and Ireland and Royalists now supported the son's claim. He was proclaimed King of Scotland after his father's death in 1649, though not crowned at Scone until 1651.

With the New Model Army, Cromwell was dispatched by Parliament to Ireland to crush Royalist support. In doing so, he earned a reputation for ruthlessness that survives him today. For forty weeks, between August 1649 and May 1650, Ireland ran with blood. The slaughter at Drogheda is the most infamous, when Cromwell's army killed around

3,000 Royalist troops, then rampaged through the town, butchering clergy, women and children. Those who surrendered were executed. Cromwell followed Drogheda with an attack on Wexford, where another 2,000 were killed. In less than a year, Cromwell assaulted twenty-five fortified towns and killed or routed Royalist garrisons. He saw Ireland as the central stronghold of Royalist Catholicism and his aim was the utter destruction of all forces loyal to Charles II. He used his army as an instrument of terror, so that Catholics would never again dare to rise against his Puritan new order. In his religious fanaticism, Cromwell allowed no mercy and his name is forever blackened by that year.

He returned to England in 1650 to lead the army against Royalists in Scotland. It would prove a harder task than the fighting in Ireland. He could not bring the Scots to battle at first. Disease and desertion reduced his fighting strength to 11,000, while the Scots had 22,000. It should have been the end for Cromwell, and before the battle, he bit his own lips until they bled, almost insane with fervour. Near Dunbar, he broke the Scottish right wing, then crumpled the lines into the centre and finally the left wing. Cromwell said of the battle: 'By the Lord of Hosts, they were made as stubble to our swords.'

It was an astonishing victory against such odds and Cromwell laughed when it was over, convinced that God had shown his hand to support him.

Throughout 1651, Cromwell's army feinted with still rebellious Scottish lords, tempting them to come south against London. They took the bait and Cromwell crushed a second army led by Charles II at Worcester, finally ending the battles of the civil war. Charles escaped from the battlefield and made his way over six weeks to France. Famously, he had to spend one night in an oak tree in Shropshire to avoid detection. Ever since, there have been both pubs and ships named 'The Royal Oak'. Charles was aided by Catholics and would eventually become one himself on his deathbed. Meanwhile, Cromwell returned in triumph to London and was received as the saviour of a nation.

His first task was to get rid of the 'Rump Parliament' which had held power without elections for more than a decade. They delayed, as men in power often will, and Cromwell lost patience and declared the parliament dissolved. He had the army, and his word carried weight. He refused to become king, but the country needed a ruler and flailed without one. Cromwell allowed the term 'Lord Protector' and assumed the role as head of state in a new parliament in 1653. His health was poor and it is doubtful that he wanted the role, but he saw it as vital to establish England as a stable republic and to tide her over the storms that had raged since the death of Charles I. Cromwell had taken part in most of them, after all.

He lived less than five years after taking up this last great office. He hammered out a constitution, rejecting the crown and title of king more than once. He did not have dictatorial powers and in fact was often overborne by the councillors and parliaments. He saw himself as a warden of the peace. His health worsened daily and he was never sure he had done enough to prevent England descending into anarchy on his death. In 1656, he wrote that he wanted to see an end to the persecution of Catholics and hoped that England would be populated by 'Godly men'. He also sought greater equity for the poor in the law. In some ways he was successful, as only 6,000 men were needed to keep the peace in England, while 40,000 had to remain in Scotland and Ireland.

Cromwell died of pneumonia in 1658. His body was buried and his effigy carried through almost empty streets to Westminster Abbey. His son Richard tried to rule after him, but lacked the strength and authority of his father. Instead, Parliament asked Charles II to return to the throne in 1661. From then on, the seat of power was with Parliament, not the monarch. The man who had done more than any other to bring about such a change became the focus for poisonous hatred.

Just a few weeks after Charles II became king, Cromwell's body was exhumed. The green and mouldering corpse was given a trial, hanged as a traitor, decapitated, quartered and buried in secret locations around England. It may have looked as if the monarchy was back in all its power, but a bloody lesson had been learned and the people had been heard. Never again would a king or queen rule in tyranny, unfettered by the will of the country.

In the centuries after his death, Cromwell has had his supporters and detractors by the thousand. For a long time, he was a heroic figure in England. He was certainly a man of enormous personal strength, who managed to overturn an entire society and leave it forever changed. He was unflinchingly brave in battle and an inspiring leader to his men. He remains difficult to like, but he was revered by many. Yet any tale of his life must reflect the words he famously uttered to his portrait painter, and be 'warts and all'.

Recommended
God's Englishman by Christopher Hill.
Oliver Cromwell by John Morrill.
Cromwell by Barry Coward.
Film: *Cromwell*, with Richard Harris, 1970.

John Churchill
1st Duke of Marlborough

A fter Cromwell, one of the MPs in Charles II's new parliament was Winston Churchill, ancestor to the British prime minister of World War II. His son, John Churchill, was born on 26 May 1650. Without exaggeration, he would become the greatest soldier of the age. He never lost a battle and the only military man of similar stature in British history is Arthur Wellesley, the Duke of Wellington. In later years, Wellington said that he could 'conceive nothing greater than Marlborough at the head of an English army.'

As with Wellington, John Churchill's time was one of extraordinary upheaval. In all, he would serve five monarchs and, for one of them, spend time as a prisoner in the Tower of London.

The Churchill family had paid huge fines for supporting Charles I during the civil war. After the Restoration, when Charles II took the throne, their loyalty was not forgotten. John Churchill was made a page in the Duke of York's household. It could not have been a better first position, as the duke would later become King James II. John Churchill wanted to be a soldier from an early age and when he was 17 the duke commissioned him as an ensign in a guards regiment.

His first active service was three years in Tangier, fighting the Moors – Muslims of North Africa. He was noted for his good looks and dashing manner even then. When he returned to London aged 20, being handsome brought both trouble and a fortune. Charles II had a number of mistresses, but one of the most voracious was Barbara Villiers, the Duchess of Cleveland. She was 30 when she met John Churchill and they began a passionate and potentially dangerous affair.

The king discovered the relationship, but in those easy-going, post-Puritan days, he was not particularly troubled. Young John did have to leap out of a window with the king coming up the stairs, but that was to save embarrassing his monarch, rather than from any fear of punishment. It is likely that John sired a child with Barbara Villiers. King Charles had a number of bastard children and did his best to give them all a start in life. Of Barbara's dubiously fathered daughter, the king said: 'I know the child is not mine, but I will acknowledge it for old times' sake.'

England was at war for the third time with the Dutch in the 1670s, a conflict between blood relatives, as the Protestant William of Orange was Charles II's nephew. As in the previous century, the struggle between Catholic and Protestant would be a driving force for change. England and Holland should have been natural allies, but Charles II was a closet Catholic and became one officially on his deathbed. He preferred to be an ally of the French, but when they invaded Holland, William of Orange ordered the dykes opened and flooded them off his land.

John Churchill's first naval action occurred during this period. He was with the Duke of York at the Battle of Sole Bay, off the Suffolk coast. The Dutch fleet trapped British ships against a lee shore, then hammered them with cannon. The duke's flagship was so badly damaged that he had to transfer to another. Churchill remained on board and survived an action in which a third of the crew were killed. As night came, he was able to get ashore and returned to London.

Churchill could not rise in rank without funds. A captaincy cost a small fortune and so could only be obtained by the wealthy, which Churchill was certainly not. It is assumed that Barbara Villiers paid the sum needed and Churchill became a captain in the marines. He travelled to Flanders (modern-day Belgium) to join the French at the siege of Maastricht, then in Dutch hands.

It was a massive assault against a well-defended fortress. British forces were led by the Duke of Monmouth, one of Charles's favourite bastard sons. Their French allies were commanded by King Louis XIV himself.

When the British regiments were driven back, French musketeers were called forward, under the command of their most famous leader, D'Artagnan. They forced their way in and Churchill went with them. He was the one who planted the French flag on the parapet of the fort. Louis XIV commended Churchill for his courage and Monmouth later praised the young man, calling him 'the brave man who saved my life'. His future looked bright indeed. Though King Charles was forced by Parliament to withdraw from the Franco-Dutch war, Churchill remained in service on the continent.

At the age of just 24, Churchill had served in Tangier, Flanders and Alsace-Lorraine, in what would one day be Germany. He remained famously handsome and was growing skilful as a professional soldier. He had also managed to collect payment for his service in the form of chests of silver. For one who had known real poverty as a boy, Churchill always expected to be well rewarded for his talents.

In London, he met Sarah Jennings, a girl with a similar background to his own. Fortunately, there was no conflict with Barbara Villiers, who had gone to France and continued her pleasantly predatory ways with the Archbishop of Paris. Churchill married Sarah Jennings in 1677. It would be a happy union that lasted for more than forty years. He also bought the position of 'Master of the Duke's Robes', which established him in the close circle around the Duke of York.

By the end of the 1670s, the Duke of York's daughter, Mary, married William of Orange, creating an alliance that justifiably alarmed the French king. Suddenly, the entire weight of British arms was behind the defence of Holland.

Churchill was made colonel of one of four new regiments and Parliament voted a million pounds to a war chest. For the Duke of York, he then travelled to Holland to meet William and decide a plan of attack against the French. He took with him an offer of 20,000 soldiers who would fight to protect Mary. She was, after all, Charles II's niece. In the end, war between Britain and France did not come about and all the alarms died to nothing.

During this time, Churchill was part of the Duke of York's most trusted circle and accompanied him to Edinburgh for two years. There, the duke persecuted Scottish Protestants without mercy. He continued to favour John Churchill and elevated him to the lowest rung of the peerage as Baron Eyemouth in Scotland.

When the duke finally returned to London in the frigate Gloucester, it ran aground and sank. He and Churchill both survived, with only thirty-eight others out of three hundred. It is said that Churchill held off those who would have swamped the boat as the duke was rowed clear of the sinking ship.

In 1685, Charles II died suddenly of a stroke and the Duke of York, James Stuart, became King of England, Scotland and Ireland. With his staunch Catholicism, it would not be a happy reign, but John Churchill was in the right place at the right time.

The first crisis of the new reign came in June that year, when the Duke of Monmouth landed with four hundred soldiers at Lyme Regis in the south of England. Monmouth was a Protestant and he intended to raise a rebellion against his Catholic uncle, James II.

John's father, Winston Churchill, was MP for Lyme Regis. It was he who received the news of the landing and both Churchills went to tell the king of this threat to his throne. More alarming still was the news that Monmouth was supported by the Earl of Argyll in Scotland, who had also raised an army.

Protestant England was already hostile to the idea of a Catholic monarch and men flocked to join Monmouth until he had a militia of around 7,000, most of them armed with just pitchforks and scythes. He entered Taunton in Somerset and was greeted as a hero.

Churchill was promoted to major general and sent to join forces with Lord Feversham, taking cavalry troops and five companies of infantry with him. Lord Feversham's soldiers attacked Monmouth first, getting the worst of the encounter. At Sedgemoor, Monmouth organised a daring night attack on the royal camp and might have been successful if a pistol had not gone off, alerting Churchill's sentries. Fighting went on in the darkness and at dawn the royal cannon opened up. It was over quickly, but the retribution was brutal, with thousands of Monmouth's rebels hanged and butchered before the day was out.

Monmouth himself was executed at Tower Hill in London and many of his supporters were tried by 'Hanging' Judge Jeffreys, who was as ruthless as his nickname suggests. In Scotland, the Earl of Argyll was caught and executed on James's orders. The Monmouth Rebellion had been crushed and King James II was grateful to Churchill for the part he had played.

The next three years were difficult ones for the country. James had learned some lessons from the rebellion and allowed Parliament to raise funds for a standing army of fifteen thousand. Yet he put Catholics into prominent positions in the army, ports, fortresses and universities, made overtures to the Pope in Rome and had Catholic priests with him as he toured the country.

Even John Churchill came under suspicion for his Protestant sympathies. He was caught in a real dilemma under a fervently Catholic king to whom he owed almost everything.

In resistance to the growing power of Catholicism in England, a cabal of powerful Protestants began to meet in secrecy. Their plan was to replace James II with his nephew, William of Orange, an undertaking described by the French king as 'the greatest conspiracy ever formed'. Both William and his wife Mary were grandchildren of Charles I, so had claims to the thrones of Britain and Ireland. The problem for the conspirators was knowing how John Churchill would jump when the time came. He was a charismatic soldier and the army would follow his lead if he supported James, or indeed William. In one letter, Churchill wrote to William: 'My places and the king's favour, I set at naught in comparison with being true to my religion. In all things but this may the king command me.' He did not, however, give an outright promise of support.

In June 1688, it all came to a head when James II's second wife gave birth to another son, creating a hereditary Catholic line. When William of Orange heard of the birth, he is reported to have said that it was 'now or never' for the rebellion. On the last day of June, seven prominent men signed a formal invitation to William of Orange and his wife Mary to take the thrones of England, Ireland and Scotland.

William gathered a fleet and an army of 20,000 in what would be the last armed invasion of England, although by invitation. On 5 November 1688, he stepped onto British soil at Tor Bay in the south-west of England.

James II needed the military mind of John Churchill and the king promoted him to lieutenant general. Churchill had become the first soldier in England and he rode with the king towards the enemy before making camp for the night.

We can only imagine what went through Churchill's mind that evening. He owed everything to the duke who had become king. Yet Churchill had seen savage persecution of Protestants in Scotland. Though he was Protestant himself, Churchill's faith was of the quiet and undemonstrative kind. He wrestled with his conscience and finally made a decision.

On the night of 23 November, Churchill left the king's camp to join that of William of Orange at Crewkerne, in Somerset. He took 400 loyal cavalrymen with him. It was a crippling blow to James II. Churchill left a letter for his old friend, explaining that his conscience and concern for his religion had prompted the betrayal. James was furious and sent men to London to arrest Churchill's wife, Sarah, but she was warned and escaped.

With his key military tactician gone over to the other side, the full state of the king's troubles became clear. James had a stammer and lacked the charisma that might have saved the day. In the end, the 'Glorious Revolution' of 1688 was a fairly peaceful handover of power. King James II was allowed to leave England for France in December. Pathetically, he was beaten up by a gang of fishermen while he waited for a ship. Judge Jeffreys tried to escape his hunters by shaving off his eyebrows, but he was caught and died a broken man in the Tower of London.

Before William and Mary were crowned King and Queen, Parliament prepared the Bill of Rights, to which their agreement was a condition of taking the throne. This was the third major stage in the evolution of British monarchy that began with the Magna Carta, continued under Cromwell and reached a peaceful state after 1689.

The Bill of Rights further limited the powers of the reigning monarch and guaranteed they would be subject to the laws of Parliament. Finally, it established William and Mary's right to continue the royal line, or if there were no children, that Princess Anne, a suitably Protestant daughter of James II, would be next in line for the throne. Even then, the final vote to elect William king was close: fifty-one to forty-nine.

Before he was 40 years old, Churchill had played for the highest possible stakes and come out on the winning side. He was made Earl of Marlborough and had sole command of William's English army. He could not have known it at that moment of triumph, but his best years and greatest battles still lay before him.

The first test of William's reign came as he was preparing for his own coronation. James II had not gone quietly into retirement. Instead, he landed in Ireland, where a 'Jacobite' (meaning 'of James') rebellion had begun in all but the Protestant north. At the same time, the French king launched an attack on William's reduced forces in Flanders.

William responded by going to Ireland himself and sending Marlborough to repel the French in Flanders. With an army of 8,000, Churchill linked up with Dutch forces and took a fortified town. When the French attacked, Marlborough swept out to hammer one flank and his allies hit the other. The French were smashed, losing some 2,000 men.

In Ireland, William defeated James's forces in July 1690. The Battle of the Boyne took place by the River Boyne near the town of Drogheda – the scene of Cromwell's brutal massacre of Royalist Catholics years before. James fled the field to Dublin, but there were still 5,000 French troops in Ireland and the country was up in arms. To make matters worse, William's fleet had been defeated at sea by the French in the Battle of Beachy Head.

Marlborough returned to England in sole command of forces there. He gathered an expeditionary force to take to Ireland, and in 1690 eighty ships sailed from Portsmouth to Cork. Marlborough knew if he could take Cork and nearby forts, he would break the French access to the country. In Cork Harbour, Marlborough was joined by 5,000 of William's troops in Ireland and forced to give overall command to the Duke of Württemberg.

They bombarded and took Cork quickly before moving on to Kinsale, a stronghold town to the west with two major forts. To take the first, Marlborough put 800 men in boats and they made a successful night attack, destroying the garrison. When his guns arrived by road, he began a bombardment that led to the surrender of the second fort in three days. In just six weeks, he had secured an area against future French invasions. He hoped to be rewarded with the position of 'Master of Ordnance' – a post that brought vast revenues and would have allowed him to purchase the title of duke. Instead, William gave the post to another. He said later that he detested Marlborough for his betrayal of James, for all that William had profited by it.

Defeated once again, James left Ireland for France and the remaining French soldiers went with him while they still could. William had secured his reign and made the Glorious Revolution a reality rather than merely a parliamentary conceit. More importantly, he now had the allied British and Dutch forces to deal with the remaining threat of the French King, Louis XIV. He had, however, lost Marlborough as a supporter.

The relationship between Marlborough and William was fragile. Marlborough had supported William against James, but William was a foreign king who surrounded himself with Dutchmen. William was also aware that if Marlborough could desert one king, he might one day do it again. In addition, Marlborough's wife Sarah was lady-in-waiting to Princess Anne, and William suspected it was Sarah behind Anne's demands for a huge living allowance. William was an ugly man and he may also have known that Anne referred to him as 'the monster' or 'the abortion'. Either way, he was wary of Marlborough's influence and never more so than when he discovered Marlborough was still corresponding with James in exile, a dangerous game indeed.

From the distance of later centuries, it is perhaps understandable that Marlborough should have kept contact with James after all he owed to him. To William, it looked like a betrayal. However, while he still needed Marlborough, he did nothing.

It was not long before France attacked again. The city of Mons in Flanders had been under the command of Dutch forces for more than a decade. In 1691, Louis XIV's forces assaulted the fortress and it fell. William sent Marlborough to command British soldiers in the area, but he made little progress in ousting the French before fighting stopped for winter. Marlborough is reported to have said that William 'had not virtue enough to value high ends or courage to punish his enemies'. All such rash comments would have been reported to the king.

Relations between William and Marlborough soured and came to a head when William received news of a conspiracy involving Marlborough to replace him with Princess Anne as queen. In addition, William suspected Marlborough of leaking information about an attack on Dunkirk.

Queen Mary ordered Anne to dismiss Marlborough's wife from her service. She refused. The following day, William dismissed Marlborough from all his official positions and exiled him from the court. To make matters worse, Marlborough had many enemies as soon as William's favour was removed. His name was discovered on a secret document pledging to restore King James II to the throne. It was later revealed to be a clumsy forgery, but in 1692, Marlborough was arrested and imprisoned in the Tower of London.

The Privy Council, William's advisers and the Cabinet, examined the forged letter and Marlborough was set free after just five weeks in the Tower. He spent his time in Princess Anne's household with his wife, removed from news of the war against the French. Though he had been cleared of treason, his status had never been lower. He had funds from the sale of his court positions and invested it in the new 'Bank of

England' which was set up around this time, making a healthy profit on the rising shares.

Meanwhile, the armies of William went from one defeat to the next in Flanders. Some historians believe Marlborough sent a secret letter to James, warning him of an attack from Camaret Bay against the port of Brest that became a disaster for William. However, the 'Camaret Bay letter' was in the handwriting of Louis XIV's secretary. Marlborough's distant descendant, Sir Winston Churchill, said later that 'you would not hang a dog' on such evidence.

At the end of 1694, Queen Mary II died of smallpox and William was distraught. He had no children and suddenly the clause in the Bill of Rights that made Princess Anne the royal heir became active. Perhaps because of this, William looked again at his life. He began negotiations with the French king and a peace accord was signed in 1697. Louis XIV accepted the peace, though he refused to expel James from France.

With Marlborough too, William was willing to forgive old wounds. In 1698, as a lonely widower, William accepted Marlborough at court once more, appointing him governor to Princess Anne's son.

In 1700, the delicate peace with France that William had negotiated was thrown into chaos by the death without heirs of Charles II of Spain. What followed would become known as the 'War of the Spanish Succession' as William scrambled to prevent the French king from adding Spain to his collection and becoming the pre-eminent European power. Louis XIV had a claim through his Spanish wife and he was quick to force the issue, placing his grandson on the throne of Spain and officially recognising him as King Philip V of Spain.

At first, William tried to negotiate a peaceful separation of Spanish territories between England and France. King Louis knew the reduced strength of William's army and he broke the agreement when it suited him, convinced there could be no threat from that quarter. Holland could certainly not contain France on its own. To make his point, King Louis sent armies into Flanders, taking the forts that were William's primary line of defence.

In England, Parliament became slowly aware that the French king would not be appeased and was in fact a serious threat. In 1701, they passed the Act of Settlement, which ensured the throne of Britain would always be Protestant. That important act complete, William appointed Marlborough as commander-in-chief of English forces in Holland and travelled there with him in the royal yacht.

It is worth pointing out that though the reasons for war were complex and mired in political alliances and negotiation, the essential purpose was a simple one: to prevent a unification of Europe under a French dictator, sixty years before Napoleon Bonaparte was born. Neither Italy nor Germany were unified at this point, except as a group of separate states such as Bavaria. France was the true power on the continent, though parts that are France today fought against Louis, as with the territory of Savoy.

King Louis XIV had up to 400,000 well-trained soldiers and massive supplies of gunpowder, shot and heavy guns. In addition, he had just achieved partial control of Spain, and if he was able to consolidate his gains, he would be the most powerful man on earth. He had threatened invasion of England before in his support of James II. The defence of William's realm therefore depended on Louis being stopped and stopped hard. William controlled the sea with his Dutch and British fleets, but the battles would be on land, where he was weak.

James II died of a brain haemorrhage in France in 1701. King Louis was quick to seize the initiative and declared James's son (also called James Stuart and later known as 'The Old Pretender') King of Britain. It was a final betrayal and blow to William, but he would not live to avenge it. After falling from a horse at Hampton Court in March 1702, he too died, and Queen Anne came to the throne, the first official queen of a united Britain.

Anne put her trust in Marlborough to save the country from French aggression. As William never had, she granted the positions Marlborough craved, from Knight of the Garter and Master of Ordnance, to Captain-General of all British forces on the continent. His income rose to more than £54,000, a vast sum in those days. He was 51, still handsome, fit and experienced. Queen Anne's hopes were well placed.

Marlborough led coalition forces including Dutch, Danes, Prussians, English, Austrian and Portuguese, during a war that would last until 1713 and throw all of Europe into turmoil. British troops wore red coats and carried flintlock muskets with bayonets, not yet replaced by the more famous Brown Bess. Marlborough drilled them endlessly in three-shot volleys: the first rank kneeling as the others reloaded in sequence, producing almost continuous fire. He also relied on the power of cavalry charges, accelerating at the last moment after trotting towards the enemy. His artillery ranged from six- to twenty-four-pounders, but it had a poor range and was rarely a major factor in the war except for sieges. As importantly, he established rules of conduct for his soldiers, so that they were forbidden looting and rape after battles. The army Wellington would one day inherit owed a great deal to John Churchill.

Churchill's four great battles in the war of the Spanish Succession were Blenheim (1704), Ramillies (1706), Oudenarde (1708) and Malplaquet (1709). Through those victories, he created a trained and professional British army which was the equal of anything in Europe.

The Battle of Blenheim, which took place by the banks of the River Danube in Bavaria, remains Marlborough's most famous victory. Despite bringing roughly similar forces to the field, the French marshal was captured and the French regiment of Navarre burned its own colours in shame. Between 10,000 and 15,000 French and Bavarian soldiers were killed, with another 24,000 taken prisoner. Marlborough lost 4,500 killed and 7,500 wounded. Bavaria fell quickly to the allies and was out of the war. More importantly, the Battle of Blenheim smashed the myth of French military superiority that had lasted on the continent for forty years.

Marlborough sent home news of the victory on the back of a tavern bill: 'I have not time to say more, but to beg you will give my duty to the Queen, and let her know her army has had a glorious victory.' The scrap of paper still survives today and can be viewed in Blenheim Palace.

Ramillies is a great open plain, near Maastricht. In 1706, King Louis XIV ordered the Duke of Villeroi to destroy Marlborough's troublesome army. As the morning mists cleared, Marlborough saw the French force of 60,000 were in sight on the plain, but badly deployed over four miles of rough ground. Marlborough drew up his men in a much shorter line and his allied force attacked on the afternoon of 23 May. Lord Orkney went for the French left, while Marlborough sent his Dutch cavalry against the French right at the village of Taviers. They took Taviers quickly and the French were forced to counter-attack or lose the entire wing. They failed to retake the village and the Dutch held the position, sending the French reeling.

In furious response, the entire French cavalry charged once again. A savage melee developed around the village and the Dutch were pushed back. The battle hung in the balance.

Marlborough personally led cavalry in a counter-attack to relieve the Dutch. His horse was killed under him and Lord Orkney said that 'Milord Marlborough was rid over'. Even so, the charge smashed the French forces on that part of the battlefield.

It was then that Marlborough used a fold of ground that hid his soldiers from view. He was able to draw off a major part of his men, leaving enough flags and banners to make the French think his forces were still there in force. The rest were marched to the centre and began the last assault. Villeroi's cavalry had been broken and the centre crumpled and collapsed, with some 6,000 prisoners being taken before darkness.

In all, the French lost up to 18,000 killed and wounded as well as some fifty of their field guns and 120 regimental colours. Marlborough's losses were around 3,000 killed and wounded, with only a small number of English soldiers lost.

After Ramillies, Marlborough had control of almost all of Flanders, including Brussels, Bruges, Dunkirk and Ostend. The French had been beaten back to just a few forts, such as Mons. They were on the defensive at last.

In July 1708, French forces threatened Oudenarde, a massive fortress town that dominated the area around the River Scheldt. Marlborough marched four columns fifty miles in sixty hours, an astonishing turn of speed for massed troops, equipment and guns. He brought 80,000 men to Oudenarde, only 8,000 of whom were British. They forded a river with pontoon bridges and caught the French completely unprepared. Confusion and panic in the French chain of command helped Marlborough to win a victory with a swift pincer movement. As evening came, the French retreated, having lost some 6,000 men and another 9,000 as prisoners. Marlborough had lost around 3,000 that day, including 200 English.

To follow up the encounter, Marlborough and Prince Eugene of Savoy decided to take Lille in France, to the south of Oudenarde. From there, they would have a base to launch an invasion and finally break King Louis XIV's power. Prince Eugene conducted the siege, while Marlborough remained in the area, fending off any attempt to retake the ground.

Lille surrendered in 1708 and the path to Paris was finally open. It was a shocking blow for the French king and he sued for peace. With the allies in such a strong position, the terms he was offered were impossible to meet. He refused and the invasion of France was on.

In 1709, Marlborough came into France with 100,000 men. The French retreated to massive fortifications around Douai and La Bassée. Faced with besieging such positions, Marlborough despaired of a quick end to the war and pulled back instead into Flanders. He took the fortress of Tournai, then moved on to attack Mons, the last major French-held fortress in Flanders.

King Louis told the Duke of Villars to protect Mons at any cost. Villars moved an army of 90,000 to the south of the fortress, close by the village of Malplaquet. Marlborough and Prince Eugene brought their force of 110,000 against him and battle began with an artillery exchange on 11 September. More than 5,000 allied soldiers were killed in half an hour of brutal cannon fire. Prince Eugene himself was struck in the neck by a musket ball, though he survived. At noon, he and Marlborough met to confer. The French centre had been thinned and it was there that Marlborough sent nineteen battalions of British and Prussian infantry. They forced their way through and Marlborough's cavalry moved up in support.

Villars began a counter-attack, but was shot in the leg and forced to retire from the battle. The cavalry forces on both sides hammered each other for hours until the French began to fall back around 3 p.m. It had been a gruelling battle and Marlborough's men were too battered to pursue them. They had won, but at the worst cost Marlborough or anyone else had seen. The French had some 12,000 killed or wounded, but the allies had lost twice that number. As a result, Malplaquet had the highest 'butcher's bill' of the seventeenth century. Mons fell shortly afterwards and the French king was forced to ask for peace a second time, only to reject the terms once more. Even so, Marlborough's reputation for military brilliance was badly shaken and he was criticised for the casualties at home.

Those four battles broke French ambition, but after such losses, another attempt to invade France was impossible. Marlborough was recalled to Britain and replaced as commander. Peace would come at last in the Treaty of Utrecht in 1713, which confirmed Philip V as King of Spain, but prevented him from also being the heir to France. So ended Louis XIV's great vision of a Europe united under France.

In England, Queen Anne had quarrelled with Sarah Churchill over the intention to build a great house for the Churchill family, a gift from the nation. They bickered and fell out over the sums of money from the public purse. Without that royal protection, Marlborough was once again vulnerable to his enemies.

In 1711, he was accused of embezzling army funds. He was eventually able to prove the allegations were utterly unjustified, but by then, he had been dismissed from his offices by the queen. He and his wife left England, returning only when Queen Anne died in 1714.

As Anne had died without heirs, the Elector of Hanover became George I of England, a claim to the throne created by marriage to Charles I's niece. George admired Marlborough and once more the Churchills were back in favour with the court. The new king gave Marlborough both position and wealth for his service in the Spanish War of Succession. Though Marlborough's health was failing at the age of 66, he would often ride out to the grounds of the great palace in Oxfordshire being built for him. It would be named Blenheim, the gift of a nation, though he ended up having to pay for a great deal of it himself. Even so, the land is still owned by the monarchy and each year, on the anniversary of the battle, the current duke has to see the reigning monarch and pay a 'rent' of a captured French flag, specially made for the occasion. If he is late by even one day, Blenheim will pass back into royal ownership.

Marlborough moved into Blenheim with his wife and family in 1719. He died after a series of strokes on 16 June 1722. That great estate would later be the birthplace of Prime Minister Sir Winston Churchill. It remains one of the most beautiful buildings and grounds in the country and is open to the public to visit.

Marlborough was relentlessly ambitious all his life, even to the extent of changing royal horses mid-stream with James and William. He was a supremely gifted general and without his victories, it can be said with certainty that France would have unified Europe under a despotic rule – with the conquest of Britain following shortly afterwards. The War of the Spanish Succession was an incredibly complex web of alliances and manoeuvres, but the future of the world hung on those battles – and Marlborough's abilities.

Back in 1712, when John Churchill was 60, a ballad was published called 'The Duke of Marlborough's Delight'. It became better known as 'Wolfe's Song' when James Wolfe sang it aloud on the night before his victory and death at Quebec.

> *"Let wine and mirth abound; The trumpet sound,*
> *The colours they do fly my boys;*
> *To fight, kill or wound; As you would be found,*
> *Contented with hard fare, my boys,*
> *On the cold ground."*

Recommended
The First Churchill by George Malcolm Thomson.
Marlborough's Campaigns by I. Beckett.
Marlborough: England's Fragile Genius by Richard Holmes.

Captain Philip Broke
and the Frigate Shannon

———◦———

While Great Britain was leading the twenty-two-year war against French dictatorship, the new Republic of the United States of America decided it would twist the British lion's tail. It attempted to conquer Canada.

Americans grandly call this diversion the 'War of 1812'. Canadians remember it as the unsuccessful American invasion of their country, while in Britain it barely registers on the horizon of history. Yet it did provide one of the greatest ship-to-ship victories in the history of naval warfare – when the 38-gun frigate HMS *Shannon* met the 50-gun frigate USS *Chesapeake*.

It all began on 18 June 1812. A British army was advancing towards Madrid in the liberation of Spain, Bonaparte was advancing on Moscow with a vast army to conquer Russia, while the Royal Navy sailed into the eastern Baltic to support Russia. The navy also supported the army in Spain as well as a hundred other duties to keep the seas free when, without warning, America declared war on Britain and invaded Canada.

America used the slogan 'Free Trade and Sailors' Rights' as its excuse for war. President Madison's true intention, however, was to conquer the colonies of Upper Canada, Lower Canada, Newfoundland and Nova Scotia and force them into the United States.

In its three-pronged attack in 1812, American troops were defeated in the west, in the centre and in the east. They invaded again in 1813, reached the capital York (now called Toronto) and burned the wooden city to the ground before retreating. After a naval skirmish in Lake Erie, America regained the territory it had earlier lost.

To the British government this was a minor irritant. The United States had sixteen warships, Great Britain some 1,000. The Royal Navy could crush the American navy at any moment it wished. Similarly, Wellington's regiments would walk through any army America might raise.

However, there were – as America well knew – more important issues in the world. In 1813, Bonaparte was in retreat after his defeat before Moscow, the British army had liberated Spain and was about to invade France and the navy was supplying every country, army and guerrilla band that declared against France. Patrolling Canada to Bermuda were just one ship of the line, seven frigates and some sloops. They would have to manage the best they could against America's sixteen ships.

One of those seven British frigates was HMS *Shannon*, under Captain Philip Broke. He had been *Shannon*'s only commander since her commissioning in 1806 and he had a well-trained and loyal crew. Since the US declaration of war he had captured more than ten American vessels along the east coast. He had chased the larger and faster USS *Constitution* for sixty-five hours before the American frigate escaped into Boston harbour, and in June 1813 the *Shannon* was again patrolling outside Boston. She had been waiting fifty-six days for an American warship to come out and face her.

In a long action the previous December, the USS *Constitution* had defeated the smaller British frigate HMS *Java* and Broke was keen to redress that loss. He sent several verbal challenges to the warships in Boston via freed American prisoners, but with no response. On the morning of 1 June, knowing he would soon have to return to Halifax to refit and reprovision his worn vessel, Broke sent a personal letter to the captain of the *Chesapeake*, beginning: 'As the *Chesapeake* appears now ready for sea, I request you will do me the favour to meet the *Shannon* with her, ship to ship, to try the fortune of our respective flags.' He then gave details of the Shannon, the size of vessel, number and calibre of guns, number of men, and so on. The Americans could not refuse such a challenge.

Cruising outside the harbour, Broke saw USS *Chesapeake*, commanded by Captain James Lawrence, prepare to sail. The beaches and cliffs filled with Americans who had come to watch the battle, expecting a decisive *Chesapeake* victory over the weather-beaten and smaller *Shannon*.

HMS *Shannon* was a 38-gun frigate with one main gun deck, the smallest vessel for a captain's command. She was 150- feet long, with a 39-foot beam and a crew of 330 experienced officers, seamen, landsmen and boys.

USS *Chesapeake* was a 50-gun frigate with one main gun deck. She was 152-feet long, with a 41-foot beam and a crew of 440 experienced officers and seamen. She was slightly larger than *Shannon*, with 110 more crew and twelve more guns. She also fired heavier shot. In a single broadside, *Chesapeake* could fire 572 lb of shot while *Shannon* could fire 510 lb. In addition, *Chesapeake* mounted an 18 lb quarterdeck cannon and Shannon a 9 lb cannon. If the battle came to close quarters, the extra 110 men on board the American frigate might make all the difference. The two vessels met east of Boston Lighthouse, between Cape Anne and Cape Cod, on 1 June 1813.

Battle commenced at 5.51 p.m. when *Shannon* opened fire at 38 yards with a broadside from her starboard guns. Initial broadsides were exchanged, but the British fired four to the American one and their impeccable gunnery beat in the bulwarks and threw back the cannon on *Chesapeake*'s deck. The American wheel was deliberately shot away in a cloud of broken wood and splinters by *Shannon*'s quarterdeck cannon, and *Chesapeake* swung stern-to before her emergency steering could be manned. *Shannon* riddled her along the length of her gun deck from stern to bow, causing chaos and dismounting more carronades.

Captain Lawrence was wounded, but at 5.55 p.m. ordered his men to board *Shannon* as *Chesapeake*'s stern drifted onto the starboard side of the British ship. It was his chance to make his extra 110 men tell. Yet Captain Broke was quicker. He called 'Follow me who can!' and boarded *Chesapeake* over her stern, leaping onto her shattered quarterdeck with his men pouring after him. As the American frigate swung alongside, British topmen lashed the ships' yard arms together and boarded that way too, sweeping *Chesapeake*'s masts clear of sharp-shooters and seamen.

On the deck 100 feet below Lawrence cried 'Don't give up the ship' as he was taken below to the surgeon. Before the wave of British seamen his men retreated below, too, and resistance came to an end. The entire attack had taken just eleven minutes before it was over – with the *Chesapeake* battered, boarded and beaten.

As the British seamen cheered, three Americans dropped from *Chesapeake*'s rigging in a last attempt to kill Captain Broke. Broke killed one, was knocked down by the swinging musket of the second and, while he was on the deck, the third slashed him across his head with a cutlass. Infuriated British seamen dispatched the two Americans before they could attack again.

The last act followed immediately when an American midshipman reached the deck from his station aloft to surrender. The wounded and bleeding Broke only just managed to save the man's life from enraged British seamen. They were angry at the attack upon their captain when the battle was won and absolutely furious at the buckets of quicklime they'd discovered around *Chesapeake*'s main deck. The quicklime was to throw into the faces and eyes of the British seamen, well beyond the accepted rules of warfare. Only the extraordinary speed of the action and boarding had prevented its use.

Chesapeake was captured at 6.02 p.m., and the Blue Ensign hoisted over the US Ensign. The audience on the shore could barely believe their eyes. On the American frigate, sixty were killed and eighty-eight wounded. On the British frigate twenty-three were killed and sixty wounded. With a prize crew in *Chesapeake*, the two ships sailed for Halifax, which they reached on 6 June. Lawrence died there of his wounds and was buried with military honours, while *Chesapeake* was taken into the Royal Navy and served until the end of the wars against France. She was broken up in 1815, her timbers used to build a mill in Hampshire.

Broke recovered from his cutlass wound and returned to Britain, where he was made a baronet and so became Sir Philip Broke. The navy sensibly drew on his expertise to change and improve its gunnery and accuracy, improvements which were used to particular effect in the victory at Acre in 1840. *Shannon* continued in service until paid off into the reserve fleet in 1831. She was broken up in 1859.

As for the 'War of 1812', Britain scraped together an amphibious force from the West Indies which sailed north in August 1814. It sailed up the River Potomac to take Washington, burning the White House and other government buildings in retaliation for the American burning of York. Canada, Nova Scotia and Newfoundland voluntarily remained British until independence in 1867. The United States revoked its declaration of war at the Treaty of Ghent in December 1814.

To this day, Canadians like to ask Americans: 'And how is your new White House?'

Recommended
The Naval War of 1812 by C.S. Forester.
The Shannon and the Chesapeake by H.F. Pullen.
Royal Navy Museum, Portsmouth, Hampshire.
Frigate HMS Trincomalee, museum ship, Hartlepool, County Durham.
Frigate USS Constitution, museum ship, Charlestown,
    Massachusetts, USA.
Chesapeake Mill, National Trust, Wickham, Hampshire.

Aphra Behn

Aphra Behn (née Johnson) was the first professional female novelist, a Royalist spy for King Charles II, a traveller, novelist, poet and renowned wit. She was also one of the most successful and prolific dramatists in Restoration theatre, yet is almost completely unknown today.

Born in Canterbury in 1640, Aphra Johnson grew up during the English Civil War and was a child when Charles I was executed in 1649. Cromwell came to power and in 1651 beat the army of the executed king's son, Charles II, forcing him to flee abroad. After Cromwell's death, Charles II was invited to return and take up his father's throne in what is now known as the Restoration. He did so in 1660, when Aphra Behn was just nineteen. Charles II was known as the 'Merry Monarch', and after the grimly puritan years under Cromwell, the Restoration would become a period of hedonistic excess. He even allowed women on stage for the first time and had one of the most famous, Nell Gwyn, as his mistress.

Aphra Behn thrived in a time when playwrights and poets were lauded as public figures. She wrote more than twenty plays, many of them light comedies. For her poetry, she was even considered as a 'female laureate' in her life, which makes her near disappearance from history all the more surprising.

Around 1663, Aphra set sail with her family for Surinam, or Guiana, at that time a disputed territory between the British and Dutch. Details about her father are sketchy, but it seems likely that Bartholomew Johnson travelled there as part of an attempt to build a British sugar plantation and colony. Such long voyages were always perilous and her father died before he reached his destination.

For his prodigious young daughter, the trip involved meeting African slaves and white owners and would one day help to produce her most famous surviving work, *Oroonoko: Or, The Royal Slave.*

She returned to England in 1664 and married a merchant of Dutch or German extraction to become Aphra Behn. He died in 1665, probably a victim of the Great Plague that swept London at that time. It was as a young and penniless widow that she met Sir Thomas Killigrew, a confirmed Royalist. He moved in circles of power and intrigue and it was through Killigrew that she would be introduced to the second Duke of Buckingham, as well as the young man who would eventually become James II of England.

At that time, England was at war with the Dutch over trade and the country was a hotbed of political alliances and factions. Information was desperately needed on the Dutch, and through Thomas Killigrew, Aphra Behn was asked to go to Antwerp as a spy for the king. As well as her brother and a maid, she travelled with Sir Antony Desmarches, a Royalist agent of long standing.

She was not well paid for the work and found her funds dwindling as she moved in society there. She identified one man as a spy for the Dutch and passed on information from other spies to England. It was not long before she had to pawn a ring to survive. In her letters, she was forced to ask for money at the same time as commenting on Dutch forces and deployment with the code name 'Astrea'. With the necessity for brief reports, she became dissatisfied with the codes she had been given and created her own.

She also used numbers for complete names: Amsterdam became 26, her contact Scot was 159, his colleague Bamfield was 38 and Astrea was 160.

Her financial situation worsened steadily, not least because she had to pay for her contact to return to England, which cost ten pounds a time. Her debts mounted to a hundred pounds by September 1666, when the Great Fire broke out in London and reduced two-thirds of the city to charred ruins. In the face of that greater catastrophe, her plea for funds went unanswered. By November, she had pawned everything she owned and wrote bluntly to one of her superiors: 'For God's sake my Lord, do something to help me out of my affliction.'

She was sent fifty pounds, which was less than half of her debt to the innkeeper where she was staying. At that time, there was very little money for the spy networks that had once thrived under Cromwell. Aphra borrowed money to return to England and, when she could not pay it back, was coerced into another spying mission to Venice by Thomas Killigrew. She was moving in a ruthless world. Some sources suggest that she spent time in debtors' prison.

She survived the experience and her debts were eventually paid, but she still had no means of support. Aphra Behn later described her solution as 'writing for bread'. There had been other female playwrights, but their work was more in the nature of a wealthy noblewoman's hobby or indulgence. Aphra Behn wrote for her very survival.

Restoration theatre was thriving at that time, with three successful companies in London. The poet laureate, Dryden, wrote three plays a year for 'The King's Company'. Aphra Behn was already fairly well known as a poet, and with Sir Thomas Gower as her patron, 'The Duke's Company' accepted her first play. *The Forc'd Marriage* was daring, tragi-comic and an instant success. She followed it with *The Amorous Prince* only six months later.

Her play *The Dutch Lover* was a failure on stage, in part due to a leading man who ad-libbed so often that Aphra Behn hardly recognised her own work, saying it was filled 'with a good deal of idle stuff, which I was wholly unacquainted with'. It was put on at the same time as a third war with the Dutch, which probably played a part in its lack of success. She followed it with more successful work in both tragedy and comedy, becoming in the process a well-known name in Restoration theatre.

In the 1670s, she met and began a tempestuous affair with John Hoyle, a notoriously bisexual atheist, lawyer, duellist and charming rogue. The romantic entanglement led to gossip at all levels of society and he became the subject of many of her poems at this time. It is likely that he was the inspiration for the hero of The Rover, her greatest theatrical success and the play which brought her the patronage of James II. Her personal experiences must have influenced lines like this one: 'Pox on Poverty, it makes a Man a Slave, makes Wit and Honour sneak, my Soul grow lean and rusty for want of Credit.' Or indeed this:

'One hour of right-down Love, Is worth an Age of living dully on.' She would later write a coronation ode for King James II in 1685.

Her path was never easy, as the slightest hint of bawdiness brought public condemnation that would never have been uttered for a male author. In comparison to some of Shakespeare's lewd verse, Aphra Behn's plays were sweetly romantic, yet she wrote about relationships and there were always enemies. After all, Charlotte Brontë didn't write *Jane Eyre* until 1847 and one critic of that later period said that if it was written by a woman, it was a disgrace.

In Aphra Behn's time, plays themselves were still considered immoral by some and theatres had been closed during the Puritan period under Cromwell. Like Jane Austen and Shakespeare, Aphra Behn wrote quickly and often while surrounded by others. Most of her plays did well enough, but some came in for great criticism and that is perhaps one factor that made her turn to prose towards the end of her life.

Aphra Behn probably wrote some of *Oroonoko* during her time in Surinam as a young woman. One of the first true novels, it predates more famous examples of the form (such as *Moll Flanders* by Daniel Defoe) by more than thirty years. In addition, its compassionate treatment of the hero is a call to end slavery more than a century before William Wilberforce became involved. It was published in 1688, just a year before her death. It was not hugely successful until after she had died, when it became the subject of a play by

Thomas Southerne, going into many editions as well as being translated into French and German.

In those days when life expectancy was incredibly low, Aphra Behn became ill and died before she was fifty in 1689, after the attentions of 'an unskilful physician'. She is buried in Westminster Abbey, an honour reserved for the great names in British history. Her tomb in the cloister is marked by a black stone with this epitaph:

> *Here lies a proof that wit can never be*
> *Defence enough against mortality.*

No one can be certain whether she wrote the line herself, or that it was written by her lover, John Hoyle.

Since her death, she has been called the Restoration's 'Dorothy Parker' or 'Mae West', and Virginia Woolf wrote of her life: 'All women together ought to let flowers fall upon the tomb of Aphra Behn, for it was she who earned them the right to speak their minds.'

Yet she did not want to be remembered as a female poet, just a poet; not as a female author, but just an author and a good one. She made her way on her own, with her wits and hard work.

Recommended
The Secret Life of Aphra Behn by Janet Todd.
The Oxford Dictionary of National Biography.

James Cook

O n a Sunday morning in Karakakooa Bay in the Sandwich Islands,
an islander struck a naval officer on the back of the head with
a club. The officer staggered and fell onto one knee. Before he could
rise, a dagger was stuck into the back of his neck. He tumbled into the
knee-deep sea and a crowd of islanders rushed to hold him underwater.
He struggled, raising his great head towards his boat for help. He was
pushed under, hit again on the head, then beaten with stones, knives
and clubs. The tropical water grew red before his body was dragged
onto the beach and torn apart.

That was the tragic end of the extraordinary life of James Cook, RN,
on 14 February 1779 – the death of the greatest explorer, navigator,
discoverer, surveyor, seaman, cartographer and ethnographer the world
has ever seen.

His ships' names are still famous – *Endeavour, Resolution, Adventure,
Discovery* – and have been used for research and exploration vessels
ever since. Today, they are also used in the exploration of Space. How
did the son of an obscure Yorkshire labourer come to die in the far
Pacific, honoured and revered by geographers and scientists throughout
the world?

Recognising his intelligence, his father educated the young James so
that he knew the three 'Rs' of reading, writing and 'rithmetic. With
education he hoped James might become manager of a grocer's or
draper's shop – perhaps even owner. However, young James saw the
masts and sails of North Sea colliers in Whitby Harbour and that was
the end of potatoes, groceries and linen.

At the age of 17, Cook was apprenticed to the collier *Freelove*,
carrying coal from north-east ports to London and sometimes to

Scandinavia and the Baltic. It was an exacting trade sailing through the shoals, sandbanks, estuaries, fogs, wild weather and lee shores of the North Sea. Good seamanship was vital there and Cook learned and excelled in his new career.

Cook was 26 and first mate when he entered the Wapping naval depot to join the Royal Navy. He was posted able seaman to the 58-gun HMS *Eagle*. From second in command of a merchant ship to nobody; from a small cabin of his own to fourteen inches in which to swing his hammock. Cook took a romantic gamble with fate, or perhaps he recognised destiny.

In a few weeks he was promoted to master's mate, a lowly petty officer, while a new captain took command. Hugh Palliser immediately noticed the tall, big-boned Yorkshireman who knew his way about ship as if he'd been there for years. Very shortly, Cook was made boatswain and given command of *Eagle's* forty-foot sloop, patrolling the English Channel and the Western Approaches. The Seven Years War, fought by Britain and Prussia against Austria, France, Russia and Spain, began in 1756 and Cook saw his first action.

Eagle captured two French ships and Cook was made prize-master of the larger to sail her to London. He was paid off when *Eagle* was refitted but, with the recommendations of both Captain Palliser and the MP for Whitby, he was made master. Such promotion was more usual after some six years in the navy; James Cook had served just two. Palliser, who went on to become Lord of the Admiralty, knew a good seaman when he saw one.

Cook was appointed master to the 60-gun *Pembroke* and in 1758 made his first ocean voyage, escorting the fleet from Plymouth to Nova Scotia for the Canadian campaign. It was an horrendous passage, the weather dead foul, and it took an amazing three months. The French, however, knew of British plans to capture Quebec and had made preparations. The city seemed impregnable, and all the navigation marks and buoys in the St Lawrence River had been removed.

Cook was ordered to survey, chart and buoy the rock-strewn and shoaling St Lawrence so that the navy could sail soldiers upriver to attack Quebec. He borrowed masters from other ships and completed the task in one week – at night. They were seen by native Canadians supporting the French and, in one attack, as natives clambered over the stern of a launch, Cook left rapidly by the bow. During daylight Cook drew a chart of the St Lawrence which was so accurate it remained in use for more than a century.

On a September night, the ships sailed up Cook's channel to reach the Heights of Abraham. Not one vessel went aground or was damaged, and General Wolfe went on to defeat General Montcalm on the Plains of Abraham to take Quebec.

In 1763, James Cook was given his first command, becoming master and commander of the schooner *Grenville*. He was known as 'Mr Cook, Engineer, Surveyor of Newfoundland and Labrador'. For five years, from spring to autumn, he surveyed and charted the east coasts of Canada, while in winter in Britain he drew his charts, wrote sailing directions for other mariners, and studied spherical trigonometry and astronomy. In 1766, there was an eclipse of the sun. Cook took many observations and measurements and presented a scientific paper to the Royal Society in London, the first of several to the world's premier scientific organisation. Yet the navy had other extraordinary plans for this farm labourer's son.

The Pacific Ocean was then a mostly unknown region where there might be – some geographers said *must* be – a continent known as Terra Australis Nondum Cognita, the 'Southern Land Not Yet Known'. The Pacific was greater in area than all the lands of the earth added together, but it was the Age of Enlightenment, and high time for Great Britain to find out whether what is now known as Antarctica existed or not. The Royal Society and the Royal Navy raised an expedition.

It was not the first venture into the Pacific by any means. The Spanish had discovered the Philippines, the Dutch western 'New Holland' (Australia) and Van Diemen's Land (Tasmania), while the British had discovered western North America, touched Japan, discovered the Tuamotus, Otaheite (Tahiti), the Gilberts (Kiribati), New Britain, New Ireland, the Carolines and other islands. Yet all had sailed through the middle and the north of the Pacific. None had sailed south, where 'Terra Australis' was expected to be. The Royal Society also wanted observations of the forthcoming transit of Venus across the sun, in order to calculate exactly the distance from the earth to the sun. Captain Wallis, returned from discovering Otaheite, recommended that island as an observatory because of its friendly people, ample food, fresh water and because its exact position was known.

The Royal Society wanted the expedition to be commanded by Alexander Dalrymple, the world's expert on Terra Australis, but he was a difficult man and refused to sail under naval authority. Someone in the Admiralty – perhaps Palliser – proposed James Cook. It was pointed out that he wasn't a commissioned officer, so he was commissioned for the task.

On 1 April, the Admiralty announced that the Whitby collier *Earl of Pembroke* had been purchased for the expedition and renamed *Endeavour*. She cost £2,307 5s. 6d., while a further £2,500 was spent fitting her out to carry people, equipment, stores and food for more than two years. The new Lieutenant Cook hoisted his commissioning pennant and took command of His Majesty's Bark *Endeavour* on 27 May, at Deptford on the River Thames.

The Royal Society accepted that Cook qualified as one astronomer and sent Charles Green of the Royal Observatory as another. Also sailing were botanists Joseph Banks and Daniel Solander, completing a ship's company of ninety-four, including a dozen Marines. A previous circumnavigator also joined – *Dolphin's* goat, a good milker and not prone to seasickness.

Cook sailed first to Plymouth, which took three weeks. *Endeavour* was a sturdy, safe but not fast vessel; her maximum speed was no more than 8 knots in ideal conditions. She was a three-masted bark, 110 feet long with a 29¼ foot beam. At 2 p.m. on 26 August 1768, *Endeavour* and Cook departed Plymouth for the South Seas, the first of the three greatest voyages of exploration, discovery and mapping ever made.

Endeavour was not equipped with one of Harrison's new chronometers, vital for the most accurate measurement of longitude. Instead, Cook and Green used the complicated lunar observations invented by Sir Isaac Newton, although Cook did have a copy of the very first Nautical Almanac (1768) containing the most up-to-date lunar tables.

Cook also took it upon himself to be ship's purser, so that the type of food was under his control. He was determined there would be no deaths from scurvy – a lack of vitamin C then guaranteed in long voyages. To this end, he packed the holds with barrels of pickled cabbage, tubs of orange and lemon juice, hogsheads of malt, portable soup (solid blocks of meat extract), wort (infusions of malt) and saloups (a drink from sassafras).

Down the length of the North and South Atlantic oceans sailed the little ship to reach the southernmost tip of South America by Christmas. Cook rounded Cape Horn in remarkably good weather and, taking the opportunity, sailed further south-west searching for land. He reached 60 degrees south, the farthest south ever recorded, to find only the fetch of the sea: deep long swells from the west indicating no land for perhaps a thousand miles. There might be land or ice to the south – Cook suspected there was – but nothing in the immediate west. In a good wind, he turned north-west for Otaheite, again sailing seas never crossed before. He found no Terra Australis and reached Matavai Bay in April 1769.

For three months, *Endeavour* remained at the exotic green island of Otaheite. The transit of Venus was observed by Cook and Green; several seamen were flogged for harshness to the Tahitians and ignoring Cook's rules of fair barter. Cook explored and charted the beautiful island; two marines deserted and took to the hills with their Tahitian 'wives', and draughtsman Buchan died of a fit. The two marines were returned by Tahitians and put in irons, and it was discovered that there was now venereal disease in paradise. King Tynah of Otaheite said it had arrived with French sailors under Bougainville.

There were tears when *Endeavour* departed in July, for many friendships had been formed, not least between Tynah and Cook. Many islanders offered to sail with their British friends, but Cook was bound for the cold south in search of Terra Australis; it would be very unpleasant for a Tahitian, and how were they to return? A priest and navigator named Tupaia pleaded to join and Cook relented.

Cook first sailed west, charting the Society Islands he named after the Royal Society. Tupaia was a great help for he knew those waters well. At exotic Tetiaroa, Huahine, Raiatea, Tahaa and Bora Bora there was a welcome for them all. There was no continent, so Cook took *Endeavour* into latitudes 40 degrees south and then to the north-west, south-west and west, searching for Terra Australis. There might have been land, rocks or reefs at any moment, but there was nothing but ocean until October, when a tall headland was sighted. Might this be the fabled Terra Australis?

Cook navigated 2,500 nautical miles around the coasts of this land and proved them to be two long islands – New Zealand – sighted once before in 1642. He surveyed and charted the coasts, met the Maori peoples with whom Tupaia had a common Polynesian language, and carried out necessary work to the ship in Queen Charlotte Sound. Cook's surveys became the basis for New Zealand charts for the next two hundred years. *Endeavour*'s artist sketched a mountain with snow on its peak and gave it the title 'Mount Egmont, New Zealand, Australia', the first definite written reference to an 'Australia'.

It took six months to chart New Zealand, half a year in which Cook became a legend and entered Maori folklore. Fifty years later a Maori chief recalled meeting Cook as a child: 'We knew that he was chief of the whole by his perfect, gentlemanly and noble demeanour. He seldom spoke ... he came to us and patted our cheeks and gently touched our heads ... My companions said: "A noble man cannot be lost in a crowd."'

However, New Zealand was not Terra Australis. By then *Endeavour* and her crew had been at sea for twenty months, so Cook called a conference of senior men to discuss their voyage home. There were two known routes: east to Cape Horn, or north around New Guinea to the Dutch settlement of Batavia (Jakarta) and then Cape Town. Typically, Cook agreed to a third unknown route – west to find the coast of New Holland (Australia), to chart it north and west to Batavia.

Cook steered for Van Diemen's Land but was blown by a storm until he was north *and* east of its position. Sunrise on 20 April 1770 revealed the south-east corner of New Holland, a cape he named Point Hicks, and so began the famous voyage along the immense east coast of what is now known as Australia, surveying, charting and naming as he went. On the 29th, he sailed into a bay to anchor 'under the South shore about 2 mile within the entrance in 6 fathoms of water'.

A boat was lowered and Cook, Banks, Solander and Tupaia rowed for the beach, where there were several Aborigines, similar to those of the far north-west of the continent discovered by Englishman William Dampier in 1688. Tupaia couldn't communicate with them and they weren't interested in trade. They were primarily defensive of their primitive canoes.

As in New Zealand, Cook raised the flag and claimed the land for Britain, while Banks and Solander collected every example of the unknown flora and fauna they could find. Cook named the bay 'Botanists' Bay' and the land 'New South Wales' because it reminded him of Wales along the Bristol Channel. They buried seaman Sutherland, who had died of tuberculosis, and continued north.

Cook was disappointed that he'd made no meaningful contact with the Aborigines as he had with other Pacific peoples, but he was no fool. He knew that contact meant change at the hands of the stronger – whether the explorers were Phoenician, Greek, Roman or British.

Cook navigated 2,000 miles northwards into the southern tropics until he was sailing between continuous reefs to the east (Great Barrier Reef) and the mainland to the west, in a gradually narrowing seaway. Inside 80,000 square miles of the largest reef in the world, Cook conned *Endeavour*, turning and twisting through narrow passages, around dangerous coral and past uninhabited islands. Inevitably, *Endeavour* ran onto a submerged reef. Seventeen fathoms had been the last sounding of the lead line in the June moonlight; suddenly the ship was aground.

After jettisoning cannon, transferring stores into the boats and floating the topmasts overside, Cook managed to haul off. The sinking ship limped to a nearby river for careening on the beach. The choice of a sturdy, broad-bottomed Whitby collier was justified. By August, after weeks of repairs, *Endeavour* put to sea once more.

Sailing north, Cook reached and named Cape York, the northern tip of New Holland. From there, he turned westward to Batavia, proving New Guinea was not joined to New Holland. He named the channel Endeavour Straits. A battered and worn *Endeavour* reached Batavia on 10 October.

Since departing Plymouth, Cook had lost three men by drowning, two from exposure, one each to drink, epilepsy and tuberculosis, but none to scurvy. Repairs to *Endeavour* took three months at Batavia, where every man contracted fever. Thirty-one, including astronomer Green and Tupaia of Otaheite, died of Batavia fever before the ship reached Britain. The last was Lieutenant Hicks in the North Atlantic.

On 13 July 1771, one month shy of a three-year voyage, *Endeavour* anchored off Deal in Kent. Of her original crew of ninety-four, fifty-six survived, and the goat from *Dolphin* had completed her second circumnavigation.

In Britain it had been thought *Endeavour* was lost. Botanist Joseph Banks was lionised as a great scientist and knighted; Cook, who'd made the decisions and done the work, was promoted to commander. Yet Alexander Dalrymple was angry that Cook had discovered no new continent other than the Pacific coast of New Holland; what we now call Australia was not the unknown southern land. However, there was still a small chance that such a continent might exist and Cook proposed a circumnavigation around the Antarctic to settle the matter.

Meanwhile, Cook returned home to find two of his four children dead, one of whom had died without him ever seeing him. It was not an uncommon story for an eighteenth-century seaman.

After the success of *Endeavour*, Admiralty purchased another two Whitby colliers and named them *Resolution* and *Adventure*. One year to the day after Cook had come ashore he was away again. What Mrs Cook thought is not recorded. *Resolution* and *Adventure* sailed from Plymouth on 13 July 1772, bound almost everywhere in the southern hemisphere. Lieutenant Tobias Furneaux commanded *Adventure*, while twenty *Endeavour* men rejoined Cook in *Resolution*. Somehow, Cook had managed to persuade the Navy Board to pay *Endeavour*'s crew their arrears of three years' pay, with an advance of two months for those who rejoined – one of his lesser-known accomplishments. He also shipped two Whitby men with Arctic ice experience.

The second expedition was even more remarkable and successful than the first. This time, Cook was entrusted with the K1 chronometer, a copy of John Harrison's prize-winning and more famous H4, so that longitudes could be calculated more exactly than ever before. They sailed to Cape Town and, after reprovisioning the two vessels, sailed due south. It was November, the southern summer, and Cook ventured far beyond 60 degrees south.

Christmas was spent deep in the Southern Ocean. On 17 January 1773, Cook crossed the Antarctic Circle, 66 degrees 33½ minutes south, to be the first to enter the Antarctic. *Resolution* and *Adventure* sailed through seas littered with icebergs before their way was barred by pack ice. From the masthead they saw only ice, for their circle of vision was no more than twelve miles. Yet they were only seventy-five miles from the ice-covered continent of Antarctica. The Whitby ice experts expressed their concerns as Cook manoeuvred between icebergs, ice floes and pack ice, but there was no passage south.

He turned north-east towards the Kerguelen Islands, to investigate French claims of Terra Australis. There was no land. In appalling weather, *Adventure* and *Resolution* were separated, but Cook had given orders for just such an eventuality and the ships continued their explorations independently. *Adventure* explored north of due east to a rendezvous in New Zealand, while *Resolution* searched south of due east following the ice edge. After 11,000 miles and 117 days from Cape Town, with no new land sighted, *Resolution* reached the south of New Zealand. Numerous pods of whales were recorded, an observation Cook knew spelt doom for the mammals even as he recorded it. In mid-May he reached the Queen Charlotte Sound rendezvous to find *Adventure* waiting. Furneaux, too, had discovered no land, but had found a good anchorage in Van Diemen's Land that he'd named Adventure Bay.

The ships were repaired and fresh food and water taken on board in exchange with the Maoris for hogs, goats and vegetable seeds. By mid-June, Cook was off into the Pacific, searching again for Terra Australis. A circular exploration took them in mid-August to Otaheite, to the delight of King Tynah, where they replenished their stores. 'And how is the great King George?' Tynah asked his friend.

Cook strove for friendly relations wherever he went, but Otaheite and the Society Islands were particular successes. Yet with the exception of the Maoris, Polynesians everywhere stole prodigiously. To counter this, Cook secured their chiefs as willing hostages until the important items were returned. This system was accepted by all with smiles and laughter until it became almost a game.

On departure from Matavai Bay there were more tears. Sailing west, Cook discovered, surveyed and charted the Friendly Isles (Tonga), where again the ships and crews were welcomed. In October 1773, Cook turned his ships south for a brief stop at Queen Charlotte Sound for provisions and water. *Adventure* became separated again and reached Queen Charlotte Sound after Resolution had left.

While *Adventure* was reprovisioning, Maoris attacked one of the boats, killing and eating the crew of ten.

After the shock of the attack, following Cook's orders, *Adventure* searched the Southern Ocean eastwards through latitudes 60 degrees south, passed far south of Cape Horn and on to Cape Town, and then headed home – yet another British circumnavigation in the eighteenth century. Spain had long considered the Pacific 'her' waters. Already it was British and, very soon, international under the freedom of the Royal Navy.

On *Resolution*, Cook ventured far south to the Antarctic ice and then east. December the 25th was spent in Antarctica at 67 degrees south, the first Antarctic Christmas. Gifts were extra tots of rum and brandy with 'wind northerly a strong gale with a thick fog sleet and snow which froze to the rigging as it fell and decorated the whole with icicles'. Cook sailed north to investigate another blank in the map, then south again to cross the Antarctic Circle for the third time.

He recorded the ice 'extended east and west far beyond the reach of our sight, while the Southern half of the Horizon was illuminated by rays of light which were Reflected from the ice to a considerable height … It was indeed my opinion that this ice extends quite to the Pole, or perhaps joins to some Land to which it has been fixed since Creation.' *Resolution* was stopped by the ice on 30 January 1774, at 71 degrees 10 minutes south, the furthest south then recorded. Cook reached the ice edge all the way around Antarctica, saw lines of icebergs broken out from the continent, but never saw the ice-covered land itself.

In a very rare personal comment, he wrote: 'I who had Ambition not only to go Farther than any one had done before, but as far as it was possible for man to go, was not sorry at meeting with this interruption as it in some measure relieved us, at least shortened the dangers and hardships inseparable with the navigation of the Southern Polar Rigions.' The hardships were many. *Resolution* was, literally, freezing cold and wet, the hammocks and bunks permanently damp. Most work had to be done without gloves and there was then no effective cold-weather clothing. The rope rigging froze solid, the canvas sails turned into stiff boards which ripped out fingernails, while metal parts froze and stripped the skin. Cook himself suffered from colic, which nearly killed him. Perhaps there is no finer testament to James Cook's seamanship, navigation and care for his men than this: in a vessel completely unsuited for the conditions, he was the first to chart the limits of Antarctica and did not lose one man.

In February, approaching Cape Horn, Cook turned north to explore the last unknown area of the Pacific where there *might* have been land. There had been a possible sighting there in the late 1500s which Alexander Dalrymple thought might be the edge of a continent. After 103 days at sea since Queen Charlotte Sound, Cook discovered Easter Island. He charted the island, met the welcoming Polynesians and uncovered the information that they also didn't know who had carved the amazing stone statues. They were there when *they'd* arrived.

In the rejuvenating warmth of the tropics, Cook sailed further north-west to discover the beautiful Marquesas Islands, sighted once in 1595 and since lost. Again he was welcomed by Polynesians as he surveyed and charted their islands and took on fresh food. There was still no scurvy in *Resolution*. He then sailed west for repairs and rest once more at Otaheite, to its green hills, its tang of wood smoke and, for the crew, other delights. Despite many offerings by chiefs of Polynesia, Cook remained celibate. He learned the language instead.

From Otaheite, Cook navigated west through the Friendly Isles, then north-west. Missing the Fiji Islands, Cook discovered and named most of the New Hebrides (Vanuatu), landing despite the cannibalism of those Melanesian islanders. Turning south again, he discovered, named and charted the New Caledonia islands and, on 10 October, the uninhabited Norfolk Island. He brought *Resolution* back to provision at Queen Charlotte Sound in November 1774.

Cook made a final sweep eastward across the Pacific Ocean through latitudes 50 degrees south, to the dangerous coast of Tierra del Fuego. He surveyed Cape Horn over Christmas, and in the new year turned south-east once more towards Antarctica. Geographers had identified 'land' there, but there was only the wild Southern Ocean. In 1775 he discovered uninhabited South Georgia Island and Clerke Rocks. He recorded in his journal the almost unbelievable number of whales, seals and birds, commenting again that these discoveries would only bring men to plunder another region of the world.

In a last dig south-east he discovered and named 'Sandwich Land' (South Sandwich Islands), which he thought may be off a southern promontory. He was right – the Antarctic Peninsula is not far away. Cook turned *Resolution* to the east once more, crossed his track of 1772 and completed the first circumnavigation of Antarctica. Finally, he turned north to reach Cape Town in March, where he was told *Adventure* had passed safely a year before.

James Cook returned to England in July 1775, to complete an incredible exploration of three years and eighteen days. He lost just four men: three drowned, one of natural causes, none to disease. In *Resolution* and *Endeavour* he'd sailed 120,000 nautical miles, twice around the world and many times around the Pacific. At 46 years old, he was truly the greatest explorer, discoverer, navigator, surveyor, cartographer and seaman of his age.

Cook was made captain and presented again to King George III. He prepared and delivered his scientific papers to the Royal Society, which awarded him its Gold Medal and elected him Fellow for his geographic and scientific achievements. Not bad for a man whose only formal education was a village school in Yorkshire.

Of Terra Australis, he concluded: 'I had now made the circuit of the Southern Ocean in a high Latitude and traversed it in such a manner as to leave not the least room for the Possibility of there being a continent, unless near the Pole and out of the reach of Navigation … thus I flatter my self that the intention of the Voyage has in every respect been fully Answered, the Southern Hemisphere sufficiently explored and a final end put to searching after a Southern Continent … That there may be a Continent or large tract of land near the Pole I will not deny. On the contrary I am of opinion there is, and it is probable that we have seen a part of it.' Captain Cook, the first Antarctic explorer, was absolutely right.

The Admiralty also made Cook captain to the Greenwich Naval Hospital, a sinecure which he accepted, but with the condition that he could leave should he be required elsewhere. For already the Admiralty was arranging a third great exploration into the Pacific and *Resolution* was refitted for further duty. This time the destination was north, to explore Sir Francis Drake's 'New Albion' west coast of North America. From there, to sail along the last unknown coastline in the world in search of a sea passage around the top of Canada, the fabled North-West Passage, and a sea passage around the top of Russia, the North-East Passage. Neither could be located from the Atlantic. If anyone could find the Pacific entrances, it was James Cook.

Having sent *Adventure* elsewhere, the Admiralty purchased another Whitby collier to accompany *Resolution* and named her *Discovery*. She was commanded by Lieutenant Charles Clerke, ex-*Endeavour* and ex-*Resolution*. Joining Cook as master of *Resolution* was the talented William Bligh; rejoining as first lieutenant was John Gore, while many more officers and seamen also rejoined. As well as taking home Omai, a Tahitian brought to Britain in *Adventure*, further gifts for the South Seas' kings were taken on board including, for the first time, horses. With goats, sheep, chickens, pigs and horses, *Resolution*'s decks looked and smelt like a farmyard when she left Plymouth on 12 July 1776. Cook had been home for less than a year, which may have been the secret of his long and happy marriage.

As soon as *Resolution* put to sea, Cook found she leaked like a sieve; her refit was appalling. Cook and his crew suffered from this negligence throughout this expedition and, ultimately, it was to be fatal. At Cape Town, Cook had almost every seam recaulked as well as replacing some masts.

Resolution and *Discovery* departed Cape Town in November 1776, sailing south-east to explore, survey and chart the subantarctic Marion, Crozet and Kerguelen Islands. There were further problems with *Resolution*'s masts and Cook anchored at Adventure Bay in Van Diemen's Land for repairs. He met the Australian Aborigines a second time, but made little progress with them. When he stopped at Queen Charlotte Sound for yet more repairs, the Maoris were surprised to find that the great Cook intended no punishment for the murder and eating of *Adventure*'s boat crew three years before. Cook understood that it was a collision of cultures and that retribution would gain nothing. Instead, he tried to explain the concept of mercy and forgiveness. The Maoris were puzzled and Omai was scornful.

Cook sailed *Resolution* and *Discovery* on a new route to the northeast, another of his Pacific wanderings in which he was destined to discover unknown islands and peoples, including another Polynesian community in what he named the Hervey Islands (Cook Islands). The two vessels nudged the occasional unknown reef and sandbank – immediately charted – then sailed west to the Friendly Isles. Cook and Bligh landed on Tofua, and King George's gifts were distributed to the island chiefs – sheep, goats, pigs and rabbits – while one of the horses was presented to the Tongan king. Cook sailed through the Society Islands to Otaheite, his Pacific home, and returned Omai to his people after several years away. The remaining gifts were presented: two horses, sheep, cattle, geese, a cock and a hen. Two *Discovery* crew deserted – desertions occurred every visit – but the Tahitians located them on another island and returned them to be flogged.

It was during this visit that Cook's rheumatism, the sailor's curse, was relieved with massage by a dozen strong women using the a'pi plant. After two treatments, it never returned. One of the Tahitians massaging Captain James Cook was Isabella, who later married a master's mate named Fletcher Christian.

In November 1777, the two ships departed Otaheite and Cook directed them directly north. On Christmas Eve he made yet another discovery, at the Equator. He named them the Line Islands and the first land sighted Christmas Island (Kiritimati). Sixteen days later Cook discovered the last great island group of the Pacific Ocean, the Sandwich Islands (Hawaii), first reaching Atui (Kauai) Island. There were more Polynesians, and Cook wondered again at these island-seamen who had sailed the Pacific in their simple outrigger canoes, from Hawaii to New Zealand, from Easter Island to the Friendly Isles.

When Cook landed on Atui on 20 January 1778, the islanders lay flat on their faces. This had never happened before and, embarrassed, Cook waved them up. It was explained that this was how these Polynesians greeted their chiefs. It was actually how they greeted their gods, but Cook was not told this. He made friends with the Polynesians in his usual way, bartering for fresh vegetables, meat and water before setting off to the east.

Resolution and *Discovery* sailed to a February landfall in North America at Drake's New Albion, north of San Francisco. The weather was cold and the seas lively, but Cook wanted to be far north by the beginning of summer for his exploration into the Arctic. The two Whitby colliers coasted northwards along what are now the states of Oregon and Washington, passing Drake's furthest point north, charting and naming as they went. Vancouver Island was named after *Resolution*'s midshipman, Cape Suckling after Nelson's uncle, Bligh Island after *Resolution*'s master and so on. Cook anchored for further repairs to *Resolution* at Prince William Sound, where *Discovery*'s crew beat off an attack by knife-wielding Eskimos. Cook ordered the men not to use firearms.

The ships were forced south again by the long Alaskan Peninsula. Cook Inlet was thought to be a possible passage east or north, but when Bligh explored he found it to be only a river mouth. The two ships reached the bottom of the peninsula at Ounalashka (Unalaska), where they passed between the Aleutian Islands and sailed northwards again through the cold Bering Sea. Cook noted the estuary of the great Yukon River and, finally, passed between the continents of America and Asia to enter the Arctic.

In the charts drawn in the great cabin of *Resolution*, Captain James Cook had mapped the last, major, unknown coastline of the world. *Resolution* and Cook also became the first ship and man to cross both Polar Circles, 66 degrees 33½ minutes south and north of the Equator – and thus the first to reach both the Antarctic and the Arctic.

Northwards, Cook navigated the little ships into the bitter polar weather. Once again, ice coated *Resolution*'s rigging until the latitude measured was almost 71 degrees north, as before it measured 71 degrees south. Once again, it was ice that stopped Cook, sea ice piled twelve feet high and impassable. Cook had indeed reached the Pacific end of the elusive North-West Passage, only to find it choked with ice. He tacked and wore his ships along the edge of the frozen sea, searching for a channel through, but there was none. He turned west for the North-East Passage.

He beat along the edge of the ice from 164 degrees west across the International Date Line to 176 degrees east. The pack ice was solid from the North Pole to the coast of Siberia. Cook had reached the Pacific end of the North-East Passage and it, too, was choked with ice. It was evident that both passages were unsuitable for commercial navigation.

By then it was September and the pack ice was beginning to re-form. Cook turned his ships back along the Siberian coast – he was charting the coast of Siberia in two Whitby colliers! – and south into the Bering Sea. *Resolution* was in a poor state once more and needed rerigging. Cook required a warm winter anchorage and he chose the Sandwich Islands, where they'd been welcomed earlier.

For two months Cook searched the islands for a suitable anchorage, surveying and charting as he went. On 17 January 1779, he found Karakakooa (Kealakekua) Bay on the west coast of Owhyhee (Hawaii) itself, the largest island. He sent William Bligh in a boat to sound the bay. The bay was open only to the south-west and the holding ground was good. It would do.

His reception was overwhelming. Thousands of islanders canoed or swam out to the ships, climbing aboard in their feathers and flowers even while the sailors were anchoring. When Cook stepped ashore with gifts of pigs, goats and iron tools the islanders again prostrated themselves before him. Elaborate ceremonies were performed and he was accompanied by priests wherever he went. In awe, the Polynesian King Kalaniopu'u visited Cook's ships. They called Cook 'Orono', 'Lono' or 'Rono'. No one aboard the two ships understood what was happening. It wasn't until many years later, after interviews with the islanders involved, that the truth was uncovered.

Orono was a Hawaiian god who'd been exiled. The legend was that one day he would return, bearing gifts of swine and dogs. Who else but Orono could the tall, noble Captain Cook be?

Cook stayed only three weeks. With *Resolution*'s rigging repaired and the ships provisioned and watered, he set sail to complete his survey of the Sandwich Islands, explore the north-west Pacific and return to the Arctic. He wrote that Owhyhee had 'enriched our voyage with a discovery which, though the last, seemed in many respects to be the most important that had hitherto been made throughout the extent of the Pacific Ocean'. Those were the final words in his journal. That he wrote 'the last' discovery is intriguing.

Resolution's log records that a strong blow caught the ship and the morning inspection revealed severe damage to the foremast and fore-topmast, one more relic of the poor refit. Repairs required a safe anchorage, for the masts had to be removed. Cook did not want to return to Owhyhee but there was nowhere else. He put about and anchored again in Karakakooa Bay on 10 February.

This time, the welcome for 'Orono' was somewhat thin. Cook went ashore to explain to King Kalaniopu'u and his chiefs the reason for his return, only to repair the masts. He believed they'd understood him, but what the priests said when he'd gone was another matter. The British seamen worked as quickly as they could, 'fished' the masts and floated them ashore for repair. It was complicated, skilled work. As it progressed, stones were thrown at them ashore and there were minor assaults. Thefts increased dramatically until the islanders actually swam under the ships to pull out the nails holding the copper sheathing to the hulls. Cook had an islander flogged as a deterrent.

On the night of the 13th, *Discovery*'s cutter was stolen from her mooring. This was extremely serious. In the morning Cook went ashore in Resolution's pinnace with ten marines in the launch to carry out his usual bloodless punishment. He would take a chief hostage until the cutter was returned. It had always worked before. Four more boats cordoned the bay to stop islanders rowing their canoes or the cutter away. Cook's reluctant orders were to fire if necessary and, unusually, he carried a shotgun himself.

Cook told Kalaniopu'u of the theft and the king agreed to go with Cook to *Resolution* until the cutter was returned. His young sons asked to go as well and, with the king's agreement, ran ahead. On the beach they heard gunfire along the bay. Cook's men had fired to stop a canoe from leaving.

One of the king's wives wailed and begged him not to go. Two young chiefs took hold of the king's arms and sat him on the beach while other islanders collected stones, spears and clubs. The lieutenant of marines lined his men along the water's edge, their muskets loaded and ready. A cry came from the crowd that a chief had been killed in the firing along the bay. Cook understood what had been said and left the king sitting on the beach. He ordered the marines to return to the ships to avoid bloodshed and walked down the beach.

A warrior rushed at him wielding a stone and a dagger. Cook turned and in Polynesian ordered: 'Put those things down!' but the man drew back his arm to throw the stone.

Cook fired his shotgun, using the barrel containing round shot, which would sting but not kill. The shot hit the warrior's coconut breastplate. He laughed and came on with his dagger raised. Cook fired the second barrel containing ball and the warrior fell to the beach.

There was a roar and the islanders attacked with stones and spears. The marines fired. The islanders came on regardless and killed four marines before they could reload. The seamen in the boat came in to help, telling the king's sons to run for it before they were hurt. The boys ran away through the shallows.

Cook stood at the water's edge, a tall commanding figure in navy-blue tailcoat and white breeches, facing the islanders. They paused. He turned to his seamen and marines with his hand held palm-up to command a ceasefire. It was then, with his back to the islanders, that he was clubbed, stabbed and killed. The marines and seamen fired their muskets into the mob and retreated to the boat. From *Discovery*, the watching Clerke fired two ship's cannon overhead into the trees. Cook's body and the bodies of the four marines were torn apart as the boats rowed into deep water. It was over.

The next day, parts of Cook's body were returned to *Resolution* by a sorrowful chief. Those remnants – missing his head – were given a naval funeral to a captain's salute of ten guns.

Lieutenant Clerke took command of *Resolution* and promoted Gore to command of *Discovery*. The masts were repaired and on a grey February day the two ships departed Owhyee. Clerke continued as Cook planned, explored north-westwards across the Pacific but discovered nothing. The two ships sailed the cold northern sea into the Arctic where Clerke found the ice further south than the year before. There was no way through. Both the North-West and the North-East were not viable passages. They are not still.

In the Arctic, Clerke died of tuberculosis. It was the worst weather for him, but he'd insisted on completing Cook's plans. Gore took command and turned south for the small Russian port of Petropavlovsk.

There, Clerke was buried. *Resolution* and *Discovery* were repaired and departed for Britain. The passage home took a year. They arrived at London in October 1780, completing a voyage of four and a quarter years. Not one man in either ship had died of disease.

The chronometer in the *Resolution* was removed, and supplied later to another ship bound for the South Seas named *Bounty*. It was removed from the *Bounty* at Pitcairn Island and is now in the National Maritime Museum at Greenwich.

Mrs Cook received a royal pension from King George, her husband's share of the royalties of his published journals and a specially struck gold medal from the Royal Society. She lived mostly alone until she died aged 93. All six of their children died without heirs, the two eldest sons in service with the navy.

In Australia, Canada, New Zealand, the United States and throughout the Pacific Islands there are memorials to Captain James Cook. In the United Kingdom, there is a statue in the Mall near the Admiralty and one on the cliffs near Whitby. It's late, but not too late, for a significant memorial in Westminster Abbey or St Paul's to the world's greatest explorer, navigator, discoverer, cartographer, surveyor, seaman and ethnographer, who just happens to be British.

Recommended
Captain Cook: The Seaman's Seaman by Alan Villiers.
The Journals of Captain Cook edited by J.C. Beaglehole.
The Life of Captain James Cook by J.C. Beaglehole.
Royal Naval Museum, Portsmouth, Hampshire.
National Maritime Museum, Greenwich, London.
Whitby Museum, Whitby, Yorkshire.
Mitchell Library, Sydney, Australia.
Endeavour Replica, Whitby, Yorkshire.
Endeavour Replica, Sydney, Australia.
Captain Cook's Cottage, Melbourne, Australia.

Edmund Hillary and Tenzing Norgay

'If you cannot understand that there is something in man which responds to the challenge of this mountain and goes out to meet it, that the struggle is the struggle of life itself, upward and forever upward, then you won't see why we go. What we get from this adventure is just sheer joy.'
　　　　　　　　　　　　　　　　　　　　– George Mallory

'We look up. For weeks, for months, that is all we have done. Look up. And there it is – the top of Everest. Only it is different now: so near, so close, only a little more than a thousand feet above us. It is no longer just a dream, a high dream in the sky, but a real and solid thing, a thing of rock and snow, that men can climb. We make ready. We will climb it. This time, with God's help, we will climb on to the end.'
　　　　　　　　　　　　　　　　　　　　– Tenzing Norgay

Less than sixty years ago, no one in the history of the world had ever conquered Everest. It is possible that George Mallory and Andrew Irvine made it in 1924, but they died in the attempt and there is no way to know if they were still climbing or coming down. Mallory's body was not even found until 1999.

The highest mountain in the world is still incredibly dangerous and climbers die in the attempt every year. More than forty bodies remain frozen on the north side of the mountain and others have been lost in avalanches, their whereabouts unknown.

Everest is part of the Himalayan range, on the border between Tibet and Nepal. In Tibet it is known as 'Chomolungma', or 'saint mother', while the Nepalese call it 'Sagarmatha', meaning 'goddess of the sky'. 'Everest' is named after George Everest, a British Surveyor in nineteenth-century India. Before World War II, ascents began in Tibet, but when China occupied and closed that country to foreigners, future attempts had to come from the Nepalese side.

Everest stands 29,029 feet high – a fraction under five and a half *miles* from sea level. For those who are interested in such things, the highest from foot to tip is actually a Hawaiian island, though obviously, almost all of that is underwater.

Above 27,000 feet, the air is too thin to breathe without severe training and months of acclimatisation. Edmund Hillary and Tensing used bottled oxygen to make their ascent. Bad weather can make climbing impossible, which leaves only a small window each year when summit attempts can take place.

The British Everest expedition of 1953 came after years of expeditions to survey the approaches from Nepal. In 1951, a potential route to the top was noted and in 1952 two Swiss attempts were made on the summit. The British team was in the Himalayas, training at high altitude and ready to climb if the Swiss failed. A French team was ready to go after them. At that time, nine of the eleven major attempts on the mountain had been British-sponsored. Such energy and risk is either impossible to explain, or very simple. As George Mallory said when he was asked why he wanted to climb Everest: 'Because it's there.'

The 1953 British expedition was led by John Hunt. It was a massive undertaking just to reach the area. More than three hundred porters were employed to bring 10,000 lb of supplies and equipment. Twenty native Nepalese guides were engaged for the task, some of whom, like Tenzing Norgay, had climbed to 28,000 feet with the Swiss the previous year. As the expedition unpacked on the lawns of the British High Commission in Kathmandu, they discovered they had forgotten the British flag to fly on the summit of Everest. Rather than go without it, the High Commissioner gave them one of the ones from his official Rolls-Royce.

More than one climb had come within a thousand feet of the summit, but then been overwhelmed by exhaustion or blizzards. At that height, the mountain has already taken a fierce toll. All equipment, including oxygen bottles, has to be carried up and progress is bitterly slow as the last reserves of strength and fitness dwindle away. As with breaking the four-minute mile, that last stretch seemed an impossible obstacle.

By May 1953, the British team had crossed crevasses and climbed sheer ice and rock to set up Advance Base Camp at 21,000 feet. The region above that height is known as the 'death zone' as climbers can endure only a few days in some of the most hostile conditions on earth.

Two-men summit teams were considered to have the best chance. The first assault on the summit was by Charles Evans and Tom Bourdillon. They came to within a few hundred feet of the top when their oxygen failed. Without warning, they were suddenly strangling in air too thin to breathe and they had to return to the lower camp.

On May 28, an advance party went up to carry equipment to the highest camp possible. In that way, they could prepare the path for Hillary and Tenzing, who were the least exhausted pair. Hillary and Tenzing carried four stone in weight of supplies up to what would be called Camp IX – about halfway between Advance Base Camp and the summit. With three other men – Alfred Gregory, George Lowe and Sherpa Ang Nyima – they rested as best they could. In a cramped tent, they slept for four hours and woke at dawn to find the weather had cleared. The temperature was around –13 °F (–25 °C), which made wind chill of the utmost importance. Winds on Everest regularly gusted up to eighty miles an hour and were a constant, deadly threat.

Both Hillary and Tenzing carried cylinders of oxygen and other equipment: 50 lb to 63 lb for each man. The plan was for Gregory, Lowe and Sherpa Ang Nyima to go first and cut ice steps as high as they could, allowing Tenzing and Hillary to make a fast ascent and perhaps push on to the very top.

Hillary and Tenzing climbed quickly, joining the first party at 27,900 feet on a ridge. There, they found the tattered remnant of the Swiss tent from where Tenzing himself had tried for the peak the year before. That experience would prove vital, as he was able to guide the team to the best route.

Their trail-breaking work done, Lowe, Gregory and Ang Nyima turned back. After cutting steps in ice all day, they were exhausted, finished, but they had given Hillary and Tenzing a chance to make the summit.

To preserve oxygen for the attempt, the two remaining men put away their breathing apparatus and gasped without it to make a camp for the night. They pitched a tent, using only their weight to hold it in place. Tenzing made soup while Hillary checked the oxygen supplies. He had less than the ideal, but the first attempt by Bourdillon and Evans had abandoned oxygen cylinders even higher and they hoped to find those and use them to get back down alive. Before they slept, Hillary and Tenzing ate sardines, tinned apricots, biscuits, honey and jam, as well as drinking hot water with lemon crystals and sugar to ward off dehydration. Hillary found his boots had frozen solid and had to cook them on a Primus stove to soften them.

In the morning, they hoisted the heavy oxygen tubes onto their shoulders. The day was bright and still and they could see the South Summit ahead of them. Making good speed, they climbed a ridge towards it, locating the abandoned oxygen cylinders on the way. They passed the cut steps and reached the South Summit by 9 a.m. on the morning of the 29th. A virgin ridge led onwards, with a 10,000-foot drop along one edge. Hillary began to cut new steps in the snow, ascending in forty-foot stages. 8,000 feet below them, they could see the Advance Base Camp as they climbed. At one point, Tenzing's oxygen tubes froze solid and Hillary freed them when he saw the Sherpa growing weak. There was no margin for error of any kind.

They had to halt at a smooth forty-foot cliff of rock, still known today as the 'Hillary Step'. Hillary said afterwards that it would have been an interesting challenge to a group of expert climbers in the Lake District, but at that height it seemed impassable. He found a place where he could wedge his body into a crack between the rock and solid snow and heaved himself up and onto a ledge at the top. Tenzing followed on the rope and began to cut steps once more as the ridge went on.

They pushed themselves to the limit of endurance and thought they had reached the top time and time again, only to find more to do. The 'false summits' were heartbreaking. Slowly and painfully, they cut steps and trudged upwards. They stood on top of the world at 11.30 a.m., the first men ever to stand on that spot. They thumped each other on the back and grinned.

Tenzing did not know how to work the camera, so Hillary took three pictures of him standing on the summit. He held an ice axe aloft, with the flags of the United Nations, Britain, Nepal and India fluttering from it. Tenzing made an offering to the gods of the summit, burying a bar of chocolate and some biscuits. John Hunt had given Hillary a small crucifix to take to the top and he placed it beside the other offerings. They also looked for traces of Mallory or Irving, as the bodies were still missing at that time, but saw no sign of them.

Exhausted as they were, they could not tarry for long, even for the best view on earth. They remained on the peak for just fifteen minutes before beginning the descent, moving as quickly as possible to reach the oxygen dump before their own supply ran out.

Hillary and Tenzing made it back to a lower camp and were greeted by George Lowe, carrying emergency oxygen and a hot lemon drink. They were too exhausted to say much, though Hillary said: 'Well, George, we knocked the bastard off.'

The following day, they climbed down to the Advance Base Camp and the rest of the team came out to see if they had been successful. George Lowe gave them the thumbs up and waved his ice axe at the summit. The highest mountain on earth had been conquered at last. The job was done and Edmund Hillary and Tenzing Norgay became famous around the world. The French team next in line to make the attempt were, frankly, gutted.

News reached England in time for the coronation of Queen Elizabeth II in June 1953. Her husband, the Duke of Edinburgh, had been the patron of the expedition and the Queen took a personal interest. Hillary was made a Knight Commander of the British Empire (KBE). In his twilight years, he was also made a member of the Order of the Garter, an honour completely in the Queen's discretion. Only the reigning monarch, the Prince of Wales and twenty-four 'companions' hold the honour at any one time. Hillary returned to England on many occasions to attend the annual service in St George's Chapel, Windsor.

Tenzing Norgay was given the George Medal by Queen Elizabeth. He was honoured by both India and Nepal and became director of the Himalayan Mountaineering Institute in Darjeeling. He lived until 1986, dying at the age of 71. His son climbed Everest in 1996.

Edmund Hillary was just 33 when he stood on the peak of Everest. Though only two men made the summit, he always praised the teamwork that had made that final push possible. He also never revealed whether he or Tenzing had stepped onto the peak first. As far as Hillary was concerned, it just didn't matter. He went on to climb ten other peaks in the Himalayas and made a successful journey to the South Pole. He spent much of his later life creating and working with the Himalayan Trust in Nepal. Nepalese people form the Gurkha regiments that have been Britain's allies for almost two hundred years and Hillary's Trust built bridges, hospitals, airstrips and almost thirty schools there.

He died on 11 January 2008, aged 88. In April of that year, Queen Elizabeth held a final service for him in St George's Chapel. Gurkha soldiers stood guard for the last time outside as he was honoured and remembered as a great man.

Recommended
The Ascent of Everest by John Hunt, published 1953. It includes the chapter 'The Summit' by Edmund Hillary.

The Abolition of Slavery
Sharp, Clarkson, Wilberforce & Buxton

There is today a vast amount of misinformation and misunderstanding about the history and origins of slavery. Slavery is, unfortunately, as old as mankind itself. The oldest oral histories, cave drawings and written histories of every race include slavery – in Africa, throughout Asia and Asia Minor, Europe, North, Central and South America, India and Oceania. It's been practised everywhere from the beginnings of history, when the British Isles were uninhabited marshes and mountains.

The great Indian civilisations of 5000 BC traded slaves. All the Middle Eastern and Mediterranean states had slaves. Classical Greek civilisation – the so-called 'cradle of democracy' – was based upon slavery. While Plato and Aristotle debated democracy, less than 1 per cent of people had any say in that society and 50 per cent were slaves. Plato's ideal republic contained slavery, while Aristotle suggested that some peoples were naturally slaves.

The Roman Empire was built on slavery. The Romans created slaves in every land they conquered, from civilians as well as defeated armies, enslaving Britons in the north, Carthaginians and Egyptians in the south. For a one hundred-year period BC, slaves outnumbered freemen by three to one, with almost 21 million slaves.

Meanwhile in Africa, slavery was already practised, both locally and in the form of exports to the Middle East. As in every continent, the nations and tribes of Africa waged war amongst themselves for thousands of years well before the British and Europeans arrived. The defeated of those wars became slaves to their victors and were either worked locally, sold on to other tribes, or used to pay debts and penalties. With the sweeping spread of Islam after AD 650, a huge slave trade in Africans was created, trading from sub-Sahara to Muslim

North Africa and to Muslim Middle East. Black slaves were sold by black Africans to Muslim traders for transportation by caravan across the deserts, by boat down the River Nile, and by sea from centres such as Zanzibar to the Arabian Gulf, Red Sea and Indian slave ports. In the late 800s, Arab geographer Al-Yaqubi recorded: 'I am informed that the kings of the blacks sell their own people without justification or in consequence of war.'

No figures exist for the number of Africans enslaved this way, but for 1,300 years of Islamic slavery, the caravan routes, River Nile and jungle paths were littered with the bones of dead slaves. During the 1800s, missionary and abolitionist Dr David Livingstone put the figure at 500,000 dead each year. That trade continues today.

Arab slavers also made raids by sea, to the Canary Islands, Madeira, Malta, Sicily, Spain, Portugal – and the British Isles. Villagers from southern England, Wales and Ireland were snatched from their homes and sold in markets on the Barbary Coast of North Africa. In the Middle East, Muslim armies raided Eastern Europe for Christian slaves and in Russia they bought slaves captured by the conquering Vikings. Turkey, France, Venice, Genoa, Spain and Morocco sentenced convicts of any nationality to be galley slaves into the 1800s.

Elsewhere, the various civilisations of Central and South America – particularly Aztec, Mayan and Incan – rose on the back of slaves. North American tribes were enslaved by their captors, especially the Haida. The Middle Kingdom of China and other Asian nations were slave societies; the Hindu and Muslim states of the Indian subcontinent used slaves. Even in Oceania, the fabled South Sea Paradise, slavery was practised, as well as infanticide and cannibalism.

The Atlantic slave trade was begun by Portugal in 1444, when 225 slaves were captured from West Africa and sold in the market at the town of Lagos, on the Portuguese coast. Papal decrees permitted the Portuguese to enslave all unbelievers and, by 1450, 1,000 Africans had been enslaved in Portugal. By 1650, Portugal had enslaved 1⅓ million from Angola alone. Meanwhile, Spain introduced African slaves to the Canary and Balearic Islands.

After the discovery of the Americas, Portugal and Spain decided to transport African slaves to their colonies for the new sugar-cane plantations. Within a hundred years, the Dutch joined the trade, transporting slaves from West Africa for sale in Brazil, the Caribbean and its North American colony of New Amsterdam (New York). They were quickly followed by the Danes, French, Prussians and Swedes.

The first Africans were brought to the English colonies by the Dutch in 1619. They were given the same status as white indentured servants so that, after ten years, English colonies had black and white freemen as well as black and white slaves. Black freemen also bought slaves; there are records in the National Archives at Kew of the purchase of white and black slaves in the colonies. Later, African slaves were preferred because three Africans could be purchased for the same price as one white slave. White slaves were more expensive because they could talk, read and, sometimes, write English. It was simple economics that favoured African slaves.

British merchants joined the Atlantic slave trade in earnest in 1663, purchasing African slaves as cheap labour for sugar and tobacco plantations in the West Indian and American colonies. At the same time, Britain also traded white slaves for labour in the colonies.

The white slaves' sea passage – in similar conditions to their cousins from Africa – were paid for by the plantation owner. The term of labour was for three, five or ten years, after which they were supposed to be freed with a small grant of land, although this rarely happened. In Britain, a profitable kidnapping trade developed to supply white slaves and ports became dangerous areas for men, women and children.

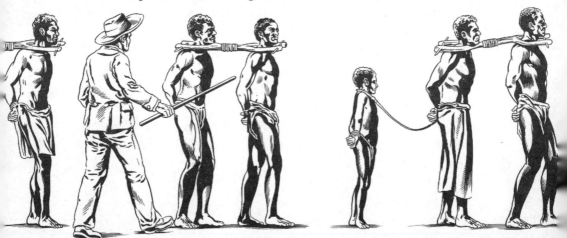

Many thousands of British convicts and political prisoners were also transported to the West Indian and American colonies as slaves.

The infamous 'triangle' shipping route developed in the eighteenth century and was used by all Atlantic slaving nations. From Europe, ships sailed with tools, hardware, weapons, beads, cloth, salt, rum and tobacco, which were traded in West Africa for gold, ivory and slaves – all delivered to the trading forts by Africans from inland as well as from along the coast. The ships then sailed the 'Middle Passage' across the Atlantic to South, Central and North America and the Caribbean, where the slaves were sold or bartered at auction. The third leg took the ships back to Europe with sugar, rum, tobacco and cotton. The American slavers began their triangle with cotton, tobacco and other American products for Europe.

The slave trade was horrific, everywhere in the world, particularly from our standpoint of the twenty-first century. Yet the only true judgement that can be made of any event in history is by the standards of those days. Was slavery considered evil in the seventeenth and eighteenth centuries? The answer is no. Slavery was an accepted practice the world over and had been since records began.

The treatment of slaves was also horrific but, in truth, was little different from the treatment of other people in those days. Sir Hans Sloane, the great doctor of the Age of Enlightenment, recorded in 1686 that for severe crimes some slaves in Jamaica had been burned to death. This is almost beyond belief, but death by burning was the statutory punishment for many crimes in Britain and European countries until replaced by hanging, garrotting, boiling or guillotining. In Spain and

Portugal, Catholic priests burned non-Catholics; suspected witches were burned or drowned everywhere, while the Salem witch executions of Massachusetts are still famous today.

Slaves were placed in wooden stocks for various misdemeanours; so in every town in England there were stocks for punishing miscreants. Slaves were flogged and, sometimes, flogged to death in punishment for crimes; so, too, were soldiers in the army, sailors in the navy and even the seamen of slave ships. Another punishment was to place slaves upon a treadmill; Oscar Wilde was punished on the treadmill of Reading Gaol – in 1895. Slaves were hanged for minor offences; so, too, were the English, Irish, Scots and Welsh. The expression 'you may as well be hanged for a sheep as a lamb' originated in 1700s Britain when stealing livestock was a capital offence. Many British felons were hanged by chains on gibbets at crossroads, their bodies tarred and left to rot as a warning to others.

Slaves were packed into the cargo spaces of ships during the Middle Passage, averaging about nineteen inches of space each in decks only five feet high; in the Royal Navy each seaman had twenty-two inches of space to sling his hammock but in two layers, one above the other, in decks five feet high. The death rate was higher among the crews of British slave ships than among the slaves. The simple reason is that the slaves were the profitable cargo of the voyage – the more who survived, the greater the profit – while the crew were the loss-making part of the voyage: they had to be paid.

This description is typical: 'During the voyage there is on board these ships terrible misery, stench, fumes, horror, vomiting, many kinds of sea-sickness, fever, flux [dysentery], headaches, heat, constipation, boils, scurvy, cancer, mouth-rot, and the like. Add to this want of provisions, hunger, thirst, frost, heat, dampness, anxiety, afflictions and lamentations, together with other trouble, as the lice abound so frightfully, especially on sick people, that they can be scraped off the body ... The water which is served out on the ships is often very black, thick and full of worms, so that one cannot drink it without loathing, even with the greatest thirst. When the ships have landed after their long voyage no one is permitted to leave ... they must remain on board the ships until they are purchased. The healthy are naturally preferred first, and so the sick and wretched must often remain on board in front of the city for two or three weeks, and frequently die.'

The voyage described was in 1750 from Britain to Pennsylvania – carrying white slaves and fare-paying emigrants. Those were brutal days.

So how was the acceptance and business of slavery brought to an end? Who were the heroes who made that amazing leap of moral judgement to declare – after 7,000 years – that slavery was wrong and that the slave trade must be abolished?

The 1600s and 1700s were the 'Age of Enlightenment' in Europe, and the major countries of this Enlightenment were England and Scotland. Scientists, philosophers, doctors, writers and radicals such as Sir Isaac Newton, Robert Boyle, Thomas Hobbes, David Home, Sir Hans Sloane, John Locke, Thomas Paine, Joseph Priestley and many more questioned, challenged and changed the accepted order of science, society, government and liberty. The 'Rights of Man', equality and modern democracy were created in Great Britain, so it's no surprise that the first slavery abolitionists were also British.

Those radicals also questioned the role of religion. Yet it was Christianity, in the form of enlightened Quakers, Anglicans and Nonconformists, which was the catalyst for abolishing the slave trade and slavery.

Quaker doctrine in England and the colonies gradually became opposed to the slave trade and slavery. Anglican philosopher John Locke described slavery as a 'vile and miserable estate'. In 1688, Aphra Behn wrote the first novel with a slave as its hero with *Oroonoko: Or, The Royal Slave*. Methodist John Wesley called the trade 'the execrable sum of human villainy', and poet and satirist Alexander Pope condemned it outright.

By the 1770s, there were about 15,000 black Africans living in England and Wales and several thousand more in Scotland. Slavery was not allowed in Britain, but was there a specific law prohibiting it? Generally in Britain, where there is no constitution, if there is no law prohibiting an act then it's not illegal, the most liberal of all systems.

Constitutions actually restrict liberty. So a test case was required to confirm whether or not slavery was illegal in Britain.

In 1765, a clerk in the Civil Service, Granville Sharp, became the first practical slave abolitionist in the world when he issued a writ of assault against a slave 'owner' for beating black slave Jonathan Strong. Sharp secured Strong's release from prison; his 'owner' responded with a counter-writ accusing Sharp of robbing him of his property. The grounds for a test case were established. Public outrage about the 'owner's' counter-writ was so immense – showing that the public did indeed consider slavery illegal in Britain – that he withdrew his writ. There was no case. Sharp tried again with fugitive black slave Thomas Lewis, but the jury decided that Lewis's master had not established his case as 'owner' and so Lewis was a free man anyway.

Sharp was able to pursue a case to its conclusion with another African fugitive, James Somersett. In 1771, Somersett escaped his Boston master while the two were visiting London, was recaptured in 1772 and imprisoned on a ship about to sail for Jamaica. Under the Act of 1679, Sharp applied for and was granted a writ of habeas corpus. This prevented Somersett being removed from England, on the grounds that he was wrongfully imprisoned because there was no such legal status as slavery.

Sharp's barrister quoted as precedent a trial 200 years earlier in Elizabeth I's reign, where the verdict determined 'that England was too pure an air for slaves to breathe in'. He argued further that a law of another country, even a British colony, had no jurisdiction in England and Wales.

Judge Lord Mansfield applied the impartial law of England and agreed: 'The power claimed [of ownership] never was in use here nor acknowledged by the law. The state of Slavery is of such a nature that it is incapable of being introduced on any reasons, moral or political, but only by positive law … It is so odious that nothing can be sufficient to support it but positive law. Whatever inconveniences, therefore, may follow from this decision, I cannot say this case is allowed or approved by the law of England, and therefore the black must be discharged.'

Judge Mansfield had confirmed the Elizabethan verdict that slavery was illegal. This judgment was the beginning of the end of slavery throughout the world. In practical terms, it meant that any slave setting foot in England or Wales was immediately a free man. There was jubilation, with Africans dancing outside the court. Scottish law followed suit, when the courts there prohibited the forced return of former slaves to Jamaica. Great Britain was the first country in the world where slavery was actually written into the statute books as illegal. Escaped slaves fled to Britain from Europe and its colonies.

With the leadership of Granville Sharp, the scattered sentiments against slavery coalesced into the Abolition movement. Sharp wrote an incredible sixty-one treatises condemning slavery. The next step was to abolish the slave trade itself.

In 1776, Abolition received unexpected support with the publication of economist Adam Smith's classic work, *The Wealth of Nations*. Smith demonstrated that slave labour was not as profitable as free labour: over time slaves were more expensive than freemen. Further, the land suffered from lack of care when using slaves, whereas freemen cared for the land because they had a vested interest.

Recent examinations of the contribution of slave labour to the British Empire and the Industrial Revolution have revealed a far smaller impact than previously thought. For example, the port of Liverpool's profit from the slave trade in the heyday of 1750–1800 was only 7.5 per cent of its total profit, while the overall profits from slave industries for Britain amounted to only 1.5 per cent of the national investment. It was not slavery but the East India Company – which at its peak controlled more than half the world's trade – upon which the British Empire was built. Adam Smith's arguments against slavery were economic rather than moral, but they were important because slavers and their supporters claimed that Abolition would ruin Britain economically. Smith showed that argument to be false.

The Society for the Abolition of the Slave Trade was formed in London in 1787. The chairman was Granville Sharp and its founding members – all of whom should be remembered for what they achieved – were William Dillwyn, Samuel Hoare, George Harrison, John Lloyd, Joseph Woods, Richard Phillips, John Barton, Joseph Hooper, James

Phillips, Philip Sansom, and 27-year-old Thomas Clarkson. Sharp, Sansom and Clarkson were Anglicans; the rest were Quakers. Potter Josiah Wedgwood devised the society's seal, a manacled slave with the legend 'Am I Not a Man and a Brother?'

Cambridge graduate Thomas Clarkson trained as a deacon but never practised. Instead, he devoted his working life to the abolition of slavery. He travelled Britain campaigning for the society, formed anti-slavery branches in boroughs, towns and cities, and collected damning information about the trade. In seven years he rode 35,000 miles. To find one witness, he travelled to five ports and visited fifty-seven vessels.

He sailed to France to persuade the revolutionaries of 1789 to include Abolition within their charter of liberties. Despite six months of meetings and submissions, he was unsuccessful. In 1791–2 he took a petition around Britain, which was signed by 390,000 people and presented to Parliament. In 1794, his health collapsed and he had to rest from the campaign.

The most important single act by Clarkson was to recruit to the society the similarly youthful MP for Yorkshire, William Wilberforce. Wilberforce became the Abolitionists' brilliant advocate in Parliament, Clarkson their passionate voice in the country and Sharp their writer and tactician behind the scenes. It was a formidable trinity.

Wilberforce's conversion to Abolition took place in stages. The first was meeting former slave captain John Newton, who had been converted to Christianity and ordained in the Church of England. He knew the slave trade and supplied details and inside information about the business to Clarkson and Wilberforce. The hymn 'Amazing Grace' was written by Newton about his redemption:

Amazing Grace, how sweet the sound,
that saved a wretch like me.
I once was lost but now am found,
was blind but now I see.

At his wedding, Wilberforce sang the hymn with pride.

The second stage for Wilberforce was recruitment by Clarkson to the society. The third was a conversation with close friend and visionary, the 24-year-old Prime Minister William Pitt the Younger. Pitt urged Wilberforce to make Abolition his special political cause and promised him his support. Pitt and Wilberforce were the young shooting stars of Parliament.

Pitt ordered inquiries into the slave trade and forced through an act restricting it and improving standards. The inquiries reported in 1789 and, after a Wilberforce speech of three and a half hours, it was agreed that a select committee would report to Parliament with details. A general election interrupted the committee but it presented its report supporting Abolition in 1791. The dying Methodist John Wesley sent his last letter to Wilberforce, urging him to continue the campaign.

After a four-hour speech by Wilberforce, two evenings of impassioned debate, and support from Pitt and the king, the Bill to Abolish the Slave Trade was still defeated, although by only seventy-five votes. It was apparent it was going to be a tough campaign. However, the Abolitionists had gained the support of another liberal from the opposition party, the hell-raising drinker Charles Fox.

Pitt and Wilberforce persisted and in 1792 Wilberforce again presented a Bill for the Abolition of the Slave Trade. The Commons debate lasted throughout the night, with Pitt speaking with such eloquence that for 'the last twenty minutes he seemed to be really inspired'. With an amendment to 'gradual abolition', the motion was passed by an incredible 145 votes. Two weeks later, a date for the beginning of Abolition was approved: 1 January 1796.

A Bill for the Abolition of the Slave Trade in the British Empire – in effect, the world – had been passed by the House of Commons. It was surely only a matter of time. The opponents of Abolition were reduced to delaying tactics, which they began immediately. In the House of Lords they moved a postponement to the next parliamentary session and then to the following year; both succeeded.

Meanwhile, Granville Sharp created a 'province of freedom' in West Africa, a settlement for free Africans living in Britain who wished to return. Supported by Clarkson and Wilberforce, he established Freetown. Black colonial loyalists who had fought with Britain during the American War of Independence also applied to go. Several thousand had escaped from the United States and were living in Nova Scotia colony. In 1792, Clarkson's brother led a fleet of fifteen ships carrying 1,196 free black settlers from Halifax to Freetown.

After France declared war on Britain in 1793, the threat of French invasion concentrated Parliament's energies on survival. The date for commencement of Abolition came and went against a background of war and elections. Wilberforce submitted motions annually for a new bill, but all were defeated. However, as the Royal Navy began to dominate the seas and as British forces defeated French, Dutch and Spanish armies outside Europe, confidence returned.

Following Pitt's victory in the general election of 1804, Wilberforce presented a new Bill for the Abolition of the Slave Trade; it was passed by the Commons but too late for presentation to the Lords. He reintroduced it in 1805 but it was defeated in its second reading. Such frustration took its toll on Wilberforce's severe colitis. Opium was then the only pain relief and he was almost addicted, so great was his pain.

Wilberforce persuaded Pitt to use an Order in Council to ban all slave trading to the captured Dutch colony of Guiana. After the Battle of Trafalgar, with the threat of French invasion virtually gone, the Government had time to address issues other than war. Abolition regained momentum, Clarkson returned to the battle and experienced lawyer James Stephen joined the cause.

At the age of only 46, worn out from orchestrating the defence against France, Pitt died in the new year. A coalition with Lord Grenville as Prime Minister and Charles Fox as Foreign Minister succeeded him. In a new tactic devised by James Stephen, Wilberforce reintroduced the Foreign Slave Bill. It banned all Britons from slave-trading outside the Empire and was passed by both Houses of Parliament. Grenville and Fox had shown their colours; the coalition leaders were in favour of Abolition.

In an agreement with Wilberforce, Fox himself moved a resolution in the Commons in June that 'all manner of dealing and trading in slaves' should be 'utterly abolished, prohibited and declared to be unlawful'. It was passed by 101 votes. Then Fox died and Lord Grenville was forced into a general election. He was returned and introduced Fox's Abolition Bill to the Lords in January. For the first time, the Lords passed the bill and returned it to the Commons.

On 23 February 1807, the bill's second reading in the House of Commons took place, the final reading if passed. The vote was a landslide, 283 to 16 – in favour. At last the bill was passed. Wilberforce was applauded by the House. Overcome with emotion, he wept at his bench.

The king signed the royal assent on 25 March. Immediately Sharpe, Clarkson, Wilberforce and others formed the 'African Institution', to promote the application of the act and to campaign for abolition of the slave trades of other countries. Ironically, because of the French wars and delays orchestrated by its opponents since 1792 when the bill was first passed, Britain was not the first country to abolish the slave trade. Denmark had abolished it in 1803. Yet – with all respect to Denmark – in global terms that abolition was irrelevant. It was what Great Britain decided which would dictate to the world the future of the slave trade. The navy began policing the ban.

With continental Europe liberated from France in 1815, Wilberforce led a campaign – including petitions of one million signatures gathered around Britain – to include in the Vienna peace treaty an anti-slave trade clause. Foreign Minister Castlereagh responded: 'The nation is bent upon this object. I believe there is hardly a village that has not met and petitioned upon it. Ministers must make it the basis of their policy.' It was also at Vienna that Britain stopped European nations from dismembering France into small states and principalities as punishment for its twenty-two years of war.

Defeated France and the Netherlands had no choice but to abolish their slave trades, but allies Spain and Portugal refused. Britain stepped forward and paid them to reduce and to end their slave trades. Despite this, all those countries continued trading slaves illegally. Between 1811 and 1870, some two million more African slaves were shipped across the Atlantic, mostly to the United States, Cuba and Brazil.

It wasn't easy for the Royal Navy to police the Atlantic in the days of sailing ships. Between 1808 and 1845 it lost 1,338 men off the West African coast alone, mostly to disease. Agreements were negotiated with many other countries, giving the navy the right to board and search their ships for slaves; the United States notably refused. From 1825 to 1865, the United States imported a further million slaves.

The Abolitionists genuinely thought that stopping the slave trade would lead the British plantations to free their slaves and employ them, as economist Adam Smith had earlier argued. The majority of transported slaves had been male. With no more arriving – ever – it was in the planters' best interests to promote free families for future labour. Through the fears and stupidity of the plantation owners, this didn't happen.

Rising again to the challenge, the Abolitionists mounted another social and political campaign. Granville Sharp, however, had died in 1813, while Wilberforce was then 67 with failing health and Clarkson was 66 and going blind from cataracts. Thomas Buxton, a young Anglican MP, led the new campaign under the banner of the Anti-Slavery Society. On 15 May 1823, Buxton moved a resolution in the Commons to abolish all slavery in the British Empire. He saw freedom in the Empire as the major step in the wider battle for freedom throughout the world, although he was realist enough not 'to suppose that we can at once, by a single effort, solve the problem which lies before us'.

That year, in the new colony of Guiana (formerly Dutch Guiana), there was an uprising by 13,000 slaves in which two overseers were murdered. The Dutch colonists proclaimed martial law, hanged forty-seven slaves, and sentenced to death English missionary and Abolitionist John Smith for complicity in the uprising. He was imprisoned and died in gaol. Smith's death, the first Abolitionist martyrdom, became a catalyst for the new cause.

Buxton forced through sweeping reforms for the West Indian and Guiana colonies. They included automatic freedom for all female children born after 1823, abolition of flogging, holidays for religious instruction, a nine-hour working day, savings banks for slaves and admission of evidence by slaves in court. In 1828, the landmark British ruling was made that 'free people of colour in the colonies' have legal equality with their fellow citizens. The planters were not pleased.

Government in the British Empire was complicated by the fact that each colony had its own separate government. This allowed local representation and administration, but also created policy differences with Parliament in London. In 1832, Jamaican colonists threatened to secede and join the United States. Slave conditions in the US were then horrific, and this threat prompted an uprising by 50,000 Jamaican slaves. The Jamaican administration was severe, executing 100 slaves after peace was restored. Upon a wave of revulsion in Britain, Buxton again moved a motion in the Commons for the Abolition of Slavery in the Empire.

On 26 July 1833, the final reading of this bill was passed by the Commons; it became law on 29 August. At a stroke, some 800,000 people were freed.

In a clever move, Parliament compensated the planters for half of each slave's market value. On the one hand it pacified the planters, on the other the money enabled them to continue the plantations and other industries and provide employment and apprenticeships for the freed slaves.

William Wilberforce died on the morning of 29 July at his home in Chelsea, aware that the abolition of slavery had been secured. He is buried alongside William Pitt in Westminster Abbey. Thomas Clarkson lived until 26 September 1846, and was buried at home near Ipswich, aged 87. His last public appearance was to address the World Anti-Slavery Convention in London in 1840.

Successive British governments in the 1800s sent the navy and the army around the world to stop slavery, particularly in Africa. Anti-slavery squadrons patrolled the African coasts, and expeditions blazed paths inland, destroying slave markets and liberating slaves at source.

The British and Foreign Anti-Slavery Society and the British Aborigines Protection Society campaigned throughout the world, while Anglican and Methodist anti-slavery missionaries such as David Livingstone worked at private expense. One missionary, Arthur West, bought the entire slave market of Zanzibar and freed the slaves. Arab sheiks, African chieftains, Turkish emirs, Egyptian pashas, Persian princes and Sudanese khedives were all coerced by the British to join foreign governments in signing slave suppression and abolition treaties. When Zanzibar became British in 1890, the slave market and stockades were blown up and the Muslim slave trade by sea almost totally stopped.

Throughout the 1800s, abolition of slave trades and slavery spread from Britain across the world, but the going was hard. The interests and moralities of African, Arab and other slavers were far more difficult to change than opinions of Members of Parliament. Slavery ceased officially in the greatest slave nation of all, the United States, in 1865 and in the second greatest slave nation, Brazil, in 1888.

Astonishingly, some modern revisionist historians criticise the Abolitionists. One found it 'reprehensible' that abolition of slavery was not the Abolitionists' avowed aim until 1823. Yet the British Abolitionists made slave trading illegal throughout the Empire, believing that without resupply slavery itself must stop. It didn't, so they then made slavery illegal.

Abolitionists were also accused of being blind to slavery in other parts of the world, in particular the colonies of Portuguese Brazil, Spanish Cuba and the United States. Yet Clarkson attempted to gain French cooperation, Sharp created the Africa Institution, and Wilberforce forced anti-slave trade clauses into the Vienna peace treaty. In addition, the British government paid Portugal and Spain to end their slave trades, the navy stopped the trade at sea and the government negotiated international boarding rights with every country it could. Short of going to war – and after twenty-two years of world war that was not an option – there's a limit to what can be achieved in a very short time. When you're first, you're breaking new ground.

As it was, the Atlantic slave trade had been stopped after a 420-year history. The Abolitionists and British governments campaigned for and abolished slavery throughout most of the world.

The simple truth is that 7,000 years of slavery was turned on its head in just fifty-five years by the British Abolitionists. Such was their fervour, their passion, that they changed public and government endorsement of an economic practice into a perception of a monstrous evil. They changed the world. An amazing grace indeed.

Recommended

A Sailor Boy's Experience Aboard a Slave Ship by Samuel Robinson.
The British Anti-Slavery Movement by Sir Reginald Coupland.
William Wilberforce by Robin Furneaux.
The Rise and Fall of Black Slavery by C. Duncan Rice.
History of Slavery by Susanne Everett.
Gottlieb Mittelberger's Journey to Pennsylvania in the Year 1750 and Return to Germany in the Year 1754 by Gottlieb Mittelberger.

Edith Cavell

One of the reasons for writing this book is to breathe new life into the extraordinary stories of heroes and heroines who were once known to all. Time and changes in education have meant that sometimes stories are forgotten where they should be remembered.

The life of Edith Cavell is one such tale. In 1915, her death rocked the world and helped bring America into the First World War. Queen Alexandra attended her funeral, the same lady who visited Robert Scott on his ship before he set off to the South Pole. Such was the outcry at her death that the German Kaiser insisted no other woman would be executed unless he had reviewed the case and given his personal order. Edith Cavell's statue stands at St Martin's Place, near Trafalgar Square in London. Very few of the thousands who pass it each day know how courageous she was, or the lives she saved at the expense of her own.

Her father was a vicar in the village of Swardeston in Norfolk. He was sometimes known as 'the one-sermon vicar' as he repeated the same one every Sunday for nearly forty-six years. Edith Louisa Cavell was born on 4 December 1865. It was a devout and stern upbringing. As there was no village school, the vicar taught Edith himself with her two sisters and a brother.

Edith discovered a talent for languages at a young age. She was engaged as a children's governess for some years, then travelled to Brussels in 1890, where she taught for five years before returning home to nurse her father through a long illness. That experience would give her life direction as she began formal training as a nurse in 1896, at the London Hospital in the Whitechapel Road. In 1903, she was promoted to assistant matron at Shoreditch Infirmary. Her efficiency and powers of organisation were said to be outstanding and she was asked by an eminent surgeon, Antoine Depage, to start the first school for training nurses in Belgium. She opened the school in 1907.

Edith was a serious woman who rarely smiled, but had the respect of all those with whom she dealt. She trained the nurses with stern discipline, coupled with a deep well of personal kindness. When she discovered one of her patients had become a drug addict, she kept the fact from the authorities until she had helped the girl break the habit. She also refused to expel one probationer nurse who had become a stripper, worrying what would become of the girl if she was turned away. In fact, the nurse gave up her second career and eventually became the supervisor of another European hospital.

As the 'Directrice' of the clinic, Edith Cavell taught anatomy, cleanliness and the importance of hard work to the trainee nurses, sometimes using Florence Nightingale as an example. On one summer day, she refused to let them kill a wasp that had got in, saying: 'Turn it free. A nurse gives life; she does not take it.'

When war broke out in 1914, Edith was at home on holiday in Norfolk. In June of that year, Archduke Franz Ferdinand was assassinated in Serbia and one by one, the great nations were dragged into the conflict. Despite the entreaties of her mother, sisters and brother, Edith knew her duty was with the nurses and patients in Brussels and returned immediately. On 20 August, German soldiers marched into the city.

As a non-combatant, Edith was offered safe passage to Holland, but she refused. Battle casualties were coming into the clinic every day and she stayed to tend them. Even then, she could have lived out the war in perfect safety if she had not felt so strongly that she must also do something for the Allies. When two British soldiers on the run asked for shelter at her clinic, she hid them in the cellar. As far as possible, Edith took this secret part of her work on herself, keeping her nurses away from the hunted men so they could not be implicated. Despite the danger, she had them smuggled out to Holland, and the clinic quickly became known as part of the Belgian underground and a safe place to hide.

Edith was aware of the danger in her activities. She kept her diary hidden, sewn into a cushion in case the clinic was ever searched. There was little money and not much to eat, but Edith and her nurses shared what they had with those who came to them, while always expecting the knock on the door that would mean they had been discovered.

She was eventually betrayed by a German spy named George Quien. He had discovered some details of the underground work going on at the clinic. He appeared one day, pretending to be a Paris doctor with a minor complaint that required him to remain in the clinic for some weeks. There, he took note of the clandestine activities and asked innocent-sounding questions of the nurses. When he disappeared without warning in early 1915, one of Edith's contacts was arrested shortly afterwards. She said to another nurse: 'I suppose it won't be long before they come for us.' Even then, under terrible strain, she continued helping Allied soldiers find their way home, passing two hundred of them back to safety. Her work was too important to give up, no matter what storm clouds were on the horizon.

In August 1915, three Germans demanded entrance at the clinic. Once inside, they produced a pistol and had the nurses line up against the wall. Edith was summoned and she came down to them in her nurse's uniform, carrying a small travelling case and gloves. They took her to St-Gilles prison, where she was charged with aiding the enemy. She remained there for two months. In her absence, one of the nurses, Sister Wilkins, sought out the American ambassador. He tried desperately to contact the German Governor of Brussels, but to no avail. The nurses sent roses to her and she kept them in her cell.

Sister Wilkins was allowed to visit Edith in prison and found her worn out and thin, but still determined to keep her dignity.

'I have done what was my duty,' Edith said. 'They must do with me what they will.' Her faith was a comfort to her and she wrote to the nurses: 'Remember that it is not enough to be good nurses; you should also be good Christian women.'

At her trial, Edith Cavell would not lie. She admitted in court that she had cared for two hundred British, French and Belgian soldiers, helping many of them to escape. The sentence was death. On 12 October 1915, a chaplain was allowed to visit her in her cell. Before she was taken out to be executed, she said to him: 'Standing as I do in the view of God and Eternity, I realise that patriotism is not enough. I must have no hatred or bitterness towards anyone.' Deeply moved by her courage, he said later: 'I came to comfort her and she has given me comfort.'

At 7 a.m., Edith was made to stand against a wall and a firing squad assembled. Some of the men fired deliberately wide and it is said that one refused to shoot. He was also killed and buried in a shallow grave beside her.

A few days later, her personal effects were returned to the clinic, with a final letter to the nurses. In it, she wrote:

> I hope you will not forget the little talks we had each evening. I told you that voluntary sacrifices will make you happy; that the idea of duty before God and yourselves will give you support in the sad moments of life and in the face of death. I know I have sometimes been harsh, but never have I been voluntarily unjust. I loved all of you more than you will ever know.

When the war ended, Edith's body was returned to England. An impressive ceremony was held at Westminster Abbey. From there, the coffin was taken home to Norfolk and she was laid to rest outside Norwich Cathedral. Every second year since, in Swardeston, a flower festival is held around 12 October in her memory. Her courage, her sense of duty, her example, is as valuable today as it has ever been.

Recommended
Edith Cavell by A.A. Hoehling.
The Oxford Dictionary of National Biography.

Douglas Bader

O n the morning of Monday, 14 December 1931, three Bristol Bulldog biplane fighters of the Royal Air Force took off from Woodley aerodrome near Reading to return to RAF Kenley.

One turned back to 'beat up' the airfield, flying slow rolls just above the grass. The tip of the lower port wing touched and the aircraft ploughed in, cartwheeling until it came to rest, a complete wreck. Trapped in the smashed cockpit, the pilot's legs were crushed, two ribs were broken and a tooth was poking through his lip. Fortunately, what was left of the plane did not catch fire.

The pilot was cut out of the wreck and taken to hospital in Reading, where he hovered for four days on that razor's edge between life and death. Against all expectations he lived. However, his right leg was amputated high above the knee and his left leg below the knee. His flying days were over. Also his sporting days, particularly rugby, at which he had hoped to play fly-half for England against the Springboks that season.

There would be no running across the Twickenham grass for that 21-year-old. In a moment of high jinks, his life had become a disaster. But the pilot's name was Douglas Bader, so it didn't turn out quite like that.

As he recovered in hospital, there were times of deepest despair. When a fellow pilot crashed and died Bader said aloud: 'He's the lucky one. He's dead. I'd rather be killed outright than left like this.' His moods swung between vague optimism and utter dejection, but the mind can be amazingly resilient.

Although rugby was out of the question, Bader was determined he would one day play cricket once more. More than anything it was the thought of flying again which drove him to recovery. Yet the first step

– literally – was to learn
to walk.

From a wheelchair he
advanced to two crutches;
from two to one crutch and a
peg leg; from a peg leg to tin legs.
At that stage in the development of
artificial limbs, no person who'd
lost most of one leg and half the
other had ever walked without a
stick, usually two. The first time
his tin legs were fitted – with
straps and supports around his
thigh for the left leg and straps
around his waist and shoulder
for the right – Bader cried out:
'Good Lord, this is absolutely
impossible!'

The limb-makers at Roehampton
Hospital told him: 'I think you ought
to face it that you'll never walk again
without a stick.' Bader looked at them
in dismay, then replied: 'Damn that! I'll
never, *never* walk *with* a stick!'

To move, he had to kick the right tin leg
forward from the hip, jerk it again like a whip to straighten it, force his
upper body over it as if he were hurdling, balance on the right leg while
swinging the left forward from the knee, then put his weight back on
his left stump. Then repeat it all again.

'This is bloody awful!' he said.

'Don't worry, you'll do it,' the doctors encouraged him. 'You can
only learn by practice, but it might take you six months.' He looked at
them in amazement.

'Don't be silly. There's a girl I want to see in a couple of days and I
want to be walking with these things then.'

They looked at him sideways, unsure if he was joking or not. In fact he wasn't. A week before, on crutch and peg leg, he'd met the woman who was to become his wife in a tea garden near Uxbridge, during an afternoon out with two other injured pilots. 'You could try a stick,' they suggested again. 'No stick!' he replied.

By summer 1932, he was stumping and staggering well enough on his new legs at Roehampton to leave his crutch and peg leg. The sticks remained unused. It was a wonderful moment when he lurched into the dining room at RAF Uxbridge for the first time since the crash without a crutch. There were cheers and yells: 'Long John's got his ruddy undercarriage back!'

Even so, it was depressing, difficult and extraordinarily painful learning how to walk with artificial legs. His stumps became blistered and raw, and he kept falling over when his metal feet dragged on the ground. He wouldn't have anyone help him up and simply soldiered on, forcing himself to keep trying over and over and over again. He reasoned that his choice was to learn to walk or be a cripple for the rest of his life.

Gradually he improved until what was initially a conscious effort became instinctive. He developed a stumping, rolling walk, with a jolting technique for going up and down stairs. He visited the tea rooms in Uxbridge many times. He passed his disabled driving licence and did play a couple of games of cricket, though his fielding, even in the slips, let him down. He began to fly once more, in dual-control planes, and passed again his flying medical and practical flying course.

However, the RAF wouldn't allow him to fly solo. 'Unfortunately, we can't pass you fit for flying because there's nothing in King's Regulations to cover your case,' he was told. He continued to fly with other pilots. They trusted him completely and never touched the dual controls, but the powers-that-be would not have that. In 1933 he was invalided out with a disability pension. He was 23 years old.

Back in civvy street, he worked for Asiatic Petroleum (later Shell), driving maniacally about Britain in an MG sports car adapted with just two foot pedals. In 1935 he married his tea-garden sweetheart, Thelma Edwards. He swam, played squash regularly – clanking around the court and falling frequently – and took up golf, at which eventually he excelled. So life continued for Douglas Bader, happy with Thelma, she happy with him, yet both knowing that in his heart he'd rather be flying than working in an office.

On 1 September 1939, Germany invaded Poland. On the 3rd, Britain was at war with Germany, Austria and Czechoslovakia. As ever, appeasement hadn't worked and, anyway, a country that actually *bans* cricket (Germany, 1934) is sure to be untrustworthy.

Bader immediately contacted the Air Ministry. Within a week he underwent another medical and was passed medically fit and flying fit. By the end of November he was back in the RAF, at his previous rank of flying officer.

In January 1940, he converted to Hawker Hurricane fighters and in his log book, under the entry 'ability as a pilot', was marked 'exceptional'. In February he was posted operational to 19 Squadron at RAF Duxford, where he converted to Vickers Supermarine Spitfires. In April, he was made flight lieutenant and a flight commander in 222 Squadron, also flying Spitfires. He was part of 12 Group under Leigh-Mallory, defending the Midlands and Wales.

Bader had his first taste of actual combat over Dunkirk, fighting the Luftwaffe above while the army was evacuated below. There he had his first victory, shooting down a Messerschmitt 109 fighter. Shortly after Dunkirk, Bader was promoted to squadron leader, a third ring around his sleeve.

He was given 242 Squadron at Coltishall in Norfolk, a squadron mostly of Canadians flying Hurricanes. It had waged a fighting retreat across France in early 1940 and was in a poor state. All its equipment and spares had been abandoned in France and it had suffered nearly 50 per cent casualties amongst its pilots and aircraft. Morale was low, as much at the shambles that was the fall of France as at their losses. Neither 242 pilots nor ground crew were impressed by 'authority'.

When Bader first met his pilots there were suspicious glances from both. They thought that with 'tin legs in a pilot, for heaven's sake!' he would lead from behind a desk. He thought they were a slovenly, undisciplined lot. They were slovenly; other than the clothes they wore they had nothing else. Bader visited both flights then climbed aboard a Hurricane and took off. For half an hour they watched a display of flying such as he used to give in the RAF aerobatic team – just about everything in the book and some variations of his own. When he landed, he didn't say a word, but merely returned to his office while his men stared at his stumping, rolling walk.

From his own pocket he paid for shirts, ties and shoes for them, trained them to his own tactics, supported them when they crossed authority, worked the ground crews and pilots together into one unit and, after a blunt signal to Dowding, got the squadron fully equipped with tools and spares. After only two weeks, Bader signalled again: '242 Squadron now fully operational' – just in time for the Battle of Britain.

The pilots of 242 Squadron were among 'The Few' who fought in that summer of 1940. Bader shot down two bombers early on, but the hard fighting for the squadron began on 30 August. Over Kent and Surrey it shot down twelve confirmed and several damaged. Bader claimed another two.

The squadron flew through the dark days of September and into October, usually operating from Duxford. With 242 Squadron, Bader led an experimental wing of four squadrons. While this was going on, Bader received the DSO (Distinguished Service Order). On 15 September – Battle of Britain Day – 242 Squadron claimed another twelve enemy shot down. By the end of October and the end of the battle, the Duxford Wing claimed 152 enemy aircraft.

Bader appeared to consider himself almost immortal. He told Thelma: 'I've a great engine in front of me, armour plate behind and tin legs below. How can they get me?' Others seemed to feel safe around him, too. Air Vice Marshal Tom Pike said: 'I think he almost eliminated fear from his pilots.'

Yet he was without doubt a prickly character. You either liked Douglas Bader or you didn't. More than a few resented him because of his bluntness and his opinions, but no one could deny he got things done.

In March 1941 he was posted to RAF Tangmere in Sussex and promoted to wing commander. There, he had 'DB' painted on the fuselage of his Spitfire so his pilots knew where he was in the air. The station commander and controller, Group Captain Woodhall, nicknamed him 'dogsbody' and it became Bader's official call sign. He was awarded a bar to his DSO and by August he had completed more fighter sweeps than anyone else in Fighter Command.

Through both Fighter and Bomber Command, the RAF was taking the war to the Nazis, attacking in France, Belgium, Holland, Norway, Denmark, Germany, Austria, Italy, North Africa and the Middle East. From Tangmere, Bader led his three squadrons of Spitfires in attacking sweeps over France, supporting daylight bombing and attacking Me 109s. On 8 August, Bader was told he would be rested on the 11th.

On the 9th, he led a high-altitude interception of Me 109s over Le Touquet. After the initial attack, he found himself at 24,000 feet with six 109s cruising ahead of him. Ignoring his own orders, he attacked alone, shot down two and was manoeuvring to slip back across the Channel when one of the remaining 109s collided with him.

Suddenly, his Spitfire was diving vertically down and the controls didn't work. He glanced behind to find that almost all the aircraft aft of the cockpit was missing. There was nothing for it but to bail out. He slid back the cockpit cover and lifted himself out into the slipstream, which then sucked the rest of him out – almost. The rigid right foot of his artificial leg caught and Bader found himself beaten back along the metal fuselage, hurtling earthwards at about 500 miles per hour and nothing he could do about anything.

The rushing air pounded and banged his body against the remains of his Spitfire. Eventually, the leather straps holding the right leg to the waist belt parted under the immense strain and he was free, his empty trouser leg flapping. He opened his parachute just above the cloud at 4000 feet and floated down to France below.

Semi-conscious, he was taken to hospital in St-Omer. The German doctor noted the missing right leg, stitched a gash under the chin, and then removed the Englishman's trousers to examine the leg. The doctor stared for some moments at the left stump with a tin leg attached, at the right stump with no leg attached, and at his RAF uniform. 'Ah!' he said in English. 'We have heard about you.'

The nearby Luftwaffe recovered his right leg from the wreckage of his Spitfire and very kindly repaired it as best they could. Meanwhile, a radio message was sent to Britain requesting a new leg be sent out. The RAF parachuted it down in a wooden crate during a daylight bombing raid.

Douglas Bader spent the remaining four years of the war in Luftwaffe prisoner-of-war camps. He'd already escaped and been recaptured twice when he met the leader of his 1930 aerobatics team, Harry Day, a prisoner in Stulag Luft III. Bader later refused to be transferred from this camp until the German Commandant arrived with fifty-six armed guards. The situation was very tense until he accepted he had to go. He stumped out to the paraded guards and then 'inspected' them as their superior officer. The prisoners loved it.

It was typical Bader; he pushed everything – himself, other people, aircraft, the enemy – to the limits. With the Luftwaffe, though, he was playing with great danger. Although fellow flyers, this did not stop the murder of more than fifty RAF prisoners after the Great Escape from Stulag Luft III in 1944.

Bader escaped once more, was recaptured and sent to Colditz Castle in southern Germany, where there were more guards than prisoners. There he met the third member of the aerobatics team,

Geoffrey Stephenson. Of course, Bader tried to escape from Colditz, but only a few ever got away.

During his travels from one camp to another, Douglas Bader saw some of wartime Germany and attempted to send a report to Britain stuck to the back of a photograph. He recorded the passage of troop trains, the general conditions, and the effects of the Allied bombing campaign. Since the war there has been much argument over whether the RAF and USAF bombing of Germany during the 1939–45 war had any worthwhile effect. Bader finished his report with: 'The bombing is doing a lot of good. Bomb the bastards to hell.'

After the war, the Nazi Minister for Production, Albert Speer, wrote: 'The strategic bombing of Germany was the greatest lost battle for Germany of the whole war, greater than all our losses in all our retreats from Russia and in the surrender of our armies in Stalingrad.'

Colditz was liberated by American soldiers in 1945 and Bader returned to Britain. He was officially credited with twenty-two and a half enemy aircraft destroyed, although Bader thought he'd shot down thirty. He was promoted to group captain and flew the first operational jet fighter, the Gloster Meteor, then the fastest aircraft in the world. On 15 September, the first peaceful Battle of Britain Day, 300 aeroplanes flew over London in remembrance of The Few. Bader and a dozen Battle of Britain pilots led the parade. Among them were two Canadian pilots from 242 Squadron, by then both wing commanders.

Douglas Bader thought that the post-war RAF was not for him. He was probably right. He retired in 1946 to rejoin Shell Aviation, where he was given his own aeroplane, a Proctor. Usually with Thelma, he flew all over the world for Shell as well as visiting disabled people, especially war veterans. It's difficult to quantify the effect his example gave to others whose legs and arms were smashed.

Because of Bader's determination, another pilot who lost his legs in a mid-air collision in 1939, Colin Hodgkinson, learned to walk with artificial legs and flew Spitfires later in the war. Soldier Richard Wood lost both legs to a landmine in North Africa. His first question in hospital was whether would he be able to walk again. He was told: 'Of course, look at Douglas Bader.' Wood walked again. There are countless others who would not have walked, if only because before Bader it had been considered impossible.

In 1976, Bader was knighted for his services to disabled people. After Thelma died, Douglas met and married Joan Murray, now Lady Bader. When Bader died in 1982, aged 72, she helped create the Douglas Bader Foundation to assist disabled and crippled people recover their lives. One of the treats it organises for children is flying in light aeroplanes.

Like Nelson, Bader set the example of there being no bar – apart from yourself – to what is possible. He swam, he played cricket, squash and golf; he danced, he married, he flew, he fought a war; he encouraged others, overcame stuffy bureaucracy and lambasted his way through rules. Yes, he was difficult, bluff, pugnacious, often rude. 'He was certainly not an angel but he was remarkable,' said one pilot. When you're proving to yourself as well as to others that life can be lived with or without legs, niceties may take second place at times. The message Bader left us is that, ultimately, what you achieve in life is up to you, not up to others.

Recommended
Reach for the Sky by Paul Brickhill.
Fight for the Sky by Douglas Bader.
Film: *Reach for the Sky*, Rank, 1956.
The Douglas Bader Foundation, England.

Sir Garnet Wolseley

Born to a British family near Dublin in 1833, Garnet Joseph Wolseley was the eldest son of Major Wolseley, whose own father had fought in the Seven Years War. Young Garnet decided early to follow in his father's footsteps, but the family had no money. After his father's death, Wolseley and his mother both wrote to the Duke of Wellington, asking for a 'commission without purchase' – an officer's post in the general's gift. In 1852, aged 19, Wolseley was offered a commission as ensign in the 12th East Suffolk Regiment. He immediately applied for transfer to the 80th Staffordshire Volunteers, who served overseas.

Knowing he would never have the funds to purchase further advancement, Wolseley intended to rise through combat and daring alone. At five foot seven, he was not an obvious warrior, but he was one of that rare breed who have no fear of anything on earth. He believed utterly that the British fighting man had no equal in the world.

At first, events were against him. He joined his regiment at Rangoon, but the second Burma war was ending and fighting had stopped. Wolseley joined an expedition to engage a small group of local rebels. He boarded a boat on the Irrawaddy River and saw the crucified bodies of British soldiers gone before him. Wolseley and around 800 others struggled through thick jungle, shot at constantly by snipers.

It took twelve days of marching to reach the rebel stronghold. The first assault failed and Wolseley volunteered for the 'forlorn hope', a group of near-suicidal attackers who would try to make a breach in an enemy position for those behind. They would advance in a hail of smoke and murderous shot and would be the first to face and reveal the extent of the enemy defences. It was a tradition of the British army that promotion was fast for those who survived.

To his great irritation, Wolseley was knocked unconscious in the first attack. When he came round, there was no sign of his companions, so he was forced to return to his own lines. Undeterred, he volunteered to lead a second forlorn hope. He wrote of the experience: 'I have never experienced the same unalloyed and elevating satisfaction, or known again the joy I felt as I ran for the enemy's stockades at the head of a small mob of soldiers, most of them boys like myself.'

The second attack was successful, though Wolseley was shot in the thigh. He cheered his men on as he staunched the bleeding. The wound was serious enough to have him shipped home, though not before he was promoted to lieutenant.

After a transfer to another regiment on its way to fight in the Crimean War, Wolseley sailed from Ireland. The campaign in the Crimea was well under way, and throughout the months on ship, Wolseley was worried the fighting would have ended by the time he arrived. The Royal Engineers seemed always to be in the thick of things, so Wolseley volunteered to join them. His bravery led to another promotion, though it was withdrawn when his superiors realised he was only 21. Wolseley protested at the injustice and his captaincy was confirmed. For a man without wealth or connections, it was a meteoric rise.

Wolseley was utterly indifferent to danger and was wounded twice more, shot once and then injured by shell fragments that killed two men standing next to him. He lost the use of one eye, had his cheek torn loose and his jaw and shin bone broken. Surgeons worked on his wounds without anaesthetic.

He was sent to recover at a monastery near Balaclava. On hearing that Sebastopol would be assaulted, Wolseley tried to mount and join the attack, though he was half-blind and appallingly battered. He could not force his body to obey him and collapsed. He was mentioned in dispatches as well as being awarded the French 'Legion of Honour' and the Turkish Medjidie (fifth class). He was also promoted to major at just 24 years old.

After a long convalescence, Wolseley was one of the last soldiers to leave the Crimea. He had done well, but worried that he 'ought to have done better'. He still wanted to make his name, to become as famous as

British heroes of previous ages. The Victorian era would provide plenty of opportunity.

In 1857, after months on garrison duty at Aldershot in England, Wolseley rejoined his regiment to sail to Hong Kong. He had seen the worst of war, but still relished the prospect of seeing the world and fighting its many inhabitants.

The journey was always perilous and the troop-carrier sprang a leak in storms before striking rocks off the coast of Malaya. Wolseley and the other survivors were eventually rescued and taken to Singapore. Despite such trials, one of the men wrote to his mother: 'I don't think I have ever been happier in my life than during the whole of the voyage here. It has been one incessant flow of excitement the whole time.'

In the meantime, the India Mutiny had begun, so Wolseley's regiment was diverted to Calcutta. There was much talk of atrocities against the British and Wolseley and the others were keen to avenge them. Wolseley wrote to his brother, saying: 'My sword is thirsty for the blood of these cursed woman slayers.'

When he joined the army under Sir Colin Campbell, Wolseley saw the aftermath of the slaughter at Cawnpore (Kanpur) and was driven to fury at the thought of the British women and children murdered there. He took part in the relief of Lucknow and was the first man to reach the defenders. However, Campbell was irritated with Wolseley for forcing his way in beyond his orders. For those who commanded Wolseley, the problem was always how to stop him. Despite this, Wolseley was promoted to lieutenant colonel at the end of the Mutiny. He became marriageable material, but like Richard Francis Burton before him, took a local woman as a 'temporary wife' during this period and learned Hindustani from her.

In 1860, Wolseley took ship for China, his original destination before the Mutiny. At that time, Britain was at war with China over opium, tea and silver and Wolseley was one of those who stormed the Emperor's Summer Palace. There were many who made their fortunes there in loot, but Wolseley retained only one small figurine to remind him of that extraordinary place, before the British army destroyed it completely. In doing so, they forced the emperor to recognise their power and, indeed, existence.

On leave after China, Wolseley kept himself busy, spending time in Paris and fox-hunting in Ireland. He also met and fell in love with Miss Louisa Erskine. The courtship had barely begun when Wolseley was sent to Canada after an incident where a British ship was stopped and two men taken off by President Lincoln's navy. In the middle of the American Civil War, Lincoln was reluctant to antagonise Britain further and released the men unharmed. Wolseley was left at a loose end and travelled peacefully with other officers to see Boston. He later called Canada 'a soldier's paradise, with rugged sports and beautiful women.' The one thing it lacked was any kind of fighting, and in 1862, Wolseley took leave to observe the American Civil War at close hand.

Wolseley later regretted the time in Canada and America, when he was not involved in any serious battle. It looked as though his tedium would be relieved in 1866, when 1,500 Irish Americans invaded Canada, but by the time Wolseley arrived on the scene, the miniature invasion was practically over, dealt with by the American government. Wolseley returned at last to Ireland, where he asked Louisa Erskine to marry him. He adored her from the first, even to having a plaster cast made of her foot to appreciate its perfection. The wedding was postponed when he was recalled to Canada as deputy quartermaster general. By that point, Wolseley was known for his ability to plan and organise as well as for insane courage. He married at last on his 35th birthday during two months' leave from that post.

In 1869, Wolseley published the product of his years of experience: *The Soldier's Pocket-Book for Field Service*. It was a comprehensive manual that dealt with everything a soldier might encounter in that era, from tactics in battle to the proper care of elephants. It sold very well and helped to make the author famous.

The following year, Wolseley was appointed to lead an expedition to root out a French Canadian rebel to British rule in Canada, one

Louis Riel. Wolseley led around 1,200 men, including three who would become the kernel of officers he used again and again. These were: Lieutenant Redvers Buller, whom Wolseley admired for his prodigious strength; Lieutenant Hugh McCalmont, who had applied to join the expedition at his own expense; and William Butler, who telegraphed 'Remember Butler 69th Foot' to Wolseley before setting off to Canada from Ireland without waiting for a reply.

Butler would later describe Wolseley as 'the best and most brilliant brain I ever met in the army. He was possessed of a courage equal to his brain power. It could never be daunted or subdued.'

Wolseley's men pursued the rebel for more than a thousand miles. Though Louis Riel escaped to America, they secured for the Crown the lands he had claimed. The expedition went like clockwork, something Wolseley said was due to it being planned and executed away from War Office meddling. It was a bloodless victory and Wolseley was knighted on his return to Britain.

In 1871, Wolseley was brought into the War Office himself, to help organise the abolition of purchased commissions. He became very unpopular in some quarters as the public face of the change. Nonetheless, it was accomplished and Wolseley was once again free to soldier for his country. He was promoted to major general and sent to Africa.

The tribes in Ghana were under British protection at that time. Wolseley was sent to quell the bloodthirsty attacks of Ashanti warriors on those more settled peoples. The Ashanti were well armed with long-barrelled muskets and preyed on those around them, practising both slavery and human sacrifice. Wolseley was given a free hand choosing his officers and took Buller, McCalmont and Butler with him. With other trusted men, they became known as 'The Ashanti Ring'. Very unusually for the time, Wolseley planned the expedition down to details such as equipping his men with tropical clothing. He had seen men freeze in the Crimea for want of warm coats and the lessons had been learned.

Very much a man of the Victorian age, Wolseley disliked the people he was meant to save from the Ashanti. In fact, he thoroughly disliked all foreigners, whether they were Indians, Africans, Chinese or American.

Nonetheless, he worked hard to recruit and train natives to take on more than 40,000 Ashanti.

His work had barely begun when Wolseley became feverish and was confined to a hospital ship. In his absence, his engineers built a road towards Kumasi, the Ashanti capital. It involved 237 bridges and a telegraph line, as well as road forts with food supplies and a hospital.

By December 1873, Wolseley was strong enough to travel. His light coach was drawn by six African men as he joined his army and ventured into Ashantiland. In January 1874, his force met the main Ashanti army around the town of Amoaful. Wolseley had formed his men with the 42nd Regiment as the front line, with two columns behind them, making three sides of a hollow square. The Ashanti were known to favour flanking manoeuvres and Wolseley's formation protected against any encirclement.

They found the Ashanti camp on rising ground across a small river and exchanged rifle fire after the Ashanti shot muskets, driving them back. In heavy jungle foliage, the 42nd pressed on and suddenly came under heavy musket fire, so that leaves rained down from the trees and bushes around them. The only sign of the enemy was drifting gun smoke and flashes. They answered with rifle volleys and the crack of two small cannon, lying down as they fired to make smaller targets of themselves. In such circumstances, it is not surprising that they fired on their own men as well. Wolseley sent a runner to the 42nd, telling them where their allied forces were.

The 42nd advanced once more, struggling through a swamp until they were forced to drop to the ground in another barrage of heavy fire. The small cannons answered with grapeshot thundering at the enemy position until their fire slackened. In the humid heat and covered with sticky mud from the swamp, they found scores of dead Ashanti as they went forward once more.

Beyond the swamp, the ground was firmer and a narrow path led up a small hill to the Ashanti's last stand. Some of the 42nd sheltered behind a tree blocking the path as musket balls snapped past them like hail. Rifle companies came up to pour fire into the area, though even then they could see very little of the Ashanti warriors they faced.

As the musket fire ceased, Wolseley gave the order to advance on all sides.

His riflemen drew their swords and searched every bush as they moved on. Five and half hours after the first shot, the Ashanti were in full retreat, having lost around 2,000 out of 15,000. Wolseley's formation had repulsed every attempt to flank or encircle and his men had forced their way uphill against superior numbers, on land that was completely unknown. More than two hundred of his men were wounded in the action, but only ten were killed outright, despite the ferocity of the engagement.

Hostile war parties still roamed around his men, attacking at every opportunity. Wolseley was running low on rations, but he pushed on to Kumasi. The Ashanti made another stand there and were defeated, so that when Wolseley rode into the city on a mule, no shots were fired. The king had fled and Wolseley burned Kumasi down behind him. Shortly afterwards, the king agreed to sign a treaty, pay tribute and recognise Britain as the pre-eminent power in the land.

Such an efficient campaign was a rarity for Britain at this time. In later years, when something was described as 'All Sir Garnet', it was as close to perfect as men could make it.

He was lionised at home. He met Queen Victoria again and was made a Knight Commander of the Order of St Michael and St George. He also received £25,000 from Parliament and was promoted again. He hoped to be sent back to fighting in India, but instead was posted to South Africa as an administrator. He took with him four of his Ashanti Ring.

In Natal, Wolseley decided the best way forward was to amend the democratic constitution, so that he could work unfettered. To this end, he charmed the legislative council with parties and browbeat those he could not charm. Assessing the local situation, Wolseley thought the Zulus would be a threat and recommended the immediate annexation of their lands. He said it could be accomplished with just a thousand soldiers. His suggestion was rejected, though it would go ahead two years later and lead to Rorke's Drift. Wolseley also favoured establishing a confederation of British and Boer colonies, though that too would not happen until 1910 and only after two bloody wars between them.

In 1878, Wolseley was called back to be appointed as High Comissioner and Governor General on Cyprus, a new British possession at the time. He started with high hopes, but an annual tribute of £93,000 to the Turks for possession of the island left very little for the inhabitants. Though he was a gifted administrator, Wolseley longed to return to active duties. The Zulu war had begun disastrously and Wolseley volunteered himself as the best man for the job. Queen Victoria did not approve of this sort of self-promotion, but Prime Minister Disraeli reassured her, saying: 'It is quite true that Wolseley is an egotist and a braggart. So was Nelson.'

With Disraeli's support, Wolseley returned to South Africa. There, he ordered Lord Chelmsford to hold and report to him. However, Chelmsford ignored the order and pushed ahead, winning the war with the Zulu king, Cetewayo, before being sent home. Wolseley sent Cetewayo to Britain after him, where the king was much admired and even met Victoria herself.

Once again, it seemed Wolseley could not find himself a proper war. With his Ashanti Ring, he led a punitive expedition against one aggressive tribe and successfully took their mountain stronghold. Victoria and Disraeli telegraphed their congratulations as Wolseley was posted yet again. By that point, he had a chest full of medals and was known and admired as a 'scientific soldier' wherever British soldiers resided. Gilbert and Sullivan had even used his fame in The Pirates of Penzance as 'the very model of a modern major general'.

Working in the War Office at home, Wolseley pressed for army reform, from improving food, pay, housing and pensions for soldiers to abolishing flogging. His work was interrupted in 1882 when Prime Minister Gladstone asked him to lead a military force to Egypt, where rebellion against British rule had reached flashpoint. Wolseley was to command almost 40,000 men – and took with him his Ashanti Ring of trusted officers. He let word leak out that he would land at Aboukir Bay, then landed at Port Said at night, taking control of the Suez Canal.

Wolseley's army fought its way west, winning battles at Tel-el-Mahuta, Mahsama and Kassassin as they headed for the heavily fortified Egyptian base at Tel-el-Kebir. The Egyptians had boasted the fortress was impregnable, but Wolseley made a night attack, with his soldiers led by naval officers who could navigate by the stars. Silence was paramount and one drunken soldier had to be knocked out before he roused the enemy.

In the last of the darkness, Wolseley's army was in the right place and pressed an attack. The fighting was hard despite their preparations, but they stormed the fortress and the Egyptians eventually fled. Wolseley sent this telegram home: 'The war in Egypt is over. Send no more men from England.'

Honours were not long in coming. Wolseley was presented with the Grand Cross of Osmanieh by loyal Egyptian forces, another £30,000 to add to his growing fortune and promotion to full general. He was also made a baron. He could not rest on his laurels, however, as trouble loomed with General Gordon, besieged at Khartoum. The Ashanti Ring were by then known as the Wolseley Ring, and in 1884 the old warhorses assembled again to rescue Gordon. Wolseley's plan was to take troops by boat up the Nile as well as overland. It was an immense undertaking and proved to be slow and dangerous work from the start.

At the oasis of Abu Klea, Wolseley's column was attacked and the square formation broken by Arab dervishes. The battle was bloody and Wolseley's soldiers also had to contend with sniper fire as they marched. Wolseley had lost a major part of his force by the time he reached the Nile and loaded his men onto steamers in January 1885. He was too late. Gordon had been killed. It was the first disaster Wolseley had suffered and it hit him badly. He was ordered back to Cairo, exhausted and made ill by his failure. His army too was recalled to counter a Russian threat in Afghanistan and Wolseley went back to his old post at the War Office.

He refused a post at commander-in-chief in India as he was hoping to command the Horse Guards. He did accept a post commanding forces in Ireland, where he enjoyed the hunting and shooting. He was made a viscount and promoted to field marshal. The following year he would finally command the Horse Guards, but his career was at an end. Tragically, the man who had once commanded tens of thousands and remembered every tiny detail was already beginning to forget. In what was almost certainly Alzheimer's disease, Wolseley lost his sharpness with shocking speed and was hurt when he was passed over for important posts. As the illness worsened, he sometimes failed to recognise old friends and colleagues. He officially retired in 1900.

His last twelve years were spent in peaceful quiet, largely forgotten by the empire for which he had fought with such energy. At one time or another, Wolseley had taken part in almost every major arena of battle in the Victorian era. With Richard Francis Burton, his astonishing and varied life was one of the inspirations for the character of Flashman in the books by George MacDonald Fraser. Wolseley died in 1913, just before the First World War began.

Recommended
The Ashanti Ring: Sir Garnet Wolseley's Campaigns 1870–82
by Leigh Maxwell.
Eminent Victorian Soldiers: Seekers of Glory by Byron Farwell.

Thomas Paine
and the Rights of Man

'If liberty means anything, it means the right to tell people what they do not want to hear.'
           – George Orwell

The United Kingdom is the originator of modern democracy. Not for nothing is Westminster called the 'mother of parliaments'. English Common Law, dating back to Alfred the Great (871–99), is the basis of many other countries' legal systems as well as Britain's. In the United States, created half a millennium after Alfred united England, its law refers back through British and English law to this common origin.

Like much progress, the spread of British democracy around the world has always been a case of 'two steps forward one step back'. The governing of Ireland should have been better, while the independence of the Australian colonies in 1901 is an example of good intentions misused. The earlier British act of 1828 decreed 'free people of colour in the colonies' had legal equality with their fellow citizens, yet two of the first acts of the independent Australian government classified Aborigines as 'sub-human' and removed their right to vote. These acts have since been overturned, yet they demonstrate the constant threat to our freedoms and 'rights', even from ourselves.

The greatest backward step for Britain was the imposition of the European feudal system upon the English free-man system. Most of the freedoms developed from Alfred's reign were lost in 1066 when William defeated King Harold at the Battle of Hastings. Feudalism created peasantry, serfdom or slavery, a class-divided society and the divine right of kings – dictatorship. It took 400 years to overturn all these, through Magna Carta, the 1381 Peasants' Revolt, to the civil war and Cromwell's Commonwealth of 1649.

Our freedoms, liberties and civil rights come at a price – human life. It's the greatest argument of all for never losing them.

Radical thinkers like Thomas Hobbes, David Home, John Locke and Thomas Paine devised the principles of our modern democratic society in seventeenth- and eighteenth-century Britain. They attacked authoritarian government, oppression, censorship and religious dogma. As a result, equality before the law, votes for everyone, freedom of speech and secret ballots are British concepts, while the first Declaration of Rights was passed into law in Westminster in 1689. Even the concept and term 'Rights of Man' was created in Britain. The later US and French constitutions are based upon Locke's revolutionary *Two Treatises of Government* of 1690.

Yet, in practical terms, no one anywhere in the world has a 'right' to anything, not even life itself. When a person is drowning, the sea does not recognise any right to survival. All our 'rights' are man-made and, while armies and navies are necessary to protect them, the first step is their creation. The man who brought all these diverse rights and concepts together – who sent shock waves through governments, churches, through society itself – was Thomas Paine, son of a humble corset-maker of Thetford in Norfolk.

Born on 29 January 1737, Thomas Paine was brought up a Quaker and attended the local Thetford school. When he was 12 years old he was apprenticed to his father. He lasted four years before running away from corsetry to the sea. He served as a seaman in the British privateers *Terrible* – commanded by a Captain Death and Lieutenant Devil – and the *King of Prussia*, preying on enemy shipping during the Seven Years War.

After his first wife and baby died in childbirth, Paine became a customs officer in Kent and then Sussex, the county of Quaker William Penn. With the separation in 1774 from his second wife, Elizabeth, came the first indication of Thomas Paine's ideals of personal freedom. Despite the patriarchal laws of the time and although poor himself, he signed his ownership to Elizabeth's inherited property back to her, permitted her to carry out business and trade with the rights of a single woman, and split the proceeds from the sale of their house and goods.

Dismissed from the customs the same year because of his labour agitation and pamphleteering, he wrote the fiery *Case of the Officers of Excise* and in London he met the British colonial free-thinker, Benjamin Franklin. With Franklin's letter of introduction, Paine sailed to the Quaker colony of Pennsylvania.

In Philadelphia, he was appointed editor of the *Pennsylvania Magazine* – just in time to campaign for the American colonies' independence from Britain. Paine had discovered his life's purpose, the campaign for individual freedom.

The background to the American War of Independence is unique. On the one hand was Great Britain, then the most democratic and liberal nation in the world; on the other were thirteen of Britain's American colonies, each with its own independent assembly and their people also British. In each land, sometimes in the same family, there was support for the other. It was almost a civil war.

Paine's magazine contributions included several essays condemning slavery, but it was his pamphlet *Common Sense*, written and published in 1776, which made his name. It was the most widely read pamphlet of the war, both in Britain and America, and in addition was translated and read widely in monarchist Europe. In *Common Sense* Paine made his arguments for independence, crystallising the vague views of radicals in Britain as well as the British colonists. He sketched a system for a united self-government, although as he asserted in another essay, his 'principle is universal. My attachment is to all the world, and not to any particular part'.

When Paine was appointed secretary to an American committee for foreign affairs, he uncovered the French supply of free arms and munitions to the colonials. He was a man of great personal integrity and despite the adverse effect it would have on the cause for independence, Paine exposed this foreign interference. Politically embarrassed, France denied the arms supply and demanded Paine's dismissal. When the American colonial congress refused to support Paine, he resigned.

Bizarrely, the French then offered Paine £700 to write articles supporting France and an alliance with the colonists against Britain. He refused. In 1782 he published *Letter to the Abbe Raynal*, a refutation of the French version of the War of Independence. He destroyed the argument – still promoted – that the war arose mainly from dispute over taxation. Paine recognised that the colonists' desire for independence was self-driven, a part of the progressive enlightenment within the English-speaking world, like an adolescent breaking free of its mother. Taxation was merely the spark that ignited the flame.

This Anglo-American revolution was only the beginning for Thomas Paine. Although given a farm at New Rochelle by the State of New York for services to liberty, he returned home in 1787 to campaign for political and social change in Britain and Ireland. In July 1789, the Paris mob stormed the Bastille. The first French revolution had begun and Paine was again in the right place at the right time. Although a symbol of the revolution, the sacking and destruction of the Bastille was not by the bourgeois revolutionaries and was not to release political prisoners; there were just seven common criminals inside. It was merely a mob looting the citadel for weapons and money.

In Britain, there was sympathy and support for this revolution at first. The excesses and tyrannies of King Louis XVI were well known and British radicals like Edmund Burke looked on with approval. At last, the French were resisting their own feudal system. When ideals degenerated into civil war, and civil war into war on neighbouring countries, most British radicals withdrew their support. Paine, however, took this opportunity to reaffirm his support for the original ideals. He used the publicity to write and publish in 1791 his watershed *Rights of Man*. That same year the first biography of Thomas Paine, encouraged by the government to be critical of him, was also published.

So radical were Paine's proposals, the first

publisher withdrew for fear of prosecution, yet *Rights of Man* became so popular that a second publisher was forced into further printings. After only two months, 50,000 copies were in circulation, an immense number in those days of smaller populations.

Paine completed a second part to *Rights of Man* in 1792, and soon sixpenny joint editions and translations abroad circulated widely. In his introduction to Part II he declared: 'If universal peace, civilisation and commerce are ever to be the happy lot of man, it cannot be accomplished but by a revolution in the system of governments.'

In *Rights of Man*, Paine advocated in Great Britain and Ireland a major redistribution of wealth, a progressive taxation system to finance poor relief, child benefits, pensions at 60, maternity grants, free education for all, accommodation for the homeless, and compensation for discharged soldiers and sailors. Internationally, he proposed treaties limiting armaments and the formation of a league of nations to prevent wars. It was 1792, the same year the Bill for the Abolition of the Slave Trade was first passed by the House of Commons. They were heady days of ideas and social change.

Argued singly, each of Paine's proposals could be accepted as a reasonable step for the improvement of society. Brought together in one document, they were dynamite. *Rights of Man* was read aloud in coffee houses and inns throughout the land. Paine's arguments commanded people to listen and to think: his proposals were debated and argued from government chambers to cottage kitchens.

However, after two overseas revolutions in thirteen years, the British government was nervous. While the United States was small, weak and 9,000 miles away, France was large, powerful and only twenty-two miles away. Under attack, Parliament introduced a law prohibiting seditious libel and publication. The publisher of *Rights of Man* was quickly charged. Despite Paine's pleas to him to make it a test case, the publisher pleaded guilty and paid the fine. A further Royal Proclamation instructed magistrates to seek out authors and printers of seditious writings; some were charged, but all were acquitted.

That June, Paine himself was charged with seditious libel, yet he refused to be cowed. He published letters criticising the repressive law, including *Letter Addressed to the Addressers on the Late Proclamation*. While his arguments were incisive, Paine's titles sometimes were not. That letter was effectively Part III of *Rights of Man*, in which he argued that true representative government must rely upon votes for all. A government's power must rest upon the sovereignty of its people, not upon itself.

Paine's prosecution was delayed until December, yet the pressure on him remained intense. Modernist societies applauded and debated his arguments, while for traditionalists it was too much, too soon. He was arrested for a business partner's debt, a charge instigated by the government. The debt was paid by Dr Johnson, creator of the famous dictionary. Paine had influential friends as well as enemies, but in September he fled to France, where he had been given honorary citizenship.

In France, he was actually appointed deputy to the French National Convention, but already the revolution was unravelling. The revolutionaries declared war on Prussia, and in November they offered military aid to all 'oppressed peoples' of other countries – an excuse to invade. In an open letter to his British prosecutor, Paine unwisely supported revolution in Britain. He was outlawed.

In the new year, the French king was executed. By February 1793, France had invaded or declared war on most western European countries, including Britain. In September began the bloody 'Reign of Terror' and the revolution was destroyed.

The uprising had got rid of the antique French monarchy and feudalism only to replace it with a republican dictatorship. That was soon followed by a military dictatorship and twenty-two years of world war. In the long term little was gained at a huge cost in lives and liberty. English radical philosopher William Blake estimated that resisting and defeating the French dictatorships set back democratic reform in Britain by more than fifty years. It was this parallel struggle for survival that made life so difficult for British radicals; the abolition of slavery was delayed, Blake charged with sedition, scientist Joseph Priestley's house set on fire, and radical William Cobbett imprisoned. Survival takes priority over freedom.

Against this background of chaos and bloodshed, Thomas Paine began his second great work, *The Age of Reason*. In December 1793, Paine himself was arrested for his opposition to the French king's execution. He was imprisoned in Paris, sentenced to death and had his honorary citizenship revoked. The translated manuscript of Part I was already with French publishers and the original English text was immediately smuggled to Britain.

Paine's health deteriorated during ten months in Luxembourg Prison, and he was nursed from death by two imprisoned British doctors. Paine completed Part II between bouts of fever and semi-consciousness. Part I was published in London and Paris at the beginning of 1794, and Part II in 1795.

In *The Age of Reason* Thomas Paine argued strongly against the religion of his time. Still a Quaker, he prefaced his work with the statement: 'I believe in one God, and no more; and I hope for happiness beyond this life.' He rejected organised religion with the argument 'All national institutions of churches, whether Jewish, Christian or Turkish [Islam], appear to me no other than human inventions, set up to terrify and enslave mankind, and monopolise power and profit.'

He also disavowed religious revelation, stating: 'A thing which everyone is required to believe requires that the proof and evidence of it should be equal to all, and universal.' Like scientist Sir Isaac Newton earlier, Paine found his proof and evidence of God in Nature. He was the first to argue that religious books such as the Bible, Koran and Torah were the writings of men, not the holy writings of God.

Once again these were ground-breaking – even dangerous – views to publish in a predominantly Christian Europe, especially in a time of world war. Understandably, they created great hostility towards Paine, and he has been much misrepresented ever since. However, in their separate fields, *Rights of Man* and *The Age of Reason* are watersheds in society as important as Charles Darwin's *On the Origin of Species*. All three are part of the framework of today's Western secular societies.

With a new French regime in place, the American ambassador took up the issue of Paine's imprisonment, claiming he was American as well as British. His sentence of death was overturned and Paine was released in November 1794, although his health collapsed again with further fevers. Because of the threat of British imprisonment, he remained in Paris for eight more years. He wrote the important essay for reforming land ownership, *Agrarian Justice*, with ownership based not upon a destructive socialist redistribution but upon commercial viability and individual freedom. He also wrote essays about how Bonaparte might invade Britain and America. Paine was still blinded to the realities of dictatorship by the original ideals of that first French revolution.

With gifts from other British radicals, Paine cleared his debts and, during the 1802 Peace of Amiens, he took ship to America. There he found himself rejected by many former colonial friends because of his writings. Once again he was temporarily arrested for a dubious debt. By that time, the revolution in the United States had also unravelled, the principles of freedom and liberty not applying to slaves and native Americans. Presidents Washington and Jefferson both were slave-owners, and the new republic was on the path to federalism and becoming the greatest slave society of them all.

Paine wrote against this new America in a series of letters *To the Citizens of the United States*. His books were burned and he was publicly booed and hissed. He was even shot at by his disgruntled farm manager, though, typically, Paine did not prosecute.

In 1809, after further illness, Paine died in New York. His request to be buried in the Quaker cemetery was refused. Ten years later, his remains were brought home to Britain, but burial there was also prohibited. His bones have since disappeared, although his skull is claimed to be in Australia at Sydney University.

Thomas Paine did not invent all the radical theories, principles of freedom and social philosophies he promoted, but in *Rights of Man* he was the first to combine them into a system of government. His ideal was not a levelling of society but one of equal opportunity. Other British radicals campaigned with and after him – Jeremy Bentham, William Godwin, Samuel Whitbread, Richard and John Carlile, Joseph Priestley, Mary Wollstonecraft, Elizabeth Fry, John Wilkes, Emmeline Pankhurst and many more. While violent, false revolutions failed abroad, a true revolution began to take place quietly and successfully in Britain.

After the defeat of military dictatorship in Europe in 1815, a catalogue of democratic, social and political reforms was enacted in Britain throughout the nineteenth century. This included repealing the law of seditious libel and publication. These principles of human rights, justice for all and liberty – begun from the first modern document of 'rights', Magna Carta of 1215 – were sent out into the world and our modern, Western society created.

Further editions of Paine's great works were published. Voting rights for everybody was slow in coming, but in 1856 the colony of Tasmania held the first secret ballot, which became British law in 1872. Women first voted in 1880 in British local elections, while New Zealand introduced the first national women's vote in 1893.

How advanced our now casually accepted rights then were is shown by events outside the English-speaking world. French women, for example, did not receive the vote until October 1944, and other countries later still. Thomas Paine was more than a century ahead of his time. His League of Nations was finally created in 1919 and its successor, the United Nations, in 1945.

Yet, now, Britain is suffering another step-back. Many of our liberties and rights hard-won by Paine and others are being lost, to British governments and to the laws and directives from the unelected European Union.

In this twenty-first century, the European Court of Justice ruled that EU institutions have the right to suppress criticism that damages 'the institution's image and reputation', or in other words, any criticism at all. This ruling is identical to the law the British government introduced to muzzle Thomas Paine back in 1792 – seditious libel and publication. Paine wrote then that only 'when opinions are free, either in matters of government or religion, will truth finally prevail.'

Recommended
Thomas Paine by A.J. Ayer.
Tom Paine: America's Godfather by W.E. Woodward.
The Light's on at Signpost by George MacDonald Fraser.

Thomas, Lord Cochrane
the Sea Wolf

O n a frozen November day in London, 1860, the funeral procession
of the man known as 'the Sea Wolf' made its solemn way to
Westminster Abbey. The hearse was pulled by six black horses and
eight mourning coaches followed, with a host of smaller carriages in
their wake. On arrival, the coffin was shouldered by two admirals, five
captains and the Brazilian ambassador. Inside, the tomb in the nave
was decorated with the arms of Greece, Brazil, Chile and Peru.

By the time of his death, Cochrane had been acquitted twice at court
martial, suffered disgrace for stock market fraud, been imprisoned,
escaped and been imprisoned again, yet seen his honours and titles
restored and his status as one of Britain's greatest naval heroes finally
recognised. His life inspired the Hornblower stories by C.S. Forester
and later formed the fictional career of Jack Aubrey in the books by
Patrick O'Brian. In the annals of lives that might be called 'classic
Victorian tales', Cochrane's would be first on the list.

He was born in Lanarkshire, Scotland, in 1775, the descendant of a
long line of knights and barons, though the family lacked the funds to
match the heritage. From an early age, Cochrane was interested in the sea
and joined the Royal Navy as a midshipman in June 1793, at 17 years
old. He was made a lieutenant two years later. In 1799, after meeting and
impressing Nelson, Cochrane was given command of the captured prize
ship *Généreux* for a single voyage. On boarding, Cochrane found the
ship barely seaworthy and when storms hit, he came close to watching
his first command sink under him. He rallied his skeleton prize crew and
climbed the mast himself in a storm to unfurl the mainsail and steady her
rolling motion. His seamanship and quick thinking saved the *Généreux*.

From the first, Cochrane was known to be quick-tempered and sharp,
even with his superiors. He was court-martialled for insulting a more

senior lieutenant, but acquitted. Nonetheless, the red-haired young Scot was considered to be a firebrand and something of a nuisance to the Admiralty. In 1800, Cochrane was promoted to command the sloop *Speedy*, a tiny ship which he would make a terror to the Spanish and French. Nelson's advice to him had been 'Never mind manoeuvres. Always go at 'em!' and Cochrane took the words to heart.

The *Speedy* had a crew of only ninety men and just fourteen four-pounder guns. Cochrane could fit the entire weight of a broadside's cannonballs into his pockets. To shave, he had to put his head out of the cabin window. However, he knew his advancement depended on winning prize money. Any ship and cargo he captured would be bought by the Admiralty for the Royal Navy and was therefore worth a fortune to every man on board. Cochrane was blunt about this being one of the chief motivations of a fighting captain. During the Napoleonic wars, there are examples of common sailors *frying* gold watches on the docks at Plymouth to show their sudden, astonishing wealth.

To that end, Cochrane employed the *Speedy* with great energy and dash along the Spanish coast. He took his first prize on convoy duty, guarding fourteen merchant ships. Having observed a strange sail, Cochrane took the risk of abandoning the convoy to go closer. He found a French privateer even smaller than the *Speedy* and captured her with barely a shot fired. When the convoy came under attack a second time, Cochrane turned back and recaptured two of the merchant ships just as their prize crews were trying to steal away from the rest. He captured three more 'prizes' in June and another three in July. Bearing in mind that the Admiral of the Fleet received the lion's share of the prize money, Cochrane's popularity was growing with some of his superiors.

At that point in history, British fleets were out in the Mediterranean to blockade the French and Spanish at Toulon, Cadiz and Brest. Napoleon had become First Consul in France and begun years of war that would pit him against every major European nation – and break him against Nelson and Wellington. In the harshest of conditions, British ships honed their seamanship while the main enemy fleets remained in port. That bitter training would bear fruit for many years after.

In 1801, the same year as Nelson's Battle of Copenhagen, Cochrane escaped a massive French frigate by running before her until darkness fell, then extinguishing his own night lamp and leaving a lantern floating on a barrel. He escaped another by flying a yellow flag indicating plague so that they would not board him. Later that year, he engaged a Spanish frigate, the *Gamo*, four times as large and with seven times his weight of shot. Cochrane had only fifty-four men to the Spanish crew of 319, having lost the rest to crew prize ships. Faced with such odds, Cochrane surprised the Spanish by attacking. He showed an American flag to confuse them, ran past under full sail, then ran up the British ensign when he was in position. He ordered treble shot in the *Speedy*'s guns then rammed the *Gamo*, tangling the rigging together. The huge Spanish ship fired uselessly overhead, while the *Speedy*'s guns ripped upwards, killing the captain and bosun as well as many of the crew.

He wrote afterwards: 'The great disparity of force rendering it necessary to adopt some measure that might prove decisive, I decided to board.' Cochrane left only his ship's surgeon to hold the wheel. At the height of the fighting, Cochrane roared for a second wave to come across, despite not actually having one. As the Spanish hesitated, they saw their 'colours struck', the Spanish flag coming down from the mast in the classic signal of surrender. It was one of Cochrane's men doing it, but they were not to know. They gave up the fight and it remains one of the most extraordinary examples of a David and Goliath battle in British naval history. Cochrane took 263 prisoners and aimed the Spanish cannons down into the hold to prevent them rising up and recapturing their ship.

For a brash young officer so recently the subject of a court martial, Cochrane was not likely to be too well rewarded. The Admiralty refused to buy the Spanish vessel as a warship, purchasing it instead as a hulk for a fraction of the price. Cochrane entered into an angry exchange of letters that made an enemy of Earl St Vincent, First Lord of the Admiralty. His vision of fortunes vanished in bitterness. In those circumstances, what should have been an automatic promotion to post captain did not come about.

When the *Speedy* visited Malta, escorting a packet boat, or mail ship, Cochrane had the packet boat anchor while he fired on Spanish ships ashore, setting them on fire. The following day, he sighted what he thought were Spanish galleons out to sea. He gave chase, only to discover they were three French warships, drawn to the light of the ones he had burned. He made a run for it under full sail, throwing his guns overboard for more speed. The *Speedy*'s stores followed the guns and Cochrane darted between two of the warships, surviving one broadside to reach open sea. The French ships overhauled him even so and Cochrane struck his colours at last. After such daring manoeuvres, the French captain would not accept his sword in surrender.

As was common practice, Cochrane was exchanged for an enemy officer and returned to Gibraltar. He was automatically court-martialled for losing the *Speedy* but was once again acquitted. At last, he was promoted to captain, but with no friends at the Admiralty, he was not given a ship and instead temporarily 'beached' on half pay. In March 1802, the peace Treaty of Amiens was signed. It looked as though the war with France and Spain was over and Cochrane's career was at an end.

With the last of his prize money, he enrolled as a student in Edinburgh to complete his education. Unbeknownst to him, Napoleon was quarrelling with Britain over ownership of Malta and had an invasion army assembling in Boulogne. Napoleon's naval men told him they needed to command the English Channel for only *six hours* to invade. He would never get those vital hours. On 18 May 1803, war was declared again between the two powers.

Cochrane wrote to Lord St Vincent, asking for a ship. The old man told him there were none available. Cochrane sent a list of ships in preparation and was told they were all promised. He then sent a list of ships under construction. Furious by this point, St Vincent replied waspishly that they were all too large for a junior captain. Cochrane was reduced to visiting the Admiralty each day and waiting with other captains for news of a ship. When he was finally allowed to see St Vincent, Cochrane said he would go back to being a student in Edinburgh if he was not wanted. With Cochrane as famous as he already was, such an event would have caused a storm of criticism. St Vincent told him to go to Plymouth, where he would be given a ship. On arrival, Cochrane was appalled to find his new command was HMS *Arab*. She looked like an ancient, battered coal ship, one of the ugliest and slowest in the fleet. It was a clever revenge on the pushy young captain, but he had been granted his wish.

Cochrane's new ship was ordered to join the fleet blockading the invasion army at Boulogne. Unlike the nimble *Speedy*, the *Arab* would sail only with the wind behind her, so Cochrane had to use oars to get back into position, over and over again. He hoped to have the *Arab* taken off the blockade and, with that in mind, deliberately stopped and searched an American ship. His plan backfired spectacularly. The protests that followed meant Cochrane was sent to patrol the Orkney Isles alone for more than a year.

St Vincent was finally replaced as First Lord of the Admiralty and in his absence, Cochrane was given the *Pallas*, 667 tons with thirty-two guns. He had to resort to a press gang to crew her and in the process his men beat up two police constables, for which Cochrane was later charged with assault. He managed to get out to sea, spending weeks in the Azores with orders to harass shipping before returning to blockade duty.

He made those weeks pay, capturing four well-laden prize vessels before three French warships put an end to his plundering. After a chase, he could not prevent the French ships from coming up on both sides of him. Cochrane ordered the sudden dropping of all sails and put the wheel hard over. The French ships shot past and he was off and running before they began to turn. The faster warships reeled him in again, pursuing for a day and night until they came upon another barrel with a candle and lantern on it. Cochrane came home in triumph with solid gold candlesticks lashed to his masthead.

Suddenly wealthy, Cochrane decided to stand for Parliament. In those days, it was a matter of contesting a 'rotten borough', effectively of buying enough votes. Cochrane was at first at a loss to understand the voters' expectation of bribery and spoke on naval corruption instead. He lost the election when his opponent offered each voter five guineas. Cochrane was so annoyed that he paid ten guineas to each of those who had voted for him. The *Pallas* went to sea again, with a captain bruised but unbowed by his first experience of politics.

Cochrane missed the Battle of Trafalgar in 1805 while on convoy duty to Quebec. In 1806, he joined a squadron patrolling the Bay of Biscay. For once, the commanding admiral appreciated Cochrane's talent for taking prizes. Cochrane had also added a secret weapon to his ship – an eighteen-oar galley he'd designed himself that could be lowered from the *Pallas*. He first used it to board a French merchantman loaded with casks of wine and quickly became so notorious that as soon as they sighted the *Pallas*, French merchant captains ran their ships aground rather than be sunk. Even so, Cochrane captured four large prizes in quick succession.

In 1806, in thick fog, Cochrane dropped anchor off the wide mouth of the Gironde, the river that leads to Bordeaux. His boats and the galley went out into the darkness, though for once, Cochrane himself stayed on board the *Pallas*. His little flotilla surprised and 'cut out' a French corvette, the *Tapageuse*, overwhelming the crew and stealing her from under French noses. The plan worked brilliantly, but at dawn, Cochrane sighted three more corvettes to windward. Between them, they had up to fifty guns and three hundred men.

It was disaster, but no one could think like Cochrane in a crisis. He had his men secure every sail with ropes, then cut them all at the same instant. The sudden spread of sail looked as if he had a full crew. As the *Pallas* leaped at them, the corvettes thought they were sailing into a trap and turned away. Cochrane pursued them, firing the only two guns he had crews to man. In panic, two of the corvettes ran aground and the third escaped. Delighted with this, Cochrane made his way to the point on the coast where he would meet his prize crew. He was even more delighted to come across the third corvette as she circled back. On sighting Cochrane, the French captain lost his head, ran his ship aground and was dismasted in the impact. It was after this that Napoleon himself referred to Cochrane in fury as 'Le Loup des Mers' – the Sea Wolf.

On the way home, Cochrane rammed and grounded a French frigate. He also blew up the French signal station on the Île de Ré. He was a famous man by the time of the next general election, when he tried again for the same seat and won. When voters came for the ten guineas he had given before, he sent them away without a farthing.

By 1806, St Vincent was back in command of the Channel fleet and not at all pleased at Cochrane's rise. With his new parliamentary authority, Cochrane forced the promotion of a lieutenant he felt St Vincent had overlooked years before, but there was a price for even that small victory. Admiralty customs officers offered him prize money less than the import duty for captured French claret. In frustration, Cochrane ordered it poured into the water at Plymouth. The Admiralty also declined to buy the *Tapageuse*. Before Cochrane could cause more trouble, he was sent to sea in the frigate *Imperieuse*.

In 1806, Cochrane's career nearly ended. The Admiralty ordered him to set sail before he could even load gunpowder or prepare his ship. Worse, no one on board had spotted the cheap iron bolts holding the ship's compass, replacing expensive copper ones. The iron meant the compass was wildly inaccurate and on a dark night, the *Imperieuse* struck the rocks of Ushant, barely avoiding being sunk. Cochrane asked to be court-martialled, but the Admiralty refused rather than have their part in the chaotic orders revealed. Cochrane took the *Imperieuse* to the blockade at Biscay between France and Spain. On the way, he captured three prizes, destroyed a French battery at Fort Roquette and set fire to seven merchant ships at anchor.

When the *Imperieuse* came home for repairs in 1807, Cochrane stood again in the general election as an advocate of naval reform. He criticised St Vincent in public, which appalled even his loyal supporters. Despite his outburst, he was elected. Undaunted by St Vincent's influence, Cochrane attacked the Admiralty as one who had personal experience of the worst sloth and corruption – such as the theft of copper bolts almost causing the loss of a ship and the appalling treatment of ships on blockade duty. His orders to return to sea came very quickly indeed, forcing him to choose between the two careers. He sailed to the Mediterranean in September 1807 to join the fleet with Admiral Collingwood, the man who had commanded the *Victory* after Nelson's death at Trafalgar.

Off Malta, Cochrane came across a suspicious-looking privateer flying the Union Jack. He sent boats to inspect her and they were fired upon as they closed. The ship was a renowned Maltese privateer. Cochrane's men boarded it under fire, including a young sailor named Marryat who would later achieve fame as an author of stirring sea tales. The privateer captain was killed in the fighting and his men surrendered. Given Cochrane's long-running feud with the Admiralty, it is perhaps not surprising that they also refused to pay a prize fee for the ship and Cochrane was instead handed a bill for their legal expenses.

Cochrane continued his prize-taking through 1808 and nothing was too dangerous or daring for him to consider. More importantly to the world, the Spanish finally turned against Napoleon in that year. French forces there became an army of occupation rather than allies. Cochrane was sent to sea to assist the Spanish in any way he could. He kept himself busy, destroying a French battery on land and stealing the guns. At sea, he was far more mobile than Napoleon's soldiers and could strike the coast of Spain wherever he wanted. He found sabotage and demolition as enjoyable, if not as profitable, as prize-taking and wreaked havoc on French positions. His one ship had the entire coast from Marseilles to the Pyrenees at his mercy. Vital French troops were diverted to protect the coast, but he was unstoppable. When he ran short of water, he refilled his casks in the River Rhone, knowing that any French ship would run at the sight of his flags.

Cochrane was wounded only once, when he walked under fire to retrieve a fallen Spanish flag at a fort. His nose was broken by a shell splinter, but he continued to command as his men repelled 1,200 French with volley fire, cannon shot and mines. Despite appalling odds, Cochrane said he 'had never run away from a Frenchman and did not intend to begin.' He eventually blew the fort up behind him. To the Spanish, Cochrane became a hero. The Admiralty, however, found little to celebrate and instead sent him a reprimand for 'excessive use of powder and shot'.

When Cochrane returned to England in 1809, he was met with news that the blockade of Brest had failed and the French fleet was out at last. They had been sighted sheltering in an anchorage known as the Basque Roads, which Cochrane knew well. Cochrane was summoned to the Admiralty in Whitehall and discussed a plan to send fireships to destroy them before they could be repaired and resupplied. For once, he was given command over the heads of more senior men.

For the task, Cochrane devised his own take on fireships, which he called 'explosion vessels' or 'coffins'. Each was packed with 1,500 lb of gunpowder, 3,000 grenades and an artillery shell, with fuses set for ten to fifteen minutes. He prepared three of these, as well as twenty-one fireships, soaked in tar and turpentine to burn slowly. This was war at its most ruthless and dangerous. The French were protected by batteries that could fire red-hot shot, but the floating bombs and fireships still had to be crewed long enough to send them in. Cochrane himself was captain of the first one into the anchorage. His biggest obstacle was a huge boom of iron chains that blocked the approaches. Coming close to it, he lit the fuses and jumped down into a boat to escape. His men rowed furiously. The boat was a hundred yards away when Cochrane realised he had left a dog on board and ordered his men back to collect it. They were barely clear for the second time when the ship exploded, breaking the boom and allowing the other ships through.

In panic, the French ships fired on each other, but there was chaos too in the fireships. Some of them were let go too soon and drifted back out, even threatening Cochrane's own ship. Braver crews did get through and the French admiral's flagship had to cut its anchor cable to manoeuvre, running aground shortly afterwards. Other French ships rammed each other as they tried to get away. Confusion and fear did more damage than fire that night and by morning, most of the French fleet was aground and helpless with a dropping tide.

Cochrane expected an order to attack, but Admiral Gambier decided it was too risky and barely acknowledged Cochrane's increasingly desperate signals. Cochrane was forced to watch as the flood tide began to save the French fleet.

At last, Cochrane could not bear it any longer. Without orders, he slipped his anchor and let the *Imperieuse* drift in as if out of control. He signalled 'In Distress' to Admiral Gambier and opened fire on the French warships. Gambier was forced to send support and four French ships were destroyed before Cochrane and the others were ordered back. Cochrane's signals and a curt exchange of letters with Gambier resulted in him being relieved of command and told to report personally to Gambier. After a furious argument with the admiral, Cochrane was sent home. He was later knighted for his part in the battle, though Gambier chose to omit his name from the official dispatch.

Napoleon Bonaparte later said: 'The French admiral was an imbecile, but yours was just as bad. I assure you that if Cochrane had been supported, he would have taken every one of the ships.'

Thoroughly blacklisted, Cochrane was once again beached. He spent time in Malta, trying to force the Admiralty court to pay him the prize money they owed. He also devised a number of new weapons, only to have his plans ignored. His worst point was yet to come, however, in the great scandal that took place in 1814.

It began with a false rumour of Napoleon's death. Cochrane had invested his prize money in shares and saw the value of his stock rise spectacularly at the news. Cochrane's uncle was certainly involved and Cochrane himself had met the man who originally spread the rumour. With so many enemies, Cochrane was quickly indicted as one of the ringleaders. Worryingly for him, the Stock Exchange engaged an Admiralty solicitor for the trial. Cochrane was found guilty, fined

£1000 and sentenced to an hour in the public stocks and a year in prison. Fearing riots at seeing a naval hero pilloried, the sentence was remitted to the term in prison. Cochrane was dismissed from the navy, expelled from Parliament and made to return his knighthood. His knight's banner was removed from Westminster Abbey and would not be restored until Victoria herself gave the order, the day before his funeral.

After that very public disgrace, Cochrane was a broken man. In prison, his only good news was being returned as Member for Westminster, as the voters showed what they thought of his treatment.

For a man of such energy, it wasn't long before Cochrane decided to escape, scaling the wall of the yard with ropes smuggled in by friends. As the wanted posters went up, Cochrane wrote from hiding to the Speaker of the House, declaring that he would take his seat in Parliament. He entered the Commons to do so and was immediately arrested and taken back to prison, this time to the darkest, dampest cell they had. He was released in 1815, after the Battle of Waterloo. His health had suffered terribly and he paid his fine with the words: 'I shall submit to robbery to protect myself from murder, in the hope that I shall bring the delinquents to justice.'

He was then tried for escaping from prison and fined another hundred pounds. He refused to pay it, but the voters of Westminster held a collection and he was free to take his seat in Parliament. From then on, however, he was publicly shunned by many who believed him a fraudster and thief.

In 1818, Cochrane was asked to take command of the Chilean navy in their war of independence with Spain. Seeing a chance for a fresh start, he left England with his wife Kitty and two sons. On arrival, Cochrane organised the Chilean navy along British lines and took the Spanish base of Valdivia as well as capturing the most powerful Spanish ship in those waters. After such success, he was asked to free Peru from Spanish rule. Cochrane brought his skill and daring to that coast and played a vital part in Peru's successful rebellion. The Chilean navy still has ships named *Admiral Cochrane* to this day, the most recent of which was commissioned in 2006. He was not well paid for his efforts, however, and disputed unpaid bills with the Chilean government until his death.

After Chile and Peru, Cochrane became an admiral for Brazil as they struggled for independence from Portugal. In just three months, outnumbered in ships, Cochrane managed to deal the Portuguese fleet a fatal blow, captured thousands of their soldiers and destroyed their major ports. Brazil too fell foul of Cochrane's desire to be paid well for his exploits and he disputed the lack of proper payment with them for another thirty years.

Cochrane then accepted the command of the Greek navy as they looked for independence from Turkey. Cochrane built them a navy from scratch, though he insisted on English and American crews. In the end, his work was overtaken by political change and a combined force of British, French and Russian ships fought his chosen enemies for him. The Battle of Navarino would be the last major battle between sailing ships. Before it began, the Royal Navy commander and hero of Trafalgar, Admiral Codrington, gathered the allied captains together for final instructions. Whether he was unaware of the feelings of the French captains or just enjoyed baiting them is unknown. His final words to them were 'No Captain can do very wrong if he places his Ship alongside that of an Enemy' – Nelson's orders before Trafalgar. The British-led fleet sank more than fifty Egyptian and Ottoman ships in the battle. Cochrane returned to England in 1829, aged 54.

At home, Cochrane sought to clear his name for the stock market fraud, appealing to anyone who would hear him, including the Duke of Wellington, who had become Prime Minister in 1828. Cochrane's old enemies were dying one by one and his chances improved as they fell. In 1831, his father also died and Cochrane became the 10th Earl of Dundonald. He could no longer sit in the Commons, but could take his place in the House of Lords. He appealed personally to the new king, William IV, asking for a fair investigation. William promised that he would look into the affair again. It would be Cochrane's wife who asked for a royal pardon, as Cochrane would not make the plea himself.

The pardon came at last in 1832. Cochrane was restored to the navy as Rear Admiral of the Fleet and congratulations came from all sides. He busied himself with designs to improve steamships and plans for a primitive rotary engine. With Victoria's accession in 1837, a new age had come and Cochrane was once again a renowned hero.

By 1843, Cochrane was becoming known as an inventor and patented one of the first designs of ship propellers. He also devised plans for saturation bombardment and gas attacks, though his ideas were seen as far too ruthless ever to be used in war. A new Liberal government under Lord John Russell saw much to admire in his history of fighting for freedom, and at the age of 72, Cochrane was offered active service as admiral of the Atlantic fleet. He accepted and held the post until 1851, when he returned to England. The Empire was at its height and the Crystal Palace was being built in London to celebrate the rise in British power.

The Crimean War loomed when Russia invaded Turkish provinces. Britain joined with France to repulse the aggressor and declared war in 1854. Cochrane volunteered for command in the Baltic, but at the age of 79, he was turned down. In the meantime, he experimented with chemicals such as naptha and potassium, looking for new weapons that would prove decisive. The war ended in 1856 with the Treaty of Paris and Cochrane retired at last. His knighthood had been restored, though his banner had not yet been returned to the abbey. He spent his last years in dispute with various governments, including his own, whom he felt should pay back the old £1,000 fine as well as his legal costs. Finally, he wrote volumes of memoirs, which sold very well and helped to secure his fame.

After his death, the British and Brazilian governments both made large payments to his heirs. Cochrane had received justice at last.

Recommended
Cochrane: Britannia's Sea Wolf by Donald Thomas.
The Life of Thomas Cochrane, 10th Earl of Dundonald
by Cochrane's son.

The Women of SOE
Setting Europe Ablaze

In Manchester, they were trained as parachutists. This began with rolling correctly on the ground, after jumping from a lorry at 30 mph, and ended by parachuting from an aeroplane at 500 feet, giving them thirty seconds before landing at 69 mph, at night.

In Inverness, they were trained in unarmed combat, in silent killing, in sabotage using the new British plastic explosive, in living off the land, in using many different weapons, including enemy weapons. In Beaulieu Estate in the New Forest, they were trained in codes and secret inks, to blow safes, forge documents and to live in enemy territory. They were woken and 'interrogated' in the middle of the night.

They became wireless operators, arms instructors, couriers, organisers, liaison officers, decoders and saboteurs. They learned new identities, code signals and passwords. They were each given an 'L-pill', a lethal capsule of cyanide to use should they be captured. They were parachuted, landed by light aeroplane or taken by sea to occupied Europe. After that, they were on their own.

They were from different backgrounds and different countries, of different ages and different education, yet they had one thing in common. They were the women of the 'Special Operations Executive' – who carried the fight for freedom behind enemy lines in the 1939–45 war and 'Set Europe Ablaze'. More than 500 SOE agents were sent into Nazi Europe to organise resistance; fifty were women.

One of those women was Violette Bushell, the daughter of a British Tommy from the 1914–18 war who'd married his mademoiselle from Armentières and brought her back to England. At the beginning of the war, Violette Bushell was working behind a counter at Woolworths in Brixton. In 1940 she met and married Hungarian Etienne Szabo of the Foreign Legion, who'd made his way to Britain to continue the fight against the Nazis. They had one daughter, Tania. Etienne died at the Battle of El Alamein in 1942 so Tania never met her father. A few months later Violette Szabo was recruited by SOE.

As well as speaking fluent French, she turned out to be a crack shot and kept her fellow SOE recruits in cigarettes by winning them at public shooting galleries. She passed her various courses, although she damaged her ankle parachuting, and became a liaison officer, code-named 'Louise'. She was commissioned as ensign and returned her L-pill, determined she would never use it.

After landing by aeroplane one April night in Normandy, Violette's first mission was in and around Rouen. With a false identity of Corinne Leroy from Le Havre, her mission was to find out who – if any – had survived from a French Resistance group that had been betrayed, and to contact them. At great risk, she located the only four survivors out of fifteen and passed on the message from London to blow up a vital railway bridge. Violette was arrested twice by the French police but talked her way out, explaining she'd come to Rouen to search for missing relatives. The night after the second arrest she left for Paris. That same night, the railway bridge was destroyed.

Violette met her British field organiser in Paris, who arranged her return to Britain for debriefing. Years before in Britain, in another lifetime, she and her husband had vowed they would buy a dress from Paris for their daughter, and this Violette did.

Her second mission, after parachuting into Limoges on D-Day plus one (7 June 1944), was to assist Resistance activity supporting the Allied invasion. She and Jacques Dufour were ambushed by German SS troops. During the skirmish Violette twisted her ankle again. She sent Dufour on while she delayed the German soldiers so he could escape, firing on them with her Sten sub-machine gun. When she ran out of ammunition she was captured with a slight flesh wound.

Imprisoned and interrogated in Limoges, Violette was then transferred to Fresnes prison in Paris and interrogated, raped and tortured by the Gestapo at 84 Avenue Foch. As well as the names of other SOE agents, French Resistance fighters and Resistance circuits, the Germans were after her 'poem', the key to her personal code for sending messages. With that, they would have been able to send false messages to London and decode her earlier messages.

Violette's poem was composed by head of SOE coding, Leo Marks. It's the most famous poem of them all and might be an epitaph for all SOE agents.

The life that I have is all that I have
And the life that I have is yours.

The love that I have of the life that I have
Is yours and yours and yours.

A sleep I shall have, a rest I shall have
Yet death will be but a pause,

For the peace of my years in the long green grass
Will be yours and yours and yours.

Violette gave the Gestapo no information and she was sent to Ravensbrück concentration camp for women. She and two other captured SOE agents made two plans to escape but each was thwarted. On 5 February 1945, Violette Szabo and her two friends were executed by a single shot in the back of the neck.

On 17 December 1946, wearing the dress her mother had bought her in Paris, Tania Szabo was presented with Violette's posthumous George Cross by King George VI at Buckingham Palace. Tania later wrote her mother's story: *Young, Brave and Beautiful*.

The first woman wireless operator sent into France was Noor-un-Nisa Inayat Khan, a Sufi Indian born in the Kremlin of Czar Nicholas in 1914. Her father was the head of a Sufi sect, an ascetic Islamic religious movement which emphasises a direct, personal experience of

God, and her mother was American. Noor was the great-great-granddaughter of Tipoo Sultan, the man Wellington came up against in Mysore in 1799. The family lived in London and then Paris, where Noor studied music for six years and played the veena, a sitar-like Indian stringed instrument, as well as piano and harp. She also studied at Sorbonne University for her degree in child psychology.

Before the war, Noor wrote children's stories for French radio, while a book of children's fairy stories was published in Britain in 1939. She spoke French like a native.

At the fall of France, the family escaped to Britain, where Noor's brother joined the RAF and she joined the Women's Auxiliary Air Force, the WAAF. From there she was recruited by SOE in late 1942 as a wireless operator. Her code name was 'Madeleine'.

A supporter of Indian independence, Noor had said: 'I wish an Indian would win high military distinction in this war. It would help to build a bridge between the British and the Indians.' Of the 36,000 Indians who died in the 1939–45 war, that person was to be Noor herself.

Noor landed by aeroplane in northern France one night in June 1943, and made her way to Paris. Many SOE wireless operators were tracked through their signals and arrested and by that autumn there was a shortage. Noor was busy throughout the day and night transmitting and receiving messages, decoding and encoding signals, as well as receiving and delivering messages to networks other than her own. Moving from one safe house to another, she remained just one step ahead of the Gestapo. At one address, she transmitted from an apartment block full of German officers. SOE twice offered Noor repatriation to Britain, but she refused and remained working.

Although there were several thousand brave men and women in the French Resistance, security was at best basic, at worst non-existent. Even with the Free French in Britain, security was a joke. Eventually,

Churchill was forced to deny all vital information to the Free French, while British intelligence fed false information to the Nazis through the Free French – it took only one or two days for it to reach Berlin.

In October, a Frenchwoman betrayed Noor to the Gestapo for 100,000 francs (£5000). Many, many SOE captures were from betrayal. Noor was arrested and taken to 84 Avenue Foch for interrogation. She escaped almost immediately but was recaptured. She was interrogated, made another attempted escape, was recaptured again and tortured. Still she gave the Germans no information.

German torture of women, as well as the usual beatings, included cutting breasts off, pulling out fingernails and toenails, sleep deprivation, laying red-hot pokers against the spine, near-drowning and other horrors. The chief of the German police, Heinrich Himmler, ordered: 'The agents should die, certainly, but not before torture, indignity and interrogation has drained from them the last shred of evidence that should lead us to others. Then, and only then, should the blessed release of death be granted them.'

Giving up on her, the Gestapo sent Noor to the German prison of Pforzheim, to Cell 1, where her hands and feet were manacled and she was kept in solitary confinement for almost a year. Her food was passed through a hatch in the door, the door itself opened only to

change her water. In September 1944, Noor was removed to Dachau concentration camp. On the 12th she was made to kneel in a sandy yard with captured SOE agents Elaine Plewman, Madeleine Damerment and Yolande Beekman. In pairs, holding hands, the four women were shot in the back of the head.

Noor-un-Nisa Inayat (meaning 'light of womanhood') Khan was awarded the posthumous George Cross and MBE.

Like Violette Szabo, Lilian Rolfe's parents were British and French. When war began in 1939, Lilian was living in Brazil. She worked for the British embassy, reported shipping movements in Rio de Janeiro and joined the WAAF in 1943. Because of her native French, she was recruited by SOE and trained with Violette to specialise as a wireless operator. Lilian's SOE code names were 'Claudie' and 'Nadine'. She landed in France in April 1944.

She worked in preparation for the D-Day invasion in June. Arranging vital drops of arms and explosives, she sent sixty-seven messages in a highly active Gestapo region. Her field organiser was arrested but she continued operating, and in July, after D-Day, took part in an engagement against German troops before she was captured. She, too, was interrogated and tortured at Avenue Foch and then sent to Ravensbrück concentration camp north of Berlin. There she joined Violette Szabo and a third friend, Denise Bloch. Lilian contracted a disease of the lungs from her forced labour and had great difficulty in breathing. Towards the end she could barely stand.

On 5 February 1945, Lilian had to be carried by stretcher to her execution with Violette and Denise. She was awarded the posthumous MBE.

Denise Bloch was French, a Jewess, and worked with the Resistance from 1942. She escaped to Gibraltar and was trained as a wireless operator in Britain at the same time as Violette and Lilian. The SOE organised, armed, supplied, trained and directed the French Resistance, and communications both ways were critical. Dedicated German radio units monitored the frequencies to take cross-bearings to track the operators. All SOE work was dangerous, but wireless operators were particularly vulnerable.

With the code name of 'Ambroise', Denise was returned to France in March 1944 to join the circuit at Nantes. In the preparations and immediate aftermath of D-Day, this circuit sabotaged the railway and high-power lines at the port of Nantes, disrupting German efforts to send supplies, soldiers and equipment to the Normandy invasion area.

On 18 June, Denise was arrested during a Gestapo raid and taken the usual route to Ravensbrück via Avenue Foch. She was shot in the back of the head with her two SOE friends that 5 February. Their bodies were burned in the crematorium along with 100,000 Gypsies, Russians, Poles, Slavs, Jewesses and other women during the period 1938 to 1945. Denise was awarded the King's Gallantry Medal for Bravery.

Ravensbrück concentration camp saw many SOE agents. Yvonne Baseden was captured and also met the three friends in Ravensbrück. The Gestapo did not realise that Yvonne was an SOE agent – they thought she was simply another Resistance worker – and no execution was ordered for her. She was included in the last Red Cross transport to Sweden and survived the war.

Eileen Nearne, with her sister Jacqueline and her brother Francis, were all SOE field agents. Eileen was captured in July 1944 in Paris. She'd just finished transmitting a signal to London when German soldiers broke in. By that time, the head of SOE codes, Leo Marks, had introduced the simple but brilliant 'One-Time Pad', a pad of unique codes written on silk. As soon as a code was used, the agent burned that silk. The only copies were in London for decoding, every agent had different pads, so if a pad was captured the Germans were unable to retrieve any messages at all. The One-Time Pad is still used today.

Eileen had burned her pad and dismantled the radio, but the German soldiers found her pistol. She was interrogated and tortured at Avenue Foch and reached Ravensbrück in September 1944. There she was reunited with Violette, Lilian and Denise. At first Eileen refused to work, so her head was shaved in preparation for her execution. She changed her mind – a decision which both saved her life and led to her freedom. In December she was sent to a labour camp near Leipzig to work on the roads, but when she was moved to another camp she escaped into a forest. All three siblings survived the war and the eldest, Jacqueline, later played agent 'Cat' in the film about the SOE, *Now It Can Be Told*.

Most agents were captured in the second half of 1944 after D-Day, when they were most active supporting the British, American and Canadian invasion. Odette Brailly, though, was one of those like Noor, captured earlier in 1943.

Born and brought up in Amiens in France, she married Roy Sansom, son of a British officer billeted with her parents during the 1914–18 war. With Roy she moved to London, had three daughters and volunteered for SOE service. Odette Sansom trained as liaison officer and, code-named 'Lise', was lifted into southern France by fishing vessel from Gibraltar in the autumn of 1942. With her field organiser, Peter Churchill, she was captured through a German double agent in 1943 and sent to Fresnes prison. From here she was taken daily to the Gestapo headquarters in Rue des Saussaies and tortured.

All ten toenails were pulled out until her feet were so mutilated she couldn't wear shoes. A red-hot poker was pressed against her spine, and she endured other tortures. Even so, Odette gave no information. She was sent to Ravensbrück and kept in solitary confinement for ten months, fourteen weeks of it in darkness, and ten of those days without food.

She hung on to her sanity by designing clothes for her daughters in her imagination, redecorating the houses of her friends room by room, and by maintaining a strict regime of smartness. Every day she rotated her skirt one inch so that it would wear uniformly, and every night, curls being the fashion in the 1940s, she curled her hair using strands from her ruined stockings. She also created the fantasy that her organiser, Peter Churchill, was the nephew of Winston Churchill and they were married. This she told the commandant of Ravensbrück.

He believed her and, with the Allied armies closing in from north, south, east and west, he took her with him when he surrendered. She denounced him immediately and he was tried and executed as a war criminal. Odette's husband had died meanwhile and she and Peter Churchill did marry after the war.

Odette Sansom was awarded the MBE and the George Cross and spent the remainder of her life helping ex-SOE agents and keeping the memory of those who died. She wrote that war taught her two great truths: 'that suffering is an ineluctable part of the human lot, and that the battle against evil is never over.'

In 1939, New Zealand/Australian Nancy Wake was already living in France. Born in Wellington and brought up in Sydney, she worked as a journalist in Paris when she met and married Henri Fiocca of Marseilles. With the 1940 creation of Vichy France in the south, the French extended the war against Britain from its colonies abroad, while at home the arrests and deporting to death camps of 75,000 Jews began. Nancy and Henri became an integral part of a successful Marseilles escape route out of Vichy France. The route through Spain and Portugal took out British airmen, escaped prisoners of war as well as refugees from the French.

By 1942, Nancy and Henri were high on the French police list of suspects, and Nancy's exploits were attributed to an agent they named the 'White Mouse'. In 1943 there was a reward of one million francs for the capture of the White Mouse. Inevitably, Nancy was betrayed, but she fled to Gibraltar via the escape route while Henri continued in Marseilles. Henri was later arrested, interrogated, tortured and executed.

In Britain, SOE recruited and trained Nancy. Commissioned captain and code-named 'Helene', she parachuted back into France to the Auvergne region in April 1944. There followed months of increasing activity with the Resistance before and after D-Day, including sabotage, guerrilla war against German troops and even an attack on a Gestapo centre. Nancy became a ferocious soldier, 'like five men' a male comrade described her.

Nancy Wake was awarded the George Medal in 1945, the US Medal of Freedom and, later, many French medals, to become the most decorated servicewoman of the 1939–45 war. 'I hate wars and violence,' she said, 'but if they come, I don't see why we women should just wave our men a proud goodbye and then knit them balaclavas.'

All the women of SOE enlisted as volunteers in FANY (First Aid Nursing Yeomanry), the first ever women's service unit, begun in 1907. As such, they were not prevented from fighting by the Geneva Convention and they served around the world. Fifty-two FANY were killed during the 1939–45 war, thirteen in the French Section of SOE. They are all our mothers and sisters.

Recommended
Young, Brave and Beautiful by Tania Szabo.
The White Mouse by Nancy Wake.
SOE: The Special Operations Executive, 1940–46 by M. Foot.
FANY Memorial, north wall, St Paul's Church, London.

Sir Henry Morgan
Buccaneer

Henry Morgan's life is simply an astonishing story. The history of Spanish colonies isn't taught in British schools, but Morgan was a pirate at a time when Britain had barely a foothold in the Caribbean Sea. Spain was the great power in those waters, with wealthy ports and cities in a vast bowl from Mexico to Venezuela and the Caribbean islands. Even today, those countries have Spanish as their first language. Morgan's combination of ruthlessness, leadership and seamanship would make him the terror of the West Indies and strike fear into Spanish settlements.

He was born in Glamorganshire, Wales, in 1635. At that time, his family were employed as soldiers of fortune under foreign flags and achieved high rank in Holland, Flanders and Germany. They also fought on both sides of the English Civil War. Henry Morgan's father, Thomas, took the Parliamentary side and reached the rank of major general under Oliver Cromwell.

In such turbulent times, it is perhaps not too surprising that few records survive of Henry Morgan's childhood. At the age of 20, he travelled as an indentured servant to Barbados. He said later that he left school early and was 'more used to the pike than the book'. It has been suggested that the young Welshman was kidnapped and sold as a white slave. In his latter, respectable days, he sued anyone who made this claim, but such events were not uncommon and the exact truth is now hidden in history. Another story is that he sailed as a junior officer on an expedition to the West Indies by Oliver Cromwell.

During the English Civil War, the West Indies was the scene of battles between Cromwell's Parliamentary forces and the Spaniards. Cromwell hated the Spanish for their Catholicism and said in Parliament: 'Abroad, our great enemy is the Spaniard.'

Jamaica was seized from Spain and in the chaos and lawlessness of war, the region became infamous for pirate ships and for 'privateers', who were exactly the same, but sailed with the approval of their governments. Tortuga, a small island off Hispaniola (modern Haiti), was a particular stronghold.

When Charles II was restored to the throne in 1660, the King of Spain petitioned to have Jamaica returned to Spanish rule. More than two and a half thousand acres of the island were producing valuable crops at that time, with huge potential for expansion and profits. Charles II refused and Parliament approved the decision. A new governor and legislative council were appointed in Jamaica, with judges and courts. The colony settled down and immigrants began to arrive from Barbados, Bermuda and even America. Virgin land was offered to them and a number of young men made their way to the West Indies, seeking to make their fortune.

It is in that context, in 1659, that Henry Morgan became captain of a privateer at the age of 24. He had taken part in several raiding voyages, but instead of squandering his share of the booty, he lived simply and saved his money until he could buy a small ship of his own.

The government in England was desperate to keep hold of the threatened Caribbean ports and not too worried about who fought for them. It suited British interests to have a raiding fleet in the area, though each ship acted alone and profit was always the first motive. A report on the fledgling colony stated: 'We had then about fourteen or fifteen sail of Privateers, few of which take orders but from stronger Men of War.'

From raids, slavery and plantation crops, Jamaica quickly became a wealthy colony. From 1662 to 1688, exports doubled to more than four million pounds' worth of goods. One law passed by Parliament said that produce from all English colonies could only be transported on English ships. It meant that every colony brought a trading fleet into existence and eventually led to the domination of the seas.

Thousands of miles from Europe, a smaller war was fought between Britain, Holland and Spain for command of Caribbean waters. New men were clearly needed and Charles II sent Henry Morgan's uncle, Edward Morgan, as senior military officer. From his years as a soldier of fortune, Edward Morgan knew the Dutch well and spoke the language. It must have been a surprise to Henry to have his uncle come out and take such a powerful position. The king made Thomas Modyford the governor and the ultimate power in Jamaica.

As governor, Modyford's first proclamation was that all hostilities with Spain were to cease. In theory, all the privateers should have returned to port and been paid off. Predictably, however, they turned a blind eye to the order, Henry Morgan among them. Attacks on rich Spanish fleets continued and King Charles II wrote to Modyford to complain about it.

Shortly after Henry's uncle arrived, one of the privateers turned pirate, raiding English shipping as well. Under the orders of Thomas Modyford, the ship was captured and the crew hanged on the docks of Port Royal in Jamaica. An example had been made, but the governor's ability to stop the privateers was limited and they carried on with their 'prize-taking' of foreign ships.

As the war with Holland intensified, battles took place in the East and West Indies, the Mediterranean, Africa and North America. In England, Parliament voted £2½ million to equip the Royal Navy for the fight. The commercial future of the world was at stake and they were determined that Britain must control the seas and trade. The privateer fleet was still terrorising Jamaican waters and rather than try to hunt them down, they offered them 'letters of marque' – official recognition and powers to attack Dutch ships on behalf of the British Crown. The alternative was to see them go over to the French colony on Tortuga island, whereby Charles II would have lost all control.

The privateer captains accepted the letters of marque and Colonel Edward Morgan led them in an expedition to seize Dutch islands in the West Indies. A fleet of ten 'reformed privateers' left Jamaica, well armed and manned. Henry Morgan was one of them and already becoming known as a good man in a fight.

Colonel Edward Morgan was old and overweight. After landing on the island of St Eustacia, he pursued enemy soldiers on a hot day, then had a heart attack and died. His privateer captains were not the sort to return home at this setback and they went on to take the island and one other from Dutch control, gathering Spanish plunder at the same time. More than three hundred Dutch settlers were deported, but his regular soldiers had to come back to Jamaica when the privateers went off to Central America in search of more prizes.

To explain how they had managed to sack Spanish settlements as far away as Nicaragua, Captains Jackman, Henry Morgan and John Morris claimed not to have heard that war with Spain had ended. It was hardly necessary. Anti-Spanish feeling was still running high in official quarters and they were in no danger of being seized as pirates.

In 1666, Modyford and his council granted new letters of marque against the Spanish to Morgan and the other privateer captains. The official record gives one reason: 'It is the only means to keep the buccaneers on Hispaniola, Tortuga and Cuba from being enemies and infesting the plantations.' Modyford may not have liked the idea of employing what was effectively his own pirate fleet, but he felt he had no choice. The privateers would defend the wealth of Jamaica if they had an interest in it and a safe port there. At the same time, the French governor on Tortuga was doing his best to bribe the privateer fleet to sail for him. It was a dangerous game, with both sides trying to feed the wolves.

By then, Henry Morgan was thirty years old and well known as a successful and wealthy captain. His uncle had left a number of children in Jamaica and Henry Morgan didn't abandon them. Far from it. The exact date is not known, but he married his first cousin, Mary, and spent a couple of quiet years on Jamaica, enjoying married life. Two of her sisters married officers on the council and so the Morgan family achieved considerable influence in a very short time.

Officially sanctioned attacks on Spanish settlements and forts continued, the combination of huge wealth and poor defences a tempting prize for fortune hunters. Privateers raided Costa Rica and Cuba as well as small islands. The Spanish attacked settlements and islands themselves, on one occasion massacring a British garrison of seventy men after they had surrendered. Some of the survivors were tortured, then sent to work in mines on the mainland. It was an unofficial war, but as ruthless as any other kind. It is always tempting to take the Hollywood view of piracy as somehow romantic, with swarthy men walking the plank and crying 'Yo ho ho!' to each other, but the reality was brutal and settlements that fell to privateers or pirates suffered torture and murders before being burned to the ground.

In 1667, Holland agreed to peace with England, and Spain renewed a peace that had never really happened in the Caribbean. British power in the West Indies remained fragile and in 1668, the Admiralty finally sent a powerful 26-gun frigate to the area, HMS *Oxford*.

Henry Morgan had been made colonel and given command of the militia in Port Royal, Jamaica. Before the *Oxford* arrived, he took a raiding expedition of ten ships to a wealthy Spanish town in Cuba. He and his men landed on 30 March and fought off an attack by Spanish militia before storming the town and stealing everything they could lay hands on. He then accepted a ransom of a thousand head of cattle in exchange for not setting the town on fire.

Other raids followed on Cuban towns and ports, often against much larger forces. However, as Morgan said: 'The fewer we are, the better shares we shall have in the spoils.' It's not quite an Agincourt speech, but he and his men caused havoc on Spanish settlements, removing anything of silver and gold from cities and churches. His crews ran wild in the sacking of towns, and only the payment of large ransoms would send Morgan away. By the time he returned to Jamaica, he had a hold full of Spanish gold.

Morgan welcomed the arrival of the *Oxford* as the most powerful ship in those waters. The Spanish had warships, but they were slow and heavy in comparison. He made immediate plans for an attack on Cartagena, the strongest fortress on the coast of what is Colombia today.

Disaster struck. The *Oxford*'s magazine exploded while Morgan was on deck. Five captains who had sat on one side of a table were killed in the explosion, while Morgan and the rest were thrown clear and survived. His choice of chair had saved his life, though he lost a quarter of his men.

Without the *Oxford*, Morgan was forced to give up the idea of an attack on Cartagena. Instead, he gathered the privateers off the eastern coast of Hispaniola. Always fiercely independent, some preferred to sail alone, so Morgan went without them and attacked Spanish ports in Venezuela. In 1669, he sacked the city of Maracaibo and went on to the settlement of Gibraltar on Lake Maracaibo. Morgan's men tortured the city elders there until they revealed where their treasures were hidden. He was not present at the time, but his name was further blackened with the Spanish as a result. The Spanish citizens of Gibraltar agreed a ransom to Morgan's captains, but could not raise all of it, so some of them were sold as slaves to make up the deficit.

It was not all raids on towns and villages. When Morgan encountered a small fleet of three Spanish warships, he and his captains captured one, sank another and watched the crew burn the third rather than let him have it. That single raid brought more than £30,000 back to Jamaica, a vast sum for the times. In port, Morgan's men taunted the captains who had not sailed with him and flaunted their sudden riches.

With new wealth, Morgan turned his hand to becoming a plantation owner. He leased a tract of 836 acres from the governor, still known as 'Morgan's Valley' today. He might have settled down, but in 1670, Spain renewed hostilities in the West Indies, capturing ships and ravaging British settlements in Bermuda and the Bahamas. In reply, the governor of Jamaica appointed Morgan in command of all warships in Jamaican waters. His fame, experience and ruthlessness made him the obvious choice. At 35 years old, Morgan was an admiral and in his prime.

With unlimited funds, Morgan equipped a fleet at Port Royal for an attack on Panama, another Spanish territory. He crewed them with six hundred men of the rough sort he knew best. The red-coat uniforms of Cromwell's army still struck fear into Spaniards, so Morgan arranged for his men to wear them.

In England, negotiations for peace with Spain were under way and Governor Modyford had orders to cease all operations against the Spanish. He made the instructions clear to Morgan and the admiral replied that he would observe them except for landing on Spanish coasts to replenish water and supplies. Morgan also added the caveat that he would of course respond if attacked, or to relieve a British settlement. With those somewhat dubious assurances, Morgan sailed in August 1670.

He sent one ship, the *Dolphin*, to the coast of Cuba, to gather intelligence on Spanish forces in those waters. The rest of his squadron anchored around Hispaniola, gathering fresh meat and water while he waited for other privateers who had promised to join him. Three French captains came from Tortuga to aid him against the Spanish and of course join him in the wealth he would take. In the sense of being a 'man's man', Morgan was a charismatic 'pirate's pirate' and national interest came second to sailing with him.

The captain of the *Dolphin* met a Spanish ship in a bay off Cuba, and though the crew were outgunned, they attacked. The Spanish panicked, their captain was killed and many jumped overboard. In the Spanish captain's cabin, Morgan's men found letters of marque from Panama, giving the Spanish authority to raid British ships and towns.

Governor Modyford sent five more privateer ships to join Morgan as they came back from taking the island of Grenada. By then, he had the most powerful fleet of privateers ever assembled in the Caribbean. It was a chance to strike a crushing blow against Spanish power.

Morgan interrogated the prisoners taken by the Dolphin and learned that Cartagena and Panama were poorly defended. He allowed his captains the final choice and they decided on Panama as the target. They set sail in December 1670, a fleet of some thirty-six ships and 1,800 men, including two or three hundred French. As it happened, peace with Spain had finally been agreed, but it took months for the news to reach the Caribbean and Morgan was not told by the time he set off.

His first stop was at Old Providence, to the north of Panama. It was a well-fortified Spanish island, but with a small garrison. Morgan landed a thousand men and the Spanish abandoned their gun battery. With Morgan's men pursuing them, they retreated to a smaller island only linked to Providence by a drawbridge. From there, they accepted Morgan's request to surrender peacefully, accompanied as it was by a threat of slaughter if they didn't.

The President of Panama, Don Juan Perez de Guzman, had been told Morgan's fleet was on the way. On the north coast, he reinforced his garrisons with men and supplies of gunpowder, convinced that the English force could not break his defences. His confidence was understandable. To reach Panama City on the south coast of the isthmus, Morgan's men would have to cross land that would one day become the site of the Panama Canal. It was dense jungle all the way, complete with deadly snakes and spiders as well as aggressive native tribes.

The jewel of Panama's fortifications was the fortress of San Lorenzo de Chagres, built on a sheer cliff and, at that time, filled with three hundred soldiers and native Indian bowmen. In addition, it had heavy artillery guns to hammer enemy ships. One of Morgan's captains, Bradley, came as close as he dared to survey the fort and decided it could only be taken from the land side. Bradley landed along the coast with 480 men and marched to a ravine leading to the rear of the fort. In normal times, there was a drawbridge, but Bradley found it had vanished. Spanish troops opened fire from the fort as he looked into the ravine.

Bradley's men retreated out of range, but were shamed in doing so. 'Thoughts of disgrace and being reproached by our Friends on board' spurred Bradley's small force into a slow descent into the ravine. They endured enemy fire the whole way until they climbed the fortress side and attacked the main gate. Bradley himself was shot in the attempt, his legs badly crushed by a cannonball. The first assault was driven back, but his men were undeterred and returned again and again, firing their muskets and throwing primitive grenades at the walls. At least one of those began a fire in the fort that took hold quickly. Wooden palisades burned to the ground, making a breach. Bradley's best marksmen then came forward and fired at anyone trying to quench the flames.

The Spanish garrison held their ground until Bradley sent a storming party armed with cutlasses and muskets. They forced their way in and the Spanish soldiers fled, leaving only the commandant, who continued to fight until he was shot. The fort was theirs. Bradley died of his wounds along with two officers and many of his men, but a crucial defence had been taken from Panama. Morgan flew the flag of England from the battlements of the fortress when he arrived in January 1671. He was only thirty-five miles from the fabled wealth of Panama City, though as yet, he had no idea of the hostile nature of the terrain in between.

In January, he and his men went inland by river until the going became too shallow even for canoes. Morgan disembarked then with the plan of marching across the isthmus for twenty-four miles through 'wild woods where there was no path'. He took 1,200 men with him, armed with just cutlasses and two muskets each. He was always a lucky man and his good fortune continued as Spanish garrisons inland set fire to their own positions and abandoned them, believing he was coming with a much larger force.

It was hard going, as every step had to be cut in dense jungle. Morgan had a group of thirty men whose sole task was to hack through the vegetation. As workers on the canal would suffer in the nineteenth century, so his men were tormented by ticks and mosquitoes and terrified by poisonous spiders and snakes, all the while labouring in a humid, stifling heat. Some of them grew sick and others fell in exhaustion and had to be sent back. By the sixth day, they had run out of food and were starving. They found some fruit and a planted field of maize, which they devoured like locusts before moving on.

On 16 January, they were attacked by local natives. The sight of half-naked tribesmen appearing and vanishing around them caused great fear in the ranks, but they fought them off, losing some thirty men in the process.

The next day, they came across a village in the wilderness and found it burning. Morgan's men discovered jars of wine in the ruined houses and drank themselves sick. Around the same time, one of them was carried off as a prisoner and Morgan gave orders that any foraging party should be at least a hundred strong.

Ten days after leaving the fortress of Chagres, Morgan climbed a hill and saw the towers of Panama City in the distance. His men had survived the jungle, the attacks and the heat. Even better, they came across a herd of cattle and shot enough to fill their bellies properly for the first time in days.

In the city, the Spanish were furious that Morgan's force had come so close. Yet they knew as well as anyone what Morgan's men had suffered to make the trip, and fancied that their Spanish gentlemen would have no difficulty in blooding their cavalry swords on a ragged group of exhausted, half-starved sailors.

As the sun rose, the cream of Spanish nobility rode to Morgan's camp, brandishing their swords and shouting elaborate and colourful insults. That task complete, they then rode away and Morgan ate breakfast with his men.

The Spanish had almost double Morgan's numbers, but on his side, his sailors were hard-bitten pirates, well used to hand-to-hand fighting. Morgan made a stern speech to them, ordering each man to make two pistols ready, but not to fire until he did, or he would shoot them himself.

When his ragged crew formed up, the Spanish cavalry charged them with great excitement and war cries. Morgan waited until the enemy were almost on top of them before he fired both his pistols. The volley that followed completely destroyed the Spanish attack. The survivors fled in panic and Morgan's men pursued them ruthlessly for three miles, killing hundreds.

Morgan's men then entered Panama City and set fire to a great deal of it, burning the wooden houses to the ground. He sent another party to seize the ships in the city docks.

At that time, Panama City was a centre of Spanish trade. Wealth mined in appalling conditions by slaves in

Peru passed through the city and rich families had collections of gold and silver plates. They had removed some of it by sea when Morgan was still far off, but most of it was recovered when one of Morgan's captains, Robert Searle, captured a Spanish ship in the port and used it to hunt fleeing vessels. Searle missed the best prize of them all, a galleon stuffed with jewels and gold, when his men became drunk on wine they found. However, they captured another ship with twenty thousand pieces of gold on board. Exact estimates are difficult as Morgan was required to pay a percentage to his superiors in Jamaica, so he was never likely to declare all of it.

Morgan stayed in the battered city for twenty days, removing everything of value and taking three thousand hostages for ransom. His men tortured some to find the location of their treasures and Morgan was later criticised, though his officers were adamant that he was not responsible for the worst excesses of his men.

In February, he and his men began the march back to Chagres. On the way, he searched his prisoners and men for hidden loot. He even took his men's muskets to pieces to check they had not stuffed jewels into the barrels. There was much ill feeling towards him because of the searches, but Morgan was not a man to let that sort of thing trouble him.

When they returned to Chagres, Morgan announced that the final division of spoils was only twenty pounds a head for his men. Many of them were furious and he lost a number of loyal captains. He returned to Jamaica with only eight ships, but almost all of the plunder. In all, he brought back some £237,000 in gold as well as silk, silver plate, jewels and lace to a similar value. In today's terms, that would be more than £100 million. It was Morgan's greatest success, but his troubles were just beginning.

As news spread of the attack on Panama, Governor Modyford was in serious difficulties. The sack of the city had taken place during peace with Spain and the Spanish court made furious demands for punishment of those involved. A new governor, Thomas Lynch, was appointed and when he arrived in Jamaica, he moved quickly. Modyford was invited on board Lynch's ship and then told he was a prisoner and would be sent home in disgrace. Lynch also began to gather information on Henry Morgan and looked over the records of all the ships involved in the sack of Panama. At the same time, he began to get reports of Spanish attacks on British territories in reprisal. He was in the same position as Modyford had been. Lynch had absolute authority in Jamaica, but needed force and ships to impose it. Worse, war with Holland looked likely once again and Lynch had to try and appease the Spanish. He had enough cause to arrest Morgan, but resisted for a time, worried that such an act would send the privateers sailing away to Tortuga.

In London, there were mixed feelings about the attack on Panama. Spain was an ancient enemy and as one royal councillor said: 'Such an action had not been done since the famous Drake.'

Modyford was imprisoned in the Tower of London, where he remained for two years before being released. He would later return to Jamaica, where he would become Chief Justice.

In 1672, Morgan was finally taken 'as his Majesty's prisoner'. He sailed home in the frigate *Welcome*, accompanied by another privateer captain who had already been sentenced to death for piracy. His hopes depended on being able to convince the king that he had not known of the peace with Spain when he set sail.

He need not have worried. At home, his explanation was accepted and it was not long before he was advising the king. War with the Dutch broke out in 1672 and Morgan put forward plans to fortify Jamaica. In 1674 he was appointed deputy governor.

When Governor Lynch heard of Morgan's easy treatment, he was considerably vexed. His own commission as military commander in Jamaica was revoked and, to his fury, Morgan was granted the same powers and knighted. The war with the Dutch came to an abrupt end in 1674, and in 1675 Morgan left England for Jamaica once more in triumph. Modyford returned at around the same time and they met with great pleasure in their old haunt.

At the first meeting of the council, Morgan had the document revoking Lynch's powers read aloud in Lynch's presence. He enjoyed confounding the man who had imprisoned Modyford and himself.

He also appointed himself as part of a committee to audit Lynch's handling of the stores and munitions on Jamaica. Carelessly, he had made himself a dangerous enemy.

Morgan's position as a wolf in the sheepfold of power was always going to be difficult. When the new governor, Lord Vaughan, ordered him to punish privateer captains, Morgan chose to advise his old friends how to escape. He also used the governor's authority and name freely in letters to privateers, telling them to regard Jamaica as a safe port. When one of the letters turned up, Lord Vaughan brought charges against Morgan and Modyford.

In Lynch, Lord Vaughan found a stalwart supporter. Lynch described Morgan as a man of 'violent humours' and alleged that Morgan had challenged two other members of the Jamaica council to duels. Slowly, the atmosphere of the council became poisoned, with many accusations of theft, piracy and corruption, until Lord Vaughan finally dissolved it.

In England, the charges Vaughan had made against Morgan and Modyford dragged through hearings with the Lords of Trade. Eventually, they decided the job was clearly too much for Lord Vaughan. He was recalled after just two years in Jamaica and replaced by the Earl of Carlisle. At the same time, Henry Morgan was confirmed in his post as deputy governor to the incoming earl, and as commander-in-chief of all military forces.

Morgan did not sit idle waiting for the Earl of Carlisle. As soon as Vaughan set sail, he ordered new fortifications and increased the guns defending the port from sixty to more than a hundred. He received news of war with France and doubled the guard on Port Royal against possible attacks. His fabled luck struck again with news that the flagship of a French war fleet had run aground on its way to the Caribbean. When its captain had fired guns in a distress signal, the other ships thought it was a command to come closer and ran aground on the same rocks. The French lost ten ships in the chaos and their threat was severely diminished in the Caribbean.

When Lord Carlisle arrived, he was very pleased with the fortified port and praised Morgan in letters home. His relationship with Morgan would always be cordial, though it was not always so with the council. Still, it was a happy time for Henry Morgan, until Lord Carlisle finally left the post in 1680.

Spanish ships continued to attack anything flying an English flag and were themselves attacked by privateers. Panama was even assaulted once more by captains who had been on the original journey with Morgan. Pirates infested Caribbean waters, beyond anyone's ability to control. Morgan captured some of his old allies when they turned pirate, but tried to prevent them being executed. Their death warrant was confirmed in London by a Privy Council growing increasingly wary of the powers being exercised in Jamaica. They lost faith that Morgan was sufficiently ruthless with the pirates, and to Morgan's horror, they appointed none other than Thomas Lynch as the new governor in Jamaica. Restored to power, the man Morgan had once humiliated would be a thorn in his side.

When Lynch returned to Jamaica in 1682, Morgan was forced to surrender his offices, which he did with strained good humour. He was still a member of the Jamaica council, but Lynch made it clear he regarded him as a ruffian and a rogue, without a redeeming feature.

Lynch's chance came when a brawl in Port Royal was referred to Morgan. Lynch ordered a full investigation and found that Morgan's account of the brawl differed from others. It was a small thing, but Lynch leaped on it, making an official complaint that Morgan was not fit for his duties. Lynch managed to have Morgan dismissed from the council in 1683. The governor's version of events reached London first and the dismissal was confirmed by the Lords of Trade.

Morgan tried to fight the decision, but his petition fell on deaf ears in London and he retired to his estates in Jamaica, putting on a great deal of weight and drinking himself insensible. Thomas Lynch did not have much time to enjoy his triumph, however. In that hot climate, death was always close and he succumbed to fevers in 1684.

Morgan was not left in peace for long. A colourful account of his career was published in a Dutch book, *The American Sea-Rovers*. Morgan successfully sued the publisher for libel, but the book made him famous even so as a bloodthirsty pirate.

Charles II died in 1685 and with that, much of the force behind Morgan's disgrace dwindled. A new governor reversed Morgan's ban from the council and restored him to public favour. Yet Morgan's health had suffered and at 53, he was old before his time. He died on 25 August 1688, leaving the bulk of his vast estates to his beloved wife Mary. He is buried in Port Royal, Jamaica, though his grave was later obliterated and lost in the earthquake of 1692. Even the earth couldn't hold him.

Though he died without sons of his own, he left part of his fortune to his brother-in-law, Robert Bindloss, and his heirs, on the condition that they took the name Morgan. One of those renamed heirs became Attorney General and another Crown Solicitor for Jamaica. Henry Morgan would have loved to see that.

After Morgan's death, it was said of him: 'He showed the world that he was qualified to govern as well as fight, and that in all stations of life he was a great man.' His talent for organising the collection of rugged individuals that were the Jamaica privateers was extraordinary, his charisma beyond dispute. Henry Morgan was a knight and a politician, a ruffian and a pirate. He dragged himself up from humble beginnings to become one of the most powerful and respected men in the Caribbean. He was without doubt a ruthless devil when he needed to be. However, it is worth pointing out that empires are never built by vicars. They are built by men like Henry Morgan.

Recommended
The Life of Sir Henry Morgan by E.A. Cruikshank.
Admiral Sir Henry Morgan: The Greatest Buccaneer of Them All by T. Breverton.

Charles Napier

'Throughout the nineteenth century, the British armed forces were filled to confusion with Napiers.' — Byron Farwell

The Napier name may have reached the pinnacle of its fame in the nineteenth century, but it first became prominent in the seventeenth, with John Napier's invention of logarithms. The name itself is said to have come from a comment by the Scottish king Alexander II to one of his lords after a ferocious battle. The king said the man had 'na peer' (no equal) and the name stuck.

Charles Napier was born on 10 August 1782. His father, George, was the sixth of ten sons and known as the strongest man in the British army. George married Lady Sarah Lennox, a woman of great beauty who had once rejected King George III's offer of marriage. Of the eight children they had together, three of the five sons would later be known as 'Wellington's Colonels'.

In the Irish rebellion against British rule of 1798, George armed the boys to protect their mother and sisters, including the youngest, Henry, who was only nine. Henry would become a Royal Navy captain, but for the three oldest boys, the future lay on land.

At the age of just 12, Charles was commissioned in the 33rd Foot Regiment, under Lieutenant Arthur Wellesley, later Duke of Wellington. The British struggle against revolutionary France would last twenty-two years, from 1793 to 1815. France had twice Britain's population, Spain as an ally and fanatical armed forces, but Britain remained steadfast and, at times, alone. The stakes were invasion and utter destruction.

At 19, in 1801, Charles transferred to the 95th Regiment. Unlike his father, he was bespectacled and short, at five feet, seven and a half inches. He described himself as 'so thin, so sharp, so black, so Jewish, so rascally, such a knavish-looking son of a gun'.

In 1802, the Peace of Amiens was short-lived and war broke out again in 1803. Charles and his brothers, George and William, were all part of Sir John Moore's grim and bloody retreat to Corunna on the west coast of Spain.

At one battle in Portugal, Charles lost his glasses and led his men right up to French lines before asking them if they could see the enemy. His men called out that they certainly could, as they were almost on top of them. 'Then blaze away!' Charles ordered.

In 1808, under Moore, Charles had his ankle and ribs broken and was bayoneted twice. Barely alive, he was captured by the French and later exchanged for a French officer, in January 1810. As Sir John Moore had died at the Battle of Corunna in 1809, Wellington was back in command and Charles joined his staff in 1810. Spain had turned against Napoleon at last and Wellington's task was to expel the French forces entrenched there. The irregular Spanish troops were the first to use 'guerrilla' tactics against the French and gave the word, meaning 'little war', to the language.

At the Battle of Busaco in September 1810, Charles was shot in the jaw. The wound was so gory that on seeing him, Wellington asked whose body it was. Hearing the words, Charles waved his hat. He was sent to surgeons who worked on him without anaesthetic. The musket ball was lodged in his jawbone and had to be shoved out from his splintered jaw using a thumb on the other side. Charles said later: 'I did not call out, but it was very painful.' For the rest of his life, the damage to his face gave him a constant, terrifying feeling of suffocation.

His brothers William and George were also wounded, with George taking a bullet in the hip. Charles later referred to their wounds as 'burning the family candle at both ends.'

Charles was a complex and interesting man. At that time, flogging was an accepted military punishment. When Charles heard evidence of theft among his men, he ordered 900 lashes for the culprit. At 200, Charles halted the flogging to give him an opportunity to confess, but the man declined. At 400 strokes, Charles put the man in solitary confinement rather than complete the sentence.

Charles turned against flogging for a time and declared his regiment would not endure a bloody back. He changed his mind when he saw a soldier kicking a woman and had the man flogged to teach him his error. In addition, Charles had great trouble with drunken men and found that flogging sobered them up quite quickly.

Like his father before him, Charles fought in America in 1812, then transferred in 1813 back to the 50th Foot. To his immense disappointment, the French war came to an end and Napoleon was banished to Elba. With his brother William, Charles went to Farnham military college to complete his education. They were not there for long before Napoleon escaped and began the bitter conflict that would end with Waterloo.

Charles went as a volunteer to Ghent in Belgium. From there, he was involved in the storming of the fortified French town of Cambrai, and though he missed being present for Waterloo, marched into Paris in 1815 with the other victors. Napoleon was banished to the island of St Helena. The French wars were over and all four Napiers had survived some of the most brutal fighting in British history. At home, William Napier began his great work, *History of the War in the Peninsula*, published in six volumes and still the definitive work of the period.

After such a young start, Charles was only thirty-three by 1815. He spent some years in Greece as Resident in Cephalonia, supporting the Greeks in their struggle against the Turkish Ottoman Empire. There he met the poet Byron, who had similarly romantic ideals of Greek independence and would eventually give his life for them. Of Napier, Byron wrote: 'a better or braver man is not easily found.'

In 1839, Napier was given command of troops in northern England, with the brief of suppressing the activity of Chartists – poor, working men organised into early versions of trade unions who rebelled against the factory owners. Napier had sympathy with their plight and wrote: 'The people are starving and the government do nothing.' His troops were called out again and again to confront angry mobs. He hated the work and wished he had gone to Australia. His own health suffered and he put pressure on his superiors for better conditions for the soldiers under him, a cause he would later continue in India.

It is true that in India he said: 'The best receipt for quieting a country is a good thrashing first and great kindness afterwards: the wildest chaps are thus tamed,' but at the same time, he was a compassionate man in private and well aware of the suffering of the Chartists.

In 1841, Charles accepted a command in India. He worried about the effect of such a climate on his wife and daughters, but the pay was better and he was short of money. At 59, he was also aware of encroaching old age in an era when life expectancy was much lower. He wrote at the time: 'If a man cannot catch glory when his knees are supple he had better not try when they are stiff. All I want is to catch the rupees for my girls and then die like a gentleman.'

He arrived in India in 1842, the year of the disastrous retreat from Kabul in Afghanistan, when 16,000 British soldiers, servants and women were massacred and only one man survived to bring the news back to the Empire. Even worse was the news that the Sepoys – Indian soldiers trained by the Crown – were threatening to mutiny. In addition, a British army was at war with China over tea, opium and silver and some of the best Indian troops had sailed to support them.

India at that time was far from unified. The British area was separated from Afghanistan by the Punjab to the north and by Sindh to the south. The British East India Company was still privately owned, but there were already forces in motion to have it taken over by the Crown.

Napier's first orders were to take command of all troops in Sindh. Despite being 60 and suffering from rheumatism, he was enthusiastic to try his hand with an army again. He wrote in his journal: 'Charles Napier! Take heed of your ambition for military glory; you had scotched that snake, but this high command will, unless you are careful, give it all its vigour again. Get thee behind me Satan!' There is a wonderful schoolboy style to his words, with a Shakespearean sense of the dangers of ambition.

Napier was not impressed with the local rulers of Sindh, the amirs. He described them as 'these tyrannical, drunken, cheating, intriguing, contemptible Ameers', which suggests his first impressions were not entirely favourable. He was also aware of British ambitions for the area and wrote: 'They are tyrants, and so are we, but the poor will have fairer play under our sceptre than under theirs.'

With the support of Lord Ellenborough, a harsh new treaty was imposed on the amirs. Popular feeling in Sindh flared up against the British and a mob of some 8,000 attacked the British Residency, forcing an evacuation.

Napier tightened his grip on the area with a ring of native spies carrying messages concealed in the one place that would not be found, even if strip-searched.

The amirs were clearly preparing a major attack and Napier was determined to strike first. He had his battle at last at Miani, facing 22,000 well-armed Baluchi warriors and eighteen field guns against just 2,200 of his own troops and twelve cannon. As well as suffering from rheumatism and diarrhoea, Napier had broken his hand hitting a camel driver for whipping his animal. 'His head was like an anvil,' Napier said.

The Battle of Miani was bloody. The Sindhi soldiers marched stolidly into frightful carnage from rifle fire and cannon. Neither side gave way and Napier later wrote to his Royal Navy brother Henry: 'I saw no safety but in butchery. It was they or we who must die.' The Baluchis suffered some 7,000 dead or wounded, while Napier's force lost sixty dead and 200 wounded. He discovered later that the amirs had planned to have him captured and his nose pierced with a ring like a prize bull, so that he could be led around. That grisly ambition had been soundly quashed.

As the battle ended, one of the amirs held back from surrender. 'Come here instantly,' Napier roared at him. 'Come here and make your submission, or I will in a week tear you from the midst of your village and hang you!'

In March, Napier went on to smash another army of 26,000 near the town of Hyderabad, in Sindh. Temperatures were over 100°F as the armies drew together. Napier chose the ground well and his men fought with extraordinary discipline, refusing to break, even in the face of overwhelming odds. By the end, Napier's men fought hand to hand with ferocious courage, but his cannon teams were again crucial as they poured shot into a close-packed enemy. On such a day, the heat of the guns meant they could hardly see for sweat, but they kept up a high rate of fire and tore bloody holes in the Sindhi forces. Astonishingly, Napier lost only 270 men in the process and nine princes surrendered their swords to him. For bravery, he mentioned lower ranks in the dispatches as well as officers, the first to do so. It has long been said that he sent his brother Henry a one-word message after the battle – 'Peccavi', which is Latin for 'I have *sinned*' – though the story may have its origin in a *Punch* cartoon. Sindh was annexed and became part of British India.

It was not an immediately popular victory, as some in Britain felt Napier had provoked the war for personal gain. False stories circulated of him stealing jewellery from the wives of the amirs. Napier was furious about this and wrote in his journal that he wanted to break his accusers' bones with a broomstick. He was decorated for the victories, but not offered a peerage. There was prize money to be had, much as Royal Navy captains benefited from taking enemy ships. Napier's share came to £70,000 and his days of poverty were at an end. He was appointed governor of the new province and set about enforcing British laws with great enthusiasm.

As governor, Napier continued to be a mixture of great compassion for the poor and a ruthless autocrat. He abolished Suttee, the practice of burning widows on their husbands' funeral pyres. When Hindus complained that it was an ancient custom, Napier replied: 'My nation also has a custom. When men burn women alive, we hang them. Let us all act according to our national customs.'

He found the population hard to convince on this point and hanged a number of men who had casually killed a wife or daughter for some small slight. In addition, he chafed at the control of the East India Company directors, whom he regarded as bureacrats and petty tyrants. He wrote to his brothers constantly, telling them of the irritations of life in the region and his deteriorating health. Napier was never a man who enjoyed the tedium of actually ruling a place. He loved great visions and grand gestures, but was not keen on the rest of it.

The war to annex the Sikh Punjab soon followed. Napier raised an army, but the first Sikh war was over quickly and he did not take part. Instead, cholera hit Karachi, where he was living. His nephew John was with him and the young man died. As a father of daughters himself, Napier had seen John as a son and suffered terribly at the loss. He sent his troops away from cities into the desert to try and protect them as the disease raged. In all, some 60,000 civilians died. Interestingly, Napier realised sewage-tainted water was the source twenty years before London built its sewers. During the nineteenth century, millions died from cholera in India, Europe, America and Britain before it was understood and controlled.

In 1847, Napier's second wife became very ill and he resigned from his post to tend her. His own health was growing steadily worse and old wounds left him unable to sleep without the sense of choking. He brought his family back to England, where to his pleasure, he was greeted as a returning hero and attended lavish banquets in his honour. Wellington chose him as commander-in-chief in India, the ultimate seal of approval for a man who idolised the Iron Duke.

Sent out to India once more, he stayed with Lord Dalhousie, who said of him: 'What a life he has led ... how riddled and chopped to pieces with balls and bayonets and sabre wounds he is.' Napier arranged for Gurkha troops from Nepal to receive the same pay as Sepoys and was reprimanded for the waste of money. He resigned and returned to England in 1851. He served as a pall-bearer at Wellington's funeral, the last honour he could give to the great man.

Charles James Napier died in August 1853, aged 71. As he issued his last breath, his son-in-law raised the colours of Napier's old regiment in Sindh and waved them over his bed. His mounted statue stands today on one of the four corners of Trafalgar Square in London, the most famous memorial in Britain.

Recommended
Arthur Bryant's *'English Saga'* in three volumes.
Eminent Victorian Soldiers: Seekers of Glory by Byron Farwell.
'The Burial of Sir John Moore at Corunna' – a poem by Charles Wolfe.

Lawrence of Arabia

'All men dream, but not equally. Those who dream by night in the dusty recesses of their minds wake in the day to find that it was a vanity. But the dreamers of the day are dangerous men, for they may act their dreams with open eyes to make it possible. This, I did.'
                                                            – T.E. Lawrence.

Thomas Edward Lawrence was a soldier, archaeologist, writer, intelligence officer and international negotiator. During his life he was known variously as 'emir dynamite', the last great crusader, the most interesting Briton alive, 'el Lawrence', the uncrowned King of Arabia and, simply, 'Lurens'. He was enigmatic, asexual, masochistic, retiring, exhibitionistic, difficult and charming. He was an extremely complex man and some parts of his life and personality remain mysteries today.

Born in 1888, he was the second of five illegitimate sons of Thomas Chapman and nursery governess Sarah Junner. Chapman made over most of his money to his wife and children, eloped with Sarah, changed their names to Lawrence and lived as husband and wife. Chapman inherited a baronetcy in 1914; officially he was Sir Thomas, but he never used the title. He died in the influenza epidemic of 1919 and Sarah went to China with Lawrence's missionary brother, Montague. By then, the name of Lawrence was already world famous through his exploits in Arabia.

After winning a scholarship to Jesus College, Oxford, Lawrence refused to play organised sports there. Instead, he walked, ran, cycled and swam. He became an excellent pistol shot and joined the Officers' Training Corps. He was quietly rebellious, independent and physically tough. Several times he broke through the winter ice to swim the River

Cherwell and was famous as one of the illegal night climbers on the university roofs. To complete his history degree he spent a summer walking and camel riding 1,100 miles through Syria, studying and recording the old Crusader castles.

He divided the next four years of his life between Oxford and excavating the ancient Biblical city of Carchemish, with archaeologist Leonard Woolley. Lawrence took to wearing around his waist the Arabian red tasselled belt of the permanent bachelor. There, he and the famous Arabian scholar Gertrude Bell met for the first time, though neither was impressed with the other. Their love and concern for Arabia and its peoples grew separately.

During those years of archaeological digs, academic reports and theses for Oxford University, Lawrence learned to speak the Arabic of the bazaars as well as to read and write basic script. From 1300, the Middle East had been part of the Ottoman Empire, the empire of the Turks stretching from Europe to the Persian Gulf, and so Lawrence learned also the ways of the Turks. He was not impressed. He and Syrian friend Daouhm were arrested and beaten by the Turks in 1912 as suspected deserters from the Turkish army.

When the Great War began in August 1914, the Turks entered in November as an ally of Germany and the Austro-Hungarian Empire. Twenty-six-year-old Lawrence was posted to Cairo as an intelligence officer in the small British army holding the vital Suez Canal. He was made lieutenant and his work involved drawing and correcting maps of the Middle East. As his Oxford lecturers had before, High Command found him difficult.

The Arab Revolt began on 6 June 1916, when Princes Feisal and Ali of southern Arabia attempted to take the holy city of Medina. They were defeated by heavy Turkish artillery fire. In punishment for the attack, the Turkish commander ordered that all Arabs living in Awali be massacred. Those dead and alive were thrown onto their burning homes.

In Mecca on 10 June Feisal's father, Sharif Hussein, fired from his window to signal the official revolt. The Turks, also Muslim, attempted a worldwide jihad to include Britain, France and Russia, but Hussein refused to sanction this and instead wanted the Turks out of Arabia.

Hussein supported Great Britain – but not France – and Britain in turn supported the Arab Revolt against their common enemy, the Turks. In June, three British ships steamed into Jeddah on the Red Sea with food, 3,000 rifles and ammunition. In July, the Turks garrisoning Mecca were defeated, the first victory of the desert revolt.

Britain's intelligence chief and instigator and supporter of the Arab Revolt was Ronald Storrs, and in his visits to Jeddah and Hamra he took Lawrence. They met all of Hussein's sons, and agreed that the most likely to succeed in co-ordinating an Arab regular force were Feisal and Abdullah. Lawrence became the first British officer Hussein allowed to visit the fighting tribes. He met Prince Feisal so many times that Feisal asked him to wear Arab dress to be less conspicuous. Feisal provided him with the white robes of a Hashemite prince, and the legend of 'Lawrence of Arabia' began.

In late 1916, Lawrence was appointed military advisor to the Arab Revolt with orders to report and liaise whenever necessary between Arabia and Cairo. He wrote: 'The position I have is a queer one. I do not suppose any Englishman before ever had such a place.' Feisal presented Lawrence with a British rifle captured by the Turks at Gallipolli, an earlier Turkish gift to Feisal. It was a gesture of friendship, humour and trust.

Supplies from Britain were trickling through and it was time for Feisal's regulars and Lawrence's irregulars to campaign. Yenbo on the Red Sea was saved from a Turkish night attack almost without a shot being fired – the only land approach was lit by Royal Navy searchlights and the Turks retreated. That success was followed by a joint advance by land and sea on Wejh. Wejh fell in January 1917 to the Royal Navy and Arab regulars as Lawrence and Feisal approached by camel over land. The only Red Sea port then left to the Turks was Aqaba. In the east, the British liberated Baghdad in March.

Lawrence initiated guerrilla attacks on the north–south railway from Damascus to Medina, a tactic continued throughout the war by Arab irregulars trained by British explosives experts. The wrecks of the engines are there today, lying on their rusted sides in the desert. Harassing rather than decisive, those attacks kept the Arab Revolt active and were ideal for mobile irregulars. That June, Lawrence trekked some 560 miles by camel through enemy Syria, converting tribes to the revolt, patching up tribal feuds and religious differences, and assuring them of British support if they fought.

Back in the south again, Lawrence, the formidable Auda abu Tayi of the Howeitat tribe and some thirty-five others quietly left Wejh. They rode a circular route, skirting the great Nefud Desert and crossing a plateau to arrive at the valleys behind Aqaba. On their camels were weapons and gold to raise the local tribes.

The inland defensive line of Turkish forts were taken one by one. In one charge to cut off a Turkish retreat, Lawrence excitedly fired his revolver and killed his own camel. On 6 July, Aqaba was liberated by Lawrence's irregulars.

Lawrence crossed the Sinai Desert by camel to take the news to Cairo and, a week later, a British ship arrived at Aqaba with food and gold.

Rifles, mortars, machine guns and explosives followed. The revolt was going well, the Turks were being stretched and, at headquarters, General Allenby took command for the British advance northwards. Yet there were failures among the successes. The Turks were tough soldiers and able to survive on poor rations and in the most hostile of terrains. It was apparent the liberation of Arabia would be hard-fought.

Deserts are not only rock, sand and sun; they are also hills, mountains, valleys and snow. The desert war for Lawrence and his Arab irregulars continued through the winter. They campaigned in rain and mud, forced their unwilling camels through snow drifts and scaled ice-covered hills in sandals and bare feet. There were many bitter moments. Of a badly wounded friend Lawrence wrote: 'We could not leave him where he was, to the Turks, because we had seen them burn alive our hapless wounded. For this reason we were all agreed, before action, to finish off one another, if badly hurt; but I had never thought it might fall to me to kill Farraj.'

Deep in Turkish territory lay Dara'a, a vital railway junction where the line from the coast joined the north–south line. In the rainy November of 1917, Lawrence entered the town dressed as an Arab to study the layout for a future attack. According to his book, *The Seven Pillars of Wisdom*, he was captured and viciously beaten by Turkish soldiers before he could escape. For many years this episode has been questioned by historians; Lawrence did not report his capture at the time and the exact details can now not be known. Possibly, it was an echo of his beating in 1912 with Daouhm. Lawrence was certainly under considerable strain for a long period. He suffered regularly from dysentery and fevers, yet continued to make many long and important camel journeys through the deserts.

For some time the Turks had offered a reward of £20,000 for Lawrence's head, and after early 1917 he usually travelled with an Arab bodyguard. There were still many tribes who worked for the enemy and perhaps half in the revolt were fighting for British gold as much as a free Arabia. Lawrence, Feisal, Auda and other leaders had to be careful; seven centuries of Turkish rule could not be changed overnight.

In December 1917, the British army liberated Jerusalem. Allenby, with Lawrence walking behind him, became the first non-Muslim leader since 1187 to enter Jerusalem when he passed through the Jaffa Gate on foot. With the Turkish withdrawal from Medina, the three holy cities of Mecca, Medina and Jerusalem were free. Damascus, the spiritual capital of Arabia where lies the tomb of Saladin, awaited.

The New Year began well when Lawrence's irregulars fought their only formal battle against the Turkish Army. The strange Englishman who spoke and dressed as an Arab was a talisman to the independent tribesmen: they chanted 'Lurens! Lurens!' when he gathered them at Tafilah. In a classic military action of pretended retreat and then encirclement, Lawrence routed an enemy column. Three hundred Turks were killed and 250 taken prisoner. There were reverses elsewhere through Turkish counter-attacks, and that Easter, many British resources were diverted to halt a new German offensive in France.

Feisal's Arab regulars became the desert right flank of Allenby's final advance north in summer 1918. The prize: Damascus. In September, 1,000 of Lawrence's irregulars took Dara'a, supported by Indian, Gurkha and Egyptian units.

During the Turkish retreat north, the villagers of Tafas, including twenty children and forty women, were massacred by a Turkish brigade. In vengeful fury, Lawrence's irregulars fell on the Turks and slaughtered most of them. The Arabs usually took prisoners and handed them to the British, but the butchery at Tafas was too much for them. Witnesses reported that Lawrence tried to stop the killing, but with only small success.

By 29 September, the armies were in the hills overlooking Damascus. Arab irregulars and the Australian Light Horse entered Damascus before dawn on the 30th and Lawrence entered later that day. By the time Allenby arrived in October, Lawrence's irregulars and Feisal's regulars controlled Damascus and had created an Arab Council to administer the city. That had been Lawrence's promise to Feisal and he had fulfilled it. Lawrence also removed the bronze wreath that the German Kaiser had added to the Tomb of Saladin. To Arabs, the wreath was a desecration, with its German imperial crown and German and Turkish script. Lawrence wanted this symbol of dominion over Arabia removed before Feisal arrived. It is now in the Imperial War Museum in London.

General Allenby and Prince Feisal met for the first time in Damascus with Lawrence as interpreter. Following his instructions from London, Allenby informed Feisal that all Syria except Lebanon was to be Feisal's, but under 'the security of France' and with a French liaison officer. Feisal replied that he would not accept French security or a French liaison officer, nor would he recognise French authority over Syria and Lebanon. The Arabs did not trust the French at all. Feisal wanted complete independence for Arabia, if necessary secured by Britain, but by no other country.

Before the fighting was even over, the politicians had moved in; British and French governments had reached an agreement to divide northern Arabia. Lawrence and Feisal had known of the discussions, but neither could believe it would actually happen. Lawrence also refused to work with any French liaison officer. Instead, he asked Allenby for leave in Britain. Two of his brothers had been killed fighting on the Western Front and he was very tired. He also realised that the next round would be fought at the peace conference and he wanted to be there.

He returned to Britain in October 1918, a colonel with a DSO, CB and a recommendation by Allenby for a knighthood. At a private investiture at Buckingham Palace, Lawrence politely refused the knighthood from King George V and informed the king: 'Your cabinet is an awful set of crooks.' He advised His Majesty that the British government was about to betray the Arabs and that he, Lawrence, would be supporting Prince Feisal, not His Majesty's government. Now one of the most famous figures of the war, he angered many with his refusal of a knighthood, however honourable his reasons. There was certainly some of Lawrence's peculiar masochism in the refusal, yet he was correct that the future of Arabia was in the hands of bureaucrats who cared little for its people.

At the peace conference in Paris, Lawrence, Gertrude Bell and others supported Arab independence. Against French wishes, Prince Feisal was also there representing Sharif Hussein, but they were outmanoeuvred by clever politicians. France was given a mandate for Lebanon and, in November 1919, the British army was withdrawn from Syria. The French invaded Syria in the spring of 1920.

It was as if the Arabs had never fought, as if the British army had fought so that France could take over part of the Ottoman Empire. There had been a small French unit fighting under Allenby in the liberation of Arabia, but they were irrelevant to the outcome. The Middle East was immediately destabilised and violence flared.

Winston Churchill, appointed Colonial Secretary, called a conference at Cairo in 1921 to sort out the mess. He appointed Lawrence Britain's 'Advisor on Arab Affairs'; Gertrude Bell and Ronald Storrs were also there. Many problems were solved by the conference but several remained, particularly the French in Syria and the warring tribes of Arabia. The tribes had continued to fight each other even while they fought the Turks during the revolt, and continued fighting under different banners of tribe and religion. For Britain, it meant another war in Syria, when French forces joined the Nazis in the 1939–45 war.

When the dust had settled, a 'John Ross' applied to join the RAF in 1922 as an aircraftman. He was refused, but returned with a letter from the Air Ministry stating who he was and that he should be admitted. The accepting officer was W.E. Johns, author of the Biggles novels, and Ross was T.E. Lawrence. It was typical of that oddly quixotic, romantic man to use a false name. After all, 'Lawrence' itself was an alias chosen by his father. The fiction also protected Lawrence from the press, who hounded him long after he had left public life. He was accepted into the RAF, the authorities believing that he wanted material for a book.

'Honestly, I couldn't tell you why I joined up,' Lawrence wrote to author and friend Robert Graves. Lawrence admitted he didn't understand many of the decisions he made.

He served in the ranks of the RAF, then the army under the name of Shaw, then the RAF again for almost the rest of his life. While there he completed, published and revised his great work, *Seven Pillars of*

Wisdom, which Churchill called 'one of the greatest books I have ever read'. Of his two other books, *Revolt in the Desert* is a précis of *Seven Pillars*, while *The Mint* is the book about his life as an RAF recruit. Lawrence continued to live his double existence, serving humbly in the ranks but at the same time moving in the circles of power of his famous friends – Robert Graves, Sir Winston Churchill, King Feisal, George Bernard Shaw, Nancy Astor, Sir Edward Elgar and others.

His enlistment in the RAF ended in 1935 and Lawrence retired to his Dorsetshire cottage, Clouds Hill. He wrote: 'My losing the RAF numbs me so I haven't much feeling to spare for a while. In fact I find myself wishing all the time that my own curtain would fall. It seems as if I had finished now.' His great friend, King Feisal, had already 'finished', dead at only 50.

On 13 May, returning on his 1000cc Brough motorbike to Clouds Hill from Bovington village post office, Lawrence swerved on the brow of a hill to avoid two boys riding bicycles. He clipped the back wheel of one, crashed and flew over the handlebars. He hit the road head first, cracked his skull and died six days later without regaining consciousness.

T.E. Lawrence is buried in Moreton Church graveyard in Dorset. Ronald Storrs, Sir Winston Churchill and many other friends attended his simple funeral.

King George V sent a message to Lawrence's only surviving brother, saying 'Your brother's name will live in history.' A memorial service was held at St Paul's Cathedral, where there is a small bust, while in the simple church of St Martin in Wareham, Dorset, there is a striking stone effigy of T.E. Lawrence in the Arab robes of a Hashemite prince.

There are few famous heroes of the 1914–18 war, but Lawrence of Arabia was certainly one. Like Richard Burton before him, he was a man in love with exoticism, while mysterious ancient Arabia captured his imagination. British archives released in the 1960s and 1970s confirmed the importance of Lawrence's work in Arabia. If anything, his *Seven Pillars of Wisdom* underplays his contribution to the Arab Revolt. Lawrence was one of the few who saw the future in independent Arab nations. He was an outsider, a romantic dreamer in many ways, yet a man who could see beyond the details to the great sweep of history.

Recommended
Seven Pillars of Wisdom by T.E. Lawrence.
Lawrence: The Uncrowned King of Arabia by Michael Asher.
Clouds Hill Cottage, National Trust, Dorset.
Film: *Lawrence of Arabia*, Columbia Pictures, 1962. There are inaccuracies but it captures brilliantly the Arab Revolt and the enigma of Lawrence.

Florence Nightingale

Victorian soldiers such as Charles Napier and Garnet Wolseley risked their lives for their country – and personal glory. Their courage in the face of enemy fire is made greater when you consider the rudimentary state of medicine and surgery at the time.

Battlefield hospitals were brutal in the first half of the nineteenth century. Surgeons did not wash their hands and operated in blood and pus-stained clothes. If a knife or sponge was dropped, it was merely dipped in bloody water before being used again. Ether, an early anaesthetic, wasn't used in surgery until 1842. Opium and chloroform were both known, but neither was in common use. Even London hospitals were places of squalor. They had no lavatories, just chamber pots under the beds. The windows were boarded up as fresh air was believed to bring illness.

It would not be until the late 1860s that Joseph Lister cut the rate of deaths from post-operative infection by making his surgeons wash their hands. He also used a spray of carbolic acid to kill germs, even though at that time they could not be seen with the rudimentary microscopes.

Antibiotics were also unknown until the twentieth century and not mass-produced until after World War II. Up to that point, fever and infection was treated with cold cloths, sulphur or sulphurous acid, mustard on the skin and occasionally mustard and salt enemas.

As a result, even light wounds could rot and corrupt a limb. Amputation was extremely common and surgeons competed for speed with a saw, trying to remove and seal the limb before the patient died from blood loss. The patient would then be very fortunate not to get one of the 'surgical fevers' – pyaemia or gangrene, which killed almost half of those who had lived through surgery.

In short, it was a different, harder world, where even measles and croup killed tens of thousands of children and a wounded soldier needed more than luck to survive. That is the context of Wolseley joining a 'forlorn hope' storming party, or Napier being shot in the jaw. Being wounded meant certain agony, likely infection and a good chance of dying in a dirty barracks hospital.

Florence Nightingale was born on 12 May 1820. Her parents were wealthy and their honeymoon in Italy lasted for four years. She was named after her Italian birthplace, an innovation at the time. They returned home to a new and very grand house in Hampshire. Florence and her elder sister Parthenope were taught by a governess, before their father took it upon himself to teach them Latin, Greek, French, Italian, German, history and philosophy. From the start, Florence found the lessons easier than her sister.

When she was 16, Florence's life changed. She always kept private notes of her thoughts and experiences, and on one of them she wrote: 'On February 7th 1837, God spoke to me and called me to his service.' Always a woman with an intense inner world, she would later record that she had heard voices at four times in her life.

She could not act on it immediately. Her mother was intent on launching her daughters into London society, but the house needed to be renovated first, so in September 1837, the Nightingales departed for the continent while the work was done. Florence loved the experience. She danced at balls and visited romantic Italian cities. When the family returned to England in 1839, her mother arranged to have the girls presented to Queen Victoria, who was just a year older than Florence. Florence's mother was pleased that her intelligent daughter had become such a beautiful and demure young lady. Marriage would clearly soon follow and Florence could live properly and have daughters of her own.

Instead, Florence threw herself into the study of mathematics. Her mother was appalled, of course. Young men were not likely to pursue a 'mathematical girl'.

In the 1840s, there was great poverty in England, both in the slums of the major cities and the countryside, where a single bad crop could mean starvation. The Nightingales spent their summers in a second home in Derbyshire and there Florence met some of the poorest labourers. In a first sign of what would become her life's work, she went out of her way to take them food and clothes, even medicine when she could get it. There was no system of benefits for the poor at that time. If a working man fell ill or was injured, his family went hungry until he recovered or died.

Florence also nursed an orphaned baby and her own grandmother. She had found her purpose, her vocation at last and she refused an offer of marriage to pursue it. She wanted proper training in a London hospital, but that was unheard of for a young woman of her social class.

In 1845, Dr Fowler of Salisbury Infirmary visited her parents. Taking the opportunity, Florence asked him to train her as a nurse. It was the first her parents had heard of her ambition and they were outraged. In embarrassment at the storm his visit had brought, the doctor left without agreeing to her request.

Florence was an unmarried daughter with no rights over her own life. Her mother forced her to continue with social engagements and her less intelligent sister never lost a chance to show her jealous resentment. Florence did her best to study on her own, visiting foreign hospitals when she travelled and reading anything medical that she could find. She made a point of stopping at Kaiserswerth hospital in Germany on one trip and found the nurses there similar to nuns in their outlook and vocation, even their dress.

Florence was 32 before her career finally began. A wealthy friend of hers, Elizabeth Herbert, put her name forward for someone to manage a new nursing home opening in London – 'The Establishment for Gentlewomen during Illness'. As Florence wrote in her private letters, it was the second time she heard a voice instructing her. She accepted the position despite the dismay of her family.

From the start, Florence introduced changes that were remarkable for the day. She insisted on clean rooms and sheets and that her patients should be warm and well fed. She even put flowers in the nursing home, an unheard-of extravagance. At the same time, she collected statistical information, always looking for ways to improve the care of patients.

She was fearless, both of authority and disease, even to the point of taking over a ward in a London hospital during a cholera epidemic. In just a year, she made her nursing home unique for its gentle care of the sick women.

In 1854, Florence's life changed again. In March, the Crimean War had broken out between Britain and Russia. Conditions there were appalling and disease and exposure were taking as many lives as the actual fighting. Cholera was a particular killer, though at that time, no one understood how it was spread. After the Battle of Alma, wounded men were laid on filthy straw without opium or chloroform or even splints for broken bones.

In the primitive troop hospital at Scutari in Turkey, the main building was filled with a thousand sick or wounded men. When news came of another thousand on their way, the senior medical officer converted an artillery barracks to hold them. Dirty and bare, with no beds, kitchen or medical supplies, it was little more than a huge hall in which to put the dying. Delirious soldiers lay in their own filth, untended and unable even to get a drink of water in oppressive heat. The stench of rotting flesh, the screaming and misery can only be imagined.

The Times newspaper brought the situation to the eyes of the public, shaming the Minister for War, Sidney Herbert. Good nurses were desperately needed and he knew and liked Florence through his wife. Herbert wrote an impassioned letter to Florence, offering to pay for her to go to Scutari with a group of nurses. For the third time in her life, Florence heard a voice telling her to go.

With the official position of 'Superintendent of the Female Nursing Establishment of the English Hospitals in Turkey', Florence was instantly famous. No woman had ever held such a post before and her mother and sister were finally able to put aside their grievances and be proud for her. Florence scoured London for the best nurses to take out to Turkey, though she preferred solid, doughty old ladies rather than young ones. She was later to regret the weight of some of them, when a bed collapsed. Twenty-four nuns joined the party and accepted Florence's authority, bringing the total to thirty-eight. They all had to be trained to Florence's standards rather than their own.

In October
1854, the nurses left
England for Paris to buy medical
supplies. News had spread of their mission
and they were welcomed and well treated by
French locals, before moving on to the great port
of Marseilles. Florence oversaw the purchases
of everything she thought she might need before
they took ship on 27 October to Malta and then Constantinople, now
known as Istanbul.

By November, after terrible gales, they reached Constantinople. The
British ambassador sent Lord Napier to greet Florence and he was
much taken with the handsome and dedicated woman who was still
exhausted from seasickness. However, she could not rest. The Battle of
Balaclava had been fought and the hospital was expecting a new rush
of casualties at any moment.

The first sight of the hospital at Scutari was not impressive. Florence
was used to dirt in hospitals, but she was not prepared to find thousands
of dying men, most of whom had diarrhoea. What drains existed were
blocked and the smell of the hospital reached right out to sea. Florence

later wrote that it should have had 'Abandon Hope All Ye Who Enter Here' written above its gate. Her most famous work had begun.

One of the reasons for the appalling state of the hospital was the lifeless hand of British bureaucracy. Even a request for a new shirt might be passed along a dozen different officials, then lost or forgotten. Her foresight in buying her own supplies was rewarded. The doctors in Scutari had no medicine, dressings or bandages. Amputation was the main treatment of wounds and the mortality rate for such butcher's work was incredibly high.

Even so, her first reception was not a pleasant experience. Apart from the sounds and smells of the hospital, the doctors were hostile to the idea of a group of women interfering in their work. They gave Florence and her group of thirty-eight nurses just six small rooms, one of which had a body in it. The following morning, the doctors made it clear that they would not allow women on the wards. Florence said nothing and put her nurses to work preparing and sorting the supplies she had brought.

On 5 November, the Battle of Inkerman took place and winter came in a sudden cold blast. Thousands more wounded began to arrive at the already overcrowded hospital. The doctors were overwhelmed and asked Florence if she would assist. It is a testament to her character that she made nothing of the small victory, just gathered her nurses and made her first tour of the hospital. 'I have seen hell,' she said later.

She had funds, both from Sidney Herbert's government purse and a collection organised by The Times itself from its readers. She sent to Constantinople for whatever was needed, from operating tables to soap, clothes, food and bedpans. In the meantime, she set about cleaning the filthy rooms. Two hundred men were hired to unblock the drains. Women were engaged to scrub and scour the floors, while Florence set the soldiers' wives to washing clothes and linen. She believed that a clean hospital was a healthy one, though this was not at all common practice, either in Turkey or England.

As the hospital began to lose its worst grime, Florence had the nurses begin their work. At last there were medicines and dressings for the wounded. She also understood the importance of small things that the army would never have considered. She bought a screen to give privacy during operations, then held the hand of soldiers as they tried to bear an amputation without anaesthetic. She made a rule for her nurses that none of the soldiers should die alone. She worked as hard as anyone, staying up for twenty-four hours at a time to tend the men. She also wrote letters home for dying men who could not write.

Despite everything, the death toll went on rising. As well as a new outbreak of cholera, the men suffered from scurvy, a disease brought on by the soldier's diet of biscuit and pork, without any vegetables. Even those with minor wounds were dying and Florence became convinced the water supply for the hospital was to blame. She set her workmen to dig up the pipes and they discovered the dead body of a horse that had been washed into an inlet. All the water in the hospital had run past that diseased flesh. Years later, it was discovered that Scutari hospital was built on an ancient cess pit, which meant human waste seeped into the water supply. Florence Nightingale could never have made it completely safe without burning it down and starting again.

Even so, little by little, Florence turned Scutari from hell on earth into a quiet, clean hospital. Each night, she would make a last tour of the wards, in a black dress and shawl and carrying a small lamp to guide her steps. It was during his time that she became known as 'the lady with the lamp'.

Before she slept for a few hours, she wrote to Sidney Herbert in London, telling him everything she had done and all that still needed doing. She urged him to keep a better record of the wounded and dying, believing that statistics would aid future generations in fighting the same diseases. In this too, she was ahead of her time.

Some of her letters were passed to Queen Victoria, who was shocked by the descriptions of such suffering. The queen wrote a reply, saying: 'I wish Miss Nightingale and the ladies would tell these poor noble, wounded and sick men that no one takes a warmer interest, or feels more for their suffering, or admires their courage and heroism more than their queen.' The words were read to the men and then pinned to a wall of the hospital. No previous monarch had written such a personal message to soldiers.

By 1855, Scutari had become the best army hospital available to British troops anywhere. However, there were two others on the Crimean peninsula and Florence saw her duty lay in visiting them and assessing conditions. She travelled to Balaclava and found them in the sort of state she had seen on her first visit to Scutari. She began another plan of attack, but without warning, exhaustion overcame her. She fainted and was found to be burning with a fever. Her best nurses came out to tend her, but for two weeks, she was close to death. Soldiers in Scutari wept when the news came in.

She recovered, but had lost a great deal of her vitality and become very thin and worn. Though she was able to return to Scutari, her health was extremely fragile and she wasn't able to go to battle with obstinate doctors as she had before. The soldiers showed their appreciation at her safe return and that sustained her over difficult months.

The Peace Treaty of Paris was agreed in February 1856 and came into effect a month later, ending the Crimean War. Almost without exception, it had been badly conceived and badly led. The cost in lives was cruelly high and in England, the public found little to celebrate. 'The Charge of the Light Brigade' by Lord Tennyson became famous, but no one wrote stirring poems about hospitals.

Gradually, the soldiers in the Crimea returned home, though Florence stayed until the last one had gone. As the hospital emptied, it still seemed full of ghosts. 'Oh my poor men,' she wrote, 'I am a bad mother to come home and leave you in Crimean graves.'

Death was often on her mind, perhaps because of her close association with it in the Crimea. Only a year later, she gave instructions to her sister Parthenope that she should be buried in the Crimea: 'absurd as I know it to be. For they are not there.' She would not get her wish.

In England, many survivors described Florence's kindness and her fame as the 'lady with the lamp' grew steadily. Soldiers contributed a day's pay for her to set up a training school for nurses. Pamphlets were printed of her time in Scutari. In London, Madame Tussaud even created a waxwork of Florence ministering to the wounded. Finally, Queen Victoria sent her a brooch that her Consort Prince Albert had designed. It has the words: 'Blessed are the Merciful' around the edge.

Huge public receptions were planned and Florence's sister and mother were in their element, overcome with the prospect of honours for the family.

Florence herself was appalled at the idea. She avoided the regimental bands and crowds by travelling under the name 'Miss Smith'. She came home alone to the house in Derbyshire and walked from the station. Her mother's housekeeper saw her coming down the road and rushed out in tears, but otherwise it was a remarkable and modest evasion of fame.

At home, Florence ignored the letters and invitations that came in, telling her sister she could open them if she wished. Instead, she threw herself into work, writing constant letters. One of her contributions to the public debate was a pamphlet, 'Mortality in the British Army', which presented statistical information with a modified form of pie chart. She followed it with other publications and visited Queen Victoria to put her case. The two women were of a similar age and mind. They worked closely together to create a royal commission on the health of the army, with Sidney Herbert as chairman.

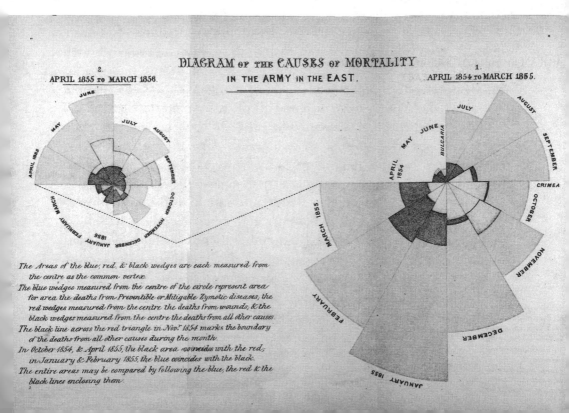

DIAGRAM OF THE CAUSES OF MORTALITY IN THE ARMY IN THE EAST.

2.
APRIL 1855 TO MARCH 1856.

1.
APRIL 1854 TO MARCH 1855.

The Areas of the blue, red, & black wedges are each measured from the centre as the common vertex.

The blue wedges measured from the centre of the circle represent area for area the deaths from Preventible or Mitigable Zymotic diseases, the red wedges measured from the centre the deaths from wounds, & the black wedges measured from the centre the deaths from all other causes.

The black line across the red triangle in Nov.r 1854 marks the boundary of the deaths from all other causes during the month.

In October 1854, & April 1855, the black area coincides with the red; in January & February 1855, the blue coincides with the black.

The entire areas may be compared by following the blue, the red & the black lines enclosing them.

At the same time, Florence's own health grew worse. She took rooms in London to work, but fell ill with fevers, almost certainly the aftermath of her exposure in the Crimea. She drove herself on regardless.

In 1858, Sidney Herbert's health also deteriorated, crushed by overwork. Florence was confined to her room with illness, but she was indomitable and forced him to continue his labours on the commission. At times, they bickered like an old married couple, but there was great mutual respect and liking between them and Herbert's wife Elizabeth encouraged the friendship.

In 1859, another royal commission was set up to investigate the health of the army in India. Sidney Herbert was made chairman, adding immensely to his workload. Unable to refuse important tasks, he was also made Minister for War by a new government.

When the Crimean Commission reported, Florence had the outcome she desired. It would create a new army medical school and reform medical provision down to the design of drains. Yet the conclusions had to be implemented and the War Office was mired in tortuous bureaucracy. Even with Sidney Herbert at its head, the attempt to reform the dusty halls of power was almost impossible.

Florence wrote that her aim was 'to simplify procedure, to abolish divided responsibility, to define clearly the duties of each head of department and of each class of office; to hold heads responsible for their respective departments.' Those words are as insightful and valuable today as they were then and all the more remarkable for it.

Sidney Herbert finally collapsed in 1861. As he died, he murmured: 'Poor Florence. Our joint work unfinished.' His statue stands today outside the War Office in London. He need not have worried: the army reforms went ahead. Barracks were redesigned, food improved and army nurses trained to a higher standard. Death rates dropped around the world as a direct result of Florence and Sidney Herbert's work.

Florence was hit hard by the death of her friend. For the fourth time in her life, she heard a voice crying out at the loss. She worked harder if anything, despite poor health. With her work on the commission, she had been unable to oversee the Nightingale Training School set up with pay from Crimean soldiers. As a result, standards had dropped.

Though she was bedridden with illness, Florence took over this last task and devoted herself to it. She was back in her element and the work made her happy. She put on weight for the first time in years and her letters grew milder in comparison with the stern missives she had sent to those in power. The Nightingale School still exists and trains nurses today.

Though she had expected death for years, it was slow in coming. Queen Victoria died in 1901 and her successor, Edward VII, awarded Florence the Order of Merit for her life's work, the first woman to receive the honour. Florence died at last in 1910, at the age of 90.

It is impossible to guess how many lives were saved or how much suffering eased because of Florence Nightingale. She made nursing a professional occupation for the first time. She opened women's medical schools and trained Linda Richards, who went on to establish nursing schools in America and Japan. She fought against the stifling attitudes and prejudices of her day, forcing new thinking in old halls of power. She won her battles and her life stands as an example of what a single individual can do with sufficient determination, faith and spirit.

Recommended
Florence Nightingale by Cecil Woodham-Smith.

The Defence of
Rorke's Drift

January in southern Africa is the worst time of year to be away from the coast. The sun is intense, the air oven-hot and dry, the thin soil dusty and parched, the plains and hills raw with heat. In the January of 1879, though, there had been unseasonal thunderstorms, so that the rivers were swollen and the grasses on the veldt were unusually green and tall.

At Rorke's Drift – a ford across the Buffalo River between Natal colony and independent Zululand – soldiers listened to distant gunfire. It had begun just before noon, to the east, where the British central column had gone, up to Isandhlwana Hill.

At first light on the 22nd, Colonel Durnford and his Natal Native Contingent (NNC) had left to reinforce the central column at Isandhlwana. Those at Rorke's Drift could hear rifle fire in the distance. Someone was catching it – Durnford, the column, or the Zulus. Still, the river was high, it was baking hot, and the work on improving the heavy wooden pontoons under Lieutenant John Chard of the Royal Engineers was demanding.

Chard, too, had ridden the eight miles to Isandlhwana that morning and returned. He reported that the bulk of the column had marched with Lord Chelmsford the day before to engage a Zulu army twelve miles away. Durnford's cavalry had been ordered up to reinforce those left behind.

Shortly after 1 p.m., the light went out of the sky and a dark shadow suddenly spread over the river. The soldiers looked up in surprise. There was a crescent across part of the sun. It was a partial eclipse, the moon passing between the sun and the earth. With the echoes of firing up in the hills, it was a strange day.

With the departure of Durnford, Major Spalding had taken command at Rorke's Drift. Originally a farm, it had become a mission of two stone buildings, converted to a hospital and storehouse. The British army in Natal had commandeered the mission as a supply depot with a small garrison to hold the ford. Mr Otto Witt, the Swedish missionary, was not pleased.

After lunch, the firing from Isandhlwana died down to a mutter and stopped at around 1.30 p.m. There was an occasional isolated rifle shot, then silence. All seemed well and at two in the afternoon, Major Spalding rode out to Helpmakaar, the nearest town some miles further west. He went to find a company of the 1st Battalion – then two days overdue in reinforcing Rorke's Drift. That left Lieutenant Chard, with Lieutenant Gonville Bromhead of the 2nd Battalion. The only other officers were Surgeon-Major James Reynolds of the Army Medical Corps and Captain Stephenson, in charge of a hundred Natal Native infantry.

All went about their various duties that hot, dry afternoon until 3.15 p.m., when two men in khaki NNC uniform came riding hard from the east and splashed across the river into Natal. Their horses were covered in white sweat.

'Isandhlwana's fallen!' they reported. 'The camp is taken by Zulus!' Chard and Bromhead were stunned. The news seemed impossible: Chard had been there only that morning.

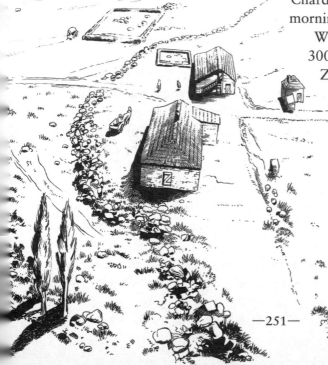

When Chelmsford had taken 3000 soldiers to meet the Zulu army, he had left at Isandhlwana 600 infantry of the 24th, 600 Native infantry, around 100 cavalry and 70 gunners, reinforced by Durnford's 340 Native cavalry. It seemed beyond belief that all 1,710 had been killed. Yet there was worse news for the soldiers at Rorke's Drift.

'There's two impis on their way here now,' said the NNC riders, both lieutenants. 'Three regiments. About one hour behind us.'

'How many men's that?' asked Chard.

'About four thousand five hundred. And they haven't been in battle yet.'

The two NNC officers rode on to warn Helpmakaar.

Although a Royal Engineer, Chard was three years senior to Bromhead and was in command at Rorke's Drift. He sent Private Wall and Reverend Smith of 'B' Company as lookouts up Oskarberg, a hill immediately south of and overlooking the mission station. Missionary Witt joined them. A third horseman arrived from Isandhlwana and confirmed the disaster.

Twenty-two thousand Zulus of King Cetawayo had attacked the British camp shortly before midday. Only 350 had escaped: five officers, six privates, and 340 Native troops and bullock drivers. The other 1,360 were all dead. The Zulus did not take prisoners. They slit open their enemy's bowels so that their 'spirit' could escape.

Zulu warriors were strong, formidable and relentless, the best in all Africa. Trained from childhood to be soldiers, the regiments of men and one of women were extremely fit, strictly disciplined, highly trained and tactically aware. They could cover fifty miles a day in a long relaxed lope then launch an attack at full sprint. Over broken country they were faster than a horse. Warriors hardened the soles of their bare feet by dancing on thorns. When they reached a river, a regiment simply linked arms and ran through and across the current. No warrior was allowed to marry until proven in battle – until he'd 'washed his spear' in his enemy's blood – giving the young regiments a certain edge to their fighting. Cetawayo had 40,000 of those magnificent soldiers.

Each warrior carried a short stabbing spear called an 'iklwa' – named after the sound it made when pulled out of an enemy's body. They also carried several long throwing spears called 'assegais', a club called a 'knobkerrie' and a large shield of hardened buffalo skin. Many used rifles as well. The impis on the way to Rorke's Drift had collected more rifles and ammunition from Isandhlwana.

Chard and Bromhead arranged their defences. They considered retreating to Helpmakaar, but with thirty-five sick and wounded to carry by bullock wagon, they would have been quickly overtaken by the Zulus and slaughtered in the open. Their only hope, small as it was, was to stand and defend the mission.

All tents were struck, fires doused and the cattle and bullocks herded into a stone kraal. The storehouse in the east was joined to the hospital in the west by two barricades of mealie sacks, ration boxes and two overturned wagons to make a rectangular compound. An inner cross-barricade was built south-to-north from the corner of the storehouse to the north wall. The work was heavy: each mealie sack weighed 200 lb and the lighter ration boxes 112 lb, the same as a sack of potatoes.

Colour Sergeant Bourne was a centre of calm and precision in the ant's nest of activity. The sick and wounded in the hospital were issued with rifles and ammunition. Firing holes were knocked through the outer walls of the hospital and storehouse, and the kraal at the eastern end was included into the defence perimeter.

At 3.30 p.m., welcome reinforcements of eighty mounted Natal Native soldiers arrived. They had been bringing up supply wagons behind Durnford's cavalry that morning but hadn't reached Isandhlwana when the Zulu army attacked. They'd seen the British camp overrun, abandoned their wagons and returned to Rorke's Drift. They were shaken men and their thoughts were very obvious: when 1,700 men had been defeated in less than two hours, what chance did their small garrison have?

However, with 104 British soldiers and twenty-one walking wounded, Stephenson's hundred NNC infantry and this bonus eighty cavalry, Chard and Bromhead had a force of more than 300 to defend the mission. They also knew that Zulus didn't like fighting against cavalry. The odds of surviving until relieved by Chelmsford's distant column had improved. Chard deployed the Natal cavalry as outriders to cover the Zulu approach.

From Oskarberg Hill, the lookouts saw the Zulu impis. Linking their arms, the Zulu regiments breasted the swollen Buffalo River and advanced on the mission. It was 4.10 p.m. As the lookouts stumbled down the hill, Private Wall gave one of the most memorable sighting reports of all time, yelling at the top of his voice: 'Here they come, black as hell and thick as grass!'

For Otto Witt it was time to leave, the massed Zulus spelling doom for his mission. He made off for Helpmakaar. The eighty Natal Native cavalry fired at the closest Zulus, then instead of riding back to the mission, deserted and fled. The soldiers building the barricades watched in anger as the horsemen disappeared, but worse was to follow.

Seeing the horsemen fleeing to the west, the hundred Native infantry also panicked. British soldiers tried to stop them with outstretched arms, but they climbed the barricades and ran for the track. When Captain Stephenson joined the wild scramble out of the mission it was too much for some of 'B' Company. They fired at the deserters, bringing down a sergeant. Chard and Bromhead were devastated, but in his report Chard merely noted dryly: 'About this time Captain Stephenson's detachment of the Natal Native Contingent left us, as did that officer himself.'

It was 4.20 p.m., the defenders had been reduced by two-thirds, and the battle had not yet begun. Remaining in the almost empty mission at Rorke's Drift were just 104 fit British soldiers with 35 in hospital, 14 of those bedridden. Encircling them were 4,500 Zulu warriors.

Eighty-seven of the British soldiers were of 'B' Company, 2nd Battalion, the 24th (2nd Warwickshires) Regiment of Foot, a Warwickshire and Welsh regiment – later the South Wales Borderers and now the Royal Regiment of Wales They wore uniforms of British red with green facings, white cross-belts, black trousers and short boots. There were forty-seven from other regiments and in hospital, wounded, Corporal Schiess of the NNC.

Lieutenant Chard saw at once that his perimeter would be too long for just a hundred men to defend. He decided to build an inner bastion to the north of the storehouse, a nine-foot-high square of mealie sacks with an inner firing step – a redoubt to which they could finally retreat. That had to wait. Private Hitch called down from his post on the storehouse roof: 'Four to six thousand Zulus advancing, sir!'

'Is that all?' Private Morris remarked dryly. The order 'Stand to' was given and there was no more time for comment. Fifteen wounded were brought from the hospital to reinforce the barricades, leaving six walking wounded inside.

The Undi Zulu regiments, commanded by King Cetawayo's brother Dabulamanzi, attacked at 4.30 p.m. It was seventy-five minutes since the news of Isandhlwana had arrived at Rorke's Drift.

Wave after wave of warriors launched themselves at the west corner of the hospital and along the north wall. Volleys, then independent fire from the single-round, breech-loading, Martini-Henry rifles swept the Zulu ranks time and again, but they still reached the barricade. There, the long bayonets fought the short iklwas, stabbing across the boxes and sacks. From the corner of the hospital Assistant-Commissary James Dalton, a crack shot, picked off Zulu after Zulu. Behind the single line of soldiers, the Reverend Smith hauled boxes of ammunition, leaving each soldier mounds of bullets on the boxes and sacks.

Meanwhile, from the trees and caves of Oskarberg Hill on the south side, Zulu riflemen fired down into the mission. It wasn't accurate fire, but every now and then a soldier was wounded or killed, until nearly a third of all British casualties were from these Zulu riflemen. It was unnerving, to fight in one direction with your back exposed to rifle fire from behind. Chard ordered soldiers at the south wall to fire at just below the puffs of rifle smoke on the hill.

Zulus broke over the north wall and were suddenly inside the compound, behind the redcoats. A reserve of Chard, Bromhead and a few privates tackled them with revolver, rifle and bayonet. Seeing the danger, Corporal Schiess hobbled out of the hospital on his crutch to join the inner battle. Orders were shouted, there were cries for help, screams of pain, desperate grunts; the Zulus were shot, spitted and forced back over the wall.

—255—

Commissary Dalton was shot in the shoulder and fell back. Schiess, now fighting at the long north wall, took another wound. Corporal Allen and Private Hitch, wounded earlier, left the storehouse medical post to continue the vital ammunition supply. Allen dragged the boxes, while Hitch left handfuls of bullets. Somehow, the defence held.

Inside the storehouse, using the former altar as an operating table, Surgeon Major Reynolds and his orderlies attended to the wounded and dying. Outside, Chard completed the final redoubt during respites in attacks on one wall or another.

Fresh waves of Zulu warriors now attacked the southern perimeter of hospital, wagons and storehouse. Bromhead led counter-attacks with rifle and bayonet. Some Zulus climbed onto the hospital roof and a skirmish took place on the thatch before they were driven off. Somehow the dry straw caught alight, perhaps from a rifle spark, perhaps lit intentionally by a Zulu.

At the western perimeter, at about 5.30 p.m., the Zulus finally broke into the hospital. That building was a series of whitewashed stone rooms, each with a single wooden door but no interconnecting doors. Above the beds, the fire in the thatch took hold, burning across the long roof and sending smoke swirling below. After killing several Zulu warriors in the western room, Private Joseph Williams was hacked to death. Private Horrigan and two patients were also killed.

With the hospital breached, Chard saw he must withdraw the western defenders to the inner cross-wall at the storehouse. Inside the hospital, the doors barricaded, the walking wounded retreated from room to room, crawling through holes made in the dividing walls by pickaxe and bayonet.

In the confined space, it was vicious hand-to-hand fighting: rifle, bayonet and fist against assegai and iklwa. Private Hook dispatched Zulu after Zulu with the bayonet, Private Robert Jones cut through the walls, William Jones and John Williams passed the patients through, from room to room. In one, a delirious soldier refused to leave and was speared to death. There were no officers, no NCOs, simply private soldiers organising and disciplining themselves, holding the Zulus at bay, removing their bedridden comrades from before the enemy.

From a high window in the eastern wall of the hospital, the patients were lowered into the main compound outside. The wounded Allen and Hitch went to help, carrying the patients across to the storehouse compound. A fourth patient was killed, but ten were brought to safety. By 6 p.m. all the British soldiers were back in the storehouse compound, the bedridden placed inside the mealie-bag redoubt.

The fire in the hospital roof had spread and the abandoned building was fully alight. The kraal on the eastern wall was abandoned as well. Sunset came and went, but the flames from the hospital blazed, giving the defenders of Rorke's Drift light to fight by.

The glow of that fire was seen by Chelmsford and his column, by then returned to Isandhlwana. It was also seen by Major Spalding as he marched up from Helpmakaar with the missing company. Spalding, aware of the defeat at Isandlhwana, thought the mission at Rorke's

Drift had been overwhelmed as well. Threatened by Zulus across his track, he returned to the town. Out in the dark veldt, Spalding and his men would have been ambushed and slaughtered, too.

Throughout the night at Rorke's Drift, assault after assault was made upon the storehouse compound. Zulu warriors came furiously out of the darkness again and again, the British desperately beating them back, refusing to be overrun – at least six major attacks were recorded. Chard, Bromhead and Bourne called the volleys. They steadied the tired men and distributed soldiers to whichever wall was weakest, but the number of wounded and dead was increasing and utter exhaustion was taking its toll. If the wounded could stand, their injuries were dressed by Reynolds and they returned to the barricades. Among those were Dalton, Schiess, Allen and Hitch, with Jones, Hook, Jones and Williams from the hospital.

The breeches of their rifles burned hot, literally dull red, blistering the soldiers' fingers as they reloaded and reloaded and reloaded. Bruised shoulders throbbed from the kicking recoil of the rifles while arms, back and stomach muscles ached from thrusting and pulling the bayonets.

At about midnight, a bayonet charge led by Chard into the main compound recovered the water cart which had been forgotten during the withdrawal. After more than eight hours of battle, still the attacks continued and still they were beaten back, until the Zulus had to clamber over their own dead and wounded to reach the barricades. The smell of death was appalling, like an abattoir, with the added smell of burning bodies from the hospital. From the redoubt, marksmen on the firing step supported weak spots along the barricades as well as targets at the edge of the firelight.

By early morning of the 23rd, the ferocity and number of the attacks gradually diminished. Sometime after 2 a.m., the Zulus took to firing out of the darkness and throwing assegais blindly into the storehouse compound. At 4 a.m., as the night paled, after eleven and a half hours of constant fighting, Dabulamanzi withdrew his Undi warriors from immediately around the mission.

As dawn lit the veldt, the defenders of Rorke's Drift stood at their barricades and saw for the first time the carnage around them. In every direction the ground was covered with mounds of dead Zulus, hundreds and hundreds of them: piled around the storehouse compound, across the main compound, in the kraal, around the smoking hospital, out into the scrub and scattered on Oskarberg Hill. Among them were thousands of weapons and shields. The defenders had fired some 20,000 bullets.

Chard would not let the men rest. He expected the attacks to continue, probably after the enemy had eaten. He knocked down the remains of the hospital so it couldn't be used as cover and stripped the thatch off the storehouse roof so that building couldn't be burned as well. He collected the abandoned Zulu weapons so they couldn't be used again and rebuilt the barricades and walls.

At 7 a.m., the Zulus reappeared. The tall, black warriors moved across the ground and grassy slopes around the mission. They paused briefly, stared at the red-coated soldiers, then turned away and forded the rift back to kwaZulu, to Zululand. They'd had enough.

In the main compound, colour Sergeant Bourne took the roll call. Seventeen men had died and sixteen been seriously wounded in the defence of Rorke's Drift. The exact number of Zulu dead is not known. It's certainly more than 600, perhaps as many as 800, with an equal number seriously wounded. After leaving Isandhlwana at first light, Chelmsford's column reached the mission at 8 a.m.

When the dead and wounded at Rorke's Drift were added to the 2,000 to 3,000 warriors killed at Isandhlwana, King Cetewayo remarked sadly: 'An assegai has been plunged into the belly of the Zulu nation.'

The Victoria Cross is the supreme medal of the armed forces. Made of bronze gunmetal from Russian cannon captured in the Crimean War, it is awarded only 'for valour and extreme courage beyond that expected of a British soldier in the face of the enemy'. In the 150 years since its inception, only 1,357 have been awarded. Eleven of those were for the defence of Rorke's Drift, against odds of forty-five to one.

They were awarded to Lieutenant John Merriott Chard, Royal Engineers; Lieutenant Gonville Bromhead, 2nd Battalion the 24th Regiment of Foot; Surgeon Major James Reynolds, Army Hospital

Corps; Assistant Commissary James Dalton, Army Commissariat; Corporal Christian Schiess, Natal Native Contingent; Corporal William Allen, 2nd Battalion the 24th Regiment of Foot; Privates Frederick Hitch, John Williams, Robert Jones, William Jones, Henry Hook, 2nd Battalion the 24th Regiment of Foot.

Distinguished Conduct Medals were awarded to colour Sergeant Frank Bourne, Reverend George 'Ammunition' Smith, Corporal Michael McMahan and Private John Roy, 2nd Battalion the 24th Regiment of Foot; Corporal Francis Atwood, Army Service Corps; John Cantwell, Royal Horse Artillery; and, posthumously, Assistant-Commissary Walter Dunne and Storekeeper Alexander Byrne, Army Commissariat. Frank Bourne died aged 91 on VE Day in 1945, the last surviving defender of Rorke's Drift. The unremarked lieutenants Chard and Bromhead were both promoted to major.

Queen Victoria called the defence of Rorke's Drift 'immortal'. It has become a military legend throughout the world.

Recommended
The Washing of the Spears by D.R. Morris.
Last Stand by Bryan Perrett.
Film: *Zulu*, Paramount, 1964.
The Royal Regiment of Wales Museum, Brecon, Wales.
Rorke's Drift, Natal, South Africa (The storehouse and re-built hospital remain).
Battle of Ulindi Memorial, Zululand, South Africa.

Winston Churchill

'The lecturer tonight is Mr Winston Churchill. By his father, he is an Englishman, by his mother an American. Behold the perfect man!'
— Mark Twain

Churchill is one name that has not been forgotten. With men like Marlborough and Wellington, he stands atop a pantheon of British, Commonwealth and Empire heroes and rarely a year goes by without a new book or television special on his life. For that reason, he nearly didn't make it into this book. Yet how can any list of heroes be complete without him? Long before he was Prime Minister, he had an extraordinary life, as a soldier, politician and writer. As a young man, he rode in one of the last cavalry charges with a sword and later he saw a nuclear bomb explode. There have been few lives in history to witness such changes. As importantly, he has come to represent a sense of stubborn Britishness, of indomitability and courage. His wit and intelligence were famous in his own lifetime, and when he died, the US ambassador said that he was 'the greatest apostle of freedom of the twentieth century. Foremost in courage, many-sided in genius.'

Churchill witnessed the end of the British Empire, seeing it battered and broken in a fight to the death against Nazi Germany. That final struggle justified the centuries of Empire, so that when the time came, there were men who could come home to fight: from Canada, Australia, New Zealand, America, India, Africa and anywhere else that felt kin to the mother country. As a result of that relationship and shared history, Hitler's Reich and his grandiose dreams died with him.

Winston Churchill was born prematurely in a bedroom at Blenheim Palace on 30 November 1874. By the time he was six, the Zulu war was being fought and young Winston thrilled to stories of Rorke's Drift. He made assegai spears out of fern stems and stalked the countryside with them.

He was a naughty child at school and earned numerous canings for his misdemeanours. He stole sugar from the school pantry and when he was punished, destroyed the headmaster's hat in revenge. He bore a grudge against that head for many years and when he was fully grown, returned to the school with the intention of birching the headmaster in front of the boys. To his disappointment, the man had died long before.

At thirteen, he went to Harrow school. His prodigious memory showed itself when he won the Headmaster's Prize for learning *twelve hundred* lines of Macaulay's *Lays of Ancient Rome* by heart. He was never particularly skilful on the sports field, but he devoured books, soaking up information at a terrific rate and creating the beginnings of an extraordinary general knowledge. At home, he played with his vast collection of toy soldiers. When his father asked him if he wanted to join the army, Winston was overjoyed. It was many years before he discovered his father had believed him unsuitable for anything else.

At Harrow, he also learned to box and fence, winning the public schools fencing championship of 1892. With his father's colleagues often in attendance at home, young Winston took a keen interest in politics from an early age. His views were Conservative and he enjoyed lively debates, while often taking the time to sit in the gallery at the House of Commons. When one of his father's friends learned that Winston had heard a speech he had made, he asked the boy what he had thought. With characteristic bluntness, Winston replied: 'I concluded from it, sir, that the Ship of State is struggling in heavy seas.'

He left Harrow and scraped into the Royal Military College at Sandhurst, where he appears to have matured almost overnight. He delighted in all things military and threw himself into learning everything he could. At the same time, his father became seriously ill. Winston and his brother John met him for the last time a month before his death in 1895.

In spring, Churchill became a subaltern in the 4th Hussars. He was keen to see active service and used his leave to persuade a newspaper to appoint him to report on a revolt against Spanish rule in Cuba. Before he left home, Churchill gave a dinner party for those 'who are yet under twenty-one years of age, but who in twenty years, will control the destinies of the British Empire'. He may have meant the other diners; he certainly meant himself.

In Cuba, Churchill saw his first fighting and took part in repulsing Cuban rebels, writing about his experiences in letters to the newspaper for which he was paid five pounds a time. For his service, the Spanish authorities awarded him the Order of Military Merit, first class. He returned to his own regiment in 1896 as his leave ended and was sent to India on a tour of duty.

British India was a strange place in those far-off days. Churchill was introduced to the parades, the heat, polo and boredom. It was a far from exciting life and it wore on him. At only 21, he wanted to see action and perhaps earn some of the glory his ancestors had won for themselves.

In 1897, when a British garrison was besieged in Afghanistan, Churchill volunteered to join punitive expeditions in Afghanistan against the Mohmand tribes of Bajaur. He found little excitement until he joined a squadron of Bengal Lancers and fought with them against the tribesmen. Churchill was mentioned in dispatches for his courage, though he was officially a non-combatant. When his leave expired, he had to return to India, where he wrote a book on the campaign.

He was regarded by his superiors as a young man in a hurry, a 'medal-snatcher' and a nuisance. Churchill tried to find action on every leave, or returned home to apply influence with those who could send him to conflicts. He was baulked by

Lord Kitchener, who disliked his brash self-confidence and refused to allow Churchill to take part in an expedition in Egypt against Arab forces. Kitchener's powers in Egypt did not extend to the 21st Lancers, however, and Churchill managed to persuade General Evelyn Wood VC to send him out to them with the condition that if he was killed, he would pay his own funeral expenses. He became a correspondent for the *Morning Post* newspaper before he went to Cairo.

Kitchener was disgusted that the young soldier had come despite his wishes and put Churchill in charge of lame horses, following the main force as they trekked into the Sudan. However, it would be Churchill who spotted the army of 60,000 Arab Dervishes when he rode out to reconnoitre an area. He galloped back to tell Kitchener.

The main charge of what would become known as the Battle of Omdurman occurred later in the day, when 400 Lancers, Churchill among them, attacked a vastly superior force. They crashed through the enemy and Churchill emerged unscathed from his first major battle. He then turned back to rescue fallen men.

He returned to England as a successful author and journalist, though that reputation had only come about from his desire to see battle. In 1898, he also expressed the ambition to follow his father in a political career. At the same time, the *Daily Mail* published a piece on him as one of the most promising young men of the day. With surprisingly accurate foresight, the war correspondent wrote: 'there will hardly be room for him in Parliament at thirty or in England at forty.'

However, before he began his political career, Churchill returned to India to take part in the regimental polo tournament. His team won and he scored three of the goals, despite his right shoulder being torn from an old injury. With that done, he resigned his commission and completed his book on the Kitchener campaign, *The River War*.

In June 1899, Churchill fought his first election for Oldham. His speeches against his opponents had the wit and verve that would become his hallmark. When his opponent, Mr Runciman, mentioned disdainfully that he had not been a swashbuckler as Churchill had, Churchill replied:

'The difference between Mr Runciman and the Lancashire Fusiliers is that, while they were fighting at Omdurman for their country, he was fighting at Gravesend for himself. And another difference between them is that, while the Fusiliers were gaining a victory, Mr Runciman at Gravesend was being defeated.'

Nonetheless, Mr Runciman won the election, though Churchill was not particularly disheartened. The Boer War had broken out in South Africa and he arranged to act as a war correspondent once more, travelling to Cape Town in the autumn of 1899. It would be the scene of some of his greatest adventures.

The city of Ladysmith was under siege by the Boers when Churchill joined other war correspondents and the main army. He met an old friend near the city and was invited to join a regular patrol that used an armoured train to survive the Boer snipers. The train was ambushed when Boers opened up on it with two field pieces and a Maxim machine gun. The driver put on full speed and the train struck a rock the Boers had laid on the tracks. The engine was in the middle of the train, with trucks before and behind. In the impact, the front three trucks were derailed and overturned. Churchill climbed out of the wreckage as the Boers opened fire on the helpless train. He ran to inspect the damage and found the driver about to run for it. As the man had already been shot, Churchill assured him 'no man is hit twice on the same day' and steadied his nerves.

Churchill then ran back to report that the train could be saved if the front trucks were dragged out of the way by the engine. He took command of the entire operation, with bullets whistling around him. Under his orders, the driver uncoupled the rear trucks and then dragged free the one blocking the line ahead. Churchill called for volunteers as the Boer fire increased and nine men helped him shove the truck off the rails. The truck jammed while still on the line and Churchill told the driver to ram it clear. By that time, the Boers had brought up their heavy guns and shells were bursting against the side of the train. In a final surge of power, the wrecked truck crunched aside.

Churchill ordered the men to push the rear trucks up to the engine, but the storm of Boer fire made it impossible. In the end, they brought their wounded onto the engine itself and Churchill told the driver to get clear, riding with him before jumping off and running back.

It was too late to save the other men. The Boers had forced them to surrender. As he lay watching, Churchill himself was captured by a Boer horseman and made a prisoner.

One of the wounded men later wrote to his mother, saying: 'If it hadn't been for Churchill, not one of us would have escaped.' It was also said that if Churchill had been a regular soldier, he would have received the Victoria Cross.

Interestingly, when Churchill later met the Prime Minister of South Africa, General Botha, Churchill told him the story. Botha replied: 'So you were the man? I was the Boer on the horse.'

Churchill was held in Pretoria, with sixty other British prisoners. His captivity was not particularly harsh and he was able to read and plan an escape. Two separate plans were abandoned and on the third attempt, Churchill climbed onto the top of the prison wall and had to wait in agonised silence while guards walked just feet away. His companions had a compass, maps and food, while Churchill had just four bars of chocolate in his pocket. He waited until one of them shouted a mixture of English and Latin, letting him know the guards were watching and they could not follow. He was on his own. He could have gone back and waited for a better chance, but that was not in his character. He climbed down the outer wall and strolled past the sentry, who assumed he had every right to be there. Churchill was in Pretoria and free, but in enemy territory and without being able to speak a word of Dutch.

He found the railway tracks and in darkness waited at a curve in the line where trains would slow, then jumped aboard an open truck as it passed. He jumped off before dawn and began life as a hunted fugitive.

'Wanted' posters went up all over South Africa and Boer newspapers were full of the escape. Meanwhile, Churchill hid by day and walked the train tracks at night, heading to the neutral frontier with Portuguese territory. For weeks he lived on whatever he could find or steal, and almost starved to death. In desperation, he knocked on the door of a lonely house and, by incredible good fortune, found it owned by an Englishman, Mr Howard.

Howard said later: 'I never saw a man with the grit that Churchill has. He simply fears nothing.'

Howard and a friend gave Churchill food and a revolver and hid him in a local mine for a time before finally smuggling him onto another train, under a tarpaulin. When Churchill saw he had passed the frontier at last, he threw off the tarpaulin, stood up, fired his pistol and shouted: 'I'm free! I'm Winston bloody Churchill and I'm free!'

Of this part of his life, he said later: 'I should not have been caught. But if I had not been caught, I could not have escaped and my imprisonment and escape provided me with materials for lectures and a book which brought me in enough money to get into Parliament in 1900.'

His second attempt to become a Conservative MP was a success and he made his maiden speech in 1901. It was not long before he fell out with his party and 'crossed the floor' of Parliament to join the Liberals in 1904. A year later, he was appointed to government office as Under-Secretary for the Colonies and was promoted to the Cabinet in 1908 under Prime Minister Asquith.

From the beginning, Churchill was fast on his feet in debate. He was often witty and, with his extraordinary memory, always able to answer any question with authority. In Asquith's government, he brought in laws forbidding boys under 14 from working in mines and with David Lloyd George, then Chancellor of the Exchequer, created the National Insurance scheme. Churchill was promoted again in 1910 to the Home Office, one of the most powerful positions in government. His self-confidence and energy seemed limitless. He said once that he felt 'as if I could lift the whole world on my shoulders.'

In 1911, Churchill became First Lord of the Admiralty and did vital work refitting an obsolete navy to answer the threat of Germany in World War I. He supported the creation of new battlecruisers and submarines as well as founding the Royal Naval Air Service. In that same year, he was involved in the famous 'Sidney Street Siege', which involved a group of armed anarchists determined to fight to the death against police in London's East End. Policemen had already been shot and killed by the time Churchill was informed. He went to the scene and authorised the deployment of Scots Guards and *a field gun* to support the police. One bullet passed through Churchill's hat while he observed. Before the big gun arrived, the building was on fire and Churchill forbade the fire department to enter the building. The authorities waited for the gang to come out through the flames, but they stayed and died inside.

Churchill's handling of the armed gang was controversial, but did little to damage his reputation as a man of action as well as politics. His calm demeanour under fire was reported across the country. After the siege, a colleague enquired: 'What the hell have you been doing now, Winston?' He replied: 'Now, Charlie, don't be cross. It was such fun!'

When World War I broke out in 1914, Churchill had brought the fleet to full war footing. He did well in organising the relief of the Falkland Islands from a German naval squadron. However, when an assault on the Dardanelles failed, Churchill was made the scapegoat and left the Admiralty. In self-imposed exile, he travelled to the trenches of Flanders and commanded the 6th Battalion of the Royal Scots Fusiliers. In 1917, he was asked to return and became Minister for Munitions, then Secretary of State for War and Air.

After the Great War, Lloyd George was the Liberal Prime Minister. In 1921, he arranged to meet Eamon de Valera to discuss Irish independence from Britain. Northern Ireland wanted to remain British and later fought with the rest of the United Kingdom in World War II.

De Valera suspected the eventual deal would not reflect well on him and sent Michael Collins to negotiate on his behalf. Lloyd George and Churchill brokered the deal, two of the most cunning and intelligent men in politics. Collins was out of his depth from the beginning. The partition between Northern and Southern Ireland was confirmed and

Ireland given Dominion status. Collins had signed his own death warrant. He was later killed by Irish Nationalists, while the 'old fox', De Valera, went on to be President of Ireland.

Lloyd George's coalition government collapsed in 1922, leaving Churchill without office or a seat in Parliament. Undeterred, he rejoined the Conservative Party in 1924 and became Chancellor of the Exchequer under Stanley Baldwin. He presented five budgets as Chancellor up to 1929, when another general election brought Labour to power.

That was the beginning of a very low period in Churchill's life. Over the next decade, he was almost completely alone in warning of the dangers of Hitler's Germany. His belief that Britain was unprepared for the inevitable conflict flew in the face of government opinion and he was considered an excitable warmonger. Still, he remained at the centre of power and in 1936 helped draft the abdication speech of King Edward VIII.

Prime Minister Neville Chamberlain famously returned from meeting Hitler in 1938, with the promise that he had delivered 'peace in our time'. When war broke out in 1939, Churchill returned to the Admiralty and the ships at sea signalled 'Winston's back'. Chamberlain resigned and Churchill formed a coalition government in May 1940 to lead Britain in the war against Nazi Germany. His first speech as Prime Minister would include one of his most famous phrases: 'I have nothing to offer but blood, toil, tears and sweat.'

Bearing in mind his previous association with Ireland, it is interesting to note that during World War II, Churchill offered to give up British rule of Northern Ireland if the Irish would allow his ships and subs to use their ports. De Valera refused the offer, believing at the time that Germany would win.

The first years of the war were brutal for British forces. Churchill made his feelings clear when he said: 'What is our policy? I will say: To wage war, by sea, land and air, with all our might and with all the strength that God can give us … What is our aim? I can answer in one word: Victory – victory at all costs, victory in spite of all terror, victory, however long and hard the road may be; for without victory, there is no survival.'

Throughout 1940, German armies seemed unstoppable. France fell incredibly quickly, prompting Churchill to comment: 'The Battle of France is over. I expect the Battle of Britain is about to begin...'

Holland and Belgium fell to Hitler's invasion forces and only by extraordinary exertions had the British Expeditionary Force been rescued from Dunkirk. Churchill uttered what may be his most famous words then: 'We shall defend our island, whatever the cost may be, we shall fight on the beaches, we shall fight on the landing grounds, we shall fight in the fields and in the streets, we shall fight in the hills; we shall never surrender.'

The Battle of Britain secured air superiority in 1940, but it was almost the only moment of hope in the first, disastrous years. Churchill held the nation together when all looked dark, but it was more than inspired oratory. He travelled all over the country to lift the spirits of the beleaguered people. At the same time, he was the overall commander of British Empire forces and took an interest in every tiny detail.

In 1941, Germany invaded Russia and Japan attacked America. Churchill had his grand alliance that would defeat Hitler and the beginning of the special relationship with America that survives today.

The fighting was brutal and British possessions of Hong Kong, Singapore and Burma were lost to the Japanese. Churchill organised massive bombing raids against Germany in retaliation for the Blitz on London. At the same time, in North Africa, he removed men from command until he found one who could bring victory against Rommel's Afrika Corps: General Montgomery.

After the vital battle of El Alamein in North Africa, Churchill said: 'Now this is not the end. It is not even the beginning of the end. But it is, perhaps, the end of the beginning.'

Churchill met Stalin and Roosevelt in a 'Three Power' conference in 1943. The tide of the war was turning and Allied forces entered Rome in 1944, hoisting the first Union flag over an enemy capital. That flag was given to Churchill and hangs from a beam at his home in Kent.

The invasion of Europe from Britain in the Normandy landings was the beginning of the end for Nazi Germany. Every foot had to be taken back by force and the death toll for Allied armies was huge. In support, Stalin overran Eastern Germany and Eastern Europe, creating what would become the Soviet bloc of countries for the next eighty years.

Mussolini was executed by his own people in April 1945 and Hitler committed suicide in his bunker two days later. German troops throughout Europe surrendered on 7 May 1945. The following day, Churchill joined the royal family on the balcony at Buckingham Palace, acclaimed as the architect of the great victory.

Britain had endured years of war and come close to the brink of utter annihilation as a nation. At the same time, immense social forces were at work and after the victory, the voters were desperate for change. In the general election of 1945, Churchill's war government was thrown out and Labour came in.

Churchill took the defeat in the polls badly at first, but he was 71 years old and needed a rest. As well as painting, horse-riding and writing, he enjoyed building brick walls, finding the work peaceful. In the Commons, he warned of an 'iron curtain' descending over the west. As with Hitler's Germany, Churchill was one of the few with the vision to see the danger of a new and aggressive Soviet Union.

In 1951, the Conservative Party was returned to power. Labour had endured a tempestuous term, nationalising industries and continuing food rationing long after the need for it had passed. As Prime Minister for the second time, Churchill enjoyed a rise in national prosperity. Queen Elizabeth II was crowned in 1953 and the country began to leave the dark years of the war behind.

Shortly afterwards, Churchill's health deteriorated. He suffered a serious stroke and, though he recovered, decided to resign in 1955. The Queen offered to make him a duke for his service, but he preferred to remain in the Commons until the end. After retirement, honours flooded in, including a Nobel prize and honorary citizenship of the USA in 1963. He spent his final years in peace, in the south of France as well as England.

Winston Churchill died in his London home in 1965, so far from the years of his birth that it is easy to forget he was a Victorian and saw the end of Empire. At the express wish of the Queen, he was accorded the honour of a lying-in-state and a state funeral, before being buried at Bladon, near Blenheim.

In all of British history, there are few lives that accomplished so much. He supported the morale of British people through the darkest years and defined the nation's spirit in his speeches and books as he crossed from the Victorian Empire to the twentieth century.

'I now put Churchill, with all his idiosyncrasies, his indulgences, his occasional childishness, but also his genius, his tenacity and his persistent ability, right or wrong, successful or unsuccessful, to be larger than life, as the greatest human being ever to occupy 10 Downing Street.'
— Roy Jenkins

Recommended
Winston Churchill by C. Bechhofer Roberts.
Sir Winston Churchill: A Memorial edited by Frederick Towers.
The Wit of Winston Churchill by Geoffrey Willans and Charles Roetter.
A History of the English-Speaking Peoples by Winston Churchill himself.

James Brooke
Rajah of Sarawak

James Brooke was born in 1803, the fifth child to an English father and Scottish mother living in India. His father worked for the East India Company as a judge. James remained in India until he was 12 and saw the height of Company rule. His life is one of those that only the Empire could have produced: a combination of comic amateurism, wild courage and fervent self-belief that led to his own kingdom and a place in history.

At 12, James had his first glimpse of England. He stayed at his grandmother's house in Reigate and boarded at Norwich Grammar School. It was a shock to the young Company child, but from an early stage, James acted as a leader among the boys of the school. His 'muscular Christianity' was also important and he became well known for never telling a lie or denying his involvement in some of the trouble schoolboys will find for themselves. At 14, he heard a friend of his had gone to sea as a midshipman and James too decided to run away. He was later discovered on the grounds of his grandmother's house. By then his parents had arrived back from India and for the rest of his time in England, he lived with them and was taught by a tutor.

Aged 16, James went back to the India he had known as a boy. Like Robert Clive before and Garnet Wolseley after him, Brooke was commissioned into the Company as an ensign.

The first major action of Brooke's life came in the war against Burma in 1824. As a young lieutenant, he volunteered to raise a troop and scouted ahead for Lord Amherst's army. In 1825, fearless and 22, Brooke led from the front and routed a Burmese force. He was mentioned in dispatches for his valour. His second battle came just a few days later and he was wounded and left for dead. With the fighting over, his colonel recovered his body and Brooke revived. He was sent to England to convalesce and given a wound pension.

The wound is worth mentioning as some biographers believe it may have been a musket ball in his genitals. If so, it would explain why Brooke remained a bachelor all his life and devoted his energies along different paths. This is a common view, but he later accepted a man named Reuben George Walker as his son, which tends to imply that he was not incapable of making one. The wound could just as easily have been in his thigh or even his lung. Brooke never spoke of it and the exact truth can never be known.

He spent four years on leave before returning to India. The ship he took was wrecked off the Isle of Wight, costing him his kit. One rule of the Company was that more than five years' absence meant his commission would be revoked, so he had to try again. By the time he arrived at Madras, he had only twelve days to reach Calcutta before he would be stripped of his rank. It was impossible. He tried to get employment in a Company office in Madras, hoping that would do, but they told him there was no work available. In a fury, Brooke resigned from the Company.

Brooke was angry enough to question the entire theory of colonial rule as a benign force. He read the history of Sir Stamford Raffles and sympathised with another who had been badly used by John Company. With all ties cut, Brooke took passage on the *Castle Huntley*, with few possessions to his name. He wrote of this time: 'I toss my cap into the air, my commission into the sea and bid farewell to John Company and all its evil ways.'

When he returned to England, Brooke was left with no path or purpose for a time. He toyed with the idea of investing in a schooner and taking it out to the East himself. He was always a man of vast enthusiasms, a dreamer who would talk one day of taking a whaling ship to Greenland, then South America or Australia the next. He was 29 and past the first flush of youth, but he had an enduring, boyish charisma that impressed all those who met him. He wanted to do *something* with his life, but he did not know what it would be.

In 1834, he met Angela Burdett-Coutts, an heiress. She fell madly in love with the young Brooke. Perhaps his wound made it impossible to marry, but it is more likely that he preferred travel and adventure to a staid life in England.

In 1835, his father died, leaving him £30,000. Brooke used the money to buy a schooner, the *Royalist*. At the age of 32, he worked hard with charts and books about the Indian Archipelago, throwing himself into the preparations. He became intrigued by what he learned of Borneo, at that time an island of pirates and mystery. Some of it had been under British or Dutch control, but European attempts to settle the land had failed.

It was Brooke's intention to take Borneo for Britain just as gentlemen adventurers of the Elizabethan age had once founded colonies. His self-confidence was extraordinary and he took the *Royalist* to Singapore, arriving in May 1838.

At that time, the British colony of Singapore was just twenty years old. Brooke found the officials there helpful, if misinformed. From them, he learned that the Borneo pirates had gone and much of the island was now under the rule of the Rajah Muda Hassim. He set sail with high hopes. In fact, two main centres of piracy – Sulu, a Philippine island, and the Sultanate of Brunei – were still extremely active. With a cargo hold full of presents of silk, gunpowder, sweets and children's toys, Brooke was sailing into a hornet's nest and terrible danger.

He sighted Borneo on 1 August. He spent time surveying the tiny islands around the coast, enjoying the sights of monkeys, turtles, coconuts and white beaches. He took the *Royalist* up the Sarawak River (pronounced with a silent 'k') to Hassim's village of Kuching. As he endured elaborate ceremonies of welcome, Brooke discovered that Sarawak was little more than the living quarters of miners working to retrieve antimony from the ground, an industrial chemical. He found the shabby collection of wooden houses and visible poverty rather depressing. Hassim questioned him closely about the relative power of England and Holland, without mentioning that he was a representative of Brunei and really needed to know which one his master the Sultan should support.

Shortly afterwards, Brooke met his first native Dyaks, the fabled head-hunters of Borneo. He was fascinated by everything and though a civil war between Malays and Dyaks was in process, Brooke's presence was welcomed in all quarters. He left Sarawak with regret, firing his guns in salute as the Rajah fired his own. He was then promptly attacked by Dyak pirates and, after fighting them off, had to return to Sarawak to have his wounded men seen to.

Brooke sailed the *Royalist* on a tour of the area, seeing Sumatra and Borneo's east coast as well as Manila. His funds were running low and it looked as if his time there was coming to an end. He returned to Sarawak to make his farewells and discovered the same civil war still going on. Hassim begged him to stay and promised that victory was very close. It wasn't.

Brooke found the local pace of war difficult to fathom. For Hassim, he agreed to command a force of poorly armed Malays, Chinese and Dyaks against a similar enemy. Brooke offered to lead them against an enemy fort, which caused much excitement and argument before they eventually refused. Local battles usually began with name-calling and insults that went on all day, so no fighting actually occurred. When one of Brooke's men proposed building a fort in a tree to shoot into an enemy camp, the native soldiers objected, saying that the tree might be cut down in revenge.

Brooke lost patience with this farcical lack of activity. He told Hassim he was going home and it was then that the Rajah offered Sarawak to him, if he did not desert his ally in his hour of need. It was too good to turn down. Brooke wrote to his mother: 'Do not start when I say that I am going to settle in Borneo, that I am about to endeavour to plant here a mixed colony, amid a wild but not unvirtuous race...'

He returned to the little war with renewed enthusiasm. He was still unable to make his mixed army do anything, so in the end it fell to his small English crew to charge the enemy fort in the middle of the name-calling. The rebels were so surprised, they fled without a shot being fired and a few days later sent word to Brooke to discuss peace. He was forced to shoot at his own men to prevent them from killing the enemy leaders and worked hard to make them understand that he would not allow reprisal attacks against them.

Rajah Hassim was reluctant to follow through on his promise to hand over Sarawak. He offered to build a house for Brooke and deliver the antimony ore. Brooke accepted his word of honour and sailed to Singapore to collect the supplies he would need to rule.

He returned to find no house and more promises. Brooke remained patient for a long time, suffering through the political games, but always demanding what he had been promised. It took the presence of the Royalist with guns aimed at the Rajah's own house to secure final agreement. In September 1841, Brooke became the Rajah of Sarawak. Both Holland and Britain were appalled at what he had taken on.

At last, Brooke had a chance to fulfil his grand dreams. He created a code of laws, allowing free trade and forbidding murder, robbery and attacks on the Dyak tribes. He imposed peace on all the tribes and began to arrange the system of weights and measures as well as the rate of tax he would impose. In later eras, he has been held up as an example of the colonial exploiter, but the fact is that Sarawak had no wealth to speak of. Brooke was instead one of those Victorians who genuinely believed they could improve the lives of 'simple savages' with a bit of order and civilisation. As he wrote at the time: 'The Sultan [of Brunei] and his chiefs rob all classes of Malays to the utmost of their power. The Malays rob the Dyaks and the Dyaks hide their goods as much as they dare.'

His first act as governor was to free Malay women and children held as prisoners. With their families returned, the Malays came back to Kuching and the population grew at an alarming rate. Brooke appointed himself as judge and held a court every day for the next six months, ruling on native disputes and allowing local people to watch. He made a point of giving equal justice to all, regardless of their race or status. As a result, his territory came to be seen as a safe place, where law and order could be trusted.

His private funds dwindled almost to nothing and he wrote to his mother and sisters, asking for materials to help educate the people he ruled. An uneasy peace was maintained while everyone waited for the 'white Rajah' to make a mistake.

In July 1842, Brooke took the *Royalist* to visit the Sultan of Brunei along the coast. Omar Ali was the uncle of the man Brooke had replaced as ruler of Sarawak. From Hassim, Brooke had heard much of the power and wealth of Brunei and was very disappointed, describing it as 'a very Venice of hovels', and 'fit only for frogs'.

The Sultan greeted Brooke with great friendliness and approved his rule of Sarawak, especially as the original agreement had guaranteed a yearly payment to Brunei.

Brooke hoped for a knighthood at home, or even that Sarawak would become a British protectorate. He had only sixteen Britons with him and though they were fanatically loyal, there was only so much they could do. After the Sultan's official approval, the story of the White Rajah was beginning to become known in England, an unusual tale even for those days. Brooke sailed again to Singapore to appeal to the governor there for support. He met a Royal Navy captain named Keppel who was very interested in the talk of pirate fleets, not least because he would receive prize money for any he captured. Even without the financial incentive, it is another example of Brooke's unusual charisma that Keppel agreed to come to Borneo. Keppel took up the cause with great determination, sending out armed boats to seize and destroy dozens of pirate vessels.

A surveying ship came out from England and Brooke charmed the crew and captain, providing houses for them on shore while the work went on. The Sultan of Brunei showed his continuing support by signing another piece of paper that deeded Sarawak to him in perpetuity. However, there was still little wealth in Borneo and Brooke did not receive the aid he desired from his own government.

Captain Keppel was eventually called back to England and in his place, Brooke dealt with Sir Edward Belcher, a surveyor and pirate hunter around Borneo. Belcher agreed to transport Hassim to his uncle in Brunei, removing his influence from Sarawak under the guise of sending him as an advisor to the Sultan. Brooke's other plan was to have part of Borneo given to England in exchange for naval defence against pirates. The Sultan agreed. The population of Sarawak had increased to five thousand families, trade was increasing and Britain looked set to make it a protectorate. Keppel had done well keeping the pirates away, but Brooke knew he really needed a dedicated warship for those waters.

In 1845, he got part of his wish and the British government appointed him 'Temporary Confidential Agent in Borneo', a peculiar title that suited his peculiar status. Brooke travelled often from Brunei to Singapore, where he met Admiral Sir Thomas Cochrane, one man who knew the value of a warship along a coast. Coal had been discovered in Borneo and suddenly the land was valuable.

A short civil war flared up in Brunei and Hassim was murdered along with his family. Brooke was enraged, taking comfort only from the fact that Britain must respond to those she had declared allies. For once, he was not disappointed and Cochrane sent six Royal Navy ships with one from John Company. They made haste for Brunei and the Sultan fled. He eventually asked for peace talks and formally ceded the province of Labuan up the coast to the British on Christmas Eve 1846. Sarawak, however, remained Brooke's private domain.

Brooke's journal had been edited by Keppel and published in England. He was famous at last and if there was ever a point where he could push for more support, funds, men and supplies, that was it. Also, by the time the squadron of ships moved on to China, Borneo was very quiet indeed. Brooke took the opportunity to return home, nine years after leaving.

He was presented with the freedom of the city of London, met Queen Victoria and had his portrait painted. He was also made official governor of the new territory of Labuan. More importantly to Brooke, he raised a small fortune to send a mission to Borneo. Though a Christian himself, Brooke never seemed interested in converting the natives, only that they be well cared for. However, mission money flowed fastest in Victorian England.

He also gathered companions and supporters, young men who were impressed by his zeal and wanted the sort of schoolboy adventures he had experienced. As a paternal figure, Brooke had the same touch as Nelson and Cook, in that many men were willing to follow him. On his return to Sarawak with Keppel, he took a new group of adventurers.

Brooke received news of a knighthood while in Singapore and returned triumphant to Sarawak in 1848, still vital at the age of 45. The natives were delighted to see the White Rajah return and his new recruits were impressed by all the beating of drums and gongs as well as a river lit with lamps in his honour. The mission centre was built quickly and he had brought a doctor from England to tend to native ailments. He also brought his nephew Johnny to train as the next Rajah. To that end, Johnny changed his surname to Brooke as well. With British recognition and support, there could be no question of a foreign nation deciding to steal away his lands. James Brooke's troubles appeared to be over.

In England, things were not going as well. Under British law, battles with pirates earned a bounty. The Borneo total came to £30,000, a large enough sum to cause great argument in the House of Commons. The fact that it went to the navy captains and crews was not enough to protect Brooke from accusations of being a bloodthirsty empire builder. Public debates were held over the 'Borneo atrocities' – this despite the fact that the Admiralty themselves had sent ships to combat the ruthless pirates of the area.

Brooke was deeply wounded by the treatment he received. Sarawak was thriving and at peace for the first time in years, making the accusations all the more ludicrous. All he could do was write to friends and supporters. He knew he had treated prisoners kindly and sent them home when others would have hanged them. He pointed out that far from being a fortune hunter, he was £10,000 out of pocket in his expenditure on Sarawak. Despite his letters, there were more than a few willing to believe the worst and he was told there would be an official inquiry. To add to his troubles, he also suffered a bout of smallpox and never fully recovered from the disease.

The inquiry was held in Singapore and was a farce from the beginning. One of the two commissioners later went insane. Brooke defended himself well and had others to speak for him, even a Dutch civil servant who described the ferocity of pirates in the area. During the days of questioning, Brooke grew tired of the accusation that he could not run Sarawak and Labuan at the same time, so resigned as governor of Labuan. In the end, he was finally cleared of any wrongdoing and returned to Sarawak.

The years that followed were generally happy ones, though smallpox and malaria had taken some of his wild energy. Sarawak was prosperous and thriving, a very different place from the collection of wooden huts he had found on his first visit.

In 1856, as war broke out between China and Britain over trade, the Chinese commissioner in Canton offered thirty dollars for the head of every Englishman. Shortly afterwards, in 1857, the Chinese in Sarawak burned Government House in Kuching. Many young Britons were murdered in the attack, some of them children. Brooke's men were driven back, but he organised a small party and retook Sarawak. That time, there really was a great slaughter and Brooke didn't mind a bit. He was getting old, but his nephew had brought out his wife and Brooke felt that he should not be there to peer over the younger man's shoulder at every moment. He considered retirement at last.

Shortly after he returned to England, a young man named Reuben George came to Brooke, claiming to be his son after an affair in Bath some twenty-five years before. That puts it later than the mysterious injury, but Brooke accepted him as his own. Brooke's family and heirs were appalled and feared he was being fooled, but Brooke was a good-hearted man and remained innocent in some respects to his dying day. We can never now be certain whether Reuben George was his son, but

Brooke believed it and would never have blamed another man for an unfortunate birth beyond his control.

Brooke sent Reuben George out to Sarawak, which caused great consternation in the family of his heir and nephew. Brooke also altered his will to give Reuben a small income after his death, though his nephew would still inherit Sarawak.

At the same time, Brooke re-established his friendship with Angela Burdett-Coutts. He worked harder than ever to have Britain take on Sarawak as a protectorate, but then suffered a stroke. He recovered very slowly and a public subscription brought in enough for him to purchase a small house on Dartmoor in Devon. His health improved with horse riding and walking.

Before his death, Brooke returned to Sarawak twice more. His heir died before him, so Brooke passed Sarawak to Charles, his nephew's son. After another stroke, James Brooke died in June 1868, at the age of 65.

Sarawak today is a prosperous state in Malaysia. Kuching is still its capital and the region has a population of 1.5 million. James Brooke would be proud.

Recommended
James Brooke of Sarawak by Emily Hahn.
White Rajah by Nigel Barley.
Flashman's Lady by George MacDonald Fraser, in which Brooke and Borneo feature.

Gertrude Bell
'Al-khatun'

'He is crazed with the spell of far Arabia,
They have stolen his wits away.'

– Walter de la Mare

Gertrude Margaret Bell was, by the end of the 1914–18 war, one of the most powerful women in the world. Mountaineer, archaeologist, historian, writer, photographer, translator and curator, she helped draw the modern map of the Middle East after seven centuries of Turkish rule. Establishing a free, independent nation when the occupying power has been removed is perhaps the greatest challenge of modern diplomacy, and Bell devoted her later life to the creation of modern Iraq.

She was born in County Durham in 1868. At three, her mother died of pneumonia, and her father married social campaigner Florence Olliffe. Gertrude was educated at home and later in London. There she lived with her step-mother and met a number of archaeologists, Middle Eastern diplomats, politicians and writers.

A brilliant scholar, Gertrude went up to Lady Margaret Hall at Oxford to study history and became the first woman to graduate with first-class honours. Slim, red-haired, personable, independent and free-thinking, she was not greatly interested in 'society' and began travelling. After visits to Romania and Constantinople (Istanbul), she decided to visit Persia (Iran), where her step-uncle was ambassador. For six months she taught herself Persian and in 1892 journeyed by train to Teheran.

In ancient Persia she fell in love with embassy secretary Henry Cadogan. He introduced her to the desert, to the mountains, to the rivers, to exotic Persia itself, and asked her to marry him. However, her father saw no future for the unknown secretary and refused permission. She returned to Britain in 1894, determined to change his mind. At home Bell wrote her first book, *Persian Pictures*, about her experiences there. She was studying Arabic for her return to the Middle East when a telegram arrived from Teheran. Her fiancée had died of pneumonia. Bell spent two years translating *Poems from the Divan of Hafiz* from the Persian, a tribute to her lost love. It remains still one of the best translations.

In sadness, Bell immersed herself in adventure. She journeyed twice around the world, instructed herself in archaeology, visited Jerusalem and became the foremost woman mountaineer of Britain and Europe. She climbed the Alps and achieved moderate fame in 1902 for hanging on a rope for fifty-three hours when trapped by a blizzard.

Her interest in archaeology and Arabia increased together. She visited the ancient cities – Petra, Palmyra, Baalbeck – and inspected major digs like Carchemish, where she first met archaeologists Leonard Woolley and T.E. Lawrence. In 1909, Bell made her own important discovery, Ukhaidir in Mesopotamia (Iraq). She reported for the Royal Geographical Society, recorded ancient Arabia in 7,000 photographs, mapped blank areas and lectured in London. She was awarded the society's prestigious Founder's Medal. Between 1902 and 1914 Gertrude Bell made six extensive journeys across Arabia by camel. The Beni Shakr tribe called her 'daughter of the desert'.

She was a white woman and an atheist. She refused to wear the Muslim veil, smoked cigarettes in public, rode camels like a man, and yet somehow became a confidante and friend of many Muslim sheiks and tribes. She was the first white person many Arabs had ever seen and it was remarked: 'If this is an English woman, what must an English man be like?'

In December 1913, she set off on a remarkable journey by camel, deep into Arabia to visit Ibn Rashid, the ruler of central Arabia. He was pro-Turkish and for the first time Bell was not made welcome. She was imprisoned for a tense ten days in his capital, Ha'il, before being released with courteous smiles. The Turks ruled Arabia through small provinces but, away from the coast and the railway, the ancient attitudes and traditions remained.

During her Middle Eastern travels, Gertrude Bell met Major Doughty-Wylie of the Diplomatic Service. She became good friends with him and his wife. Doughty-Wylie received a commendation for bravery for intervening in the Turkish massacre of Armenians at Adana. Gradually, Bell fell in love with the dashing young officer.

In July 1914, continental Europe fell apart, as alliances brought many nations to war after the assassination of the Austro-Hungarian heir. 'War is a biological necessity,' wrote Germany's General von Bernhardt. Great Britain remained apart from the domino-like declarations of war until 4 August, when Germany invaded neutral Belgium. In the creation of Belgium in 1830, Britain had guaranteed its permanent neutrality, and thus Britain was at war with Germany.

In November, Germany persuaded the Turkish Ottoman Empire to enter the war on its side. The Turkish army attacked Russia in the north, advanced on Basra in the east, and in February 1915, attacked British forces along the Suez Canal. There, they were defeated. Gertrude Bell's detailed knowledge of Arabia and its intricate alliances made her indispensable to British strategy. Her Middle East assessment, written before the Turks entered the war, was instrumental in Britain supporting the later Arab Revolt.

Other Middle Eastern archaeologists such as Woolley and Lawrence were posted to Cairo in December, but Bell had to wait. She joined the Red Cross, worked in France, then learned that Doughty-Wylie had been killed in the Gallipoli landings. She was devastated. At last she was posted to Cairo and sailed for Egypt in November 1915. She was then 47 years old.

She found herself the only woman working for the Arab Bureau of British Intelligence, but a respected and valued contributor. The following year she was posted to Basra, close behind the British advance in the east. When British forces liberated Baghdad in March 1917, Bell was appointed Oriental Secretary to Sir Percy Cox in Intelligence and moved to the ancient capital. Her particular responsibility was British–Arab relations and she interviewed sheiks, politicians, Sunnis, Shias and Kurds. In only a few months she met every person of consequence in Mesopotamia to determine their histories, needs and expectations for a post-war independent Arabia.

It was difficult work, especially for a woman. In May she wrote home: 'Until recently I've been wholly cut off from [the Shias] because their tenets forbid them to look upon an unveiled woman and my tenets don't permit me to veil.' Later that year she was awarded the CBE for her work.

The Ottoman Empire collapsed when the Turks were pushed out of Arabia by the British army and a full armistice was declared on 11 November 1918. Bell became an important figure in the complicated peace negotiations in Paris, where she worked with Prince Feisal, Lawrence of Arabia and others negotiating for an Arabia of independent

countries. France insisted on administering Lebanon and Syria and the peace process stalled. France based her claim to Syria on the Crusades of the 1180s. Prince Feisal replied: 'But you lost the Crusades!' Britain made no claim. She was involved because the Ottoman Empire had fought Britain and she had defeated it.

Bell proposed that the United States instead of France take the mandate over Syria from the new League of Nations. Feisal agreed, but the US Congress prevaricated. In 1920, the League of Nations created British mandates over Mesopotamia, Trans-

Jordan and Palestine while France was given mandates over Lebanon and Syria. However, Prince Feisal was crowned King of Syria by the General Syrian Congress in March and still refused to accept French authority. He proclaimed Syria's independence and warned the League of Nations that France was preparing to occupy all of Syria.

When the British army withdrew, France invaded Syria, sweeping aside an Arab army defending Damascus. The Syrians were oppressed by the French as the Turks had oppressed them before, and King Feisal was deposed. The newspapers were controlled and the French language imposed in courts, schools and government.

Elsewhere, the independent emirates of the Persian Gulf remained self-governing, their freedom guaranteed by Britain since the 1880s. Oil was discovered there in the 1930s. Southern Arabia was independent but divided between the Sharif Hussain of Mecca, Ibn Saud and Ibn Rashid. Saud soon overran the others to create Saudi Arabia. In Mesopotamia, there were bitter and bloody revolts against the League of Nations mandate.

Returning to Baghdad, Sir Percy Cox and Gertrude Bell attempted to negotiate alliances between Iraq's three main provinces and the different Islamic sects to create an independent Arab administration. Yet there was also division amongst the British: some colonialists wanted Iraq administered from India. To the Arabs, Gertrude Bell became known as 'al-Khatun', the Lady, and her Baghdad house saw many meetings. The pro-Indian lobby referred to the house dismissively as 'Chastity Chase'. Regardless, Bell presented the first-ever white paper by a woman to Parliament, the important 1920 'Review of the Civil Administration of Mesopotamia'.

Her negotiations involved 700 years of complicated history and Bell found it particularly difficult dealing with religious leaders. She wrote in frustration: 'There they sit in an atmosphere which reeks of antiquity and is so thick with the dust of ages that you can't see through it – nor can they.' In another way, some of the modern leaders were as difficult. One, Pasha Sayid Talib of Basra, simply murdered those who opposed him. At one meeting, Bell respectfully asked in Arabic: 'Tell me, Pasha, how many men have you done to death?' He replied, equally politely: 'Nay, Khatun, it is difficult after all these years to give the exact number.'

Britain's new Colonial Secretary, Winston Churchill, called a conference in Cairo in 1921 to find a settlement. Gertrude Bell was again the only woman among forty delegates and, with Cox and Lawrence, directly advising Churchill. He announced that Britain was willing to relinquish control of Mesopotamia apart from the British oil wells near Basra and this cleared the way for an Arab government. A final resolution was obtained which al-Khatun Bell had a very significant part in negotiating.

Britain revoked the League of Nations mandate over Mesopotamia to create an Arab-ruled Iraq with a small RAF security presence. Britain similarly revoked her mandate over Trans-Jordan to create the modern Arab-ruled Jordan, while Palestine remained a League of Nations mandate administered by Britain. Controlled immigration of Jews, agreed to in the Balfour Declaration of 1917, would continue but no separate Jewish nation would be created. Palestine was intended to be the Palestine of the Bible, mixed Arab and Jew.

In the negotiations by Bell, Cox and Lawrence, Feisal was proposed for King of Iraq while his brother Abdullah was proposed for King of Jordan. Both Feisal and Abdullah had fought in the Arab Revolt against the Turks, Feisal raising the standard in 1916 beneath the walls of Medina. Bell hoped that this honoured Arab Hashemite dynasty – directly descended from Muhammad – would unite the different factions in both countries.

Bell observed in June: 'We can't continue direct British control, though the country would be better governed by it, but it's rather a comic position to be telling [Iraqi] people over and over again that whether they like it or not they must have Arab, not British government.' Referendums were held and Feisal and Abdullah were approved, though not by the margin published. In Baghdad, on 23 August 1921, Feisal was crowned King of Iraq. Bell, Cox and Wilson were there, Lawrence was not.

Bell and Cox remained in Baghdad to advise King Feisal. There was a long way to go for Iraq; the Turks who'd settled there wanted their region to be part of modern Turkey, the Kurds wanted to be part of a Kurdish republic. In the south, Ibn Saud demanded parts of Iraq and Kuwait for Saudi Arabia. Cox and Bell devised borders so that the suspected oil fields would lie under all three countries, sharing the future oil revenue.

The religious and tribal complexities of the Middle East are all represented in Iraq, which Bell and Cox sought to unite for long-term stability. If the various factions and religions there could not live together under a single government, there was no hope for a single Arabia, the original aim of the Arab Revolt.

When Cox departed Baghdad, Bell continued as Oriental Secretary to the High Commission. In 1923, King Feisal appointed her Honorary Director of Antiquities to preserve the archaeology and artefacts of ancient Mesopotamia. In this position she helped create the prestigious Baghdad Museum. She also promoted the education of girls and women in the new Iraq, an innovation in Muslim society.

With Gertrude Bell, the Baghdad Museum became the finest in the Middle East. Yet by 1926 she was depressed. Her father wanted her back in England but she knew the museum still needed her experience. That July, Feisal was away from Baghdad and most of her friends had also escaped the summer heat. On Sunday the 11th she was weary from swimming in the Tigris and went to bed early. She took an overdose of sleeping tablets, whether by accident or design is not known, and died during the night. She was three days short of her 58th birthday.

Gertrude Bell was buried with full military honours by the Iraqi army. King George sent a message to her father: 'The nation will with us mourn the loss of one who by her intellectual powers, force of character and personal courage rendered important and what I trust will be lasting benefit to the country and to those regions where she worked with such devotion and self-sacrifice. We truly sympathise with you in your sorrow.' In her will, Bell left £50,000 to the museum.

The following year, the second largest oilfield in the world was discovered in Iraq. King Feisal led Iraq's constitutional monarchy to complete independence in 1932 and it became the first independent Arab nation to be accepted into the League of Nations. Unfortunately for Iraq, Feisal died suddenly the following year to be succeeded by his young son, Ghazi. In 1939 there was a military coup during which King Ghazi died, possibly murdered, in a car crash. His four-year-old son was proclaimed King Feisal II, under a regency of his uncle, but the military government remained.

During the 1939–45 war, German and Italian agents infiltrated the government so that Iraq supported the fascists. The regent fled. From French Syria in 1941, German, French and Italian aircraft operated into Iraq. British forces from India and Egypt quickly took over the country and invaded and liberated Syria from the French. Britain withdrew from Syria and Iraq at the end of the war.

King Feisal II assumed the throne in 1953 but five years later there was another military coup. Feisal was assassinated and Iraq proclaimed a military republic. There followed many coups and military juntas until, in 1979, Saddam Hussein emerged and proclaimed himself everything – President, Prime Minister, Chairman of the Revolutionary Council, and Secretary-General of the Ba'ath Socialist Party. Since then, for one reason and another, Iraq has been a mess.

It's easy to criticise Gertrude Bell for what Iraq is today, for she drew the pencil lines which became the international borders. Yet it's surely unreasonable to expect her to have foreseen the death of Feisal, the rise of fascism and another world war, the events which destabilised Iraq. Jordan did not suffer this destabilisation and survived, as have the Emirates, the Trucial States (United Arab Emirates) and Saudi Arabia. Bell understood the peoples, the problems, the ancient faiths and the intricate tribal histories of Iraq far better than most of those who've come after her. Now, Britain and America are embroiled in the region again, and the great Baghdad Museum was looted in 2003.

Gertrude Bell left behind some 16,000 letters, sixteen diaries, seven notebooks and 7,000 unique photographs of Arabia. Her notes and photographs in particular are invaluable, for they record a world and a history which would otherwise have been lost for ever.

Recommended
Gertrude Bell by H.V.F. Winstone.
Gertrude Bell: Queen of the Desert, Shaper of Nations by Georgina Howell.
The Robinson Library, Newcastle University, Newcastle-upon-Tyne, Durham.
Archives and Special Collections, Durham University, Durham.

Cecil Rhodes

When Cecil Rhodes was a young boy, he came across a retired admiral who kept acorns in his pocket and planted them. With the brashness of youth, Rhodes asked why he did it, as the old man would never see them grow into oaks. The admiral replied that he had the 'pleasure of the conception of their glory'.

The life of Rhodes is one of great dreams. He was a man who tried to bend the world to suit him, to carve a country in a wilderness and even give his own name to it.

He was born on 5 July 1853 in Hertfordshire, the fifth of seven sons. His father was the vicar of Bishop's Stortford. At 13, in answer to the question 'What is your motto?', Rhodes wrote in the family album: 'To do or to die'. Another of his answers suggests that he considered celibacy preferable to marriage. Like James Brooke and T.E. Lawrence, he would never marry.

At 16, Rhodes showed signs of having a weak heart and lungs. His brother Herbert was a planter in South Africa, so with funds from his aunt, Rhodes sailed to join him. He said later: 'They will tell you I came on account of my health, or for a love of adventure, and to some extent that may be true, but the real fact is I could no longer stand the cold mutton.'

He arrived in South Africa in 1870, at the beginning of the diamond rush. At that time, there were two Dutch Boer republics, two British colonies (Natal and the Cape) and two Native Territories. Cecil joined his brother on a farm. It was in dire straits as the first cotton crop had failed completely. Cecil came up with the idea of planting maize at intervals to draw insects away from the cotton and the two brothers won a prize for the idea at an agricultural show.

Cecil also put some of his aunt's money into a railway being built between Durban and the Cape. His brother was lured to the diamond fields to make his fortune and Cecil was left in charge of the farm until October 1871, when he joined Herbert. He left the farm thriving and when he encountered obstacles in later years, he would say: 'Well, they told me I couldn't grow cotton.'

At 18, Rhodes crossed the Drakenberg mountains and saw the landscape of Africa. He read Homer, Plutarch, Marcus Aurelius and Aristotle on the trip before joining his brother in Kimberley, where Herbert had staked three claims in the midst of 600 others on a hill.

Though he was a vicar's son, Rhodes enjoyed the lawless mining site and its tented community. The work was hard and required large numbers of natives to remove shale to get at the diamond-bearing soil. Yet it was a rich seam and both brothers saw diamonds of all sizes dug up. Before long, their claims were bringing in around thirty carats of diamond a week and Rhodes used the profits to buy more sites. Before his eighteenth year ended, his holdings were valued at more than £5,000 – an immense sum for the time.

When his older brother Frank joined them, he was amazed to find Cecil was already well known and respected in the diamond fields. However, the hard work caused Cecil to fall ill and in 1872 he left Frank in charge and set off on a journey to recover his health that took him as far as Mafeking and Pretoria. On that trip, Rhodes fell in love with Africa. In almost messianic style, he wrote of this time: 'For four months I walked between earth and sky, and when I looked down, I said this earth should be English, and when I looked up I said the English should rule this earth.'

He was financially independent, but his manners and education were incomplete. To that end, he returned to England. Before he left, he bought claims in the mine known as 'Old De Beers' and made investments in diamonds, gold claims and new land. He knew his future lay in South Africa and he intended to return.

At home, Rhodes went to Oriel College, Oxford, once the college of Sir Walter Ralegh. He loved the university and its history. While there, he read Gibbon's *The History of the Decline and Fall of the Roman Empire* and confirmed his belief that Britain was Rome's natural inheritor. At a later point, when someone expressed surprise at Rhodes trusting a man with a day's collection of diamonds, he said: 'That's all right. He's an Oxford man and an English gentleman.'

On his death, Rhodes left the university £100,000 in his will, to fund the Rhodes scholarships that continue to this day. Many of the Rhodes scholars have gone on to become famous in their fields, such as astronomer Edwin Hubble, Australian Prime Minister Bob Hawke and American President Bill Clinton.

At the age of 25, in 1878, Rhodes returned to Africa and began to work towards his ambitions. He had a band of close friends around him and was referred to as 'the chief'. He cared only for what wealth could bring him: power.

The first step was to stand for the Cape Parliament. Rhodes was elected by Boers to a seat he would retain for the rest of his life. On election, he immediately bought a large share in the Argus newspaper, to be certain his speeches would be well covered.

His maiden speech so impressed his parliamentary colleagues that they appointed him to a commission of inquiry into a native uprising in Basutoland. There, he met General 'Chinese' Gordon. When Rhodes heard of Gordon's death at Khartoum seven years later, he said: 'He was a doer, a man who could move mountains and gain the objective he had set himself.' From Rhodes, there could be no greater praise.

In 1885, Rhodes bought claims in gold mines in the Transvaal. A town grew up to support the miners there, later to be known as Johannesburg. The Transvaal was Boer territory and the Dutch were worried by British interest in the area. Paul Kruger was their president, an old-fashioned puritan by style, who detested the hard-drinking 'Uitlanders' or foreigners. He allowed the English no part in the state government or the new town's administration. Kruger detested Rhodes and once said of the foreign settlers: 'I shall never give them anything. I shall never change my policy. And now let the storm burst.' The Transvaal president would be a thorn in Rhodes's side for the rest of his life.

In partnership with Alfred Beit, Rhodes achieved the amalgamation of the De Beers claims in 1887. With two others, they formed a new company with complete rights over South African diamond production

– the De Beers Consolidated Mines Ltd. At the age of 35, the mine was earning Rhodes around £50,000 a year. With his partners, he controlled 90 per cent of the world's diamond production and had gold-field stakes that would bring in £400,000 per year, an astonishing sum for the time. In London, the annual pay for a nurse at that time was just ten pounds. Rhodes had reached the point where vast wealth brought vast influence.

In 1887, Rhodes met the British Governor of the Cape Colony, Sir Hercules Robinson. Rhodes told him of a plan by Kruger to sign a treaty with the Matabele tribe that would put a crimp in any future British designs on the land. Robinson was overwhelmed by the younger man's fiery enthusiasm. He asked where Rhodes would draw the line for British possessions. Rhodes took a map and pointed to the south of Lake Tanganyika, a thousand miles north of Johannesburg. Robinson was astonished at this naked ambition, but agreed not to interfere or hinder the young man.

The next stage was to arrange mining rights in Matabeleland and adjoining Mashonaland. Rhodes sent three friends to arrange this and they secured a treaty with the Matabele king for £100 a month, rifles, ammunition and a steamship. With this treaty, Rhodes was able to create the 'British South Africa Company'. For those familiar with the wealth and power of the ancient British East India Company, the very name suggests imperial ambition.

Rhodes returned to London to secure a royal charter. He had an extraordinary talent for persuasion and, of course, great wealth was part of that. He asked key men to become directors of the company and succeeded in gaining the charter – a free hand from the Crown to make treaties, promote commerce, good government and civilisation, to create a police force and to suppress slavery. Rhodes issued a million one-pound shares and De Beers bought a fifth of them. In one stroke, the company had been granted the powers of a sovereign nation – *over an area larger than France and Germany put together*.

Back in Africa, Rhodes organised an expedition to Mashonaland. The Matabele king was justifiably wounded that mere mining rights appeared to have become a foreign invasion, but he was a man of

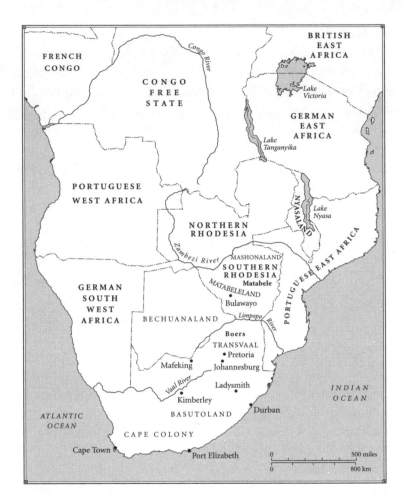

great honour and would not go back on his word, no matter how his permissions were abused or interpreted.

Rhodes's pioneers marked out a road as they went and built forts. Rhodes could not go with them as he had just been made Prime Minister of the Cape Colony. He received word of the column's successful arrival and said: 'I do not think there is a happier man in the country than myself.'

However, the first year was almost a disaster. Administration costs, such as building roads and keeping a police force, rose to £250,000. To make matters worse, there was no sign of the gold for which his investors hoped. Rhodes visited his colony and increased their holdings into Nyasaland, dreaming of a British railway that would stretch from the Cape all the way north to Egypt. He established another police force and applied British law throughout the territory. Foreign imperial nations, such as Germany, Portugal and Belgium, looked on aghast at this interloper into their area of influence. However, the British government remained firm in its support of Rhodes, perhaps in part because he had the foresight to name forts after members of the royal family.

In 1890 and 1891, Rhodes agreed treaties with Portugal and Germany, paying vast sums to give him access to a harbour and new lands to administer. He pressed on regardless of the feelings of the Matabele king, who was growing more and more dissatisfied with the agreement between them. In 1893, Matabele warriors launched a great raid on the colonists and, in doing so, gave Rhodes a free hand to engage them. Once again, economics would play a part. Rhodes sold shares to cover the expenses of a war and his volunteers were promised a farm each. The armed men descended on Matabele land and an ultimatum was issued, telling the king to leave.

In the face of such a threat, the Matabeles were in fact leaving when a single shot was fired. Fighting broke out instantly. The warriors were routed and the king's personal holdings, his 'kraal', taken. The king himself died of smallpox a few months later and is a tragic figure in this story as one who never broke his word and still lost his land. When he heard of the king's death, Rhodes felt enough guilt to pay for the education of his three sons.

After the short campaign, Rhodes was in control of all territory between Bechuanaland and the River Zambezi. His fortunes were still on the rise. In London, he had lunch with Queen Victoria and was surprised to find her well informed and interested in his exploits. One of her maids told the queen that Rhodes was known to dislike women. She replied: 'Oh! But he was extremely kind to me!' Queen Victoria made him a privy councillor and the Postmaster-General's office approved the name of 'Southern Rhodesia' and 'Northern Rhodesia' for the conquered territories.

By 1895, when Rhodes was still just 42, Company shares stood at nine pounds. New cities were springing up, like Bulawayo, which had a telegraph line, hotels and even newspapers. Railway tracks were being laid across Rhodesia. As a man of Empire, Rhodes saw himself as one of a greater brotherhood. He used some of the Cape wealth to aid Australia, and as Prime Minister sent envoys to Canada to settle tariff questions. He regarded South Africa as a federation under Britain, but he also respected the Dutch colonists and raised statues to their great men. As his company charter allowed him to do, he opposed slavery throughout his lands and delighted in the native terms for him: 'Father of the people' and 'The Old Man'.

Rhodes the man appeared to have little or no superficial vanity, though his dreams were boundless. He dressed in mismatched clothes and cared little if they became grubby. He was once turned away by a Cape Town doorman for being improperly dressed – this, when he was Prime Minister. He gave money to anyone who came to him in serious need – perhaps because on one occasion when he refused, the petitioner committed suicide.

His memory was extraordinary. He could soak up vast amounts of information and then repeat it almost word for word. When the business of government became tiresome, his habit was to go off on his own, with just a gun and a valet, out into the wilderness. His health was always poor and in his forties he suffered a series of heart attacks. The constant pain seemed to inspire him to greater efforts, as if he knew he had only a short time to complete his life's work.

As a result of Kruger's unwillingness to share power, relations with the Boers were deteriorating. Neither Kruger nor Rhodes was capable of compromise. In 1895, Rhodes's friend Jameson, a doctor, raised a militia to raid Boer territory. He signalled Rhodes that he was going in and then cut the telegraph wires, so that he did not hear Rhodes ordering him to stand down. Jameson took 700 men into the Transvaal and Kruger quickly organised 5,000. The Boers were accurate snipers and used the terrain to encircle Jameson and kill his men from astonishing distances. One of Jameson's officers said later: 'We were fighting against puffs of smoke.' Sixty-five of Jameson's men were killed and thirty-seven wounded before he surrendered and was imprisoned in the Boer capital, Pretoria. Rhodes's brother Frank was with him.

It was a disaster for Rhodes, politically as well as personally. As the news came in, he stayed awake for eight days and nights, driving himself to the brink of heart failure. He resigned as Prime Minister of the Cape Colony and from the board of the Company. The British government disowned him for the actions in his name. Public opinion at home was against Rhodes until the German Kaiser sent a telegram to Kruger, praising him and suggesting German support. When the telegram was released to the press, Rhodes was almost forgotten in the righteous fury it provoked.

Jameson was sentenced to death for his raid, but political support had swelled and Kruger was pressured to hand him over for trial in London. Jameson served a year in prison there before returning to Rhodesia as a hero. Other ringleaders were also sentenced to death, but Rhodes agreed to pay a fine of £25,000 to free them. In the end, he was the one who suffered most as he had lost all his public positions, but he never complained at the twists of fate and refused to allow anyone else to be blamed.

In 1896, the Matabeles revolted against the Company; 15,000 of them surrounded the new city of Bulawayo. Rhodes was no longer in power, but he was not the sort of man to let that minor detail stop him. He took command of Company troops and his reputation and charisma were such that no one dared question his right to do so.

He organised a fast column and quick rout of the Matabele warriors, but Rhodes preferred negotiation to battle. He pitched his tent near some caves where they had gone into hiding and waited, unarmed. The Matabele chieftains were suspicious at first, suspecting a trap. After some days, they invited him to a safer location in the hills. There, he listened to their demands and offered concessions in return. Finally, he stood before them and asked: 'Now for the future, is it peace or is it war?' In response, they dropped their spears on the ground. Of that moment, he said later: 'It is occasions like that which make life worth living.'

He spent two months with the Matabeles before telling them to go and sow their fields. The fact that they accepted his authority, though it was based on no official position, shows the sort of man he was. In October 1896, peace was officially declared with the tribe. Rhodes used his personal wealth to pay for a million sacks of grain to tide them over the winter. Ever after, the Matabele referred to him as 'the separator of fighting bulls'.

In London, Rhodes was called before a commission of inquiry to answer for the disastrous Jameson raid. As always, he was astonishingly persuasive and escaped with just a reprimand. While at home, he met the French Minister for Foreign Affairs and expounded on his philosophy, talking of a future in which Africa was ruled jointly by France, Britain and Russia – with Germany the real enemy. For 1897, this was a prescient comment. Rhodes also told the man: 'What do we look for in this life? To leave something worth remembering. I have left something to remember. I have built a country.'

In South Africa, Rhodes continued to expand his holdings, creating industries as they became needed, from hotels to dynamite factories. He was elected again to the board of the Company and Jameson was back at his side. His rail and telegraph lines had to cross the territories of Belgium and Germany, so Rhodes travelled to Europe to meet both leaders. Surprisingly, he liked the Kaiser more than the King of Belgium, who was such a cunning negotiator that Rhodes complained he lost a province to him at every lunch. Nevertheless, both men agreed to let his telegraph cross their territory.

Meanwhile, the relationship between Boers and British was worse than ever. 'Uitlanders' were by then the majority in the Transvaal, but Kruger allowed them no votes or concessions of any kind. Rhodes made a rare misjudgement when he said: 'Nothing will make Kruger fire a shot.'

War broke out in 1899 and the British settlements of Ladysmith, Mafeking and Kimberley were besieged. Lords Roberts and Kitchener took command of a large army, mostly consisting of New Zealand and Canadian troops. Rhodes was very ill, but he ignored constant chest pains and organised supplies for them. He also had a new field gun made, named the 'Long Cecil'. Each of its shells had 'Compliments from C.R.' inscribed on them.

In May 1900, the army under Roberts marched on Pretoria, taking Johannesburg on the way. Kruger was forced to flee to Europe rather than be captured and held for trial. The war was quickly won and on 25 October 1900 the Transvaal was officially annexed as a new British territory. It turned out to be a lot harder to hold than to take as a continuing guerrilla war grew in ferocity. Government buildings and train tracks were blown up by the Boer commandos. Sniping was a constant hazard. Rhodes spoke publicly on the subject, saying that the future lay only in cooperation.

As well as a young Winston Churchill, journalist and poet Rudyard Kipling was in South Africa and Rhodes spent many evenings with him.

Rhodes despaired of seeing a solution to the conflict and left them to it, travelling to Italy, then Egypt and finally back to England, where he bought another house. A law case where his signature had been forged required him to return to Africa and his health worsened. He required constant care as his heart slowly failed. The one bright spot for Rhodes was Kitchener's announcement of an amnesty and peace negotiations with the Boers. The day after he heard, Rhodes was lying down. He was heard to say: 'So little done, so much to do.' He was dead before the doctor reached him, at just 48 years old.

In April 1902, a train bore his body from Cape Town to Rhodesia. Boers and English gathered at every stop to pay their respects to the Old Man. When his coffin reached the hills where he would be buried, thousands of Matabele warriors gathered to see him entombed as a king. One of the chieftains said:

'I was content to die knowing that my children and my people would be safe in the hands of Mr Rhodes, who was at once my father and my

mother. That hope has been taken from me and I feel, indeed, that the sun has set for me.'

History has not been kind to Cecil Rhodes. He epitomised the manic self-belief of an empire builder. While he lived, the American author Mark Twain said of him: 'I admire him, I frankly confess it; and when his time comes I shall buy a piece of the rope for a keepsake.'

He has been portrayed as the worst kind of imperial exploiter. Yet, he was a dreamer of great dreams and such men are extraordinary and rare. He once said: 'I would annex the planets if I could.' His Rhodes scholarships continue and the De Beers company he founded is still the world's largest diamond producer. For achievement alone, he was, without a doubt, a great Englishman. In his will, he wrote: 'I contend that we are the finest race in the world and that the more of the world we inhabit the better it is for the human race.' Perhaps his most famous words are these: 'Remember that you are an Englishman and have consequently won first prize in the lottery of life.'

He had many of the beliefs of his day in regard to races and cultures not fortunate enough to be English, but at the same time was a passionate defender of the rights of natives and Boers in South Africa.

At a dinner in England, in 1899, he said: 'Sometimes, in pursuing my object, the enlargement of the British Empire and with it, the cause of peace, industry and freedom, I have adopted means in removing opposition which were the rough and ready way and not the highest way to attain that object. But you must remember that in South Africa where my work has lain, the laws of right and equity are not so fixed and established as in this country. It is among those men that my own life must be weighed and measured.'

The Cape to Cairo railway has never been completed. Northern and Southern Rhodesia have been since renamed Zambia and Zimbabwe. Their borders are still the ones Cecil Rhodes drew in pencil on his maps.

Recommended
Cecil Rhodes by André Maurois.
Cecil Rhodes by Basil Williams.

The Gurkhas

'The Almighty created in the Gurkha an ideal infantryman, indeed an ideal Rifleman, brave, tough, patient, adaptable, skilled in fieldcraft, intensely proud of his military record and unswerving loyalty. Add to this his honesty in word and deed, his parade perfection, and his unquenchable cheerfulness, then service with the Gurkhas is for any soldier an immense satisfaction.'
– Field Marshal William Slim (1891–1970)

The father of the authors of this book flew in bomber command during World War II and later, the Fleet Air Arm. One of his jobs was training parachutists and he tells a story of a group of Gurkhas, fresh to England from Nepal to begin their training. The Gurkha soldiers spoke no English and their senior officer only understood a few words. After a final lecture, they were taken up in a plane for the first practice drop. Even at that late stage, the RAF crew weren't at all sure the soldiers had understood what was going on. One of them went back to the waiting Gurkhas and tried to explain once more.

'We are rising to an altitude of five hundred feet,' he said, 'at which point, a green light will come on and you and your men will jump.' He mimed jumping.

The Gurkha officer looked worried, but went back to his men to explain. When he returned, he said: 'Five hundred feet is too high. We are willing to try three hundred feet.'

The RAF officer went pale. 'You don't understand,' he said. 'At three hundred, your parachute will barely have time to open. You'll hit the ground like a sack of potatoes.'

The Gurkha officer beamed at him and went to tell the men. They all beamed as well. They hadn't realised they would be allowed to use the parachutes at that stage of the training.

Now that story must surely be apocryphal, but it was told at the time and it demonstrates how the British armed forces saw the regiments from Nepal – keen, tough, uncomplaining and unbelievably courageous. They have always been held in the highest regard, a respect they have earned, time and time again in their history.

The Gurkhas have been part of the British army for almost two hundred years, beginning in 1816 when the British East India Company signed the Peace Treaty of Sugauli with Nepal that allowed them to recruit local men. Gurkhas had fought them to a bloody standstill on a number of occasions and the Company was very keen to have such a martial race on their side. Lieutenant Frederick Young was one of those fighting the Gurkhas in 1815. His troops ran away and only he refused to run as he was surrounded. The Gurkhas admired his courage and told him: 'We could serve under men like you.' He is known as the father of the Brigade of Gurkhas. He later recruited 3,000 of them and became the commander of a battalion, later named '2nd King Edward VII's Own Gurkha Rifles'. They still serve today as part of the Royal Gurkha Rifles.

Gurkhas are small men, drawn from a rugged and inhospitable land, the sort of herdsmen who must once have formed the backbone of Genghis Khan's armies. They are famous for carrying the 'kukri' blade, a curved knife that, once drawn, must be blooded before it can be sheathed.

Along with the Sikhs, Nepalese Gurkhas remained loyal to Britain during the Indian Mutiny and have fought for Britain in every major conflict since then, winning thirteen Victoria Crosses in the process. The British officers who commanded them won another thirteen. It is part of the legend of the Gurkhas that their officers have to be as enduring and self-reliant as the men themselves, or they don't get to command.

They have seen service in Burma, Afghanistan, the North-East and North-West frontiers in India, Malta, Cyprus, China and Tibet. At the beginning of the 1914–18 war, the King of Nepal placed the entire

Nepalese army at the disposal of the British Crown. More than a hundred thousand young Nepalese men fought in France and Flanders, Mesopotamia (Iraq), Persia (Iran), Egypt, Gallipoli, Palestine and Salonika. Twenty thousand of them were killed or injured, an almost unimaginable loss to a nation with a population of just four million. In 1915, they captured and held heights at Gallipoli, some of the worst fighting in the war. It is interesting to note that when Australian infantry battalions made a suicidal charge into Turkish and German machine-gun positions, taking them after fierce fighting, they were nicknamed 'The White Gurkhas' by their allies afterwards.

In World War II, there were 112,000 Gurkhas in British service, serving as rifle regiments, special forces and parachutists. In 1940, the bleakest part of the war for Britain, permission was sought to recruit another twenty battalions to match the first twenty. The Nepalese Prime Minister agreed, saying: 'Does a friend desert a friend in time of need? If you win, we win with you. If you lose, we lose with you.' Once again, the whole Nepalese army was placed under the disposal of the British Crown. They fought in all theatres of operation, from North Africa to Italy and finally Burma, where they repelled a massive Japanese invasion from Thailand.

As infantry, they have a reputation for incredible toughness, but it is not a historical footnote. In 2006, in Afghanistan, just forty Gurkhas held a police station against massed attacks over ten days by Taliban fighters. One of them, Rifleman Nabin Rai, was hit in the face by a rifle bullet, but refused to leave his post. When he was dazed by another round that struck his helmet, he had a cigarette to recover, then returned to his position. The Taliban attackers eventually left to seek out an easier target, leaving a hundred of their dead behind. The Gurkhas had suffered three wounds and lost no one.

Their history abounds with such examples, including the true story from 1931 of a mule kicking a Gurkha in the head with an iron-shod hoof. He wore a sticking plaster over the gash, while the mule went lame. Another tale from World War II involved Havildar Manbahadur being shot through the spleen, then gashed in the head by a Japanese officer. Left for dead, he walked sixty miles to catch up to his unit. Medical orderlies told him he should have died from his wounds, but he just grinned and asked to rejoin his men.

In 1943, having understood that a soldier must never lose his weapon, one Gurkha had to be rescued by Brigadier Mark Teversham after sinking to the bottom of a river. The weight of his gun was holding him underwater, but he would not let go of it. Their reputation for stoicism and macabre humour only grew in that time.

Against the Japanese, the Gurkhas earned a reputation as relentless and skilled hand-to-hand fighters. They cleared machine-gun positions by approaching under heavy fire and then leapt among the enemy, wielding their kukris' blades with terrible efficiency. The Japanese developed a grudging respect for the fearsome little men. The British commander in Burma, Field Marshal Slim, told a story with relish of a Japanese officer who challenged a Gurkha to a duel with blades alone. The Japanese officer lunged with his sword and the Gurkha swayed away from it, untouched. The Gurkha then stepped in close and swung his kukri.

'You missed as well,' the officer said.

The Gurkha replied: 'Wait till you sneeze and see what happens.'

In June 1944 in Burma, a Gurkha unit was faced with Japanese tanks and unable to move forward. Bhutanese Rifleman Ganju Lama went on his own with an anti-tank gun. Although he was shot three times and his left wrist was broken, he used the gun to destroy two tanks, then stood up with bullets whipping around him and used grenades to kill the other tank crews. Only when the way was clear for his unit to move forward did he allow his terrible wounds to be dressed. He won the VC for that action, yet it is only one story of hundreds that go some way to explain the enormous affection and respect the Gurkhas have earned for themselves.

After Indian Independence in 1947, there were ten Gurkha regiments in the army of British India. Four of them transferred to the British army as a brigade: 2nd King Edward's VII's Own Gurkha Rifles (The Sirmoor Rifles), 6th Gurkha Rifles (later Queen Elizabeth's Own), 7th Gurkha Rifles (later the Duke of Edinburgh's Own) and the 10th Gurkha Rifles (later Princess Mary's Own). They would play a vital role in the Malayan Emergency (1948–60) and the Brunei Revolt (1962–6). They also took part in the defence of Cyprus in 1974 after a Turkish invasion and as a garrison in Belize in 1978.

In the battle for the Falkland Islands in 1982, the Gurkhas were involved in the final assault to liberate Port Stanley from Argentinian troops. They were particularly feared by the Argentinian soldiers, whose own propaganda had led them to believe the Gurkhas were savages who killed their own wounded, slit Argentinian throats and sometimes even ate the enemy.

While the 2nd Scots Guards took Mount Tumbledown and 2nd Para took Wireless Ridge, the Gurkhas' objective was the key position of Mount William. To the north of Tumbledown, there was a minefield the Gurkhas could either go round or feel their way through. At dawn, the Gurkhas chose to go through. They came under artillery fire, but didn't falter as fourteen were wounded.

Meanwhile, some 300 Argentinians were retreating before the Scots Guards when they ran into an advance Gurkha patrol. They immediately turned about and surrendered to the Guards.

The main force of Argentinians on Mount William then saw they were faced by the Gurkhas. They left their positions, threw away their rifles and bolted for Port Stanley. The Gurkhas were bitterly disappointed to take Mount William without resistance.

'They knew we were coming and they feared us,' said Lieutenant Colonel David Morgan, then commander of the Gurkha Rifles. 'Of course, I think they had every ground to fear us.' The Argentinian lines of defence were broken wide open.

Gurkha regiments also served in Iraq and Afghanistan at the beginning of the twenty-first century. Despite their history, they are in every way modern riflemen, but they maintain an age-old spirit and discipline. They see courage as the greatest aim and honour in life and regard those of their number who have won the Victoria Cross as an elite group of Nepalese national heroes. Every young man who joins the regiments today cherishes the idea that he may one day be part of that small, valiant number.

One problem faced by Gurkhas from World War II is that they did not qualify for a pension unless they had served a full fifteen years. Others who had fought in Malaya, Borneo and Brunei were sent home with just a small gratuity in 1967–71 as the overall numbers were reduced. More than ten thousand of those who returned to Nepal after risking their lives for Britain are still alive today and depend on the work of charities such as the Gurkha Welfare Trust for support.

In a landmark ruling in September 2008, the High Court ruled that Gurkha soldiers who retired before 1997 should have the right to live in Britain. That was a huge step forward for a group who have rarely been rewarded as they deserve. Even so, after so many decades of being forbidden the right or the pension to live in Britain, a large number will prefer to spend their final years in Nepal, where the continuing work of British charities is vital.

Recommended
The Gurkhas by Byron Farwell.
Supreme Courage: Heroic Stories from 150 Years of the Victoria Cross by General Sir Peter de la Billière.
Journeys Hazardous: Gurkha Clandestine Operations: Borneo 1965 by Christopher Bullock.
The Gurkha Museum in Winchester.

Horatio Nelson
– The Immortal Memory

The 29th of September, 1758: the Wife of the Rector
of Burnham Thorpe Parish, of a Son.

All Saints' Church, Burnham Thorpe, Norfolk is today much as it was in 1758 when a son of the rector and his wife was baptised and christened. The most notable additions to this quiet Anglican church since that christening are the wooden lectern and rood – carved from the original oak of HMS *Victory*. For the boy born that autumn was Horatio Nelson, destined to become the most famous naval commander in the world – with his and *Victory*'s name forever joined.

Horatio's boyhood was normal beneath the flat skies of East Anglia. Although the family was educated, it was not wealthy. He attended local schools, went bird-nesting, and scrumped apples and pears from orchards with his friends. His mother died when he was nine years old, but it was through her family that there was a connection with the sea – Captain Maurice Suckling, an uncle serving in the Royal Navy. Horatio asked his father for permission to join his uncle in a ship being commissioned for possible war with Spain over the Falkland Islands. It was agreed. In January 1771, aged twelve years and three months, Horatio Nelson joined his first ship, the 64-gun *Raisonnable*, at Chatham Naval Dockyard, Kent.

Across the dock from *Raisonnable* was the new first-rate *Victory*, a 100-gun ship of the line launched in 1765 but held in reserve. There's no doubt that Midshipman Nelson noticed her. It's likely he boarded and looked her over, for she was a most impressive ship: 2000 English oak trees had been used to build her.

Five months later, Spain withdrew her claim to the Falklands and Captain Suckling and Nelson transferred to the 74-gun *Triumph*.

Suckling arranged for his nephew to ship for a year to the West Indies in a merchant vessel. Most seamen in the Royal Navy of that era spent time in the merchant service; it was the best training in seamanship available. One such officer, James Cook, had returned from a voyage around the world that July and all Britain was talking about him.

A year after his return, Nelson joined an Arctic expedition seeking the North-East Passage through the ice around the top of Russia to the Pacific. Aged 14, he wangled a berth in the bomb ketch *Carcass* as coxswain, a petty officer in charge of one of the small boats. Ice-bound one polar night, Nelson left the ship on foot to hunt polar bear across the sea ice. He wanted to send his father a white bearskin for his hearth, but the bear escaped when Nelson's musket misfired. Nelson himself escaped the enraged bear only after *Carcass* fired a cannon to frighten it off. Heavy ice turned the expedition back north of Norway.

At the end of 1773, Midshipman Nelson joined HMS *Seahorse*, a 20-gun frigate in a squadron sailing to the East. He served in *Seahorse* for two years, visiting Africa, India and the Spice Islands before he contracted malaria and almost died. Semi-paralysed, Nelson was invalided home but was to suffer from the after-effects for the rest of his life. Yet only a few days after his return, five days before his eighteenth birthday in 1776, Nelson was appointed acting lieutenant to the 64-gun *Worcester*, escorting convoys to Gibraltar and elsewhere. The following year, having served the required minimum six years on board ship, he sat and passed his lieutenant's examination.

The bitter American War of Independence was then being fought and Nelson was posted to the West Indies station in the frigate *Lowestoffe*. In her he obtained his first command, the captured American schooner *Little Lucy*. A year later, Nelson was promoted to first lieutenant to the flagship HMS *Bristol*. In December 1778, he was promoted again, to be master and commander of the brig *Badger*, his second command. Only six months on, aged just 20, Horatio Nelson was posted captain. That same year, in the far Pacific, Captain Cook was killed.

Although Nelson was 'known' at the Admiralty through his uncle, promotion on the West Indies station was due to the fact he was keen, imaginative and good at almost everything he did. Most superior officers appreciated his talents, most contemporaries enjoyed his company, and most seamen liked and worked willingly for him because he looked after them – their health, their conditions and their few comforts.

On being appointed to the 20-gun frigate *Hinchinbrooke*, replacing a captain killed in action, Nelson wrote: 'I got my rank by a shot killing a Post-Captain, and I most sincerely hope I shall, when I go, go out of the World the same way.'

He contracted yellow fever during a combined naval and army assault up the shallows and swamps of the San Juan River on the Spanish Main. His efforts were the main reason the expedition finally succeeded in capturing Fort San Juan, but in 1780 he had to be invalided home. By the spring of 1781 he'd recovered, to be appointed captain of the frigate *Albemarle* for convoy work into the Baltic and to Canada. In 1783 a treaty with the colonial Britons was signed by which the independent United States of America was created. *Albemarle* and many other vessels returned home and were paid off and Nelson took leave to visit France.

Before he himself was paid off the active list, Nelson served once more on the West Indies station, from 1784 to 1787. He incurred the displeasure of British planters and traders for enforcing the new trading laws with America, and the displeasure of his king, George III, for associating with his womanising sailor son, Prince William. On the Isle of Nevis in March 1787, Nelson married 'Fanny' Nisbet, a widow with one son. Prince William gave away the bride.

In his career to that point, Nelson had accumulated some very talented friends and admirers, both senior and junior to him – Admirals Parker, Hood and Jervis; Captains Cornwallis and Ball; Lieutenants Collingwood, Troubridge, Saumarez, Berry and Hardy. During the twenty-two years of French wars, these men became household names in the long fight for freedom from tyranny.

Yet in 1787, Horatio Nelson was 'on the beach', a captain without a ship, living on half-pay in the Burnham Thorpe parsonage with his wife, stepson and father. He was 29 years old. He was also beginning to go blind, from a then untreatable disease of the conjunctiva spreading slowly across each eye.

Nelson remained on half-pay for five years, concerning himself with the conditions of farm labourers and campaigning for improvements. He thought he might never go to sea again, but in 1792 revolutionary France declared war on Austria, Sardinia and Prussia and invaded the Austrian Netherlands. Despite Britain's neutrality in continental politics, the die was cast in early 1793, when French batteries fired upon HMS *Childers* without warning or provocation. Nelson was appointed captain to HMS *Agamemnon*.

The British government still refused to respond, but on 1 February France declared war on Britain and Holland. Thus a world war began that was fought from Ireland to Russia, from Norway to South Africa, in the North and South American continents, in India and in South East Asia, and across almost every sea in the world. France further inflicted on the world a gunnery corporal named Napoleon Bonaparte, the man responsible for the greatest destruction in Europe until the rise to power of Adolf Hitler. During the war against French oppression Nelson grew to despise Bonaparte.

Ship of the Line *Agamemnon* was a 64-gun vessel from Hampshire; strongly built yet fast, manoeuvrable, and with a crew mostly of volunteers. She was Nelson's favourite command. Soon after joining, he was offered the command of a 74-gun ship. He declined. In a fleet under the command of Admiral Hood in HMS *Victory*, Nelson sailed for Gibraltar and the Mediterranean.

Nelson and *Agamemnon* were deployed continuously for three years throughout the western Mediterranean. During the capture of Corsica, Nelson received a severe wound to his right eye from a stone chip, leaving it virtually useless. However, he never wore an eyepatch; it was over his weakening left eye that he occasionally wore an eyeshade to protect it from glare. At sea, he usually wore a green shade beneath his cocked hat to protect both eyes. The Trafalgar Square statue depicts him accurately with no eyepatch.

In *Agamemnon* Nelson hoisted his commodore's pennant, fought a series of successful actions against the French and Spanish, and wrote a brief autobiography, 'Sketch of My Life'. A weather-beaten *Agamemnon* was sent home for a refit in 1796 and Nelson transferred his commodore's flag to HMS *Captain*. In February 1797 came the first great sea battle of the war – and of Nelson's career. It was named the Battle of Cape St Vincent, fought in the waters off south-west Portugal.

On the morning of St Valentine's Day, a Spanish fleet of twenty-seven ships of the line – the 130-gun four-deck *Santissima Trinidad*, six 112-gun ships, two 80s and eighteen 74s – was intercepted on its passage to the English Channel by Admiral Sir John Jervis. Jervis's fleet comprised only fifteen ships of the line, including the 100-gun *Victory* and *Britannia*, three 98s, one 90, eight 74s and one 64. As the enemy vessels gradually emerged from a bank of fog, Captain Calder in *Victory* counted them for his admiral: 'There are eight sail of the line, Sir John.' 'There are twenty sail of the line, Sir John.' 'There are twenty-five sail of the line, Sir John.' 'There are twenty-seven sail of the line, Sir John.'

'Enough, sir. No more of that!' Jervis thundered. 'If there are fifty sail, I will go through them!'

Go through them he did. *Culloden* led the British fleet and opened fire at 11.30 a.m., splitting the Spanish line in two. The majority of Spanish vessels on the right altered course to the north, engaging the British sailing on the opposite course. Jervis ordered his captains to tack in succession to pursue the main body and to prevent the gap being closed by the eight Spanish ships on the left. Broadside after broadside drove those ships out of the battle.

Close to the rear of the British line in the north, Nelson saw that the majority of Spanish ships were attempting to escape. Disobeying orders, he hauled the 74-gun *Captain* out of the line and engaged the 130-gun *Santissima Trinidad*, the largest warship in the world. Collingwood followed Nelson in *Excellent*. With Troubridge in *Culloden*, Frederick in *Blenheim* and Rear-Admiral William Parker in *Prince George* arriving from the south, a fierce battle within a battle took place as those five British ships attempted to stop the Spanish fleet escaping.

All the vessels suffered heavy damage. At one stage *Captain* was fighting five ships at once, and Nelson was wounded in the stomach by a flying splinter of wood. Then the Spanish first-rates *San Jose* and *San Nicolas* ran onto each other and were locked together. Nelson saw his chance. He steered *Captain* onto the *San Nicolas*. 'Calling for the boarders, I ordered them to board,' he wrote later.

From *Captain*, Nelson led the British marines and seamen onto the 80-gun *San Nicolas* and captured her. Seeing no reason to stop, he then led them onto the 112-gun *San Jose* and captured her, too. On the quarterdeck of *San Jose* he received the sword of the dying Spanish admiral and handed it to bargeman William Fearney, who 'placed it, with the greatest sang-froid, under his arm.' Pursuing the Spanish fleet, *Victory* passed by and her crew lined the rails and cheered the amazing sight of the three ships all now flying Royal Navy ensigns. This unique action of boarding one enemy ship via another was referred to as 'Nelson's patent bridge for boarding first-rates'.

Although his understanding of tactics was supreme, he had taken an enormous risk, disobeying both Jervis's order of battle and Admiralty Fighting Instructions. Jervis had told him to use his initiative, but it might have been a court-martial offence. Instead, after the battle, Jervis welcomed him to the deck of *Victory* with open arms. The last shots were fired at 5 p.m. and the Spanish retreated into Cadiz. They had lost four ships and 3,000 men killed, wounded or captured; the British lost no ships, but 73 killed and 400 wounded. Jervis was created Earl St Vincent, Nelson made a Knight of the Bath and, unknown to the fleet, was already promoted rear-admiral, though the news didn't arrive until April. He was just 38 years old.

Elsewhere, there was mutiny in the Channel Fleet. The cause was partly due to ill-treatment by a few captains but primarily the government not paying the seamen. One of those vessels, *Theseus*, was ordered to Jervis's fleet. Jervis transferred Rear-Admiral Nelson, Captain Miller and a handful of former *Agamemnon* seamen to her.

Theseus was under-provisioned, lacked most of her military stores, had never seen action, and her seamen were still mutinous. It's indicative of Nelson's leadership and care for his men that within one month a note was left on the quarterdeck. It read: 'Success attend Admiral Nelson, God bless Captain Miller, we thank them for the officers they have placed over us. We are happy and comfortable and will shed every drop of blood in our veins to support them, and the name of *Theseus* shall be immortalised as high as Captain's. Ship's Company.' It was all part of what came to be called the 'Nelson touch'.

A month later, Nelson experienced his greatest defeat. He devised and led an attempt to capture the port of Tenerife in the Canary Islands and a Spanish treasure galleon lying there. He was soundly beaten. He lost a quarter of the landing force – 250 men killed or wounded – as well as his right arm. It was shattered by grapeshot and amputated below the shoulder in *Theseus*. There was no anaesthetic in those days, only the surgeon's saw, a leather pad to bite upon, and rum or opium afterwards. The next day, using his left hand, he wrote a request for sick leave. Nelson was sent home to convalesce, the first time he'd been in England for more than four years.

At that stage of his life Horatio Nelson had seen action against the French and Spanish more than 120 times. He'd become the man we recognise from the portraits: slightly built, five foot six inches tall, white-haired, a sightless right eye, a poor left eye, one-armed, with his decorations worn proudly upon his blue uniform coat. Behind this public image, he sometimes wore, for fun, a diamond wind-up clock in his cocked hat. He famously suffered from seasickness as well as the continuing effects of malaria and yellow fever, and the splinter wound to his stomach caused him great distress. He was in almost constant pain. Yet the three greatest achievements of his career, three of the most important naval battles of all time, were yet to come.

On 29 March 1798, Nelson hoisted his flag as Rear Admiral of the Blue – the Blue Ensign – in the *Vanguard* at Portsmouth. Through the Royal Navy, Britain was taking the offensive. Under overall command of Earl St Vincent, a fleet was sent back into the Mediterranean to wrest control from the French. Intelligence reports had indicated that Bonaparte was about to make a major attack there – perhaps Greece, perhaps Constantinople, perhaps Egypt – then move on India. It was a pivotal moment in world history.

Admiral of the French fleet transporting Bonaparte and his 30,000 strong Army of the East was François Brueys, a very capable tactician. Skilfully, he avoided the hunting British squadrons and landed Bonaparte in Egypt. Alexandria fell by 2 July and, leaving his fleet in Aboukir Bay by the estuary of the River Nile, Bonaparte marched on Cairo. That city fell on 24 July and Bonaparte declared himself a Muslim. In France he had declared himself an atheist revolutionary; during his invasion of the Italian principalities and Rome he'd become a devout Catholic.

Although the fall of Egypt was not known to Nelson, he was certain that Bonaparte was somewhere in the east and continued searching. On 1 August 1798, the lookout of HMS *Zealous* reported the topmasts of the French fleet in Aboukir Bay. Brueys had anchored hard up against sandbanks along the western side of the bay to force any attacking ships to approach from the east. He'd also landed guns on Aboukir Island at the head of the bay. Accordingly, Brueys had the majority of his men manning all the guns on the eastern, starboard, side of his ships. It was a tactical position of great strength. Nelson summoned his captains to *Vanguard*.

In the anchorage were more than twenty-two French warships; thirteen ships of the line comprising the 120-gun flagship *L'Orient*, three 80s and nine 74s, as well as four large frigates, two brigs, three bomb ketches and several gunboats. Approaching from the sea, the sun about to set, were fifteen British warships, comprising thirteen 74s, one 50 and a brig.

Brueys did not expect Nelson to attack that evening – in the dark, in an unchartered bay, in shallow water, outnumbered and outgunned.

However, at 5.30 p.m. Nelson signalled his fleet: 'Form line of battle as most convenient.' The 74s swept past Aboukir Island into the darkening bay.

Almost immediately, *Culloden* went aground to become a helpless spectator of the battle. Brueys now had 250 more guns than Nelson. As the remaining twelve British 74s reached the head of the French line, they split into two divisions; six and the 50 taking positions along the eastern side of the French fleet as expected, while the other six proceeded along the western side – between the French and the sandbanks. Nelson had told his captains: 'Where there is room for a French 74 at single anchor to swing, there is room for a British 74 to attack.' There was. The first shot was fired at 6.28 p.m.

Despite his careful preparations, Brueys's ships were attacked on both sides. Nelson leapfrogged his ships along the enemy line, sweeping the ships from port and starboard with broadside after terrible broadside, destroying or capturing one ship after another. The *Conquérant* surrendered after twelve minutes. By 8 p.m., four more had surrendered. Nelson was once again wounded, cut to the bone above his left, good, eye. Bleeding heavily and severely concussed, he was carried below to the surgeon and the horrors of the cockpit.

In *L'Orient*, Brueys was also injured, both his legs cut off below the knee by shot. The French ships surrendered or fought on until they were incapable, mast-less hulks. After intense gunnery from HMS *Bellerophon*, *Swiftsure* and *Alexander*, *L'Orient* caught fire. Brueys was dead. In *Vanguard*, Nelson insisted on being helped back to the quarterdeck.

The fire spread in the enormous French flagship until the flames illuminated the battle like a giant candle. It was soon evident there could be only one outcome. Nelson and the captains of nearby British ships lowered their boats to rescue the French seamen leaping into the dark waters. Shortly after 10 p.m. the fierce blaze reached the magazine.

The mighty *L'Orient* disintegrated in a shattering explosion that was heard thirteen miles away in Alexandria. Flying debris set *Swiftsure* and *Alexander* briefly alight. All ships stopped firing for about twelve minutes, in awe at the destruction. With *L'Orient* went gold plate and bullion looted by Bonaparte from Malta. Only seventy of her crew were found by the British boats.

The great battle resumed, continuing through the warm night. The perspiring crews, stripped to the waist with handkerchiefs bound over their ears, worked their guns continuously. The tongues of flame illuminated the darkness like a series of paintings. By mid-morning, eleven French ships of the line had been captured or destroyed, the two which escaped being captured shortly afterwards. Two frigates were also destroyed. It's estimated that 1,700 French seamen lost their lives, 1,500 were wounded and 3,000 taken prisoner. Not one British ship was lost, although 218 men were killed and 678 wounded.

The Battle of the Nile is the most comprehensive naval victory ever achieved – and its effects were immense and far-reaching. The Royal Navy had taken control of the Mediterranean. Bonaparte and his Army of the East were isolated and the Egyptians and Arabs willingly turned against him. Eventually, Bonaparte abandoned his army and fled back to France in a fast frigate, a Muslim no longer. A force from India under General Abercrombie later disposed of this army. In thanks to Nelson and Abercrombie for their liberation from the French, Muhammad Ali, the Viceroy of Egypt, presented to Britain Cleopatra's Needle, from 1500 BC. It stands today on the Victoria Embankment in London.

Other countries saw that the French could be defeated, inspiring Austria and the Italian states to resume the struggle. Although there were to be a further seventeen years of warfare, Nelson and the navy had shown that victory was possible.

Overnight, Nelson became a hero to Britain and Europe. He was created Baron of the Nile and of Burnham Thorpe, a wonderfully unlikely combination of place names.

Nelson's private life also changed. In Naples, he began the affair which lasted the rest of his life – with Emma Hamilton, wife of British ambassador William Hamilton, Nelson's friend. The affair caused society outrage, yet the three lived much of their lives together and remained steadfast friends until their deaths. With Emma, Nelson had his only child, Horatia.

In 1801, a 'treaty of armed neutrality' of many Baltic Sea nations led by Russia had closed the Baltic trade to Britain. The trade in timber, flax, tar and other supplies was vital for the navy to continue the fight against Bonaparte. Russia seized 300 British merchant ships, while Denmark closed all her ports. The treaty was effectively an alliance with France. Britain sent a fleet to the Baltic under Admiral Hyde Parker with Nelson, now vice admiral, second in command.

Negotiations between Parker and the Danish court failed in March and an attack on Copenhagen began. The Danes had protected their port capital by anchoring their ships in an unbroken line of floating batteries and gunboats between the city and the Öresund channel that led out to sea. There would be no British attack to both sides of their fleet here. The channel markers had also been removed, yet Nelson had a plan.

The Danes expected the British to attack from the north, the main channel into Copenhagen, whereas Nelson planned to sail a division of ships through a narrow channel outside and attack from the south. Admiral Parker's division would still attack through the main channel from the north to engage the formidable guns of Fort Trekroner.

Nelson shifted his flag to the 74-gun *Elephant* for the battle. In all, the Danish had 380 guns, the British 400, but the Danish had immense superiority in the calibre – the size – of their guns. In addition, Fort Trekroner, the ships, floating batteries and gunboats were continually replenished with fresh men and ammunition from Copenhagen. Nelson relied upon the superior rate of fire of his seamen to counter these disadvantages.

On the morning of 2 April, Nelson sailed ten 74s, one 54 and one 50 to the southern and central Danish defences. Positioned behind *Elephant* in the 54-gun *Glatton* was Captain Bligh of the *Bounty* mutiny. Seven bomb ketches firing mortars were anchored beyond *Elephant*.

Battle commenced at 10.05 a.m. but Nelson's plan had to be changed immediately. Parker could not bring his ships down from the north because of a dead foul wind, while three of Nelson's 74s went aground in the unmarked channel and were out of the battle. Nelson now had only seven 74s and fewer guns to attack the Danes.

He sent five frigates to the north to prevent any Danish ships coming south against him.

In the chill Baltic spring, the great guns thundered outside Copenhagen, the Danish putting up a strong resistance. Firing continued uninterrupted until 1 p.m., when Admiral Parker sent his famous signal of recall.

In fact Parker was not retreating; he was shouldering the blame for what he thought may become a defeat. Both Danes and Britons were suffering heavy losses in what was simply a slugging match, for no further manoeuvring was possible in the confined waters. By his signal, Parker gave Nelson the opportunity to withdraw under his commander's orders if he wished.

Nelson said to the captain of *Elephant*: 'You know, Foley, I have only one eye – I have a right to be blind sometimes.' Then he put his telescope to his blind right eye and exclaimed: 'I really do not see the signal!' The expression 'turning a blind eye' entered the language.

Gradually the fire from the Danish ships and batteries slackened. The flagship *Dannebrog* caught fire, struck her colours and drifted out of control. Like *L'Orient* she blew up, but British boats were prevented from rescuing her crew because of fire from the Danish shore batteries. By 2.30 p.m. the Danish firing had almost stopped. Nelson offered a truce, which at just after 4 p.m. was accepted and an armistice later negotiated. Seventeen Danish ships were captured, burned or destroyed, with a loss of almost 1,700 men killed or wounded and 3,500 taken prisoner. Yet again Nelson lost not one vessel, although 941 British were killed or wounded.

It was a brutal battle and one which both nations – usually friends and allies – regretted having to fight. It's indicative that only two honours were awarded for the Battle of Copenhagen. Nelson was made viscount and his second in command, Rear Admiral Graves, invested with the Order of the Bath. Yet the victory was vital to the progress of the war against France. It kept the Scandinavian countries and Russia neutral, it maintained Britain's Baltic trade, and it affirmed that, although Bonaparte's armies ruled the continent, the Royal Navy controlled the seas. French military dictatorship ended where the sea was deep enough for Britain to float a boat.

The 1802 Peace Treaty of Amiens lasted barely a year before Bonaparte broke it. He had used the peace to rebuild his navy, invade Switzerland, the Netherlands and Elba, and assemble some 7,000 barges to carry the 200,000 Grand Army across the English Channel to invade Britain. In May 1803, war resumed.

Nelson hoisted his flag in the refitted *Victory* as Vice Admiral of the Red – the famous red ensign now used by the merchant navy. St Vincent was at the Admiralty, Admiral Cornwallis was in charge of the Channel and Western Approaches, and Nelson was given charge of the Mediterranean.

Despite controlling the seas, the situation for Britain remained critical. A change of wind might blow the Royal Navy blockading fleets away and the same wind allow the rebuilt French and Spanish fleets out of port. If they could combine and take control of the English Channel for a single day, Bonaparte might slip his army across and French boots would march up Whitehall.

Cornwallis's brief was to blockade the French fleet in Brest and control the Western Approaches while Admiral Keith's division held the Channel. Nelson's orders were to blockade the French fleet in Toulon. With St Vincent at the Admiralty, those four men controlled the destiny of the world. A single mistake, a single error of judgement, would have tipped Europe into a military abyss.

Nelson commanded *Victory*, nine ships of the line, a frigate and two sloops. Captain of *Victory* was Thomas Hardy, Nelson's old friend who'd been present at both the Nile and Copenhagen. For two years the blockades were maintained, two years in which the British fleets were continuously at sea. Such a time at sea without refitting in a dockyard has never been surpassed by any fleet. Those square-rigged sailing ships, constantly patrolling the Channel, off Brest, off Cadiz and in the Mediterranean, were the 'wooden walls' of Britain. Nelson never left Victory, though his eyesight deteriorated further and his stomach wound bothered him constantly.

Finally, in April 1805, under the very capable Admiral Villeneuve, the French fleet slipped out of Toulon while the majority of Nelson's ships were taking on water. A great chase ensued; over the western

Mediterranean, through the Straits of Gibraltar, across the Atlantic to the West Indies, and back to Ferrol in northern Spain by the end of July. Yet nothing had changed. The French fleet still avoided major action, the French army remained camped by the Channel ports, and the invasion barges sat waiting. Nelson was given leave and set foot off *Victory* for the first time in two years.

At the end of August, Villeneuve slipped his fleet south to Cadiz where, with Spanish reinforcements, it numbered more than forty ships. Bonaparte ordered him to combine with the fleet in Brest and gain control of the English Channel.

Nelson was recalled from leave. When he rejoined *Victory* at Portsmouth, a large crowd collected. Some were in tears, some cheered and lifted their children high to see him, others knelt and blessed him as he passed. He said to Hardy: 'I had their huzzas before. I have their hearts now.' *Victory* arrived off Cadiz on 28 September.

The combined French and Spanish fleets under Villeneuve's command put to sea on 19 and 20 October and assembled south of Cadiz. The British under Nelson lay out of sight while his inshore frigates relayed the enemy's movements.

During the night, Nelson manoeuvred his fleet. At daybreak on the 21st they were positioned so that if Villeneuve continued south to Gibraltar he would have to fight, if Villeneuve sailed north-west to the Channel he would have to fight, and if Villeneuve returned to Cadiz he would also have to fight. Importantly, Nelson had maintained the commanding, windward position.

As Nelson had predicted, when Villeneuve sighted the twenty-six waiting British ships at dawn he altered course to return to Cadiz. At 5.40 a.m. Nelson signalled his captains: 'Form the order of sailing in two columns.' This signal was repeated at 6 a.m. so that the captains knew this was also the order of battle.

In *Victory*, Nelson commanded the northern column of eleven ships of the line which included *Temeraire*. Vice Admiral Collingwood, second in command in *Royal Sovereign*, commanded the southern column of fifteen ships of the line. A latecomer, 64-gun *Africa*, was ten miles to the north-west, sailing to join Nelson.

His Majesty's ships were *Victory, Royal Sovereign, Britannia, Temeraire, Revenge, Prince, Tonnant, Belle Isle, Mars, Neptune, Spartiate, Defiance, Conqueror, Defence, Colossus, Leviathan, Ajax, Achille, Bellerophon, Minotaur, Orion, Swiftsure, Polyphemus, Agamemnon, Dreadnought, Thunderer* and *Africa*.

East and downwind of the Royal Navy, the French and Spanish fleet of thirty-three ships of the line sailed northwards in a curved formation, roughly two abreast. It included Villeneuve's flagship *Bucentaure* and the largest and second largest warships in the world, the 130-gun *Santissima Trinidad* and the 112-gun *Santa Ana*. The enemy fleet had superiority by six ships of the line, 474 guns, and 8,124 men. In addition, Villeneuve had seven frigates to Nelson's four.

A total of seventy-one warships, sixty of them ships-of-the-line, slowly converged at the shoals of Cape Trafalgar off Spain on the morning of 21 October 1805 – the day ever after known as Trafalgar Day. Although the wind was only light from the west-north-west, drawing the fleets together at just 1½ knots, the swell was gradually increasing, indicating a coming gale. It would blow hard by the end of the day. The British ships – flying the white ensign for easy identification – set all sail including stun'sails instead of the usual, reduced, fighting sails so as to close the enemy as quickly as possible. In the tense waiting Nelson remarked to his officers: 'I'll now amuse the fleet,' and so was hoisted the most famous naval signal ever made.

It began as 'Nelson confides that every man will do his duty'. At the suggestion of another officer Nelson amended it to 'England confides that every man will do his duty' (there was a single code flag meaning 'England' but not for 'Britain' or 'Nelson') and, at the suggestion of the flag lieutenant in order to use even fewer flags, it was finally hoisted as 'England expects that every man will do his duty'. The fleet cheered, although Collingwood said: 'I wish Nelson would stop signalling. We all know well enough what we have to do.'

The plan of battle, an improvement on the Battle of St Vincent, was already agreed. Instead of one column, two British columns would break the enemy line from windward, turn port and starboard to lay alongside from leeward and so prevent the enemy from escaping downwind. It was simple and brilliant. Nelson's last words to his senior officers were: 'No captain can do very wrong if he places his ship alongside that of an enemy.'

In his diary he wrote the prayer he had composed that morning: 'May the Great God, whom I worship, grant to my country and for the benefit of Europe in general a great and glorious victory, and may no misconduct in anyone tarnish it, and may humanity after victory be the predominant feature in the British Fleet. For myself, individually, I commit my life to Him who made me and may His blessing light upon my endeavours for serving my country faithfully. To Him I resign myself and the just cause which is entrusted to me to defend. Amen, amen, amen.'

It was Collingwood in the 100-gun *Royal Sovereign* who first came under fire, just before noon, from 112-gun *Santa Ana*. Minutes later *Victory*, feinting as though to attack the head of the enemy fleet, came under fire from several ships. Her wheel was destroyed and she had to be steered by emergency tackle from below. *Royal Sovereign* broke the enemy line astern of *Santa Ana*, the eighteenth ship, into which Collingwood fired double-shotted broadsides.

Nelson steered *Victory* back towards the 120-gun *Santissima Trinidad* and 80-gun *Bucentaure*, thirteenth in the line. After sustaining twenty minutes of unanswered fire, *Victory* passed astern of *Bucentaure* to fire a running port broadside, double-shotted, through Villeneuve's stern windows and the entire length of the vessel. French reports state that twenty guns were destroyed and 400 men killed or wounded from that first broadside alone.

Victory passed on, turned alongside *Redoutable* and fought that ship with her starboard guns while her port guns fought *Santissima Trinidad*. *Redoutable* under Captain Lucas was one of the best-manned French ships and it was hard going for *Victory* – she was almost boarded – until HMS *Temeraire* approached and fired a series of broadsides into *Redoutable*. Then *Fougueux* came to *Redoutable*'s assistance and the four vessels fought it out for a further three hours. One after another, the British ships broke the line, turned and engaged one or more enemy ships, until the ships and the sea itself were obscured by greasy cannon smoke.

At about 1.15 p.m., on the quarterdeck of *Victory*, Nelson was shot. A marksman above in the mizzen mast of *Redoutable* – her only surviving mast – fired and the musket ball passed through the gold epaulette on Nelson's left shoulder. It broke two ribs, severed a main branch of the pulmonary artery to the heart, and continued on to break two vertebrae. He sank to his knees and then slid to the deck as Hardy went to his assistance. 'They have done for me, at last,' Nelson said to him. He was carried below to the cockpit – on the way ordering damaged tiller ropes to be repaired – but there was nothing surgeon Beatty could do for him.

Nelson asked for Hardy to come to him, but the fighting was fierce. At 1.45 p.m. Villeneuve surrendered flagship *Bucentaure* to HMS *Conqueror*. *Bucentaure* had been dismasted and her decks and gangways were filled with wreckage and the dead. At 2.15 p.m., *Santa Ana* struck her colours to *Royal Sovereign*. It wasn't until *Fougueux* and *Redoutable* surrendered to the *Victory* and *Temeraire* that Hardy could leave the quarterdeck at 2.20 p.m.

'Well, Hardy, how goes the battle?' Nelson asked weakly. 'How goes the day with us?' Hardy reported that twelve or fourteen enemy ships were already captured, but another five were bearing down upon *Victory*. 'I hope none of our ships have struck, Hardy?' 'No, my lord,' Hardy replied, 'there is no fear of that.' Hardy shook his friend's hand and returned to the deck.

Some fifty minutes later Hardy returned to the surgeon's cockpit, took and held Nelson's cold hand, and this time was able to congratulate him on a brilliant victory. The Royal Navy had carried the day, again without the loss of a single ship. The news of Nelson's mortal wound was passed only to Collingwood in *Royal Sovereign*.

'Don't throw me overboard, Hardy,' Nelson whispered, and then: 'Take care of my dear Lady Hamilton ... Kiss me, Hardy.' The tall, angular Hardy knelt down and kissed his cheek. Nelson murmured: 'Now I am satisfied; thank God, I have done my duty.' Hardy stood gazing at his friend for a moment and then knelt again and kissed his admiral's forehead. 'Who is that?' asked Nelson. It appears his sight had gone. 'It is Hardy,' the captain replied. 'God bless you, Hardy.' Then Hardy returned to the quarterdeck.

Nelson lingered a little longer, saying again: 'Thank God, I have done my duty.' *Victory*'s logbook records in pencil: 'Partial firing continued until 4.30 p.m., when a victory having been reported to the Right Hon. Lord Viscount Nelson, KB, and Commander-in-Chief, he died of his wound.'

At 5 p.m. there was a massive explosion. The French *Achille*, dismasted and on fire, had blown up. The tally that day was twenty-eight French and Spanish ships of the line surrendered and one destroyed. Eleven of those surrenders, including *Santa Ana*, escaped during the gale to reach Cadiz. One was wrecked on the beach, while the remainder were found to be so severely damaged they never put to sea again. In addition, three more French ships of the line were wrecked in an attempt to retake captured French ships the following day, while the final four ships that escaped to the south were captured fourteen days later.

Ultimately, twenty-six enemy ships were captured or destroyed by the Battle of Trafalgar, 5,860 French and Spanish killed or wounded, and 20,000 taken prisoner. No British ship was lost but 1,600 seamen were killed or wounded. The Battle of Trafalgar was Nelson's third total victory.

That night, when the gale lashed the fleets and the British seamen risked their lives to rescue French and Spanish crews from their battered ships, it was observed with dismay that the three admiral's lanterns at the stern of HMS *Victory* were not lit.

Nelson's body was preserved in a cask of brandy and returned to Britain. Battle-hardened, tarred and pigtailed sailors wept when they learned of his death. One wrote home: 'All the men in our ship are such soft toads, they have done nothing but Blast their Eyes and cry ever since he was killed. God bless you! Chaps that fought like the Devil sit down and cry like a wench.' Britain mourned.

On 9 January, 1806, in the first state funeral for a commoner, Horatio Nelson – in a coffin made of timber from *L'Orient* – was placed in a tomb of black marble in the crypt of St Paul's Cathedral, exactly below the centre of the dome. He was posthumously created earl. Memorials to Captains Duff of *Mars* and Cooke of *Bellerophon*, who also died at Trafalgar, are nearby. So also is the modest tomb of Admiral Collingwood. Succeeding Nelson in the Mediterranean, controlling all the seas and coasts from Gibraltar to Turkey, Collingwood literally worked himself to death only five years later in the cause of freedom.

Nelson and his 'band of brothers' gave Britain command of the seas for some 140 years. The famous uniform worn by sailors of the

Royal Navy, most Commonwealth navies, and copied by almost every other navy in the world, remembers Admiral Nelson. The three white stripes around the border of the shoulder flap record the three great victories of the Nile, Copenhagen and Trafalgar. The black silk neck-scarf echoes the mourning bands worn by the seamen who pulled the gun carriage carrying his coffin, from Whitehall steps to the Admiralty and St Paul's.

Horatio Nelson's most enduring qualities are his humanity and care of others – both the enemy as well as his own men – and a leadership inspired by love rather than dominance. Lord Montgomery of Alamein judged him on all counts to be 'supreme among captains of war'. In the French language, a sudden decisive blow is called a 'coup de Trafalgar'. At Trafalgar Day dinners, the toast is a unique silent toast – to 'The Immortal Memory'.

HMS *Victory* is now preserved in Portsmouth as she fought at Trafalgar, and is the honoured permanent flagship of the Commander-in-Chief, Naval Home Command. She is the oldest commissioned vessel in the world. Because of battle, decay and rot from over 250 years, little of the original oak remains today. Yet, in All Saints' Parish Church of Burnham Thorpe, Norfolk, you can touch still the timber that was afloat off Cape Trafalgar on 21 October 1805.

Recommended
The Authentic Narrative of the Death of Lord Nelson by William Beatty.
The Life of Nelson by Robert Southey.
Nelson and his Captains by Ludovic Kennedy.
Nelson the Commander by Geoffrey Bennett.
Trafalgar Square, London.
HMS *Victory*, HM Naval Dockyard, Portsmouth, Hampshire.
Royal Naval Museum, Portsmouth, Hampshire.
National Maritime Museum, Greenwich, London.
Chatham Naval Dockyard, Chatham, Kent.
St Paul's Cathedral, London.
The Guildhall Monument, Guildhall, London.
The Trafalgar Cemetery, Gibraltar, UK.

Billy Bishop –
The Courage of the Early Morning

At 3.57 a.m. on 2 June 1917, a lone Royal Flying Corps fighter took off from Filescamp airfield near Arras in France. It was still dark, with that hollow predawn cold when the body is at its lowest ebb. The Canadian pilot had pulled his clothes on over the top of his pyjamas to keep his bed warmth, drunk a cup of hot tea and walked out to his Nieuport 17 and waiting mechanic. Soon he was across the front, high above the road to Cambrai.

In June, the sun rises early and the first colour spread across the Great War battlefields below. At his target airfield near Cambrai there was no activity, so pilot Billy Bishop searched for another target. Near Esnes, twelve miles behind enemy lines, he found an airfield with aeroplanes wheeled out for battle; a single two-seater reconnaissance plane and six grey-blue Albatross scouts – enemy fighters. Bishop swooped low at two hundred feet through ground fire, spraying the aircraft below from the Lewis machine gun on his top wing. He saw a mechanic fall.

An Albatross started to take off, so he flew in behind and shot it down sixty feet above the ground, the machine disintegrating as it slid along the grass. Its pilot survived. A second Albatross began its take-off. Bishop turned tightly, fired but missed. The German pilot swerved away into a tree, tearing off the aeroplane's right wing. By then, two more Albatrosses had taken off and Bishop duelled with one while the second watched and waited. He manoeuvred in tight turns until he was below the enemy and emptied his gun into the Albatross's engine. The aeroplane fluttered away and crashed near the airfield.

Gripping the stick between his legs, Bishop stood in his cockpit and replaced the empty ammunition drum of the Lewis gun. The fourth Albatross flew in to attack, but Bishop turned the Nieuport head-on towards it and fired the full drum. The German fled and Bishop turned away for home.

Above him at 2,000 feet he saw a dawn patrol of Albatrosses. He flew unseen directly below them until he reached the front line trenches and dived for friendly territory. German pilots rarely pursued across the front, but the guns on the ground fired up at him. Bishop landed back at Filescamp, one hour and forty-three minutes after taking off. His Nieuport had been raked by machine-gun and anti-aircraft fire along its lower wings, elevators and fuselage. Mechanic Sergeant Nicod noted the damage in his report.

Bishop's commanding officer of 60 Squadron, Major Jack Scott, recommended him for the Victoria Cross, Bishop's second recommendation. It was gazetted in August to be Canada's first aerial VC. General Trenchard, commanding officer of the RFC (soon after renamed the Royal Air Force), called it 'the greatest single show of the war'.

Captain William Avery Bishop was already well known along the Western Front of Belgium and France. By June 1917 he had twenty-one confirmed 'victories' against German flyers, making him an ace four times over. He was holder of the Military Cross. Yet in those early years of aerial combat, success was a lottery, determined by the aeroplane itself as much as the enemy. Bishop flew first in 21 Squadron, flying the experimental RE7 reconnaissance aeroplane. It was known as the Suicide Squadron. 'The RE7s are nearly as manoeuvrable as ten-ton trucks,' Bishop commented, 'but by no means as safe.'

At that point, British ace Captain Albert Ball VC of 60 Squadron had the most victories of the 1914–18 war, with forty-four. A victory was given if 'an enemy aircraft was seen going down out of control, in flames, to fall apart, driven down or forced to land'. It was different from the later Battle of Britain, when an aircraft had to be destroyed to claim a 'kill'.

Bishop learned his tactics from Ball. After Bishop downed his fifth enemy plane to become an official 'ace', he painted the front of his engine a bright blue so as not to be mistaken for Ball's red aeroplane. German flyers called Bishop the 'Blue-nosed Devil'. It was Ball who'd first suggested a surprise dawn attack on a German airfield, but he'd been shot down and killed that May. After Ball's death, Bishop was determined to exceed his total.

He was more a lone hunter than one of a team, although he commanded 'C' Flight at Filescamp. With their rare level of skill, Ball and Bishop were two of the very few pilots allowed to hunt alone. Bishop similarly sought the advantage of height, of surprise, of attacking out of the sun, and hunting deep behind enemy lines. He was a superb shot, developed from game shooting in Canada. He had excellent eyesight, and possessed that three-dimensional awareness of airspace vital for a successful fighter pilot. He also made many more flights than most pilots, for he flew both squadron patrols *and* alone. It increased his chances of victories. It also increased his chances of being someone else's 'victory', but that's war.

April 1917 was known as 'Bloody April' in the RFC – the average lifespan for a pilot was forty-five days; in Bishop's sector only seventeen days. Flying was increased to support the Battle of Arras below, in which the Canadian Corps captured Vimy Ridge. 60 Squadron suffered particularly badly, for they were opposite the red-painted 'Flying Circus' of Baron Manfred von Richthofen, the most successful squadron of the war. Richthofen claimed eighty victories before he was killed in April 1918. Bishop battled with the Circus and, some claim, with Richthofen himself on 30 April, although that is doubtful.

During Bloody April, thirteen of the eighteen pilots in 60 Squadron were shot down as well as seven replacement pilots – a 110 per cent casualty rate. Yet thirty-five of the enemy were also shot down, twelve of those by Billy Bishop, so April wasn't exactly a honeymoon for German flyers either. It was that May that Major Scott first recommended Bishop for a Victoria Cross, for 'prolonged gallantry'. He was awarded the Distinguished Service Order instead.

In July, the squadron's out-of-date Nieuports were replaced by the excellent SE5 fighter and Bishop shot down even more enemy aeroplanes – two-seater fighters, reconnaissance, single-seat fighters, even German observation balloons – until on the 28th his SE5 was hit by the slashing shrapnel of anti-aircraft fire. Still two miles from Filescamp airfield, the spluttering engine caught fire and Bishop crashed into a stand of poplar trees. Wire snapped, wooden struts splintered, canvas wings tore, and Bishop was left hanging upside down in his harness. He passed out. Rain put out the fire and he was rescued by passing soldiers. Understandably, he was shaken. He wrote home: 'I find myself shuddering at chances I didn't think about taking six weeks ago'.

Nonetheless, by the time he was given extended leave on 1 September, he'd overtaken Ball's total, with fifty victories. He took a steamer to Canada and married his sweetheart, Margaret Burden. Thousands lined the Toronto streets to see Canada's air hero and his bride.

When the United States entered the war in April 1917, Captain Bishop VC, MC, DSO and bar, was posted to the British War Mission to help

America build an air force. While in America, he wrote a quick autobiography, *Winged Warfare*, which, more than anything, was propaganda for recruiting drives. The truth was embellished and the preface baldly stated that the book would provide 'inspiration to every young man in the army "wings" or who contemplates an army career.' Bishop said later: 'It turns my stomach.'

It wasn't until March 1918 that Bishop was posted back to Britain. He was immediately promoted to major and given command of the new RAF's 85 Squadron at Hounslow, near Heathrow. Given a relatively free hand in the selection of pilots, more than two hundred volunteered to join Bishop. There were Australian, British, Canadian, South Africans, New Zealanders and even the first Americans. In May, flying SE5a scouts, one of the best aeroplanes of the entire war, the squadron flew to Petite Synthe near Dunkirk for operations over Flanders. They were known as 'The Flying Foxes'.

On 27 May, Bishop shot down a two-seater over Passchendaele, and on the 28th two Albatross fighters over Ypres. His phenomenal – and deadly – marksmanship continued until 17 June, when his squadron was operating from St-Omer. He was advised he'd been posted to Britain to help create a Canadian Flying Corps and he had to leave his squadron by noon of the 19th. 'I've never been so furious in my life,' he wrote to his wife. 'It makes me livid with rage to be pulled away just as things are getting started.' However, the Canadian government was worried about him. With the best aeroplanes and better tactics, the RAF commanded the air over the battle fronts, yet it was feared that, like his mentor Albert Ball, Bishop would be killed. He was more important to the war effort alive than with a few more victories and dead.

On the morning of the 19th Billy Bishop flew his last patrol. 'One last look at the war,' he described it. He intercepted a flight of German Pfalz fighters and in a ferocious fifteen minutes of flying was credited with three more victories, although he claimed five.

In August, he was awarded the RAF's new Distinguished Flying Cross in recognition of his recent twenty-five victories in just twelve days of combat. Two days later he was promoted to lieutenant colonel and appointed Officer Commanding-designate of the Canadian Air Corps. In all, he was credited with seventy-two aeroplane victories and two observation balloons, making him the greatest ace of the RAF and one of the few great aces to survive the war.

Billy and Margaret Bishop's post-war years were up-and-down. They moved to England in 1921, had three children and ran a successful business until bankrupted by the stock-market crash of 1929. Returning to Canada, Bishop was appointed honorary group captain in the Royal Canadian Air Force and, eventually, honorary air marshal.

During the 1939–45 war Air Marshal Bishop helped expand the Royal Canadian Air Force. He was also instrumental in creating the 'Commonwealth Air Training Plan', in which thousands of flyers from the Commonwealth and Empire were trained in the peaceful air spaces of Canada. He had the pleasure of presenting his own son, Arthur, with his pilot's wings. Arthur Bishop flew Spitfires during the Battle of Britain to become one of The Few, and one of the few of The Few to survive that war.

In 1942, after the United States entered the war, Billy Bishop appeared in a Hollywood propaganda film, 'Captains of the Clouds', and so became one of the rare actors actually to play himself. More importantly, King George VI made Bishop a Companion of the Order of the Bath in the Birthday Honours List of 1944, while at home he was awarded the Canadian Efficiency Decoration. After the war, he wrote another book, *Winged Peace*. That book and Bishop himself helped the formation of the International Civil Aviation Organisation. Bishop retired in 1952 at the age of 58, to die in his sleep in September 1956.

Billy Bishop's honour seemed safe. He'd played his part in two world wars, defeating respectively militarism and fascism. Many books were written about him, including one by his son, and there is even a play, 'Billy Bishop Goes to War'. Yet it seems nothing is sacred. In 1982, a 'documentary' film was released by the National Film Board of Canada called 'The Kid Who Couldn't Miss'. It caused controversy throughout Canada and a Senate Inquiry.

Using fictional 'interviews' with people long dead, played by actors giving fictional replies, Bishop's whole 1914–18 war record was questioned – in particular, the dawn attack of 2 June 1917. The film alleges Bishop lied about this attack. As his Victoria Cross is, so far, the only VC awarded for a specific action not officially witnessed, Bishop was an easy target for defamation. The accusations of lying were built around the argument that (1) there are no German records of an attack on Estourmel, (2) a Nieuport 17 could not have flown that distance and remained in the air for that time, (3) the damage to the Nieuport was self-inflicted by Bishop, (4) Bishop landed in Allied territory and used the aeroplane's machine gun to make that damage, and (5) Bishop then hid the machine gun.

It's the classic defamation of a hero. He's dead, the witnesses are dead, most of the records are destroyed or lost, and the event took place in another era with different standards of honesty. Yet with Billy Bishop, fortunately there is evidence against the defamation.

According to Bishop's own combat report, written that 1917 morning, his attack was against an airfield at 'either Esnes or Awoingt' – not Estourmel, as the film claims. Bishop wasn't sure which, for both were temporary airfields, both were four miles from Estourmel and Bishop was fighting a war, not making a documentary. That 1st and 2nd of June there were six Albatrosses on a temporary airfield at Esnes, during a German squadron transfer to the British front. It's not surprising no German report survives, because squadron transfer reports were not required. The squadron diary where it might have been mentioned was destroyed by British bombing during the 1939–45 war. The confusion with Estourmel actually comes from a mistake in Bishop's son's book of 1965.

The flight described in Bishop's combat report that lasted one hour and forty-three minutes was within the capabilities and range of a Nieuport 17. The damage report by mechanic Sergeant Nicod recorded 'both machine-gun and heavier anti-aircraft damage'. How can a pilot fake anti-aircraft damage to the underneath of his wings? Further, the Nieuport 17s were renowned for structural weaknesses in their wing struts; Bishop's squadron had already lost five from this dangerous fault. It defies argument that an ace with twenty-one victories would land his aircraft, remove his machine gun from the top wing, and shoot his already weak wing structures.

In addition, it was impossible for the pilot to leave the cockpit of a Nieuport 17 with the engine turning. With no hand or wheel brake and a high-revving rotary engine, the aeroplane would motor away from him. A pilot had to switch off the engine – but the aeroplane had no self-starter. A second person had to swing the propeller, with the pilot in the cockpit, to restart the engine. As to the alleged hidden machine gun, why would Bishop hide it, whatever the circumstances? His combat report does not mention a lost Lewis gun, and the weekly squadron reports record no lost or jettisoned Lewis at all for June. Again, the origin is in Bishop's son's book, written from memory nine years after his father died.

Finally, Bishop's attack was corroborated by British balloon observer Louis Weirter, twelve miles away at the British front line. Visibility was good that mid-summer dawn and, from 4,000 feet, equipped with military field glasses, Weirter would have clearly seen a single-fighter attack at Esnes – as he reported. From that height he would have seen clearly thirty miles away.

For confirmation of Bishop's other victories, because he fought deep behind enemy lines it's no surprise that witnesses to some were hard to find. Yet in fact, Bishop had a very high confirmation rate by witnesses, second only to James McCudden of those pilots given commissions to hunt alone.

In Berlin in 1928, Billy Bishop became the only Allied fighter pilot to be inducted into the German Aces Association of the 1914–18 war. They had no doubt about the 'Blue-nosed Devil' from Owen Sound, Ontario, Canada.

Let's leave Bishop's honour to the 1956 obituary by the Montreal Gazette:

'Death came to Air Marshal Billy Bishop in the early morning. He died at the chill hour before the coming of the dawn – an hour when he must often have been making ready for his solitary flights. Perhaps, if he had had his choice, this would be the hour he would have preferred. For he had that courage which Napoleon Bonaparte once said was the rarest – the courage of the early morning.'

Recommended
Over the Front (Volume 10, No 3) by Philip Markham.
The Courage of the Early Morning by Arthur Bishop.
Billy Bishop Museum, Owen Sound, Ontario, Canada.
RAF Museum, Hendon, Middlesex.

Bletchley Park
and the First Computers

‘The geese who laid the golden eggs and never cackled.’
– Winston Churchill

In the north Buckinghamshire countryside lies a sprawling country house built in Elizabethan, Jacobean, Georgian and Victorian styles, two storeys high with a small central tower and battlement. It’s set in a Domesday estate of 480 acres and is listed by English Heritage. It’s called Bletchley Park.

In early 1939, the Secret Intelligence Service took over Bletchley Park for its ‘Government Code and Cipher School’ – GC&CS. After the success of Room 40 during the 1914–18 war, the government appreciated the vital role intelligence could play. Nowadays it’s located at GCHQ in Cheltenham, Gloucestershire. It is without doubt the most successful secret service in the world, if only for what its men and women achieved in Bletchley Park from 1939 to 1945.

Bletchley Park is where the codes of the German ‘Enigma’ machines were broken, where the Japanese military and diplomatic codes were broken, and where the world’s first electronic computer was invented to break Hitler’s top-secret codes. The computer age began at Bletchley Park, Buckinghamshire.

The ‘golden eggs’ to which Churchill referred was the intelligence Bletchley produced, and the 7,500 women and 2,500 men who worked there were the ‘geese’. Not one word was spoken about their role until it was declassified in the mid-1970s – the geese never cackled. That thirty years of silence is significant in another way. The vast majority of men and women at Bletchley were not silver-haired professors; most of the code-breakers were under thirty. Many were under twenty and a few were straight from school. It was young brains that did the job, assisted by daring raids in the field by other young brains.

By 1939 there was already a history of GC&CS success. Intercepts and code-breaks of communist Russian signals between the wars had uncovered attempts to sow a communist revolution in Britain – funding left-wing newspapers, the British Communist Party, union unrest and strikes.

From the efforts particularly of John Tiltman, Hugh Foss and Australian Eric Nave, GC&CS also broke Japanese codes regularly from the 1920s. American intelligence didn't make its first Japanese code-break until 1940. However, the surprise 1941 attack on Malaya and Pearl Harbor was *not* uncovered. The 1941 German attack on Russia was uncovered by Bletchley; Churchill warned Russia but was not believed.

By 1940, GC&CS was breaking twenty-six diplomatic codes of both enemy and neutral countries. The Americans were then working only four countries. Later, GC&CS gave almost all its keys, ciphers, code-breaks and equipment to American intelligence for it to catch up.

The greatest challenge that would face the Bletchley park codebreakers was the German Enigma machine. Resembling a typewriter, it had the advantage of being able to encode messages at typing speed. They were a vital part of Germany's war effort and were used by all its armed forces and diplomatic networks. Britain's Polish allies copied the first Enigma machine in 1939 and passed it to GC&CS. When Poland fell in 1939, Polish cryptanalysts fled to France, and when France fell they fled to Britain. Polish intelligence also made the first Enigma code-break in January 1940, while GC&CS made the second code-break in February.

There are three parts to a coded message: the plain language, the key to the code used, and the resulting encoded message. Any two parts are required to uncover the third. To operate an Enigma machine, the code designated that day was entered in the code-board to prime the machine. For example, letter A became letter P, B became Q, C became R and so on. The plain-language message was then typed and the machine automatically substituted letter for letter. The coded message was then passed by the machine through three separate rotors, each set to one of twenty-six alphabetical positions according to that day's code. That encoded the message three more times. A reflector rotor then 'reflected' the message back in the opposite direction, so that the message was encoded another three times. That produced an almost random encoded message with nearly three million combinations. The coded message was then transmitted.

At the receiving end, the coded message was typed into an identical Enigma machine set to that day's code and the plain-language message was revealed, letter by letter. The one weakness of the Enigma machine, not realised by German cryptanalysts, was that it was not 100 per cent random. Crucially, A could not be encoded as A, B could not be B. This gave the brains at Bletchley Park the tiny window they needed in order to, slowly, break each day's code.

To speed decoding, the brilliant Cambridge mathematician Alan Turing invented an electro-mechanical machine utilising banks and banks of rotors and code-boards into which an intercepted coded message was entered. It was called a Bombe, after an earlier but different Polish machine.

The Bombe was not a computer; that came later. Turing's Bombe worked by eliminating every wrong decode for a message to leave only the few possible correct codes. Those were then entered by hand, tested, and the correct code for the day uncovered. A Bombe was then programmed with that code and every message in that particular Enigma network could be decoded.

There were different Enigma networks for Germany and for Italy, for the army, navy, U-boats, and air force, for High Command, for field units, for the Gestapo, embassies overseas, German spies in Britain and

so on. Network after network, each using different types of Enigmas –
100,000 of them – and different codes.

Thousands of radio operators throughout Britain, the Empire and
the Commonwealth monitored enemy radio frequencies to intercept
the messages. Those intercepts were passed to huts built in the grounds
of Bletchley Park. There, teams of women and men decoded their
particular network. Cross-feeding of information between the different
sections was carried out by the head of each team. In the early part
of the war there were not enough Bombes to handle the number of
intercepts. When America entered the war in December 1941, Bletchley
Park sent a Bombe to American intelligence for it to copy.

Inevitably, the Germans increased the complexity of their codes and
improved the Enigma machines. Very early, a plug-board like an old-
fashioned telephone exchange was added, increasing possible codes to
159 trillion – 159,000,000,000,000,000,000. Improved rotors were
introduced, rotor wiring changed, and when a fourth rotor was added
to naval Enigmas (increasing decoding possibilities to 26 x 159 trillion)
it almost won the war for the Nazis. Until a break-in could be found,
Bletchley was working blind. It was then that the men in the field played
their part.

Captures of code books and pieces of equipment took place
throughout the war, unknown to Germany. Rotors VI and VII were
captured from submarine *U-33*, and code books were recovered from
patrol boat *Schiff* 26 in 1940. In 1941 Enigma parts and a key-list
were taken from the trawler *Krebs* during the brilliant Lofoten Islands
commando raid, and the surrender of *U-570* yielded the lid from the
new four-rotor naval Enigma. Australian soldiers captured Japanese
code books in New Guinea in 1943.

The most vital and famous capture was of the weather and convoy
code books for the naval four-rotor Engima from *U-559* in the
Mediterranean. Lieutenant Fasson and Able Seaman Grazier of HMS
Petard descended into the sinking U-boat on 30 October 1942, to
recover the books. With 16-year-old Tommy Brown, they passed out
code-papers as the water poured into the sinking submarine. Brown
escaped, but both Fasson and Grazier drowned as they tried to salvage

the new Enigma machine itself. They did not give their lives in vain. That code-book capture gave Bletchley Park the break-in to the four-rotor naval code known as 'Shark'.

Before that capture, GC&CS had broken Shark only three times. It caused the crisis in the Battle of the Atlantic, when merchant ship sinkings by U-boats reached their peak and it was thought the United Kingdom might be blockaded into defeat. In the first half of 1942, U-boats sank more than three million tons of shipping, carrying vital men, food, fuel and military supplies. With the breaking of Shark that December, intelligence flowed again to the Admiralty, ship sinkings decreased and U-boat sinkings increased.

Of the 1,550,000 naval Enigma signals intercepted, 1,120,000 were successfully decoded at Bletchley Park. How that intelligence was used required very careful decisions. Often, intelligence was not acted upon, for to have done so would have alerted the enemy that its codes were being broken.

One success in March 1941 was by Dillwyn Knox's girls, decoding a message from Italian naval Enigma. The intelligence forewarned the Royal Navy, so that Admiral Cunningham's ships sailed from Egypt to surprise and defeat an Italian fleet at the Battle of Matapan. Italian ships never put to sea again during the whole war. Believing its Enigma codes unbreakable, Germany accused Italy of harbouring a traitor, but it was Dilly Knox's girls at Bletchley.

Intelligence is a game of bluff, counter-bluff and apparently unrelated events. For example, RAF Bomber Command dropped mines into various continental sea lanes, apparently to disrupt enemy shipping. In fact, it was not primarily to sink enemy vessels but to generate enemy signals. The coded signals announcing the sea lanes had been cleared were intercepted and passed to Bletchley. Knowing roughly what those signals concerned allowed codebreakers to decode them, then use the decodes as 'cribs' to break more important messages and ciphers.

Similarly, Nazi spies in Britain and Ireland were captured or 'turned' without the Germans realising. Carefully compiled accurate but not vital information was sent to German intelligence as if from these agents. The coded responses were intercepted and passed to Bletchley, where another crib was obtained.

Some codes were unbreakable. 'Pike' German naval code was never broken and 'Staff' only once. Of Hitler's three 'Fish' codes 'Thrasher' was never broken, 'Sturgeon' was solved, but was mostly duplicated by other signals, while 'Tunny' was solved and exploited without German knowledge. Tunny was used mostly for top-secret messages between Hitler and German High Command.

The absolute brilliance of the women and men at Bletchley Park is demonstrated there, because a Tunny machine was *never* captured, never photographed, never even seen. Nevertheless, purely from intercepted signals, the brains in Hut 11 worked out that it was a teleprinter, that it used strings of characters from different combinations of five positive and negative dots and crosses, that the machine used twelve wheels to create the code, and so on.

John Tiltman and Bill Tutte first worked on Tunny in 1941, beginning a two-year-long analysis of the code. Alan Turing joined Hut 11 in the summer of 1942, specifically to help with the complex maths needed to break the Tunny wheel patterns. He invented a solely mathematical solution called the Turingery. The breaking of Tunny remains still the greatest cryptanalysis ever achieved by any intelligence service, but to take advantage of the break-in, a computer was needed to decode the signals quickly enough for the intelligence to be used.

Another amazing Cambridge mathematician, Max Newman, joined Hut 11 in November 1942. Initially he devised a photo-electric machine using mechanical relays and valve counters. It compared fast-moving teleprinter tapes of Tunny signals against a decoding tape. It was built in Hut 11 by Post Office engineers. It looked physically impossible, like an iron bedstead on end, a boffin's dream, and so was named the Heath Robinson. Most importantly, Newman's machine brought Newman and Post Office engineer Tommy Flowers together. The result was the world's first electronic computer.

A computer is simply a piece of equipment – mainframe, palm-pilot, desktop, laptop, pocket calculator or calculating machine – capable of following the instructions and completing the calculations that a human being can do, only quicker. The first modern computers or calculating machines were built by the 3rd Earl of Stanhope in about 1777, but development was slow.

In 1935, Alan Turing devised the vital breakthrough of controlling a machine with a program stored in the machine's own memory. He was just 23 years old. He turned the concept into a practical design he called the 'Universal Turing Machine'. At that time calculating machines were electro-mechanical – they used electrically operated on–off switches called relays. Turing himself built a small electro-mechanical binary multiplier. Several such computers were built, but they were slow and they were not electronic. The development of electronic valves for radio and radar – in turn replaced by diode and transistor technology – opened the door to electronic computers.

Tommy Flowers realised that electronic valves were reliable enough to be used as on–off electronic switches and would be hundreds of times faster than mechanical relays. Using those concepts, he invented the world's first electronic telephone exchange, operating in Britain in 1939.

Max Newman had his Heath Robinson photo-electric machine up and running in June 1943. It operated at 1000 to 2000 characters per second. Tommy Flowers was unimpressed. He said electronic valve equipment would be four times as fast. Perhaps understandably, the powers at Bletchley thought it would take too long to make and would be less reliable. Flowers went ahead regardless and built his concept at Dollis Hill in London. Working flat-out, Flowers' team had it completed and operating by December 1943. It was called *Colossus*, the first electronic digital computer in the world. It went online at Bletchley Park in February 1944 to decode Tunny signals.

Colossus used 1,600 electronic valves, operated at 5,000 characters per second, weighed a ton and was the size of a small cupboard. It was a semi-programmable as opposed to a stored-program computer. A basic Pentium 2 laptop today has the same power as that first computer. Flowers' much-improved *Colossus II* was brought on-line in May 1944 shortly before D-Day. It used 2,400 valves and operated at 25,000 characters per second.

German High Command Tunny signals were decoded regularly and speedily by *Colossus*. Almost the entire German battle order in France was revealed at Bletchley before the D-Day invasion. As a result, Bletchley Park was involved in the deception called Operation Fortitude, where the Nazis were deceived into believing the invasion would be at Calais, not Normandy. In addition, a thirty-two-page report sent by the Japanese military attaché in Berlin was decoded by the Japanese section at Bletchley, filling important gaps in the German battle plan. A late change of German positions in Normandy was also decoded by *Colossus*, which stopped US paratroopers landing in the middle of a German division.

Two vital items of military intelligence were not decoded because they were, unfortunately, never sent. The first was the position of the 21st Panzer (tank) Division. That division attacked the left wing of the British landings at Sword Beach and prevented them from taking Caen that 6 June 1944. As a result, the British and Canadian armies were forced into a slow and bloody battle for Caen lasting almost two months. It was the bloodiest fighting in western Europe, with 66,000 German and 80,000 British and Canadian casualties.

The second item never sent was the position of the German 352 Division. They were near Omaha Beach and hammered the US army in its landings on 6 June. From those two gaps in intelligence it can be seen that, without the codebreakers of Bletchley Park, the invasion might well have failed.

Message decoding at Bletchley reached a peak of 18,000 a day shortly after D-Day then gradually decreased. After D-Day, German High Command changed its Tunny codes every day, so that by the end of the war nine *Colossus* computers were online in Hut 11.

American historians claim that America invented the first electronic computer, the *ENIAC*. Like *Colossus*, *ENIAC* development began in June 1943, but was not completed until 1946. *Colossus* was operating in December 1943, and *Colossus II* in May 1944. There was another American machine, the Automatic Sequence Controlled Calculator, but that did not operate until 1945. It was a Bombe, not a computer, using seventy-eight adding machines and desk calculators.

After the war, Max Newman and Alan Turing left the GC&CS and began their own separate projects to design and construct the first stored-program computer. Their designs were both based upon Turing's ground-breaking 1937 paper 'On Computable Numbers'.

Turing designed his stored-program computer in 1945, using his earlier Universal Turing Machine. He completed the technical report – 'Proposed Electronic Calculator' – by the end of the year, the first complete specification for an electronic stored-program digital computer. Its high-speed memory was equal to the chip memory of the early Macintosh computers of the 1980s. However, Turing had problems with production and soon was eighteen months behind schedule. Max Newman, meanwhile, wrote his own logico-mathematical design for a stored-program computer. He invited the brilliant electrical engineers Frederick Williams and Thomas Kilburn to join him.

Newman's team produced the world's first stored-program electronic computer in 1948. It was called *The Manchester Baby* and incorporated the first high-speed random access memory (RAM), called the Williams Tube. *The Manchester Baby* ran its first program on 21 June. So far ahead in production was Newman's team that Turing joined them that year.

With Turing on board, a redesigned input and programming system was built for *The Manchester Baby*, including a programming manual. That improved computer was called *The Manchester Mark I*. The *Mark I* became the first computer mass-produced for public sale.

Very soon Turing was using the *Mark I* to model biological growth – what we now call 'Artificial Life'. By 1950, Turing was already devising how to program a computer to think. A fragile genius of the first order, he had always been a shy and retiring man. He committed suicide in 1954 by eating an apple laced with cyanide. He was just 41 years old. He did not see the modern computer age he helped begin at Bletchley Park.

All the messages decoded at Bletchley came under the general heading of Signal Intelligence, or 'Sigint'. However, there were other people working at Bletchley Park. Sigint people referred to them as 'the other side'.

The 'other side' specialised in Human Intelligence – 'Humint'. None of the Sigint people knew what Human Intelligence was, nor what the 'other side' did. Even today they don't know, for Humint has not been declassified. There are secrets still to come from Bletchley Park.

Recommended
British Intelligence in the Second World War, volumes 1 & 2,
by F.H. Hinsley.
Codebreakers: The Inside Story of Bletchley Park edited by F.H. Hinsley and Alan Stripp.
The Emperor's Codes: Bletchley Park and the Breaking of Japan's Secret Ciphers by Michael Smith.
Action This Day edited by Michael Smith and Ralph Erskine.
Bletchley Park Trust, Bletchley Park, Buckinghamshire.

William Bligh's Boat Voyage

In 1789, the twenty-ninth year of the reign of His Most Gracious Majesty, King George III, occurred the most famous naval mutiny of all time: the Mutiny in the Bounty.

At dawn on 28th April, Lieutenant William Bligh and eighteen crew were cast adrift in the *Bounty*'s 23-foot open launch. Bligh had been obliged to order some of them out for safety and four loyal seamen remained behind with the mutineers. Even then, the launch rode only seven inches above the surface of the sea.

In 1787, the Admiralty had appointed Lieutenant Bligh commander of the *Bounty*, to be addressed as captain on board. His orders were to sail to Otaheite (Tahiti), there to collect breadfruit plants as a crop to feed plantation slaves. Bligh's experiences with Captain Cook and his previous visit to Otaheite made him the obvious choice.

Bligh was allowed to choose the master's mate from the many who applied. He chose his friend, Fletcher Christian, who had sailed with him twice before. The Admiralty saddled Bligh with a drunken surgeon, Thomas Huggan, though Sir Joseph Banks found Bligh an assistant surgeon, Thomas Ledward. The Admiralty would not promote Bligh to captain, would not appoint any commissioned officers, and would not give him marines. Cook had considered commissioned officers and marines essential for discipline in his three voyages to the Pacific and Bligh agreed. There, the Admiralty made a bad decision; Bligh knew the South Seas, the Admiralty did not.

Knowing Bounty's voyage would take two years, Bligh divided her crew into three watches instead of two. With two watches, watchkeepers work four hours on, four hours off. It's a tiring system. With three watches they work four on and eight off. The advantage of three watches is the opportunity for decent sleep. In a long voyage this is invaluable. Bligh promoted Fryer, Peckover and 23-year-old Manxman Fletcher Christian as watch-leaders. There was also another Manxman in the *Bounty*, 14-year-old, unqualified Midshipman Peter Heywood, distantly related to Christian. Through Bligh's Manx wife, the Heywood family had requested a berth for Peter.

One of the first signs of a troubled voyage came from carpenter Purcell, who was insubordinate at Cape Town. He refused to obey an order from Bligh and an order from the master, and when they reached Otaheite, he refused another order from his captain. Bligh was enraged by this disobedience. Under the 22nd Article of War, Bligh could have hanged or flogged Purcell for the offences. He did neither. In fact, he ordered only seven floggings in sixteen months, fewer than the great and beloved Nelson, fewer even than the humane Cook. Seven floggings a month was not unusual in those times.

Bligh knew the temptations of Otaheite from his voyage with Cook. The women were bare-breasted, their skins a smooth brown. They were attractive, sensual and they bathed every day. They had no inhibiting morals. The climate was languid, the lush greens of the hills contrasting pleasantly with the blue tropical sea. The food was plentiful, and the Tahitians friendly. They did practise human sacrifice, they did use infanticide to control their island population, and some of their rituals involved sexual intercourse. It was a heady, seductive mix, very different from the grim streets of Georgian Britain. Cook's men had deserted there on every voyage, only to be recaptured and flogged.

With no officers and no marines, Bligh knew it would be impossible to stop his men going ashore. With the permission of King Tynah, Bligh worked a rotating system where some crew maintained the *Bounty* while others lived ashore to tend the breadfruit nursery.

In five months on the island, only three men deserted and were recaptured. They'd stolen a ship's boat, arms and ammunition while the mate of the watch, Thomas Hayward, was asleep on duty. Bligh disrated Hayward, placed him in irons for four weeks and flogged the deserters. Desertion on a foreign station was a hanging offence.

At the time, an exasperated Bligh wrote: 'Such neglectful and worthless petty Officers I believe never was in a ship as are in this – No orders for a few hours together are Obeyed by them, and their conduct in general is so bad, that no confidence or trust can be reposed in them – in short, they have drove me to everything but Corporal punishment, and that must follow if they do not improve.' Yet only one more man was flogged, for 'neglect of duty'. This, perhaps, was Bligh's problem: he was too humane for his time.

As well as *Bounty*'s log and Bligh's journal, there is another day-to-day account: the journal of boatswain's mate Morrison – a mutineer. It was recovered in Otaheite. It agrees with Bligh's journal in every detail and includes the list of possible deserters. There is no recording of cruelty, excessive flogging, gagging, inhumanity, excessive duties or extra punishments by Bligh. In the journal of mutineer Peter Heywood there is also no mention of cruelty, excessive floggings or punishment by his captain. In the notes written by John Adams in Fletcher Christian's Bible after the mutiny, there is no mention of cruelty by Bligh.

After five months at Otaheite, the *Bounty* prepared for sea with breadfruit plants in pots around the quarterdeck. There had been minor incidents with the islanders, mostly breaking of 'tabu', but the most unsavoury involved the master. Fryer had sex with a woman but did not give her the agreed piece of cloth. Bligh apologised to the woman and ordered Fryer to give her the cloth. Like Fryer, Bligh was a married man, but like Cook, he remained celibate.

Surgeon Duggan drank himself to death on Otaheite from his own private supplies. He kept notes of the patients he'd treated, including those for venereal disease. Among them were Christian and Heywood.

Bounty departed Otaheite on 4 April, bound for the West Indies. Bligh stopped at Anamooka island on the 25th for fruit and water. There, he became angry with the crew for letting islanders steal their tools, and brandished a pistol at McCoy for not paying attention. Bligh's temper was well known. Cook had a temper, too, but the anger of a captain is not cause to mutiny.

At sea, someone in Christian's watch stole coconuts from the supply stowed on deck. Stealing coconuts may appear petty, but one of the codes of behaviour on board ship is not to steal anything. A ship is a small community and possessions cannot be locked away. In the navy it's a criminal offence.

Bligh called Christian 'a damned hound' after the theft and the men of Christian's watch 'scoundrels'. He might have flogged them. Many captains in 1789 would have flogged a thief without a second thought.

That evening, Bligh invited Christian to dinner in the cabin. The incident had obviously not been important to Bligh, but Christian refused, saying he was unwell. Purcell, Morrison and Lebogue all reported that Christian drank heavily that night.

After dinner in the *Bounty*, Bligh slept, leaving his door open as usual. Shortly before dawn, he was shaken awake by Christian, with a cutlass in his hand. Behind him, carrying loaded muskets and bayonets, were Churchill, Mills and Burkitt. They tied the captain's hands behind him and pushed him out on deck in his nightshirt.

Christian ordered boatswain Cole to lower the launch. Heywood assisted, and those of the crew who refused to join the mutiny were called on deck and told off into the boat. The sea was very calm. As daylight came, Christian ordered a dram of rum for each mutineer to steady them through the confusion. Bligh's clerk, Samuel, managed to take a quadrant, compass and the journal into the launch, but was warned by Christian 'on pain of death' to leave charts, surveys, sextant, chronometer and navigation tables.

When Bligh had to order some men back to the *Bounty* from the overladen launch, Fryer was told he'd be shot if he returned. Bligh asked Christian if this treatment was the 'proper return for his friendship' and Christian answered: 'That, Captain Bligh, that is the thing; I am in hell – I am in hell!' In the last moments, with Heywood standing by Christian, Bligh called again for Christian to come to his senses, begging him to reconsider. According to Bligh, Christian replied: 'I am in hell,' while Morrison recorded: 'I have been in hell this fortnight passed and am determined to bear it no longer.' It was three weeks since they'd left Otaheite.

Bligh and the launch crew were all aware that midshipmen Peter Heywood, Stewart and Young were among the mutineers. Morrison recorded it was Stewart who first suggested that Christian take the ship. Christian said: 'Come, Captain Bligh, your officers and men are now in the boat, and you must go with them; if you attempt to make the least resistance you will be instantly put to death.'

As the launch veered astern of the ship, the mutineers jeered and threw breadfruit plants from the quarterdeck. The *Bounty* sailed slowly to the west-north-west, although Bligh assumed correctly that it was a false course and the mutineers would eventually return to Otaheite.

At the time of the mutiny the *Bounty*'s crew numbered forty-three. Twenty-two remained loyal to their captain. As the launch and the *Bounty* parted company, those forced to remain called down to Bligh for him to remember they were loyal.

'Never fear, my lads,' he said. 'I'll do you justice if ever I reach England!'

In fact, Bligh had greater worries on his mind. He was in the middle of the South Pacific Ocean in an overloaded boat, with no charts, no surveys, no sextant, no guns, no stores, and small odds of surviving. So began the greatest open-boat voyage in history.

As the *Bounty* sailed away, the launch crew also knew their chances were virtually nil. Certainly they could sail for an island where they could rot until disease, starvation or the islanders killed them. That is what the mutineers expected them to do. They'd thrown cutlasses and food and water for five days into the launch. However, William Bligh wanted more than mere survival. He was determined to get his men home.

First, he sailed thirty miles to Tofua, in the Friendly Isles (Tonga). There they took on water and food – coconuts, breadfruit and fish. Yet there had been changes since Bligh had visited the island with Captain Cook. This time the sailors would not be welcomed by the islanders.

On Tofua, Bligh heard a sound he dreaded, the loud clacking-together of stones. He knew it as a call to arms for the warlike islanders. His men had refilled the water barrel and found food, but now it was time to leave. As Bligh and Purcell walked down the beach to the launch, the islanders crowded around and stones began to fly. One hit Bligh's shoulder and drew blood, but he staggered through the shallows to the launch, Purcell ahead of him. Quartermaster Norton leaped into the water with a cutlass, to cut the mooring line.

Purcell and Bligh clambered aboard but Norton was still cutting the line when a flying stone knocked him down. The islanders beat him to death in the warm, shallow water. With no pistols, there was nothing the men in the launch could do but watch in horror. Bligh himself cut the mooring and the islanders pitched stones at the launch as they rowed away. They were followed by war canoes until Bligh and others threw their blue uniform jackets into the water to divert them.

At sea once more, Bligh called his men to order. He knew the Pacific as well as any navigator alive. He had sailed it for four years, two of those with his mentor James Cook. To the west, a new colony was being settled in New South Wales, yet there was no guarantee the colonists had reached Botany Bay or even survived. However, there was an established settlement to the north-west in Dutch Timor. Bligh had not been there, but two others in the launch had: botanist Nelson and gunner Peckover, who'd also sailed with Cook. Bligh had spent days poring over Cook's charts and he remembered Timor's approximate latitude and longitude. He thought it was within reach. Either way, it was better than rotting on an island.

He discussed the navigation with the master, the gunner and boatswain. With tight rations, they had food and water for six weeks – at one ounce of bread and a quarter-pint of water per man per day, supplemented by scraps of meat and occasional teaspoons of rum. Bligh spoke to all the men, wanting their views – indeed, their approval for the voyage. They gave it and Bligh pointed the launch at Timor, 3,500 nautical miles away.

During the great voyage, Bligh recorded the names of the mutineers in his log, as well as the loyal men he'd been forced to leave behind. Those were: Joseph Coleman, Charles Norman, Thomas McIntosh and Michael Byrne, the half-blind fiddler. He knew he must stand by those men, if he ever reached home.

Bounty's launch had seats for ten, so it was incredibly crowded for eighteen. Bligh divided his crew into two watches under the master and gunner. Those two, the boatswain Cole and Bligh himself would steer. Everyone else would rotate their position to ease their cramped and aching joints, while two men could lie outstretched on the bottom boards. The launch was a sailing lugger with six oars. It was a sound boat, but it wasn't designed for a 3,500-mile ocean voyage.

Bligh was also concerned about the crew themselves. There were only two malcontents but two might have been enough to destroy them all. One was master and second in command of the *Bounty* John Fryer, who had been shown in the previous sixteen months to have limited abilities. He was disliked by the crew and even the mutineers had refused to have him. The second malcontent was carpenter William Purcell. Most ships have a 'sea-lawyer' and in the Bounty it was Purcell. He was insubordinate, argumentative and asserted his 'rights' at every opportunity, spreading discontent in the crew. Yet when invited to stay in the *Bounty* he'd replied: 'I'm not staying with a pack of mutineers,' and entered the launch with his tools.

The remaining fifteen admired and liked their captain. They were William Peckover, William Cole, Thomas Ledward, David Nelson, William Elphinston, Thomas Hayward, John Hallett, Peter Linkletter, Lawrence Lebogue, John Smith, Thomas Hall, George Simpson, Robert Lamb, John Samuel and 12-year-old Robert Tinkler.

For his part, Bligh had lost his ship to mutiny, an almost unheard-of event. What was he thinking as he stared at his overcrowded command? Somehow he had to navigate his loyal men to safety, in a small boat on a vast ocean.

The next morning, a gale overtook the launch, increasing to storm force and soaking them all. They bailed water continuously as they ran before heavy seas. It was a foretaste of the weeks to come, although bad weather helped them to survive. It was the southern winter, and the voyage was beset by fogs, rain and cold nights. Yet they didn't suffer greatly from thirst because of the rain and suffered little from sunburn or heat, or the madness that comes with those. You can last for a month without food as long as you have water. The damp and cold, the cramps from lack of movement, those were their greatest hardships. At times they craved tropical heat. The teaspoon of rum in the morning became a necessity rather than a luxury.

Back in the *Bounty*, there was a surfeit of rum. The mutineers were: Edward Young, Peter Heywood, George Stewart, Isaac Martin, Charles Churchill, John Mills, James Morrison, Thomas Burkitt, Matthew Quintal, John Sumner, John Milward, William McCoy, Henry Hillbrant, William Muspratt, John Adams, John Williams, Thomas Ellison, Richard Skinner, Matthew Thompson and William Brown, led by master's mate Fletcher Christian.

Fletcher Christian: the most famous name of them all. It was his third voyage with Bligh. They had met first in HMS *Cambridge*, on which Bligh was fifth lieutenant and Christian a volunteer seaman. Christian was a Manxman and Bligh was then living on the Isle of Man. Bligh later sailed as captain on merchant ships for four years, and in 1786 Christian applied to sail with him as midshipman on *Britannia*. All berths were taken, so he volunteered as seaman and was accepted.

Nevertheless, Captain Bligh and first mate Lamb instructed and taught Christian as an officer and to navigate.

Bligh sailed through the Cannibal Isles (Fiji) without stopping. Tales of brutality were legend in the area and he would not risk another attack. Two canoes chased them and they rowed desperately to escape. While they threaded their way through the islands, the first white men to sail those waters, Bligh surveyed, named and charted positions using quadrant and watch. 'Boat Passage' still marks the reef through which *Bounty*'s launch entered the Fijis.

Succeeding days passed slowly, with incessant bailing, increasing hunger, and more aches and cramps than it seemed possible to bear. On 12 May, Bligh observed: 'At length the day came and showed to me a miserable set of beings, full of wants, without anything to relieve them. Some complained of great pain in their bowels, and everyone of having almost lost the use of his limbs. What sleep we got was no ways refreshing, as we were covered with sea and rain.' Botanist Nelson was already weakening.

Bligh discovered the Banks Islands, north of the cannibalistic New Hebrides (now known as Vanuatu). He sketched them, charted their positions, and named them after Sir Joseph Banks. He sailed west towards the Great Barrier Reef and the north of New Holland, as Australia was then known. He wrote on the 23rd: 'The misery we suffered this night exceeded the preceding. The sea flew over us with great force, and kept us bailing with horror and anxiety. At dawn of day I found everyone in a most distressed condition, and I began to fear that another such night would put an end to the lives of several. I served an allowance of two spoonfuls of rum'.

Bligh was forced to reduce rations further. They now received, twice a day, 1/25th of a pound of bread plus the usual quarter pint of water and any food they might catch. Several seabirds blundered into the sails and this raw flesh – including eyes, claws, intestines and stomach contents – restored a little interest in the weakening men. In navy fashion, the portions were offered by 'Who shall have this?', while a man with his back turned called a name.

On the night of 28 May, Fryer heard the breakers of the Great Barrier Reef. In daylight, Bligh navigated through a gap in the reefs and they were inside, in relatively protected water, with slight damage only to the rudder. The following day they stopped at an island. It was their first time out of the cramped launch in four weeks. They stumbled onto the sandy beach. Some collapsed, some fainted, others rested on their knees or staggered a few steps before falling. For two days they rested on the island Bligh named 'Restoration', eating oysters, hearts of cabbage palm, some berries that Nelson thought edible, and fern roots. When they weren't suffering from stomach cramps, they stretched out on the ground to sleep.

In the meantime, Purcell had repaired the rudder. Bligh put to sea hurriedly when a large party of naked Aborigines assembled on the mainland. They carried spears and shouted at the castaways. No one knew whether they were friendly or threatening, so wearily they sailed on, north-westwards inside the reefs. Bligh decided to stop again soon after, for Nelson's health had worsened and others were visibly weakening.

He beached the launch again on Sunday Island, where Nelson, Ledward and Lebogue crawled up the sand and collapsed. The others argued bitterly about who was to forage for food. 'I'm as good a man as you are!' Purcell argued with Bligh. They shouted at each other and Bligh flourished a cutlass. Why not after five weeks cooped up together in a 23-foot boat? Bligh faithfully recorded this incident in his log. The amazing thing is that no one came to blows.

After two days recuperating on Sunday Island, Bligh sailed north to Cape York and on 3 June turned west through Endeavour Straits on a course for Dutch Timor – all from his memory of Cook's charts. In open seas again, they resumed bailing the launch. By then, the weather was hot, but they had enough water to continue the quarter pint a day.

They caught a fish, their first, but the part given Bligh by 'Who shall have this?' made him violently ill. He vomited again and again over the side of the boat, his head burning hot. When he'd stopped retching, he looked at the others who very worriedly stared at him. Their legs were swollen, their joints bruised, their skin ulcerated. He said how sorry he was they were all so ill. Boatswain Cole replied:

'I really think, sir, that you look worse than anyone in the boat.' There was actual laughter.

Bligh's entry for the 12th June 1789, reads: 'At three in the morning, with an excess of joy, we discovered Timor bearing from WSW to WNW, and I hauled on a wind to the NNE till daylight.'

At dawn, the launch was six miles offshore, so Bligh steered south-west along the coast through yet another gale. He wrote: 'It appeared scarce credible to ourselves that in an open boat, and so poorly provided, we should have been able to reach the coast of Timor after leaving Tofoa, having in that time run, by our log, a distance of 3618 miles; and that notwithstanding our extreme distress, no one should have perished in the voyage.'

The eighteen men spent one more night at sea and *Bounty*'s launch arrived at the town of Coupang (Kupang) on Timor the following morning. It was Sunday, 14 June 1789, forty-seven days after they were cast adrift in the South Pacific, 3,670 miles away.

Although himself sick with fever, the Dutch Governor of Timor met Bligh and expressed his sympathy at the mutiny, incredulity at the voyage of the launch, and amazement that only the one man had died. A Dutch surgeon treated their sores, ulcers, cuts and swellings, and they were given the only uninhabited house in Coupang in which to recuperate. Bligh ordered Fryer to give his bed to Nelson, who was still desperately ill. Bligh was determined to report the mutiny as soon as possible, but he had to wait for a ship to take him home.

Bligh wrote to his wife from Coupang, seven weeks after the mutiny: 'Besides this young villain [Christian] see young Heywood, one of the ringleaders, and besides him see Stewart joined with him ... I have now reason to curse the day I ever knew Christian or a Heywood or indeed a Manks man.'

Nelson succumbed to the fever which also killed the Dutch Governor. He died on 20 July, mourned by Bligh as a friend and as the only non-naval witness to the mutiny. After transport by ship to Batavia (Jakarta), all the castaways came down with fever, Hall the next to die. Bligh had brought his crew through an incredible voyage only to see them perish ashore. The first ship departing Batavia had only three berths. Bligh had to be one, but who else? He chose Samuel and Smith, ex-Britannia men, knowing the choice might condemn others to death.

It was so. Within a fortnight, Elphinston and Linkletter died. Lamb died during the voyage home, while Ledward's ship disappeared. Bligh had brought seventeen men safely over 3,670 miles, yet only eleven reached Britain. He, Samuel and Smith arrived in Portsmouth on 14 March 1790.

In October, after the surviving launch crew returned, Lieutenant Bligh was court-martialled at Portsmouth for the loss of his ship. He was honourably acquitted. Purcell was court-martialled for refusing to obey orders and insubordination. He was found guilty and reprimanded.

William Bligh became a national hero for his brilliant navigation and command of that amazing open-boat voyage, the greatest ever completed. He was promoted to captain at last.

Many years passed before the fate of the mutineers was known. Bligh thought he had heard them cry 'Huzza for Otaheite!' Morrison wrote they were keen to return to Otaheite, where 'they might get weomen without force'.

The *Bounty* had sailed first to Toobouai (Tubuai) Island, 350 miles south of Otaheite, arriving there on 24 May 1789. They stayed a week there before sailing to Otaheite for livestock – and women. Lies were told to deceive King Tynah, and in June, the *Bounty* left with livestock, nine women, eight men, seven boys and one girl. The mutineers lived for three months on Toobouai, fighting amongst themselves and fighting the islanders. In one battle,

sixty-six islanders were killed. It was not the life of ease the mutineers had desired and in September the different factions agreed to return to Otaheite.

In *Bounty*'s final visit to Otaheite, Christian stayed aboard. The four loyal men, most of the Tahitians and twelve mutineers went ashore, while other island women came aboard in welcome. According to Tahitian woman Teehuteatuaonoa (known as Jenny), who escaped from Pitcairn Island in 1817, all but three of seventeen Tahitian women were kidnapped by Christian when he cut the *Bounty*'s anchor cable and sailed from Otaheite. Those kidnappings are confirmed in the Pitcairn journal of Midshipman Young.

In January 1790, after four months searching for a hideaway, Christian located Pitcairn Island, marked on the charts as 'position doubtful'. The ship was stripped of valuables – including the chronometer and Christian's Bible – and then burned. There would be no going back, no change of mind.

The twelve mutineers left at Otaheite included Heywood, Stewart, Churchill and Morrison. Churchill was murdered by mess-mate Thompson, who was in turn sacrificed by the Tahitians to their gods as a punishment.

A year later, in 1791, Captain Edwards in the frigate *Pandora* apprehended those fourteen who remained at Otaheite. Assisting the search for the mutineers were Hayward and Hallett of *Bounty*'s launch. Edwards locked loyal men and mutineers alike in a wooden cage on *Pandora*'s quarterdeck so that there could be no subversion of his crew. There was no sign of the others and after three months of searching, he set sail for Britain. It was to be a troubled journey.

In August 1791, the *Pandora* ran aground on the Great Barrier Reef and sank. Thirty-one crew and four of the mutineers drowned. Captain Edwards and ninety-eight survivors sailed four boats 1,100 miles to Coupang, the second open-boat voyage to Timor for Hayward and Hallett. From there, they were repatriated via Batavia and Cape Town.

Meanwhile, the Admiralty had appointed Bligh captain to the frigate *Providence* and, with the brig *Assistant*, he was sent to Otaheite to complete his original task of transplanting breadfruit to the West Indies.

On that occasion, the Admiralty appointed commissioned officers and marines. Interestingly, four *Bounty* crew volunteered to sail with Bligh – Peckover, Lebogue, Smith and Samuel. He took all except Peckover. Bligh stated he didn't want to sail with any Bounty warrant officer ever again.

They arrived at Otaheite in April 1792, where Bligh was welcomed by King Tynah. He met Heywood's Tahitian wife and the children of other mutineers. Disagreeable changes in Tahitian life were noted by Bligh and others – particularly swearing – from the mutineers living there for more than a year.

At Portsmouth, the surviving ten of the *Bounty*'s recaptured crew were court-martialled for mutiny in September 1792. The four loyal men – Coleman, Norman, McIntosh and Byrne – were honourably acquitted. Bligh, as he had promised, had registered their innocence with the Admiralty.

Peter Heywood, Morrison, Burkitt, Muspratt, Millward and Ellison were all found guilty and sentenced to death. Muspratt was discharged on a legal technicality and pardoned. Heywood was given a royal pardon, possibly because he was young, but probably because of his family's naval connections. Morrison was pardoned because he had not actively supported the mutiny. Three were hanged.

Far away, on Pitcairn Island, the murders began. Williams's wife died and he demanded one of the Tahitians' wives instead. The Tahitian men were furious. They rebelled and in one day murdered Williams, Christian, Mills, Martin and Brown. They then fought each other, and the survivors of those murders were murdered in turn by the four surviving mutineers and their Tahitian wives. McCoy committed suicide. In 1799, Quintal was murdered by Young and Adams, and Young died of asthma in 1800, leaving Adams the sole survivor.

Fletcher Christian was identified by both loyal and mutinous crew as leader of the mutiny. Peter Heywood had been tried and found guilty of mutiny. Despite his later pardon, not one loyal man or mutineer had said Heywood was not part of the mutiny. As a result, the only avenue for the Christian and Heywood families to salvage their reputations was to find an acceptable reason for the mutiny. The only way to do that was to blame the Bounty's captain. So began the slander of William Bligh.

In a letter dated 5 November 1792, the pardoned Peter Heywood wrote to the Christians and offered to provide evidence of 'false reports of slander' against Christian by one whose 'ill report is his greatest praise' [Bligh]. The vilification of Bligh began, with inventions of floggings, gagging, maltreatment and sadistic cruelty.

Morrison's journal was rewritten to include accounts of cruelty, though Sir Joseph Banks stopped its publication. The Christians arranged a private 'inquiry' into the mutiny by their friends, then published its 'verdict' as well as a fictional appendix to the courts martial, containing inventions of cruelty by Bligh. They altered dates, names, sequences and facts to support the lies. When Bligh returned home, he rebutted the 'appendix', but ignored most of the libellous stories about him. Some of his shipmates would not.

One, who had been with Bligh and Christian on *Britannia*, wrote: 'When we got to sea and I saw your partiality for the young man, I gave him every advice and information in my power. Though he went about every point of duty with a degree of indifference that to me was truly unpleasant; but you were blind to his faults ... In the Appendix it is said that Mr Fletcher Christian had no attachment among the women of Otaheite; if that was the case he must have been much altered since he was with you in *Britannia*, he was then one of the most foolish young men I ever knew in regard to the sex.'

If Christian had no attachment with the women of Otaheite, how did he contract venereal disease? Before Otaheite, Bligh had his surgeons inspect the men of *Bounty* for VD and found none. Before the mutiny, Bligh reported that Christian's hands were sweating badly and affected everything he touched. Heywood's family admitted that Christian 'was a man of violent temper' and Rosalind Young, mutineer descendant, wrote in her 1890 history that on Pitcairn, Christian was 'a violent man'.

In all the accounts written before, during and immediately after the mutiny, in all the evidence given at all the courts martial, there is not *one* accusation of ill treatment by Bligh and not one allegation that the mutiny was caused by cruelty. All those came later, via the Christian and Heywood families. If a reason for the mutiny must be found, it lies in the simple words of the last survivor, Adams, who said: 'We only wanted to return to our loved ones on Otaheite.'

William Bligh died as Vice Admiral of the Blue in 1817, having served with distinction at the battles of Camperdown (1797) and Copenhagen (1801), where he was personally commended by Admiral Nelson. In 1805, he was appointed governor of the colony of New South Wales, with specific instructions to stop the illegal rum trade in Sydney. Unfortunately, it was the New South Wales Corps under his command that organised most of the trade. The Corps refused Bligh's orders and he was faced with another rebellion. He was completely exonerated and the officers and colonists concerned were punished.

In 1825, after both Bligh and Sir Joseph Banks had died, Peter Heywood published a 'Biography of Peter Heywood, Esq'. It was based upon Morrison's rewritten journal, bought from Morrison by Heywood's family. It's this biography and Morrison's doctored journal that is the source of the films, stage shows, and books portraying Bligh as an evil sadist. Some fifty films have been made about Bligh's 'cruelty' causing the mutiny.

The tragedy of the Christian–Heywood slander is that it destroyed the recognition and fame due to Admiral Bligh for his command of the 3,670-mile voyage in *Bounty*'s launch. Like his mentor Captain Cook, he was a brilliant navigator, a brilliant seaman, a brilliant surveyor and a humane man. The honour owed him for that voyage is long overdue. Simply, it is the greatest open-boat voyage of all time.

Recommended

A Voyage to the South Seas by William Bligh.
Mutiny of the Bounty and Story of Pitcairn Island 1790–1894
by Rosalind Amelia Young.
*The Voyage of the Bounty's Launch as Related in William Bligh's
Despatch to the Admiralty with the Journal of John Fryer*
by William Bligh and John Fryer.
The Bounty by Caroline Alexander.
Bounty replica, Hong Kong.

Arthur Wellesley,
Duke of Wellington

No collection of heroes could ever be complete without the man known as the Iron Duke. There are few for whom becoming Prime Minister is only a small part of their life and honours. Winston Churchill was one of those, Arthur Wellesley certainly another.

He never lost a major battle and is famous as the man who stopped Napoleon on land, as Nelson stopped him at sea. It is no exaggeration to say that without the military talent of this particular man, Britain would not have remained a free nation. It is interesting to consider that the pantheon of British, Commonwealth and Empire heroes has as its brightest stars not those who conquered, but those who resisted dictators and oppression.

Arthur Wesley (originally 'Wesley' until the family adopted an earlier spelling of 'Wellesley') was born in 1769 to a Protestant family in Ireland. In the same year, a boy was born in Corsica who would go on to be Emperor Napoleon Bonaparte.

Arthur Wesley's father was the Earl of Mornington and owned land in Ireland, so that young Arthur was born with the title 'the Honourable'. In regards to his Irishness, he later said famously that being born in a stable does not make one a horse.

His earliest years were spent in Dublin before his family moved to London. His father died in 1781 and his older brother Richard inherited the title. Arthur attended Eton in the same year. However, his family lacked financial security and he left that school after only a short time. His mother then moved to Brussels.

At that time, the army was not regarded as a suitable career for noble sons, in part because of its use as a police force at times of national unrest. Even so, Arthur was sent to be trained at the Royal Academy of Equitation in France. He learned basic French as well as becoming a decent hand at the violin before returning to England in 1786.

His brother wrote to the Lord Lieutenant of Ireland to secure a commission for Arthur and, like Robert Clive before him, he was gazetted as ensign, joining the 73rd Highland Regiment of Foot. His brother's support aided his rise and a year later Arthur Wesley was promoted to lieutenant in the 76th Regiment, then transferred to the 41st, who were on their way to Ireland.

In Ireland, Arthur Wesley also tried his hand at politics for the first time. He spoke well at public meetings and was elected to the Irish House of Commons as MP for Trim. Around the same time, he met Kitty Pakenham, the daughter of the Earl of Longford. However, when he asked formally for her hand in marriage, her family refused. In great distress, Arthur Wesley burned his violins and never played again.

With that defeat behind him, Arthur borrowed money from his brother and purchased the ranks of major, then lieutenant colonel, commanding the 33rd Regiment. In later years, when men like Garnet Wolseley were reforming the system that allowed men to purchase commissions, it became generally accepted that the practice had allowed great incompetence and corruption. That may be true, but it also gave us the man who would become the Duke of Wellington.

In 1794, the 33rd were sent to Flanders to resist a French invasion. There, Wesley was promoted to command a brigade of three battalions and saw his first major military action at Breda in September. Wesley and his men stopped a French column with steady fire from their flintlocks.

In 1795, faced with overwhelming French forces, the army was evacuated in chaos and Wesley saw at first hand the incompetence of senior officers. The experience taught him a great deal and stood him in good stead in later years. He suffered with illness caused by damp and a frozen winter and had a good idea of the horror and misery that was a part of the soldier's life.

In 1796, at the age of 27, Wesley travelled as Colonel of the 33rd to India, leaving behind a troubled Ireland that would erupt into violent rebellion just two years later. In the same year, Napoleon married his mistress Josephine and took command of the armies of Italy.

The India of that time was experiencing the last great days of John Company before it was taken over by the Crown. The British East India Company, for whom Clive had fought the Battle of Plassey, was in almost sole control of the subcontinent and there were still fortunes to be made when Wesley landed at Calcutta in 1797. France, Holland and Spain had all declared war on Britain and advancement could be quick for a competent young officer. It could not have hurt that his brother Richard was being sent as governor general of British India. It was his brother who changed the spelling of the family name back to a much older form. Young Arthur accepted the change readily enough and used 'Wellesley' first in a letter announcing the arrival of his brother in India. Another brother, Henry, also came as Richard's private secretary.

Arthur Wellesley went with the 33rd to Madras in 1798, a harsh sea journey during which fifteen of his men died from fevers brought on by bad water supplies. He joined the staff of General Harris for a time, handing command of the 33rd to Major John Shee. By December 1798, Wellesley was in command of a mixed force of British and Indian units intent on battle with the forces of Tippoo Sultan, known as the Tiger of Mysore. As an open ally of France, Tippoo Sultan was seen as a potential threat.

With his men, Wellington travelled to the Sultan's fortress of Seringapatam. Another large force under Harris moved up from the east, while a smaller one marched from the Malabar coast.

On 10 March 1799, Tippoo Sultan's cavalry attacked the rearguard. Wellesley led the counter-attack and saw them off without major losses. In another attack, the 33rd routed the enemy with bayonet charges. Tippoo Sultan withdrew to the fortress.

Wellseley took part in a night attack on an outlying village, but it was chaotic in the darkness and the 33rd were beaten back by Tippoo Sultan's rocket teams and musket fire. In the fighting, Wellesley was hit in the knee by a spent musket ball, though not seriously wounded. He took the position easily enough the following day, but said later that he had learned 'never to attack an enemy who is prepared and strongly posted, and whose posts have not been reconnoitred by daylight.'

Seringapatam fell after British guns made a breach in the walls. Tippoo Sultan was killed in the fighting that followed, his body found by Wellesley himself. He returned to his camp, bathed and slept. Overall command was not his and he could do nothing while British soldiers looted and gutted the fortress.

The following morning, Wellesley was appointed governor of Seringapatam. He strode back in, hanged four soldiers and flogged many others to suppress the orgy of looting and destruction. He was paid £4,000 as prize money for his part and offered to pay his brother Richard back for the loan to purchase a commission. His proud brother refused the offer. Despite recurring sickness, Wellesley completed his duties as governor. He was promoted to Major General shortly afterwards.

In 1802, he was ordered to battle against the Maratha Confederacy, a number of Hindu principalities in opposition to British power in India. Arthur Wellesley planned the campaign in great detail, which was already a habit of his, but still unusual for the time. In 1803, he took around 15,000 of his own men and 9,000 Indian troops six hundred miles to a Maratha fort. He had decided that a long defensive war was impossible, so moved quickly and boldly. His men took the defended local town in less than an hour.

As one of the Maratha officers said: 'The English are a strange people, and their General a wonderful man. They came here in the morning, looked at the Pettah wall, walked over it, killed the garrison and returned to breakfast! What can withstand them?' The fort itself surrendered only days later.

The brilliantly fought Battle of Assaye followed on 23 September. Wellesley's men were outnumbered seven to one, but he was still intent on quick victory as the only possible plan. Under heavy cannon fire, his army had to cross the River Kaitna, then attack a vastly larger force. He briefed his officers in person once they were across the river, impressing them with his calm demeanour as shot whistled on all sides. The 78th Highlanders were the first to meet the Maratha infantry. Wellington had his horse killed under him and calmly mounted another. It was a chaotic scene and Wellesley's regiments were battered by cavalry as they advanced and eventually routed the enemy. 1,584 of Wellesley's men were killed or wounded in the fighting, while the Marathas lost around 6,000 as well as all their guns. It had been a costly victory and Wellesley said later that it was 'the bloodiest for the numbers that I ever saw'.

Other battles followed and in December Wellesley took the key fortress of Gawilghur, a loss which was the final straw for the Maratha forces. They sued for peace, giving up disputed territories and disbanding their men.

Wellesley was made a Knight of the Bath in 1804 and had amassed a personal fortune of some £42,000. He applied for leave to return home in 1805. On the way, his ship stopped briefly at the island of St Helena, which would one day be the final prison of Napoleon Bonaparte. He had learned his trade in India, from the need for personal fitness and moderation, to the logistical importance of planning a campaign down to the vital supplies of food, water and ammunition.

In England, an expeditionary force was being prepared to fight against Napoleon. Wellesley was keen to command it and travelled to the Colonial Office in Downing Street to put his case to Lord Castlereagh. In the outer office, he waited for a time with an admiral named Horatio Nelson. Wellesley recognised him, but at first Nelson did not know the general fresh from India. When Nelson found out who he was, they talked for some time and Wellington said later that he'd never had a conversation that interested him more. The following day, Nelson joined HMS *Victory* and went out to the Battle of Trafalgar and his death.

While Napoleon was winning the Battle of Austerlitz, perhaps his greatest victory, Arthur Wellesley was given a brigade at Hastings in England, a long way from the action he desired. There, he offered marriage to Kitty Pakenham for a second time. He was no longer a penniless young man without a future and she agreed to marry him in November 1805. He also returned to the political debates of the day. He was elected as MP for Rye in 1806 and used his position to support his brother when Richard was accused of wasting public money in India.

Wellesley married Kitty Pakenham in April 1806, though with an extraordinary lack of grace, he muttered to a friend that 'She has grown ugly, by Jove!' It was not to be a happy marriage and may have come about in part because of the obligation and challenge he felt after the first proposal was turned down. After a brief honeymoon, he returned to his brigade.

In 1807, Wellesley was given command against the Danes. In what is known as the Second Battle of Copenhagen, he bombarded the Danish capital until they surrendered. The British aim of securing Danish ships for their own fleet was accomplished. More importantly, it denied those ships to the Napoleonic fleet. Wellesley was promoted to Lieutenant General.

In 1808, Wellesley prepared to take command of an army heading to defend allied Portugal. His years there in what would become known as the Peninsular War would secure his fame and Napoleon Bonaparte's eventual downfall.

At that time, Spain had deserted its alliance with France and was using guerrilla tactics against French forces there. Britain was keen to support any European nation willing to fight Napoleon. Wellesley had a small army of around 15,000 and his first action was to march from Mondego Bay on the west coast, to join up with 1,600 Portuguese soldiers. He faced two active French armies in Portugal as he pushed on south to Lisbon, the capital.

He reached Obidos by August 1808 and climbed a church tower to view a French army only miles away. The following day, he attacked. The French army under Delaborde were forced into a fighting withdrawal. Though it was not a rout, it was an auspicious beginning and reinforcements arrived for Wellesley, so that he had around 17,000 men.

The Battle of Vimeiro followed on 21 August. Wellesley's forces met two large French columns. His riflemen engaged them as they approached, killing many before the enemy were close enough for his artillery to fire one round from cannons. The French column then met a British line and were hammered by concentrated musket volleys. The French broke quickly and the rifle regiments ran out again to shoot them as they left the field. Wellesley used the new shrapnel ordnance to great effect against the massed French forces, though he felt his cavalry could have done better, having lost their heads and many lives by galloping wildly after the fleeing French. In all his career, he preferred infantry to cavalrymen, whom he regarded as having very little common sense.

The battle was over by noon, and shortly afterwards, senior British officers agreed the Convention of Cintra, a French request to evacuate peacefully from Portugal. Wellesley was among those who imposed very generous terms and allowed the French to take even looted supplies with them. It took the rest of the summer to organise and would later be ridiculed at home. He was summoned home to an inquiry, leaving Sir John Moore in command of the force in Portugal.

Wellesley was eventually cleared in the inquiry, but by then, Sir John Moore had been killed in the famous retreat to Corunna and successful evacuation from Spain. It was around that time that Wellington visited his bootmaker in London to commission a pair of calfskin boots that would resist being waterlogged. Though they were not made of rubber until the 1850s, the 'Wellington boot' became extremely popular in his lifetime and remains so today.

Wellesley returned to Portugal in overall command in 1809. By then, French Marshal Soult had overrun much of Portugal and two veteran French armies were in almost complete control. Wellesley had around 20,000 under his command. He made a lightning march north to Oporto, but Soult was too experienced to be trapped in the city and had destroyed bridges across the River Douro. Wellesley was forced to rely on barges to get slowly across, but there was no help for it. His army retook the city of Oporto and forced Soult's men out, killing or wounding 4,000 in the process.

Moving east into Spain, Wellesley was not impressed by his Spanish allies, though they brought around 20,000 men to join him. With reinforcements, Wellesley had 55,000 to move against the French under Marshal Victor and Napoleon's brother Joseph. However, when he approached the area and looked for the Spanish, there was no sign. His messenger was told that the Spanish were too tired to fight that hot day and the French escaped the trap.

The French attacked first at the Battle of Talavera in Spain towards the end of July 1809. Their skirmishers very nearly captured or killed Wellesley as he observed the distant French forces with a telescope. He reached his horse and managed to escape, with shots fired after him. His Spanish allies had assembled for the battle and fired a volley at the French. To Wellesley's astonishment, around 2,000 Spaniards 'were frightened only at the noise of their own fire' and ran away.

As night fell, Wellesley rode across to investigate some firing and was again almost killed by French skirmishers. In pitch darkness, he was dragged from his horse and his aide was shot dead. He managed to regain his saddle and returned to his lines, shaken but unhurt.

The following morning, the French bombardment began and Wellesley ordered his men to lie down on the far slope of a small hill while the riflemen engaged the French skirmishers. This 'reverse slope defence', using the lie of the land to protect his men, was one of his favourite tactics. The French columns advanced confidently into the gun smoke, expecting the British forces to be smashed and reeling. Wellesley's men rose to fire point-blank volleys. They drove the French back and once again the wide British line, where all the guns could bear, broke the French column, a hallmark of the Peninsular War. Even so, the fighting was brutal and often came down to hand-to-hand and bayonet charges.

Wellesley saw a large French force of infantry coming to a breach in his lines and sent a single battalion to stop them with more of the devastating volleys. His talent was in his coolness, and he never lost the overall sense of a battle, even when the shot was flying around him and men just paces away were being killed.

That night, Joseph Bonaparte withdrew the surviving French forces in defeat. Wellesley was later made Viscount Wellington of Talavera for that victory and others.

In 1810, Marshal Masséna was ordered to retake Portugal with an army of 138,000 men. Wellington moved to block the French advance into the country, while Portuguese irregulars attacked the French wherever possible. He also ordered the creation of the 'Lines of Torres Vedras' – a system of fortified positions to protect Lisbon that stretched right across part of southern Portugal. At that time, before the trenches of the 1914–18 war, it was one of the most efficient and impressive fortification lines ever created. On his orders, 108 forts, 151 redoubts and more than a thousand heavy artillery pieces formed the Lines, with almost 70,000 men in place to defend them.

A brief battle was fought at Busaco, where the French lost more than 4,500 men to Wellington's 1,252. Even so, Wellington justified the immense expense and labour that had gone into the Lines when he was forced to retreat to them against overwhelming numbers. Behind him, he used a 'scorched earth' policy that meant his men stripped the land of anything that might feed the French soldiers coming south. It was successful. The French began to starve and Marshal Masséna had to leave for Spain to resupply his army. In all, Masséna lost some 30,000 men over that winter. In 1811, he returned to Portugal and attempted to relieve the fortress city of Almeida on the eastern border with Spain.

The war continued with Wellington defending Almeida, while part of his force under Beresford besieged the French-held fortress of Badajoz in the south. Marshal Masséna launched a massive attack on Almeida to relieve it, but could not break Wellington's forces.

At Badajoz, without Wellington's watchful presence, things were much worse. The siege of the fortress had begun in May 1811, though its massive and ancient walls proved resistant to the guns. Marshal Soult arrived to relieve Badajoz and fought a fixed battle after pinning the British forces down. For once, the Spanish allies held their ground long enough for reinforcements to arrive during vicious fighting. Even then, British forces were almost cut to pieces in French cavalry charges. A rainstorm had soaked the gunpowder in their flintlocks and for a time they were almost overrun. Lowry Cole brought up his 4th Division and they moved forward slowly against the French, hammering them with volleys.

That Battle of Albuera was over before Wellington arrived, despite him having killed two horses riding to reach his men. It was a slender victory for the British forces, though it cost them 6,000 dead. Famously, when Wellington visited the field hospital, he told the wounded men that he was sorry to see so many of them there. One replied: 'If you had commanded us, my lord, there wouldn't be so many of us here.'

At that time, French armies were always in range and poised to retake Portugal. Wellington's forces began to besiege Ciudad Rodrigro, a fortified town across the Spanish border. Like Badajoz, it guarded one of the two main routes into Portugal from Spain.

Artillery made a breach in the walls of Ciudad Rodrigo and the assault on the town took place on 18 January 1812, against ferocious French resistance. After their surrender, Wellington went south and took Badajoz at last, after a month of siege and heavy bombardment. It is said that he broke down at the sight of the British dead in the breaches there, weeping for the only time in front of his men. The Spanish made Wellington a Duke of Ciudad Rodrigo for his part in the defence of their nation.

1812 would also see the Battle of Salamanca in Spain, when Wellington's Anglo-Portuguese force routed a French army of around 50,000. It was a triumph of manoeuvre as well as force. Wellington was watching the French positions when he saw a weakness in their lines as they moved. He shouted: 'By God, that will do!' before ordering the attack.

The defeated French marshal said that Wellington had manoeuvred his men 'like Frederick the Great'. The road to Madrid was open and that battle, as no other, established Wellington as the most able general Britain could field, though his greatest victory was still to come.

A new allied offensive in 1813 included the Battle of Vitoria, where Wellington beat the army of Joseph Bonaparte. Seeing his men loot abandoned wagons after that battle, Wellington made one his most famous comments: 'We have in the service the scum of the earth as common soldiers.'

By 1814, French forces had been forced to withdraw from Spain and Portugal and Wellington had crossed the Pyrenees to invade France, his men the first foreign troops to enter France at the beginning of Napoleon's downfall. Napoleon's armies were in disarray.

The self-titled French Emperor abdicated in 1814 and was exiled to the island of Elba. Before Wellington returned to England, he published a final word to his army, in which he wrote: 'The Commander of the Forces, being upon the point of returning to England, again takes this opportunity of congratulating the army upon the recent events which have restored peace to their country and the world.'

He was made a duke by a grateful nation, the highest order of nobility, to add to his previous titles of viscount, earl and field marshal, among many others. The tyranny of France had been broken over Europe and peace was at last possible.

Wellington visited Paris for a time, where he met the abolitionist Thomas Clarkson. Clarkson found him well informed. Wellington had previously promised Wilberforce that he would do everything in his power to help abolish slavery. Wellington was in fact baulked in this desire by those who had made fortunes from the trade. It would be many years before slavery was eventually abolished across the Empire.

Wellington attended the peace negotiations for the Treaty of Vienna in January 1815. It was still going on when he heard the news that shook Europe. Napoleon had escaped.

With the help of a French ship, Napoleon Bonaparte set foot in France once more in March 1815. On news of his return, King Louis XVIII of France sent a regiment to intercept him before he could reach Paris. Famously, Napoleon threw open his coat to reveal his military decorations and said: 'Let him who has the heart kill his emperor!' Instead, they cheered him and followed him back to Paris. The Hundred Days War began as he gathered 118,000 regular soldiers, 300,000 conscripts and another 100,000 support personnel. Finally, he had the veteran Army of the North around Paris – another 124,000 men.

Against him, Wellington had an Anglo-Dutch and Hanoverian force of 92,000 in Flanders and a Prussian army of 124,000 under Marshal Blücher. The Austrians also had 210,000 men and an Austrian army of 75,000 more stationed in Italy. There was also a Russian army in the east of 167,000 mobilising to march against this threat of another reign of terror. The stakes had never been higher and only Napoleon could have tried to win against such odds. He might even have been successful if the commander facing him had not been the Duke of Wellington. Before Wellington left Vienna, Tsar Nicholas of Russia laid a hand on his shoulder and said to him: 'It is for you to save the world again.'

Napoleon's only hope was to try and crush the armies against him one by one rather than allowing them to join forces. No one else could have done it, but he was a superb military tactician and, like Wellington, always kept a clear sense of the vast tapestry of units that made up a campaign area. His armies moved quickly into Belgium, but Wellington was also on the move and his allied force stopped one of Napoleon's marshals at Quatre-Bras, south of Brussels. As a result, the beleaguered Prussian forces were preserved after losing a battle at Ligny, where the French failed to follow up for lack of support.

Wellington moved his forces to the south, taking command of the ridge 'Mont St-Jean' near a village named Waterloo. That night, 17 June, it rained in torrents.

The Prussian General, Blücher, had given his promise to Wellington that he would support and reinforce his men. His deputy, Gneisenau, was convinced that Wellington would be quickly routed by the French army and wanted to leave the area. Though Blücher was 72 years old and already wounded in previous fighting, he held to his word.

On 18 June 1815, the French bombardment began. Napoleon had a force of around 74,000 compared to Wellington's 67,000. His guns, known as his 'belles filles' or beautiful daughters, hammered the allied force before his veteran troops marched forward to take the British-held ridge. They endured artillery fire themselves, but climbed the ridge in the teeth of it, fighting with bayonets and rifles against Wellington's men. The Earl of Uxbridge then smashed them with a cavalry charge over the ridge.

Napoleon was by then aware of the approach of the Prussian forces under Blücher. He sent almost his entire reserve force of nearly 15,000 infantry and cavalry to hold that flank. He kept back only his elite soldiers, the Imperial Guard. They had never been defeated in battle and their reputation made them a feared force on any European battlefield. It was a vital decision. Delaying the main attack on Wellington to repel the Prussians may well have lost Napoleon the battle.

At the same time, Marshal Ney tried to break the British centre with cavalry alone. Wellington responded with small square formations that were weak against infantry, but almost impossible for a cavalry charge to shatter. Horses will not leap into a solid mass of men with bayonets.

One British captain later recalled the French horse as an 'overwhelming, long moving line, which, ever advancing, glittered like a

stormy wave of the sea when it catches the sunlight. On they came until they got near enough, whilst the very earth seemed to vibrate beneath the thundering tramp of the mounted host. One might suppose that nothing could have resisted the shock of this terrible moving mass.'

Massed artillery and musket fire poured into the French cavalry as they came close, driving them back again and again as the light faded. It was around that time that the Earl of Uxbridge had his leg smashed by grapeshot as he sat in the saddle by Wellington.

'By God, sir, I've lost my leg!' he said, in surprise.

'By God, sir,' Wellington replied. 'So you have.'

Marshal Ney gave up his attempt to attack with cavalry alone and ordered French guns to fire grapeshot into the British squares, some of whom were beginning to run out of ammunition. The carnage was terrible and the British forces wavered. Napoleon saw the moment, felt victory in his grasp. His main reserves were still embroiled with battle against the Prussians on the flank. Yet his Imperial Guard had not fought that day and they were fresh and straining at the leash. He sent them in at last, to break the British centre.

Their morale was high as they marched in three columns through a storm of skirmisher and canister fire. One of the columns smashed a British force of Grenadiers and then their own flank came under fire and they were charged down and routed. Another Imperial Guard column marched towards British Guard regiments under Colonel Maitland. They were lying on the ground to survive French artillery attacks. When Wellington saw the Imperial Guard closing on their position, he roared: 'Up Guards and at 'em!'

The British Guards met the French with massed volley fire and a bayonet charge. With the 52nd Light Infantry, who wheeled in line to attack their broken flank, the Imperial Guards and Napoleon's last hope were smashed and broken. Famously, their bearskin hats were taken by the victorious regiments and are still worn by British Guards today. As the French soldiers ran in shock and terror, they shouted 'La Garde Recule!' – the Guard retreats.

The Prussians attacked once more, coordinating with Wellington's own counter-attack. The French army collapsed and Napoleon withdrew from the battlefield, returning to Paris where he would be forced to abdicate again and surrender. It had been his greatest gamble and Wellington later said of Waterloo that it had indeed been a 'close-run thing'.

Napoleon was taken to the island of St Helena off the coast of West Africa, one of the most isolated British possessions in the world. He died there six years later, in 1821.

Waterloo was Wellington's last battle, as well as being his finest hour. He spent some time in Paris before finally coming home. In England, he was lionised as he returned to his career in politics. He also enjoyed hunting and shooting, though he was a terrible shot and managed on different occasions to hit a dog, a keeper and an old lady as she did her washing.

Wellington represented Britain at an international congress in Verona in 1822 and took on various roles, such as Master General of the Ordnance, so was still connected to the military. He was part deafened by being too close to guns being tested, and he never recovered from the treatment, which involved a caustic solution being poured into his affected ear. He travelled to Vienna and Russia, where he met the Tsar once more.

In 1828, Wellington became Prime Minister and held his first cabinet meeting at his home, Apsley House in London. Interestingly, he had a statue of Napoleon at the bottom of the stairs there which remains today. Wellington used to hang his hat on it.

He found the idea of a cabinet somewhat trying, saying that 'I give them my orders and they stay to discuss them!' By then, he was close to 60 years old and had lost much of his youthful energy. Even so, he forced through a bill on Catholic Emancipation, in the face of much opposition. The English people were still very wary of giving Catholics any rights whatsoever and mobs threw stones at Wellington's home, smashing the windows. He ordered iron plates to be put in place and carried on. For this action, rather than any military success, he became known as 'The Iron Duke'.

When the Earl of Winchilsea said that Wellington planned to infringe liberties and introduce 'Popery into every department of the State', Wellington demanded satisfaction in a duel, which took place in March 1829. In the end, both men fired deliberately wide and the earl apologised to Wellington. At that time, duelling was illegal and it was an extraordinary thing for a Prime Minister to undertake, even one with Wellington's history.

The bill was passed and a reluctant king gave it royal assent. Wellington went on to create the Metropolitan Police in 1829. The continuation of that work would fall to his successor, Robert Peel, whose policemen were known as 'Bobbies' or 'Peelers', nicknames which endure today.

Wellington retired from political life in 1846. As Lord Warden of the Cinque Ports, he spent part of his final years at Walmer Castle and died there in 1852 at the age of 83. He was given a state funeral and finally interred in St Paul's Cathedral, where his tomb lies in the room next to Admiral Nelson.

Britain has since survived perhaps even darker moments and greater dangers than Napoleonic ambition, so that it is difficult to imagine the threat of foreign tyranny in those times. There is even a tendency to romanticise Napoleon in a way that has never been applied to Hitler. Yet Napoleon wanted nothing less than the complete subjugation and destruction of British freedoms. Nelson stopped him at sea and Wellington stopped him on land. That is his enduring legacy, far more than any marble tomb in London.

Recommended
Wellington: The Iron Duke by Richard Holmes.
St Paul's Cathedral, London.

Alcock and Brown
– Transatlantic, Non-Stop

When the 1914–18 war ended, the new world of aviation turned its attention from military to peaceful challenges. Flying an aeroplane in those glorious, dangerous, pioneering years meant sitting in a wooden cockpit open to the elements, with a wooden propeller in front and the wind roaring too loudly for speech. Both pilot and passenger were burned by the sun and soaked by the rain. Aeroplanes were called flying machines, stringbags and birdcages, with fragile wings of wood and canvas. It was the closest thing possible to being a bird.

When the *Daily Mail* offered a prize of £10,000 for the first non-stop flight across the Atlantic Ocean by an aeroplane, 'from any point in the United States, Canada or Newfoundland to any point in Great Britain or Ireland, in 72 consecutive hours', there was much shaking of wise heads.

The traditional first aeronautical challenge, the English Channel, had fallen as long ago as 1785. In an Anglo-French effort by Jean-Pierre Blanchard and Dr John Jeffries, a hydrogen balloon flew from Dover to Calais, but only by throwing all non-essentials out of the wicker basket – including Monsieur Blanchard's breeches. Being British and realising that the first crossing was also the first international flight, Dr Jeffries retained his breeches.

It was 124 years before an aeroplane crossed the Channel. In a tiny 25-horsepower, home-built monoplane, Frenchman Louis Blériot flew from Les Baraques to Dover in 1909 to claim a *Daily Mail* prize of £1,000. He very nearly crashed as he landed on the white cliffs, proving Australian flyer Charles Kingsford-Smith's observation: 'Flying is easy. It's landing that's difficult.'

Dover to Calais is twenty-three miles, yet only ten years later the talk was of crossing the Atlantic Ocean non-stop: 1,880 miles at its narrowest. The *Daily Mail* first offered the prize before the war as an incentive to aviation, but with the advances made in aeroplanes – in particular by Britain and Germany – such a flight had entered the realms of the barely possible.

By April Fools' Day, 1919, six contenders announced they would attempt the crossing that year. There were five British and one Swedish, but almost immediately Swede Hugo Sundstedt crashed his biplane during a test flight in America.

Major John Wood was the first to fly, on 18 April. He took off from Eastchurch, on the Isle of Sheppey in Kent, and flew westwards across Britain in a two-seater seaplane named *Shamrock*. Slung between the floats was a massive extra fuel tank. Twenty-two miles west of Wales, his engine seized and he was forced down into the Irish Sea. He and his navigator were picked up by a passing ship. Wood's enterprise embraced the pre-war spirit of aviation – adventurous, against the odds, glorious and extremely dangerous. Disappointed, the flying major declared 'The Atlantic flight is pipped!'

The remaining four transported their aeroplanes by ship to Newfoundland to fly west-to-east with the prevailing winds to reach Britain or Ireland. The intrepid flyers, engineers and riggers assembled at St John's, capital of Newfoundland, in early May 1919. The four teams were experienced aircraft manufacturers: Sopwith, Martinsyde, Handley-Page and Vickers, proud names in the history of aviation.

Sopwith Aircraft Company chose for its pilot Harry Hawker, a lean Australian and the company's chief test pilot. His navigator was Lieutenant Commander Kenneth 'Mac' Grieve, Royal Navy. For the attempt, Sopwith chose its new biplane called *Atlantic*. It was powered by a single Rolls-Royce Eagle Mark VIII engine. At that time, it was the most powerful aero-engine in the world. In the *Atlantic*, it produced a speed of 100 knots and a range of 3,000 nautical miles. After take-off Hawker could ditch *Atlantic*'s undercarriage in the sea to give an extra 7 knots of speed. Every knot might be needed. Hawker made two 900-mile test flights of *Atlantic* in Britain and the team were the favourite to succeed. As Hawker Company, Sopwith later produced the superb Hurricane fighter.

Martinsyde Aircraft Company also chose a small aeroplane. Its *Raymor*, a two-seater biplane, was powered by a single Rolls-Royce Falcon engine. Cruising speed was 110 knots with a range of 2,750 nautical miles, making *Raymor* the fastest entrant. Its pilot was Freddie Raynham, 26. Raynham's navigator was Captain C.W. Fairfax 'Fax' Morgan, a Royal Navy flyer. During the war he'd been shot down over France and used an artificial cork leg as a result. Fax was a descendant of the buccaneer Sir Henry Morgan. *Raymor* was named after its pilot and navigator.

Handley-Page Ltd then produced the largest aeroplane in the world, the V/1500 bomber, and selected a three-man crew for its attempt. Overall commander was 55-year-old Admiral Mark Kerr with a Handley-Page pilot and navigator. The V/1500 was powered by four Rolls-Royce Eagle Mark VIIIs. The fuselage of the V/1500 was even large enough to have an enclosed cabin. Handley-Page later produced the *Victor* nuclear strike bomber.

Vickers Ltd, the last entrant, chose 26-year-old Captain John 'Jackie' Alcock, DSO, as pilot and Lieutenant Arthur 'Teddie' Brown, as navigator. Alcock was born in Manchester and

Brown in Glasgow. They were both ex-RAF flyers and both had been brought down during the war. Brown had a gammy left leg to remind him of his crash. He was engaged, but delayed the wedding when offered the position as navigator.

Vickers chose its *Vimy* bomber for the Atlantic attempt, an aircraft named after the Battle of Vimy Ridge. The *Vimy* was the second largest aircraft in the world, 43½ feet long with a wingspan of 68 feet. A good-looking biplane – and good-looking aeroplanes are usually good-flying aeroplanes – it was powered by two Rolls-Royce Eagle Mark VIII engines. By removing the bomb racks and the gunner's equipment and fitting two extra petrol tanks in the fuselage, the *Vimy* had a cruising speed of 90 knots with a range of 2,800 nautical miles. Vickers later produced the brilliant *Supermarine Spitfire* fighter.

The strong naval presence may seem odd now, but in 1919 the majority of air navigators were seamen. Both flyers and sailors navigate using the heavens and land features. Both use rudders, both use port and starboard, both use cockpits and cabins, and so on. The different airflows above and below a wing which 'lifts' an aeroplane into the air are exactly the same as the airflows in front and behind a sail which 'draws' a vessel through the water.

The four aeroplanes had at least 1,880 nautical miles to fly – by a long, long way the greatest distance ever attempted – yet the biggest obstacle to success was the Atlantic weather. Unpredictable, unknown and dangerous, with no weather ships and no weather satellites, conditions could change in moments. Gales and wind shear can blow an aircraft miles off-course. Cloud and fog can blind and disorientate pilot and navigator. Ice can form on wings, destroying the 'lift' of the machine and, in those days, instruments and engines often packed up in such extreme conditions.

In their favour was the west-to-east prevailing wind, so that even if they met contrary winds within a weather system, the system itself usually moved east. Yet even prevailing winds sometimes don't blow, and weather systems don't always follow the rules laid down by meteorologists.

'It's a piece of cake!' said Jackie Alcock after a test flight in England. 'All we have to do is keep the engines going and we'll be home for tea.'

Fields long and flat enough for aircraft to take off from were rare in rugged Newfoundland. Sopwith and Martinsyde were first to arrive and found meadows suitable for their small aircraft – just. Handley-Page located fields 60 miles from St John's at Harbour Grace and spent a month clearing and joining them together. Vickers took down hedges, dismantled walls, felled trees, rolled boulders, filled ditches, and even removed a stone dyke to create a 500-yard airfield close to St John's.

Every Newfoundlander knew what was at stake, of course. Willingly, they helped the four teams prepare. Alcock christened Vickers's airfield 'Lester's Field', after the drayman who hauled the crated aircraft from the dockside. To ease the hard labour new words were added to a local folk song:

Oh, lay hold Jackie Alcock, lay hold Teddie Brown,
Lay hold of the cordage and dig into the ground.
Lay hold of the bowline and pull all you can,
The *Vimy* will fly afore the Handley-Page can.

However, it was Sopwith's *Atlantic* which first left Newfoundland, on the afternoon of 18 May. That morning Hawker described the weather as 'not yet favourable, but possible', and began to fill his fuel tanks. Raynham made the same optimistic forecast and fuelled Martinsyde's *Raymor*. The V/1500 was not yet assembled, while Vickers still awaited its aircraft's arrival.

At noon, Hawker and Grieve decided they'd fly and informed the other teams. In a gentleman's agreement it had been decided to let each team know each other's plans. At 15.40 Hawker called cheerily from the cockpit: 'Tell Raynham I'll greet him at Brooklands,' and sent *Atlantic* swaying across the soggy field. After 300 yards the wheels lifted, cleared a row of trees and the aeroplane was away.

Harry Hawker and Mac Grieve circled once above Martinsyde's field alongside Lake Quidi Vidi to wave, crossed the coast, jettisoned

Atlantic's undercarriage and headed for the British Isles. In six minutes they were out of sight in the Atlantic murk.

Two hours later, the faster *Raymor* was ready and about 2,000 Newfoundlanders had gathered to watch the take-off. Freddie Raynham and Fax Morgan waved. Raynham opened the throttle and began *Raymor*'s run across Quidi Vidi field into a crosswind. There is less lift from a crosswind than a headwind. After 300 yards, *Raymor*'s wheels left the ground and she rose about ten feet – and obstinately stayed there, drifting slightly sideways. *Raymor* dropped to the ground, the undercarriage collapsed, the propeller dug into the turf and she crashed. Raynham was not seriously injured and crawled from the cockpit with a bang to his head, but Fax had to be lifted out and taken to hospital. He was told he'd lose an eye.

Alcock and Brown visited Martinsyde's flyers in hospital that evening. Raynham offered them Quidi Vidi field so that they could assemble the *Vimy* for test flights while Lester's Field was completed. Meanwhile, no radio message had been received from *Atlantic*. In itself this was of no concern, for 1919 was also the pioneering age of radio; they frequently stopped working.

When *Atlantic*'s maximum flying time of twenty-two hours was reached next afternoon, there was still no word from Britain or any ship. It was evident the aircraft was down, somewhere in the Atlantic Ocean.

The dismantled *Vimy* arrived at St John's harbour on 26 May – the day after good news had arrived by telegram. Hawker and Grieve had been picked up from the Atlantic Ocean by a Danish steamer and reached Scotland on the 25th. *Atlantic*'s radio had broken immediately after take-off. The weather had worsened with heavy rain squalls and after four hours the engine began to overheat. The problem was a blockage in the cooling system. By repeatedly switching off the engine, diving, then switching on again, Harry Hawker had partially cleared the blockages. They'd continued until dawn on the 19th, but it was clear the engine was not going to take the aircraft to Britain. With a gale approaching, Hawker and Grieve had searched for a ship and ditched *Atlantic* alongside. Half an hour later the gale came through.

In Newfoundland, the *Vimy* was assembled in record time, working in the open through rain and snow. Only a fortnight after arriving, the aircraft made its first test flight from Quidi Vidi field. The same day, the V/1500 made its first test flight from Harbour Grace. On 8 June, Alcock and Brown flew the *Vimy* in its second test flight to Lester's Field.

At Quidi Vidi, engineers and riggers were also repairing *Raymor* and a navigator was found to replace Fax Morgan. Raynham was trying for another attempt. The V/1500 made her second test flight but also encountered engine cooling problems. It was a toss-up which of the three aircraft would depart next.

Alcock drained the cooling systems of the two *Vimy* engines of water, boiled it twice and filtered it to remove any matter that might block circulation. He thought that the sediment in the Newfoundland water might have caused the *Atlantic* and V/1500 cooling problems. The weather closed in again with successive gales before clearing on the morning of the 13th.

Alcock made another decision at Lester's Field, possibly taking a leaf from *Atlantic*'s book. He removed the *Vimy*'s nose-wheel in order to reduce 'drag'. The nose-wheel was there only for landing, to stop the aeroplane pitching forward should the undercarriage snag in grass. The *Vimy* normally rested and landed on the four wheels of the main undercarriage beneath the wings and a small tail-wheel. Without a nose-wheel Alcock would have to ensure he made a decent three-point touchdown when he landed.

Riggers and engineers worked throughout the day and night and by the morning of the 14th the *Vimy* was refuelled and ready to fly. Stowed on board were 197 letters, potentially the first transatlantic airmail. Alcock and Brown spoke together briefly and decided to fly. They sent a message to the V/1500 at Harbour Grace and a telegram to Vickers. The *Daily Mail* sent a telegram to London. Raynham came to see them off.

Early that afternoon, with the Rolls-Royce engines running smoothly, the *Vimy* jolted across Lester's Field and gathered speed, heading slightly uphill into a west wind. The picnicking Newfoundlander crowd watched interestedly then anxiously: 100 yards, 150 yards, the tail lifted, 200 yards, 300 yards, 400 yards. Only 100 yards of field remained.

Brown wrote later: 'We were almost at the end of the ground tether allowed us.' He glanced at Alcock. 'The perspiration of acute anxiety was running down his face.' The distance between success and disaster would be just feet. The watching Raynham knew how Alcock would be at the controls, the throttles wide open, gently coaxing the machine up.

The jolting stopped as the undercarriage finally left the ground, the four wheels skimming the grass. Alcock eased back the stick a touch – only a touch – or the aircraft would stall and crash. Brown held his breath as they reached the end of the field. The *Vimy* rose, cleared a stone dyke, cleared the first trees, then disappeared behind rising ground 300 yards away. The crowd gasped and began running towards the hidden ground. The St John's doctor ran with them.

Then the big *Vimy* reappeared beyond the crest in a shallow climb, rising slowly into the grey sky. Brown waved his arm above the cockpit, Alcock concentrated on his airspeed. At 1.42 p.m. on Saturday, 14 June 1919, they were away.

Alcock gained height, banked the *Vimy* in a gentle turn to the east to fly over St John's harbour where ships' whistles blew farewell. At 1,200 feet, Brown took a departure position from the Newfoundland coast and sent a radio message: 'All well and started.' They flew out over the Atlantic Ocean and thirty minutes of steady climbing took them to 5,000 feet.

In the previous attempts to fly the Atlantic non-stop, one aeroplane had ditched in the Irish Sea, one had ditched in the Atlantic Ocean and one had crashed on take-off, but no one had been killed. Now the fourth was finally airborne, the first of the heavies.

Looking from their windy cockpit to the north, to port, Alcock saw icebergs on the horizon; beyond was Greenland and the Arctic. Ahead there was only ocean until Europe, sixteen to twenty hours away. To the south, to starboard, there was also nothing but ocean. Behind and diminishing rapidly was North America.

At 5 p.m., they passed over sea fog below and the ocean disappeared. Cloud gathered above and the sun disappeared, then the fog reached up to them and everything disappeared, no clouds, no horizon, nothing. Alcock steered his compass course, holding the bubble in the turn-and-bank indicator central to keep the wings level and checking the altimeter to keep the nose level. He flew 'blind' for more than an hour.

The small propeller of the radio generator sheered off in the slipstream and their communications were finished. Suddenly, the starboard engine clattered. The two men looked to their right in alarm.

'A chunk of exhaust pipe had split away and was quivering before the rush of air like a reed in an organ pipe,' wrote Brown. 'It became first red then white-hot and, softened by the heat, it gradually crumpled up. Finally it was blown away.' The clattering stopped.

They dined on sandwiches and coffee, Brown feeding Alcock, who kept one hand lightly around the control stick. When darkness fell, Brown wanted an accurate position, so Alcock took the *Vimy* above the cloud at 6,000 feet. It was cold up there and Brown's fingers were numb as he took star sights of Polaris and Vega at 10 p.m., using an artificial horizon fixed to his sextant. He calculated their position while Alcock came down to a lesser cold at 4,000 feet.

After eight hours' flying they had covered 850 nautical miles, a speed over the ground of 106¼ knots. A light tailwind and less drag without the nose-wheel had given them a greater speed than expected. They were almost halfway across the Atlantic Ocean.

Flying through cold misty moonlight, the aircraft skimmed across the top of the clouds. Beneath them were silvery grey valleys, above the distant starred heavens. Brown found an aura of unreality about the flight. He recorded in the logbook: 'The distorted ball of a moon, the weird half-light, the monstrous cloud shapes, the fog, the misty indefiniteness of space, the changeless drone, drone, drone of the motors.' On they flew, growing stiff and numb on the wooden bench seat. 'I looked towards Brown and saw that he was singing,' Alcock said later, 'but I couldn't understand a word!'

Behind them the moon set and ahead, perhaps above Ireland and Britain, came the first suggestion of the pale dawn. Suddenly, a massive cloud towered in the darkness ahead, silhouetted for the first time against the eastern sky. There was no way around: they flew straight in. It was 3 a.m. on the 15th.

Inside the black cloud a storm was raging. The temperature plunged, the air heaved and roared about them, and the *Vimy* shook and twisted in violent wind and rain.

'The aircraft swung, flew amok and began to perform circus tricks,' Brown said. 'Until we should see either the horizon or the sky or the sea and thus restore our sense of the horizontal, we could tell only by the instruments what was happening.'

The bubble in the turn-and-bank indicator had disappeared, giving no indication of how level the wings were. The airspeed indicator had jammed at 90 knots, while the roar of the storm masked the roar of the engines. Only the altimeter registered, just under 4,000 feet. The aircraft pitched and tossed like a cork and, with Alcock disorientated in the roaring cloud, flew slower and slower in the darkness.

Without warning, the aeroplane shuddered and stalled. The nose dropped, and immediately the big *Vimy* slipped into a spinning dive, the most dangerous and deadly condition for any aircraft.

In 1919, a spinning nose-dive was called a Parke's Dive, because Lieutenant Parke was one of the very, very few pilots who had managed to fly out of it. Unfortunately, even Parke wasn't sure how he had done it. Once begun, a diving spin more often than not continued down and into the ground – or sea. Early aeroplanes often disintegrated in a spin, their wings torn off.

The theory is that with enough height, you get out of a spin by putting the stick forward into a steeper dive to regain airspeed and thus 'lift'. Apply rudder opposite to the direction of the spin, then the plane will stop spinning and you can level out. Even in daylight, when you can see the ground and the horizon, it's about the greatest test for any pilot.

In the *Vimy*'s cockpit, inside the cloud, the altimeter reeled away the height down and down. The compass spun continuously, which in reality was the aircraft spinning around the compass, while Alcock tried to fly out of the spin in complete blackness. 'How and at what angle we were falling we knew not,' wrote Brown. 'Jackie tried to centralise [the aircraft] but failed because we had lost all sense of what was central.'

Spinning through 3,000 feet, 2,500 feet, 2,000, 1,500, 1,000 feet, the altimeter unwound until Brown could hear, somewhere about them, the hissing and churning of the ocean. He thrust the logbook into his Burberry flying jacket. If they ditched, one of the extra fuel tanks would become their lifeboat and it was his responsibility to drag it out.

Abruptly, the *Vimy* dropped out of the bottom of the immense cloud a few hundred feet above the Atlantic Ocean – almost upside down. Alcock saw the luminescence of the wave-tops above his head, flipped the aircraft over, kept the nose down, opened the throttles, countered the spin with the rudder, and levelled out fifty feet above the water. The propellers clawed at the air and dragged the aircraft from danger, hauling her slowly away from the sea. Pilot and navigator exchanged glances.

Alcock eased back the stick and set the aircraft climbing between the clouds. They had to get height, away from the turbulent air over the surface of the sea. 'The salty taste we noted later on our tongues was foam,' Alcock said.

A check of their situation showed that the instruments were registering again. There was no damage to the aircraft, there was still plenty of fuel and dawn had broken. They needed a position to reset their course since the last 10 p.m. position, another very good reason to climb above the clouds into the sun.

Heavy rain drove into the cockpit, onto their leather helmets, their goggles and their flying jackets. It drummed upon the canvas of the wings and fuselage. As they gained more and more height, the rain became lighter and changed into snow. At 8,000 feet, still climbing, still in dense grey cloud, the snow coated the aircraft and froze to ice. Alcock kept working the controls of the aircraft to stop permanent icing: rotating the stick and moving the rudder pedals backwards and forwards. As yet there was no danger to the aerodynamics of the *Vimy*, but some of the instruments would be affected.

While Alcock kept the aeroplane level, Brown slipped out of his harness. He stepped up onto the seat, clutched a wooden wing strut with one hand, pushed himself out into the slipstream of 100 knots with the other and knocked away the ice from the instruments. The propeller blades swished nearby. He cleared the air tubes of the speed indicator and the glass faces of the fuel gauges, for once ice formed the only way to melt it would be to descend again to near sea level.

Four times they completed those manoeuvres, until at 11,800 feet they finally broke clear of the cloud. There was the red-yellow morning sun, low in the east. There was no warmth in the rays at that altitude and with stiff, frozen hands Brown took his sextant shot and calculated their dead-reckoning position. Alcock maintained the hard-won altitude.

Eventually, Brown leant across the cockpit to Alcock with a new course and a written message: 'About eighty miles to the Irish coast!'

The starboard engine backfired. Ice had formed over the air intakes, which Brown had no way of reaching because of the spinning propeller, so Alcock switched the engine off. Closing the throttle of the port engine to idling speed, he put the *Vimy* into a shallow glide along the new course. At a lower height, the seal of ice would melt and he'd start the engine again.

They were still over the Atlantic, so there was no danger of flying into a mountain, yet no pilot enjoys losing height in cloud. There was the altimeter, but altimeters work according to air pressure, and their instrument had been set sixteen hours ago in Newfoundland. They had no way of knowing how accurate it was.

They levelled out in clear air 500 feet above the sea, grey and white beneath them. Alcock opened the port throttle for flying speed, then started the starboard engine and opened that throttle too. The Rolls-Royce Eagles roared. All was well so they stayed just below the cloud, peering through their goggles for the continent of Europe.

They saw first two small, rocky islands in the distance, with a low smudge across the horizon further on. Twenty minutes later they flew over Eeshal and Turbot Islands. Ten minutes after that, they crossed the west coast of the Emerald Isle. Turning to starboard, they flew south along the desolate coast until Brown identified the tall masts of the British wireless station at Clifden. They'd reached Ireland over Connemarra, only ten miles north of the planned route.

'What should we do?' they discussed, shouting and using hand signals.

'We had plenty of fuel, enough to fly on to England,' Alcock said later, 'but there didn't seem any point.' In fact they'd used only two-thirds of their fuel, with enough left to reach France if they'd wished. They cruised above Clifden looking for a suitable landing field. They flew over a long, green field with no trees near the wireless station and Alcock decided that would do.

On the ground, people had come out to see the flying machine, for it was evident it was going to land. Those by the green field waved at the *Vimy*. Alcock and Brown saw waving arms, mouths opening and closing. The two flyers grinned from on high and waved back. That was good, an Irish welcome. They could do with a drop.

Alcock completed his circuit, turned into the final upwind leg and brought the aircraft down for a three-point landing – nose a little higher, tail a little lower than the bottom wings. Without the safeguard of the nose-wheel, he concentrated on a good landing. The *Vimy* touched down, the large wheels of the two undercarriages and the small tail-wheel almost at the same time. It was 8.40 a.m. on Sunday, 15 June 1919.

The aircraft bounced over the tufted grass, slowing down, when suddenly the undercarriage wheels dug in, the tail flew up, the nose tipped forward, and they came to a sudden halt. In a land of many bogs they had very carefully selected and landed on one of the flattest. The waving people had actually been waving them away.

The two men clambered out of their cockpit, now at ground level, Brown with a bump to his nose. They pushed their goggles up and grinned tiredly at each other. They had been in the air for 16 hours and 27 minutes. They had flown 1,890 nautical miles. They had crossed the Atlantic Ocean non-stop.

'What do you think of that for fancy navigation?' navigator asked pilot.

'Very good!' pilot replied. Beside the *Vimy*, Alcock and Brown shook hands.

Soldiers from the wireless station arrived, feeling that an unidentified aircraft landing near a military installation was possibly in their jurisdiction. 'Where're you from?' asked one.

'St John's,' replied Alcock. No one knew St John's. Was that Scotland?

'Newfoundland,' Alcock explained. No recognition.

'North America?' he tried.

'Get away!' the soldiers laughed, thinking it was a joke. It took a while for the truth to sink in: they'd witnessed the completion of the greatest flight ever made. The flyers' hands were shaken, their backs were slapped, their shoulders gripped, their hands wrung again. 'North America, eh?'

In Newfoundland, the news of Alcock and Brown's safe arrival on the other side of the Atlantic was greeted with rapture.

Lester's Field was indeed the first transatlantic aerodrome. North America to Europe, non-stop, in 16½ hours.

Telegrams announcing their amazing feat flashed around the world. It was a sensation. In the year 1919, the achievement was almost unbelievable. Only ten years after the first aeroplane had struggled across the English Channel, Jackie Alcock and Teddie Brown had flown the vast Atlantic Ocean. They'd blazed the trail. Others would surely follow in the years ahead, but they were the first.

They were driven to Dublin, where a telegram from the king awaited them. From Dublin, they travelled to Liverpool by ferry, from Liverpool to London by train. Alcock and Brown made a triumphant journey and were feted wherever they stopped. These were the men who had conquered the Atlantic. Occasionally, Vickers and Rolls-Royce were mentioned.

The Times reported: 'In Crewe station there was yet another crowd which insisted on the airmen leaving the train during the halt. Suddenly an Australian soldier called to a porter "Up with him" and Lieutenant Brown was lifted shoulder-high so that all the people could see and cheer him. Another soldier with assistance hoisted up Captain Alcock.'

Waiting crowds in London cheered them through the streets of the capital, where they were driven in an open Rolls-Royce limousine. The Royal Aero Club (the Royal Aeronautical Society) honoured them with a reception and officially validated the flight. They successfully delivered to the Post Office the first transatlantic airmail. At a grand luncheon at the Savoy Hotel the Minister for War and Air, Winston Churchill, presented them with the *Daily Mail* prize of £10,000, which was shared with the Vickers team.

They were summoned to Windsor Castle. There King George V knighted the two airmen with the same sword Queen Elizabeth had knighted Francis Drake in 1581. Alcock and Brown, their surnames forever joined, were national and international heroes.

Significantly, they had flown the Atlantic in a production aeroplane with production engines. The *Vimy* hadn't been redesigned for the flight; it was the standard model. The weight reduction achieved by removing the bomb racks and machine guns was replaced by the weight of the extra fuel tanks. It was the thirteenth built, it cost £3,000 and it had crossed the Atlantic non-stop. There was the future of aviation.

Barely three weeks later, on 2 July, airship *R34* of the RAF took off from East Fortune, east of Edinburgh, and flew westwards to North America against the prevailing winds. Under the command of Major G.H. Scott, *R34* reached New Jersey through terrible weather in a non-stop flight of four and a half days. Airships were new to America, so Major Pritchard parachuted down to organise the landing. *R34* then flew back to Britain to land at Pulham in Norfolk. Major Scott and his crew became the first to fly the Atlantic Ocean east-to-west non-stop and the first to fly both ways non-stop. Alcock and Brown had certainly started something.

Their 1919 conquest of the Atlantic remains the greatest pioneering flight of all. It was the first non-stop ocean crossing and the first long-distance flight. It encountered bad weather and overcame it. It convinced the sceptics that aeroplanes were for civilian use as well as for war, and it carried the first oceanic airmail. Intercontinental air travel had begun.

Outside the Queen's Building at Heathrow airport there is a statue carved in stone of Alcock and Brown. The Vickers *Vimy* they flew is on permanent display at the Science Museum in London.

In December 1919, Sir Jackie Alcock delivered a Vickers *Viking* to France. Landing in thick fog, his wing tip snared a tree and he crashed and struck his head. He died a few hours later without regaining consciousness. Sir Teddie Brown married that October, decided he wouldn't fly again and died in England in 1948.

Recommended
Flying the Atlantic in Sixteen Hours by Sir Arthur Whitten Brown.
Our Transatlantic Flight by Sir John Alcock and
Sir Arthur Whitten Brown.
The Vickers Vimy by P. St-J. Turner.
Queen's Building, Heathrow Airport, London.
The Science Museum, London.

General James Wolfe

T he history of the last five hundred years can be summarised in just a pair of sentences: The nations of Europe exploded outwards into the world, claiming territories as their own. One by one, they came into conflict with Britain, were beaten and sent home again.

During that time, 'New Amsterdam' was renamed New York, 'New France' was renamed Canada and 'New Holland' was renamed Australia. The island nation of Britain fought Spain, France, Denmark, Holland, Germany, the Holy Roman Empire, Russia and Italy, emerging battered but victorious from centuries of war.

There is no obvious reason why Britain became the pre-eminent power over five centuries, before passing on the torch to America. The Spanish were as hungry for land and trade, French ships were better built, Napoleon Bonaparte was a brilliant tactician and the armies of the Kaiser and Hitler were vast and well organised. The difference seems to have been just a handful of men and women who were in the right place to bring about huge change. Henry V, Edward III, Elizabeth I, Wellington, Nelson, Clive, Napier, Prime Ministers Pitt and Churchill – Britain seemed to produce a higher calibre of leader and warrior at exactly the right moment. The one time there was no one of quality on the walls, the American colonies were lost. In the end, that too has worked out reasonably well.

The Seven Years War (1756–63) had as great an effect on the history of the world as any other before or since. Battles took place as far away as India and Canada, and it is that vast sphere of interest that makes this the first true world war, though the Napoleonic wars also have a claim. It was a conflict between autocracy and democracy, as the France of Louis XV was a very different place from the Britain of George II and III.

While Robert Clive was in India, another professional soldier was battling the French in their North American colony. At that point, Canada was the French colonial jewel and would not be taken without a fight. James Wolfe would give his life at the moment of his triumph and enter the pantheon of great names.

Wolfe was born on 2 January 1727, in Kent. He had red hair and blue eyes, a beak of a nose and a receding chin that completely failed to predict his temperament and determination. His father had been with Marlborough in Flanders and his grandfather reached the rank of major. Wolfe knew from an early age that he would 'follow the drum'. His younger brother Edward became a lieutenant and died of tuberculosis at only 16, while on active service. Like the Napiers in the following century, the Wolfes were expected to give their lives to the army.

At 14, James joined his father's regiment of marines. In 1742, he transferred to the 12th Foot and travelled to Ghent in Flanders to fight against the French in the War of the Austrian Succession. He was rapidly promoted, becoming a captain at 17 and a brigade major at 18. Wolfe was a born soldier and despite an explosive temper, he impressed his superiors with his courage, tactical thinking and ability to lead men.

In 1745, the second Jacobite rebellion took place (after the first in 1715). Those rebellions were the attempt to restore a Catholic, Scottish monarchy with James Stuart ('The Old Pretender'), then Charles Stuart ('The Young Pretender'). Wolfe served with his regiment at the battles of Falkirk and Culloden – the latter being the last land battle fought in Britain.

The Duke of Cumberland commanded a predominantly Scottish force at Culloden, where the fighting was particularly brutal. More than a thousand Scots were killed and Cumberland gave orders for the wounded to be slaughtered, earning himself the nickname 'The Butcher of Culloden'. He is said to have ordered Wolfe to shoot a wounded colonel of the Fraser regiment, but Wolfe famously refused, saying his honour was worth more than his commission. Later, when Wolfe commanded the Fraser regiment, they were fanatically loyal to him. Interestingly, Wolfe's view of war could be as ruthless as any other professional soldier of the day. He was sometimes merciful, but never at the expense of a victory.

While still in his twenties, Wolfe engaged tutors in Latin and mathematics, determined to better himself and complete his education. He also spent his leave in Paris, where he learned French. His meteoric military rise continued. He saw other battles on the continent and in Scotland and became a major at 22, with an acting rank of lieutenant colonel, confirmed in 1750. By 1756, when the Seven Years War began, Wolfe was an experienced, seasoned officer of just 29, with the fires of youth still undimmed. He was considered too young to promote to full colonel, though he had been in four major battles and a host of successful minor engagements. He ran his regiment efficiently and was well known and admired by his superiors. It was said of him at the time: 'He looked upon danger as the favourable moment that would call forth all his talents.'

In 1757, Wolfe was ordered to take part in an expedition against Rochefort, a heavily defended French port at the mouth of the Charente near the Basque Roads – an area of France that Thomas Cochrane would assault some fifty years later. Wolfe joined a fleet that included Richard Howe, in command of the *Magnanime*, and one William Hamilton. Hamilton was friendly with Wolfe and had known him for years, but he is most famous for being the husband of Emma Hamilton, later to become Nelson's mistress.

Batteries protecting the Basque Roads were on the Île d'Aix, an island in the main channel. Richard Howe sailed the *Magnanime* to within sixty yards of the guns, ignoring their fire. His crew then pounded the batteries until the French lowered their flag and surrendered. Wolfe was one of the naval party who landed on the island to take command, but he was baulked in his desire to follow it up with a general landing of troops. His commanding officers dithered and the chance was lost.

Wolfe's words on the subject would later become famous: 'We have lost the lucky moment in war and are not able to recover it.'

For his zeal at Rochefort, Wolfe was mentioned to King George II and promoted to colonel. In later years, when Wolfe's detractors said he was not stable enough to be given independent command, the king replied: 'Mad, is he? Then I wish he would bite some of my other generals!'

In 1758, Prime Minister Pitt the Elder planned an assault on the massive French fortress of Louisburg in Canada, the strongest military base in the country. As the author G.A. Henty later wrote: 'It had been manifest for some time that the continent of North America was too narrow to hold both Great Britain and France.' Another fleet was assembled under Admiral Boscawen, known as 'Old Dreadnought' to his men. An army of 12,000 under General Amherst was assembled to storm the fort. Wolfe was one of three brigadiers. The plan was to take Louisburg as quickly as possible, then to move on to the French stronghold at Quebec, up the St Lawrence River.

The campaign did not begin well, as the British forces landed exactly where the French expected them. The battalions forced a landing in the face of hostile fire, though many were killed or drowned when their boats overturned in the surf. Wolfe was in charge of the landing party and led his men on foot, capturing French batteries with musket and bayonet. With a dash of luck and courage, they avoided what could have been a complete disaster. Away from the shore, Wolfe and his men laid down mortar positions to bombard the remaining French batteries. In support, the British fleet pounded the anchored French ships, setting most of them on fire. Boscawen then sent in raiding parties to cut out the two surviving French ships, though one ran aground in the attempt and had to be burned.

Without ships, the French surrendered and nearly 6,000 were taken as prisoners. Amherst and Wolfe wanted to move on Quebec without delay – to seize the 'lucky moment' of war – but Boscawen's ships were already stuffed with prisoners and provisions were running low. Instead, Amherst was sent to reinforce another attack to the south and Wolfe was ordered to carry out raids in the area.

Given a free hand, Wolfe destroyed French towns and settlements during September 1758. In one of the raids, he learned that a French admiral was coming down the St Lawrence with eight fighting ships. Always impetuous, Wolfe advised an attack, but to his disgust, was overruled. He sailed home at the end of 1758. Louisburg had been taken, but with the strongholds of Quebec and Montreal still in French hands, the future of Canada was in doubt.

In December 1758, Wolfe was summoned to a meeting with Pitt's military adviser and discussed future plans for Canada. Pitt was impressed with the young officer and recommended him for another expedition to take Quebec.

Around that time, Wolfe met Katherine Lowther, a society beauty. They became engaged, but did not announce it publicly. This may have been because Wolfe's mother had occasionally been hostile to the women in his life and he did not want her to sour the relationship. Wolfe was ordered away before they could be married.

The fleet to take Quebec was assembled under Vice Admiral Charles Saunders. One of his officers was James Cook, later to become famous as the greatest navigator of the age. Another was John Jervis, later Earl St Vincent, who would one day be both an enemy to Thomas Cochrane and a great supporter of Horatio Nelson. They sailed from Spithead on 14 February 1759.

As Commander-in-Chief, Amherst decided to attack Montreal, while Wolfe went after Quebec. With the new rank of major general, Wolfe had around 8,000 experienced soldiers under his command, including a regiment of Fraser Highlanders. His men were equipped with the flintlock musket known as the 'Brown Bess', with a four-foot barrel and attached bayonet. A British redcoat could shoot three times a minute, a rate of fire that was devastating for the period. In Canada, Wolfe also assumed command of six companies of American Rangers, troops raised by the Crown in what were British colonies at that time.

The French military commander at Quebec was Louis-Joseph de Montcalm-Gozon, known as the Marquis de Montcalm. Like Wolfe, he was a professional soldier who had fought in the War of the Austrian Succession. Montcalm had a citizens' militia of around 10,000 as well as 2,400 regular French troops. Vitally, he also had the entire British plan from an intercepted letter written by General Amherst. Montcalm was instructed to hold and defend while he waited for reinforcements from France.

Wolfe's army assembled at Louisburg. While there, Wolfe heard of the death of his father and wore a black armband to mark the loss. He spent months preparing the expedition, overseeing every detail of uniform and supplies before the army finally embarked in the summer of 1759.

The St Lawrence River had never been properly surveyed and the French were certain British ships would run aground. They were mistaken. As sailing master of the *Pembroke*, James Cook played a vital role in mapping and surveying the river approaches to Quebec before the main fleet came in.

When the British force made its way up the St Lawrence, they anchored at the western point of the island of Orleans, a little below the city. From there, Wolfe had his first sight of Quebec. To say the least, it was a daunting prospect for an assault.

Quebec is built on a cliff above the river, with the Upper Town rising some two hundred feet above the water. In addition to that natural obstacle, the French had built a floating battery of twelve heavy guns and a pontoon bridge to allow their soldiers to move freely across the St Charles River to the north of the city. They had shallow-draught boats with bow cannons and crews who knew the waters far better than the British. They had also prepared for the attack with a line of well-manned defences, blocking a landing for six miles along the northern banks. Finally, the French had a flotilla of fireships that could be sent out into the river to burn the British fleet.

On the night of 27 June, seven of the fireships were sent towards the anchored British vessels. Each had a small crew, whose task was to fire the ship and then take to boats to escape. Surprise is vital for such an enterprise and the nervous crews set the fires too soon, so that the British were able to react without panic. The *Centurion* was closest and her captain cut her cable and moved clear. After that, British crews took their own boats out in the darkness, grappling the flaming vessels and towing them to shore, where they burned merrily and harmed no one.

In July, Wolfe found the siege hard going. British ships could not get as close to shore as he wanted and the French gunboats were a constant threat, able to slip in and out of the shallows with impunity. In addition, a storm hit one night and caused terrible damage to the British fleet. The winters in Quebec were too harsh to continue an assault and Montcalm knew he only had to hold out for a few months before the river iced up and Wolfe had to leave.

Wolfe chafed at every delay. Naturally impetuous, it was the worst sort of warfare from his point of view. He also suffered a bout of dysentery and a bladder ailment that reduced him to misery for some time. From Orleans Island, he sent men to Point Lévis, on the opposite bank to Quebec. The French believed the move was a feint and did not react. That was a serious error. The soldiers on Point Lévis

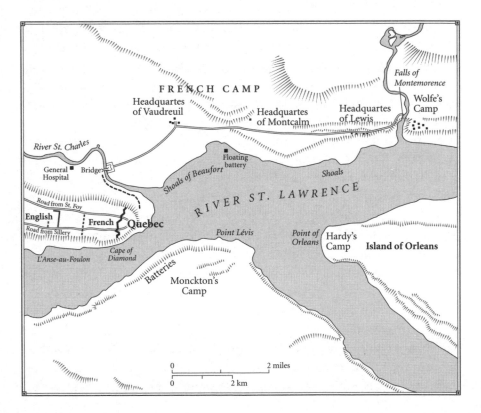

dragged cannons to high ground that overlooked the city. From there, they began to bombard Quebec and reduced a great deal of the city to smoking ruins. The French sent a message to Wolfe: 'We do not doubt that you will demolish the town, but we are determined that your army shall never get a footing inside its walls.' Wolfe replied: 'I will be master of Quebec if I stay here until the end of November.' By then, he commanded the river and sent ships above Quebec to intercept any supplies coming down.

Despite that success, the British forces were at an impasse. The enemy was too entrenched to force a landing anywhere near Quebec. When his men scouted the land around the city, they were ambushed and scalped by natives working for the French.

Wolfe turned his attention to the Montmorency River, east of the city. He went himself to see if he could land and then move west to attack Quebec from the rear. Seeing his ships, the French sent a party of natives to harass the landing party, but they were repulsed. Hand-to-hand fighting followed in the woods and more than forty of Wolfe's men were killed or wounded. He found a fording place, but it was well defended and he withdrew in frustration.

Recklessly, Wolfe then tried a landing on the north bank of the St Lawrence. Two ships ran in as fast as possible and French cannon fire hammered them. Wolfe was struck by flying splinters three times. His men assaulted the bank in small boats, then waded through bloody water under constant fire. The slaughter was terrible, with more than two hundred killed and the same number wounded. It would have been worse if a sudden rain squall hadn't ruined French supplies of gunpowder. Wolfe's ships were also badly damaged, but he was able to take the survivors off. Wounded men were scalped on the beach as those in the boats got away.

It was a shocking defeat for Wolfe and he was furious with himself. He shouldered the lion's share of the blame, though at the same time, he rebuked his men for running wild on the shore instead of holding the position.

By the end of August, Wolfe heard that General Amherst had taken

Fort Niagara, far to the west. The news spurred him on. Wolfe knew his entire campaign would be wasted if he failed to take the city before winter. His cannons had reduced much of Quebec to rubble, but he had yet to break the main French defences.

As September advanced, Wolfe gambled it all on a massive assault. He sent his regiments to Point Lévis, where they could march west, cross the Etchemin River and join British ships and boats upstream. The plan was to stage a boat landing to the west of Quebec, then climb the cliffs to the Plains of Abraham behind the city. His orders were read to his men, so that there could be no possible misunderstanding.

In darkness, his boats crossed the river to a bay known today as Wolfe's Cove, but at that time was called L'Anse-au-Foulon. It was a tense trip and they were challenged more than once by sleepy French sentries. Some of the Scots spoke fluent French and they answered in that language. In no small feat of boat navigation, the entire force reached the rendezvous intact. Ahead lay steep cliffs and, in darkness, Wolfe's men began to haul heavy guns up on ropes. They climbed through the night, scrambling up as best they could with the weight of their musket and kit. At the same time, Admiral Saunders fired guns and manoeuvred in the St Lawrence River all night to keep Montcalm's attention away from the west and Wolfe.

By dawn on 13 September 1759, Wolfe's first battalions were at the top of the cliffs and able to form in line. The Plains of Abraham stretched before them, but there were woods on one side and native forces skirmished and sniped at his men as he deployed. Wolfe took a position on the right flank, ready to lead the attack on Quebec. He had around 4,500 men in all and faced at least that many on the French side, though only 2,600 of them were regular soldiers. Wolfe was visibly confident and his men's morale was high.

Montcalm had no choice but to form his battalions and meet Wolfe's army on the plain. He was aware that Wolfe had brought only two field guns up the cliffs and would raise many more if given time. Montcalm gave the order to advance in the late morning and the British waited, their Brown Bess muskets 'double-shotted' with two lead balls for a devastating first volley.

The French fired first and too early, then reloaded as they came forward. Wolfe was hit in the wrist and bound the wound with his handkerchief. The British redcoats did not answer at first, as Wolfe waited to make the first volley as potent as possible. When he finally gave the order, the French lines were almost on them. The volley tore through Montcalm's battalions and was followed immediately by a bayonet charge. That volley has since been described as the most perfect ever fired on a battlefield. Montcalm's army was shattered in one sudden crack of sound. They broke instantly, running from the British soldiers with kneeling marksmen covering the retreat.

Wolfe was in the front ranks and was wounded again in the groin as he advanced, though he was able to keep moving. He had survived two wounds, but a third shot hit him in the chest.

He staggered and his men laid him gently down on the grass. One of them asked if Wolfe wanted a surgeon and he replied: 'It is needless. It is all over with me.' Another man cried out: 'They run, see how they run!' Dazed and in pain, Wolfe asked who they meant. His men replied, 'The enemy.' Wolfe gave a final order to cut off the retreat, then lay on his side. His last words were: 'Now, God be praised, I will die in peace.' He was 32 years old.

Montcalm had also been shot in the stomach and the French forces were in disarray. He died the following day and was buried in a Quebec chapel. The French surrendered on 18 September, signing a capitulation in the British camp. That evening, British artillery troops hoisted the Union flag in the city for the first time.

In England, King George II told Pitt: 'Quebec is certainly a great acquisition, but 'tis gold bought too dear. Wolfe is an irreparable loss, such a head, such a heart, such a temper and such an arm are not easily to be found again.'

Today, Quebec is host to statues of both Wolfe and Montcalm. It is a city that owes much to its French past. Yet because of that single battle, Canada would become a jewel of the Empire and later, the Commonwealth. Decades of war with France would follow. Napoleon would threaten even the shores of England with invasion as the nineteenth century dawned. Yet Wellington and Nelson would be there to resist him, just as Wolfe once stood against the French in Canada.

Recommended
With Wolfe to Quebec by Oliver Warner
With Wolfe in Canada by G.A. Henty. Henty's books begin with a masterly summation of the events, then the book itself is written as historical fiction.

Sir Walter Ralegh
and Sir Francis Drake

The Elizabethan age was a time of extraordinary optimism in England. Queen Elizabeth I's reign lasted from 1558 to 1603 and during that period, the Renaissance flowered in literature, music, art and exploration. Shakespeare and Marlowe were at the peak of their powers, the wealth of the world was brought home and the foundations laid for the British Empire. In many ways, it is still considered a golden era.

It was also a time of relative peace when compared with the upheavals of the seventeenth century. The monarch held absolute power and Parliament did not challenge the divine right to rule. As a queen, Elizabeth was a skilful mistress and dominated the court for decades, surrounding herself with the best men of the age. The great leaps in science that would mark the next three centuries had their beginnings in her reign, but the foundation stone of power and wealth lay with men like Sir Walter Ralegh and Sir Francis Drake, as they discovered new lands and brought riches to England. At the same time, the natural resources of timber, coal, wood, wool and iron were exploited on a massive scale in the beginnings of what would eventually become the Industrial Revolution.

The great enemy of the period was Spain. By the time Elizabeth reached the throne, the Spanish had established settlements in Central and South America, a cultural influence that continues today in countries as far apart as Mexico, Peru, Argentina and Nicaragua. Great wealth flowed back to Spain from those colonies and their ships were dominant in that part of the world. Inevitably, the fleets of England and Spain would come into conflict, for the highest stakes.

Walter Ralegh was born in Devon in 1554. There are few surviving details of his early life before he attended Oriel College, Oxford, at around the age of 16. From the first, he was possessed of restless energy and a desire for adventure. He spent only a year at Oxford before joining a unit of mounted volunteers in France, where he fought at the Battle of Moncontour in 1569. Returning home, he trained as a lawyer for a time, but took no special interest in his studies. He was tall and handsome, with a sharp wit and a furious temper. Around that time, he spent six days in Fleet prison for a public brawl, and on another occasion in a tavern grew so angry with a man that he sealed up his mouth with wax to stop him talking.

His half-brother, Humphrey Gilbert, was a renowned sailor. When he was granted a patent to mount an expedition to the 'New World', or the Americas, Ralegh decided to join him. They sailed in November 1578 from Plymouth, with Ralegh in command of one of seven ships.

This first expedition ended in complete failure and would introduce Ralegh to the dangers of Spain. As well as violent squalls, Gilbert's small fleet met a squadron of Spanish warships off the west coast of Africa. They fought and lost, so that the battered and damaged ships returned to Plymouth. There was no official war with Spain at the time, but both countries were capable of that sort of action if the odds were right. With sufficient force and enough wealth at stake, there was simply no law at sea. At that time, Spain's Catholic Inquisition was at its most powerful and captured English sailors were sometimes handed over to the torturers as enemies of the Pope.

After that chastening experience, Ralegh used Gilbert's connections to secure a commission to put down an uprising in Ireland. Irish Catholicism made them the natural allies of Spain and France, right on the doorstep of Elizabeth's court. It was Ralegh's first opportunity to show his abilities. English forces marched across Ireland, attacking castles and strongholds and massacring garrisons much as Cromwell's men would do in the following century. Ralegh became known as a captain of particular dash and ruthlessness. He took the castle of Lord Roche by talking his way in to discuss peace, then gradually brought more men in as he ate dinner with the host. When he had enough men, he threatened to destroy the castle if Roche refused to surrender. Some sources say Ralegh held a knife to his throat as he made his offer.

A force of a hundred mainly Italian mercenaries authorised by Spain landed to support the rebellion, but they were pinned down on land in the Bay of Smerwick. Ralegh and another captain went in after their surrender and hanged or slaughtered everyone except for twenty officers held for ransom. It is perhaps worth pointing out that it was a perfectly normal action by the standards of the day. The threat of Spanish invasion was a constant danger and both sides were utterly ruthless in a struggle to the death. Ralegh was unmoved by horrors, though he wrote letters of complaint about the inept decisions of his military superiors. It was an early example of Ralegh's complete lack of subtlety in political matters. He never learned to guard his tongue.

Ralegh's unit was disbanded in 1581 and he returned to London with a growing reputation for both gallantry and courage. He prepared to meet Queen Elizabeth with great care, spending almost everything he owned on ostentatious clothing. She was extremely taken with the young soldier from Devon. She enjoyed his accent as much as his forceful manner, grand apparel and good looks. It was not long before he was regularly called to court and it was around that time that one of the most famous incidents of his life took place.

Elizabeth and Ralegh were walking in Greenwich when they came to a marshy patch of ground. Ralegh whipped off his jewelled cloak and placed it over the wet ground. That act of conspicuous gallantry was completely in character and cannot have failed to impress the queen. It is too cynical to suggest that he saw her simply as a way to gain power and wealth. Elizabeth was in her late forties at the time and there was genuine affection for her among the dashing young blades of the day. A female monarch was a rarity in England and her relationship with men at court was often one of adoration, almost reverence. There was also an element of flirtation that would not have gone down well with Henry VIII. Ralegh, for example, was a gifted poet. He scratched a line on a window for Elizabeth to see: 'Fain would I climb, yet fear I to fall.' She added another line with a diamond ring: 'If thy heart fail thee, climb not at all.'

Queen Elizabeth favoured Ralegh with a house in the Strand and the right to export woollen cloth, a hugely lucrative licence. He had arrived at the highest levels of society and quickly became very wealthy. Like the equally famous Francis Drake, he came from a minor Devon family, but with royal favour, he rose quickly.

Francis Drake had been born around 1540, to a very poor family. In later years, the motto on his coat of arms would be 'Sic parvis magna' – great things from small beginnings. His sailing career began at the age of 14 in a merchant ship carrying grain. On that small vessel, he began to learn the skills of navigation that would play such a part in his later life. When the owner of the ship died, he left it to Drake, which shows the respect he had earned in just a few years. Like Ralegh, he was a staunchly Protestant, restless young man, always with his eye out for ways to make his fortune.

In 1564, he sold the ship he had inherited to join Captain John Lovell on a trading expedition to Spain. It was his first experience of ocean navigation and the first time he would encounter the Spanish. In a Spanish port, Drake saw his cargo confiscated. He hated them with a passion after that.

In 1567, Drake joined his cousin, John Hawkins, in a fleet sponsored by Queen Elizabeth to capture Spanish treasure ships. Drake and Hawkins sailed to Africa, then the 'Spanish Main' – the coasts of Central and South America. Storms forced them to make landfall in Mexico, just as the annual Spanish treasure ship was about to set sail. Drake and Hawkins were vulnerable after the storm and needed repairs and supplies. They anchored by a small island, but that night, the Spanish struck them in force. English sailors on shore were slaughtered and Spanish ships sailed out to attack Hawkins's battered fleet. Only two of the ten ships escaped – the pair commanded by Hawkins and Drake. They limped home to Plymouth and from then on, it was a very personal war for both men.

In 1572–3, Drake raided Spanish settlements on the coast of Panama, seeking the gold and silver that came from the slave mines of Peru. In February 1573, Drake heard of a mountain where it was possible to see the Pacific on one side and the Atlantic on the other. When he made the climb, he was overcome with excitement and made a vow to navigate and explore the new world that had opened up to him. At the same time, he ambushed a Spanish mule train heavy with silver and captured two Spanish ships before returning to Plymouth a very wealthy man. However, Queen Elizabeth could not publicly acknowledge his success while she negotiated with the Spanish king.

By 1577, the talk in London was of finding the fabled North-West Passage that would allow ships to reach the Pacific without having to go around South America, a lengthy and extremely dangerous journey. Hawkins was one of those who organised an expedition to seek out new territories and Drake was given command. He met the queen in secret to discuss the plans and understood that Elizabeth wanted revenge on the Spanish king. Drake was certainly the man for that. He sailed with five ships in December of that year and crossed the Atlantic to land on the Brazilian coast. By August, Drake reached the Straits of Magellan, a notoriously difficult passage through the tip of South America. To mark the event, he renamed his ship the *Golden Hind*. It took sixteen days to navigate through the straits. Drake and his crew were the first Englishmen ever to make the trip and reach the Pacific by that route. Storms battered them in the Pacific, driving the ships south and east so that Drake realised he had not crossed a continent, only the southernmost tip of it in modern-day Chile.

With a better idea of the geography, Drake raided Chile and Peru for silver, fresh fruit and water. At Lima, Peru, he discovered twelve merchant ships and took their cargoes before sailing on a rumour of a treasure ship, the *Cacafuego*, which was heading for Panama. Drake used all his sailing skill to catch the *Cacafuego* and captured her easily, breaking her mast with his third shot. It took *days* to transfer the vast cargo of pearls, jewels, silver and gold. Drake's ships were stuffed with treasure, so he set sail for home. He suspected the Magellan Straits would be blockaded by the Spanish, and he ran north, looking for the legendary passage through to the Atlantic.

He landed for a time on the coast of what is now California. Drake named the area 'New Albion' and while he was there native Americans crowned him as a king. From there, he sailed west across the largest ocean on earth, looking for a path through to circumnavigate back to England. He reached the Spice Islands (the Moluccas), off Indonesia, then ran aground on a hidden reef and almost lost the *Golden Hind*. The damage was not too great, however, and he made landfall at Java, a thousand miles north-west of Australia. From there, he crossed the Indian ocean, rounded South Africa's Cape of Good Hope and eventually returned to Plymouth on 27 September 1580, three years after he had set out. In doing so, Drake was the first man to return alive from a circumnavigation of the world. Magellan had managed it earlier, but died before reaching home. When he came home, Drake asked if the queen still lived.

In that voyage, Drake had demonstrated to the world the new English power on the seas. He was summoned to meet the queen and, like Ralegh, had the sense to take gifts of jewels. She ordered him to bring the *Golden Hind* from Plymouth to London and she knighted him on the ship's quarterdeck in 1581. Both Ralegh and Drake were high in royal favour and she allowed Drake to remove £10,000 from the treasure before the official tally was taken. The queen used the riches Drake brought back to found what would one day be known as 'The British East India Company'.

At home, Sir Walter Ralegh had become an MP for Devon. A favourite at court, the queen also made him Captain of the Yeoman of the

Guard, the men responsible for her personal safety. She adored the dashing young courtier and made him a gift of vast estates in Ireland. In his London house, he invited poets and friends such as Christopher Marlowe and Edmund Spenser. At the same time, he prevailed on Elizabeth to grant him a patent to explore the New World and claim territories for her. Drake's success was the talk of the country and as a fellow Devonian, Ralegh was hungry for similar adventures. It was not enough for him to wear jewelled clothes and have the queen hang on his words. He was too vital and energetic for that sort of life.

Ralegh was no professional sailor, like Drake or Hawkins. In a sense, he was a talented amateur when he sailed with Sir Humphrey Gilbert to America in 1583, in command of five ships. That voyage was a disaster, as four ships were lost and only one managed to make it back to Plymouth. Gilbert's own ship went down in a storm. Ralegh had failed, but he showed his mettle in organising another expedition the following year. In 1584, he reached America and named an area 'Virginia' after England's virgin queen. It was an inspired name that survives today. Ralegh was knighted on his return, four years after Drake received the same honour.

Ralegh sent colonists out in 1585, but they ran into trouble and had to be rescued by Drake, who was cheerfully raiding Spanish settlements in that part of the world. Drake lent them a ship to get home and only fifteen men stayed behind to keep the colony alive. All fifteen were murdered by natives by the time Ralegh sent new colonists to relieve them. In that group, the first Christian baby was born in America, a little girl appropriately named Virginia.

The constant war with Spain was growing in intensity and Ralegh had enormous trouble getting ships to support his Virginian colony. He sent two ships only to see them turned back by French pirates. He had practically bankrupted himself in the venture and was forced to turn over the queen's patent to a company of London merchants with funds to continue the work. Even then, it was a failure. The native Americans killed everyone there. Later, he wrote: 'I shall live yet to see it an English nation.' He did live to see a permanent English colony established in 1607. His name is remembered there, and in 1792 the seat of government in North Carolina was named 'Raleigh'. As with Shakespeare, his name has always been spelled in different ways.

Though the exact truth cannot be known, Ralegh is often credited with having brought potatoes to England. Tobacco was already known, but with a long silver pipe and gold tobacco box, Ralegh also made smoking fashionable in London. It became a widespread luxury and later a major source of national revenue. He also made fortunes by growing potatoes from the New World in his Irish estates. However, though he made the wealth he wanted, Queen Elizabeth never saw him as a military commander. When the great fleet known as the Spanish Armada sailed to invade England in 1588, Ralegh was not chosen to command.

The Armada was first sighted off Cornwall on 19 July. It would have come earlier, but Drake had been sent by the queen to 'distress' Spanish shipping and disrupt the invasion plan. He had succeeded brilliantly, destroying or disabling more than thirty ships in Cadiz. He later referred to this as merely 'singeing the King of Spain's beard', but it delayed the Armada for a full year. Philip of Spain put a reward on his head of 20,000 ducats, the equivalent of millions of pounds today.

Famously, Drake was playing bowls with Lord Howard on Plymouth Hoe when the news of the Armada reached them. Tradition has it that Drake replied to the messenger with the words: 'There is time to finish the game and beat the Spaniards too.' He was correct, in that the tide was against him at that moment and he could not sail for another three hours. By noon the following day, Lord Howard and Drake were out at sea. Howard had the fleet's flagship, the *Ark Royal*, while Drake, as his vice admiral, commanded the *Revenge*. At the start, they had eighty ships against the Spanish force of 127. The Spanish had come in a great crescent down the English Channel and brought more than 18,000 men to invade. The stakes were at their highest. Not until Napoleon and Hitler threatened invasions in later centuries would England be in such direct peril again.

Drake and Howard engaged the Armada, alarming the Spanish officers with the agility of their ships. They skirmished with the

Spanish for two whole days, preventing a landing. By chance, one enemy ship blew up and caused chaos in the crescent as they dropped sail to pick up casualties. Even so, they reached the Isle of Wight by 24 July. The English captains knew those waters better than any others on earth and manoeuvred to drive the Spanish onto rocks. The enemy ships barely avoided the trap and tacked towards Calais. By then, every English ship had joined Drake and Howard, so that they had a fleet of 197 under sail. Howard sent fireships amongst the Spanish, causing some to scatter east into the North Sea without reaching a safe haven in France. At the same time, Drake engaged the Spanish flagship, firing into her.

The Spanish managed to re-form north of Calais, but they were under constant fire and forced to retreat still further. It was then that a squall hit and blew the fleets away from each other. By then, the Spanish had lost their taste for the fight and intended to head north and round Scotland to make their way home. Drake's captains harried and fought them all the way up the east coast, still fearing a landing in force. He and Howard pursued the Spanish right up to the Firth of Forth before they turned back.

The surviving Spanish fleet limped past Scotland. Many were lost on rocks around the Irish coast in waters they did not know well. Some of them were washed ashore on Ireland and killed on the beaches. Of the 130 ships that had set out, sixty-three were lost in the attack. Protestant England had been saved from Catholic Spain.

Flushed with success, Drake organised a raiding fleet the following year. It was not successful, however, and he lost his investors a small fortune, the queen among them. From hero and saviour, his star fell quickly and he retired to Devon to tend his estates. His last voyage took place in 1595 to the Spanish Main. He raided Panama and other settlements, though he had been so successful in the past that there were few riches to be plundered. There, he became ill with dysentery and donned his armour for the last time, determined to die as a soldier. He died on 28 January 1596, at the age of only 55. He was buried at sea. Famously, the drum from his ship was returned to England and remains at Buckland Abbey, his home. It is said that whenever

England is in peril, the drum sounds across the land, summoning men in her defence. The Spanish poet and contemporary of Drake, Juan de Miramontes, wrote:

> *This realm inconstant, changeable in faith*
> *Has raised a captain whose glittering memory*
> *Will last undimmed through future centuries.*

Ralegh's fall from grace was more tragic. It began in 1587 with the arrival at court of Lord Essex, a youth of such unusually handsome figure that he captured the queen's attention at Ralegh's expense. Ralegh and Essex quarrelled bitterly over the queen's favour, each jealous of the other. After the Armada had been sent home, Ralegh and Essex arranged a duel, but the queen forbade it, rather than lose one or both of her favourite men. Essex used his influence with Queen Elizabeth to have Ralegh sent to his estates in Ireland for a time.

In Ireland, Ralegh wrote poetry with Edmund Spenser, at the same time as that man created his masterwork, *The Faerie Queene*. Both were around 37 and at the peak of their powers. Sadly, only a small part of Ralegh's own poetry and prose survives.

Ralegh found favour with Elizabeth for a time in the reflected glory of *The Faerie Queene*'s publication. It also helped that Essex had married without telling Queen Elizabeth, who preferred her handsome admirers to remain single and devoted to her.

However, in 1591, Ralegh made a serious error. He fell in love with one of the queen's maids of honour and married in secret, just as Essex had done. Elizabeth regarded it as a betrayal. She had both husband and wife sent to the Tower of London. By happy chance around this time, an expedition he had organised captured the *Madre de Dios*, the greatest Spanish treasure ship ever taken. Queen Elizabeth took the lion's share of the riches and Ralegh and his wife were released. A son, also named Walter, was born shortly afterwards, in 1594.

Free, Ralegh returned to his life as a privateer for the Crown, mounting an expedition to seek out 'El Dorado', a legendary place of fabulous wealth somewhere in South America. Ralegh spoke both Spanish and French fluently and spent many months reading everything he could find on the subject. He was granted the right to search for it by Queen Elizabeth and sailed in 1595. He and his crew explored Guiana on the north-east coast of the continent, but found no fabled cities. He considered Guiana to be a worthy possession for England even so, but the lack of gold meant his entreaties fell on deaf ears at court. The era of the great English pirates was ending and the queen herself was ageing and growing weary. Ralegh spent fortunes on other expeditions to Guiana, but the queen had other concerns and remained unmoved.

In 1596, a huge fleet of ships was gathered to attack Cadiz in Spain, then one of the richest cities in the world. Ralegh commanded a squadron and was badly wounded in the fighting, so that he had to be carried back to his ship, the *Warspite*. The victory came quickly and Cadiz was taken and sacked. Unusually for the times, the English crews were forbidden violence and the Spanish king later commended them for their conduct. Ralegh won great goodwill for his conspicuous bravery, and in 1597 he was allowed at last to return to court.

The next five years were relatively tranquil. Ralegh was back in the queen's favour as well as being wealthy and famous. He still had enemies at court and perhaps relied too heavily on the queen's shadow to protect him. Essex had fallen from her favour to the point of raging arguments and Elizabeth walloping him around the ears. She sent Essex to suppress a rebellion in Ireland, but he negotiated instead of crushing them as Elizabeth wanted. When Essex returned, he was arrested, though she later relented and cancelled his trial in 1600.

Essex became an enemy of the queen and conspired to remove her from the throne. Ralegh was one of those who fought against the plot, which involved a few hundred armed men riding through London. Essex had hoped to create a mass rebellion in the English, but they quite liked Elizabeth and merely looked at him in astonishment. Essex was beheaded in 1601, aged only 36.

When Elizabeth died in 1603, James I, King of Scotland, was the next in line for the throne. He was no friend to Sir Walter Ralegh and distrusted anyone who had risen so high under the queen who had executed his mother, Mary Queen of Scots. He also desired peace with Spain and Ralegh was the last of the raiding captains known and hated by the Spanish king. King Philip of Spain demanded that Ralegh be executed. To appease him, James convicted Ralegh of treason. Ironically, the charges involved passing information to the King of Spain in return for huge sums of money. That part is almost certainly true and a clear trap laid for Ralegh. He was locked up in the Tower of London for the second time in his life. Abandoned by friends and supporters, Ralegh would remain there for fifteen years. He was allowed to live in a suite of well-appointed rooms, but not to leave. Alone, he wrote poetry and books and experimented with chemistry.

Ralegh was allowed out in 1616 at the age of 62 on the promise to King James that he would bring back a shipful of gold from Guiana. When the Spanish ambassador heard, he wrote to the King of Spain to advise that all ships travel only in convoy. Such was their alarm at the prospect of Ralegh back on the high seas. Ralegh was aware that he was being used as a pawn, but he had no choice. He remained youthfully optimistic that he could win back his place, fame and fortune. Sadly, the odds were stacked against him, not least because King James gave all the secret plans to the Spanish ambassador.

The expedition was doomed before it began, though Ralegh reached Guiana and began looking for gold mines. As he searched, Spanish soldiers harassed his men and Ralegh's son was killed in the fighting.

No gold was found. Ralegh was distraught and wrote at the time: 'What shall become of me now I know not. I am unpardoned in England, and my poor estate consumed.'

He wanted to press on, but his men mutinied and deserted him, so that he returned in only one ship to Plymouth in 1618, ready to face his king. He was put under house arrest shortly after his return. His argument that Guiana was not Spanish territory held no weight with a monarch determined to be rid of him. Ralegh considered escaping to France, but a servant betrayed the plan and Ralegh was taken to the Tower for the third time in his life. He was already under sentence of death for his previous conviction of treason and James merely had to lift the temporary reprieve that had allowed Ralegh his last trip to Guiana.

The King of Spain took a keen interest once more and wrote to James to demand Ralegh's execution. All appeals at home failed and Ralegh prepared for death with great courage and calm.

On 29 October 1618, Ralegh walked out into the Palace Yard, Westminster, and addressed the gathered crowd. He talked of his innocence and his loyalty to the king, then added: 'So I take my leave of you all, making my peace with God. I have a long journey to make, and must bid the company farewell.' He was asked if he wanted a blindfold and he scorned it, saying: 'Think you I fear the shadow of the axe, when I fear not the axe itself?' He prayed for a time and then, when the executioner hesitated, Ralegh snapped: 'What dost thou fear? Strike, man, strike!' Moments later, he was dead.

His body was buried in St Margaret's Church, Westminster, though his head was embalmed and kept by his wife until her death, when it was finally buried. Ralegh was much loved by the people of England and his passing caused enormous resentment towards the Stuart dynasty. They had killed the last of the great captains, just to appease Spain. It has been said that Ralegh's execution began the unrest that ended with the execution of Charles I, which took place only a quarter of a mile from the site of Ralegh's final moments.

Ralegh and Drake were opposite sides of the same Elizabethan coin. Ralegh was the gentleman, the diplomat, the dreamer and elegant courtier. The way he was treated by his queen and then his king makes his story one of the great romantic tales of the era. Drake was the rumbustious seaman and privateer. Both were vital to the flowering of Elizabethan England.

Recommended
Sir Francis Drake by George Malcolm Thomson.
Sir Walter Raleigh by Philip Magnus.

Scott of the Antarctic

A fter Captain Cook's 1774 circumnavigation of Antarctica there had been only the one determined exploration south, despite the continent being first sighted in 1820 by Britons Bransfield and Smith.

James Clark Ross, discoverer of the North Magnetic Pole, sailed south to search for the South Magnetic Pole in his great expedition of 1839–43. He forced his two ships, HMS *Terror* and HMS *Erebus*, through the pack ice south of New Zealand to discover and chart the Ross Sea, the active volcano Mount Erebus, determine the Magnetic Pole was inland, and land on the islands to claim the territory for Britain.

In 1898, the Royal Geographical Society and the Royal Society announced a new scientific expedition to explore Antarctica inland from the Ross Sea. Commander Robert Falcon Scott was appointed leader. Thirty-two-year-old Scott was a modern and innovative officer, carving a promising career for himself in the Royal Navy. He specialised in the new torpedoes, marine electronics and mines. The Admiralty commented that Scott would be 'relinquishing a brilliant Navy career' in commanding the Antarctic expedition, but the First Sea Lord recommended him and his commanding officer wrote: 'He is just the fellow for it, strong, steady, genial, scientific, a good head on his shoulders, and a very good naval officer.'

Officers and seamen from Scott's Royal Navy ship volunteered to join him in the new 172-foot *Discovery*, while the balance of the expedition consisted of merchant navy officers, seamen and many scientists. Scott ran the expedition along modified navy lines, and despite recent suggestions, it was completely successful.

Other Antarctic expeditions of the era – Amundsen (Norwegian), Shackleton (British), Borchgrevink (Norwegian/British), de Gerlache

(Belgian), Mawson (British/Australian), Drygalski (German), Nordenskjold (Swedish) – suffered insurrection, mutiny, shipwreck and even insanity. Antarctica is perhaps the harshest environment in the world, yet Scott's two explorations, with more than 100 scientists, officers, seamen, soldiers, sledgers, dog-handlers, skiers and photographers, had not one major problem.

Australian scientist Louis Bernacchi wintered with both Borchgrevink (1899–1900) and Scott (1901–4). He recorded that Scott's broad formality and discipline 'helped to preserve an atmosphere of civilised tolerance such as has seldom been found in polar expeditions' and was 'of infinite benefit'.

As he made his preparations, Scott sailed first to Norway for advice from Fridtjof Nansen, scholar and great Arctic explorer of the time. Nansen had made the first crossing of Greenland by man-hauling his sledge and attempted to reach the North Pole using dogs. He recommended dogs but admitted that over rough ice they were not much use – in those conditions only man-hauling would get you through. Scott and Nansen became good friends and Scott followed his mentor's advice. His second in command, Lieutenant Armitage, had also made several Arctic sledging trips; he recommended Siberian ponies. Previously, Ross and McClintock of the navy had made a 1,175-mile Arctic journey averaging nearly seventeen miles-per-day man-hauling. As no one knew the conditions of inland Antarctica, Scott took dogs, ponies and motor-sledges and used all four methods of sledging.

Discovery left Britain in August 1901, bound for Antarctica. Before he sailed, Scott was made a Member of the Royal Victorian Order by the newly crowned King Edward VII and Cadbury supplied 3,500 lb of chocolate.

The expedition crossed the Antarctic Circle on 3 January and landed at Cape Adare to inspect Borchgrevink's hut – where Bernacchi had completed the only previous wintering-over in Antarctica. In *Discovery*, Scott explored the limits of the Ross Sea: eastward he discovered King Edward VII Land, while southward all was bound by the Great Ice Barrier (Ross Ice Shelf).

The Ice Barrier reaches five hundred feet high from sea level, in massive vertical cliffs of floating ice. It stopped Ross in 1843 and has stopped every ship since. In a natural inlet in the ice at the Bay of Whales, Scott sailed *Discovery* south for twelve more miles to reach the southernmost water in the world. Beneath twelve-foot cliffs, a landing was made for the first scientific journey inland by Armitage and Bernacchi.

Scott, followed by third mate Ernest Shackleton, made the first Antarctic flights there in February 1902, in a British army hydrogen balloon named *Eva*. They rose to 800 feet, tethered by cable in what Scott termed a 'very inadequate basket', to take the first aerial photographs of Antarctica. Seals basking on the ice were slaughtered in great numbers. Scott – like Cook before – ordered their killing for fresh meat, a vital preventative against scurvy. Nowadays, we know a lot about scurvy, but at the beginning of the twentieth century, little more was known than at the time of Cook, in 1770.

Scott established winter quarters at Hut Point on the southern promontory of Ross Island, next to the Ice Barrier. In a fortnight, the expedition erected the main thirty-ton hut, two magnetic huts, kennels for twenty-three huskies (from Nansen's supplier) and landed stores and scientific equipment. Sledge-training parties with dogs immediately set out into the white wilderness and skiing exercises began.

For the skiing, only minimal training was required. Norwegian skis then weighed 10 lb each and a single stick was used. It took longer to organise the dogs, yet within a month the first dog-sledge expedition set off; within two months they were on the Ice Barrier, laying stores depots for the following summer's explorations. Scott learned quickly.

After the winter months of total darkness, scientific parties set out in the bitter cold spring, sledge-training continued and more depots were laid. Navigation was difficult so close to the Magnetic Pole, so Scott improvised. He invented a shadow-scale for navigating by the sun, and devised a simple way to calculate the sun's daily declination changes. He also invented tapered sledge runners, designed a face hood to deflect the wind when sledging, and a trawling net for the marine scientists. Some of his inventions, including the 'face funnel', are used today.

For the Southern Exploration, Scott selected a party of three, which was considered safer than two for crevasse work and emergencies. As well as himself, he chose Dr Edward Wilson, a medical doctor, scientist and artist, and Ernest Shackleton. The three men got along well and respected each other – one Royal Navy, one civilian, one merchant navy.

On 2 November 1902, the Southern Exploration departed, the first expedition into southern Antarctica. Before them stretched the Ice Barrier towards the South Pole, 740 miles away. Between lay the last unexplored continent in the world. They set off with twenty-two huskies, their skis, sledges and a support team led by second mate Michael Barne. After a fortnight they were on their own.

They experienced the alarming 'Barrier Shudder', eerie echoing reverberations when suspended ice and snow suddenly collapse underfoot. They were traversing an immense, featureless, white wasteland of ice and could not help but wonder if it was like that all the way to the pole.

By the 25th, they'd reached 80 degrees south, 600 miles from the Pole, and individual features were visible in the south-west. Wilson sketched as often as possible. They left a supply depot for their return and continued with lighter sledges. They tried to leave the Ice Barrier several times but the dogs could not cross the ice-joint – the tumbled ice linking the floating ice to the land ice on their right. They drove the dogs further south.

On 19 December, Wilson killed the first dogs to feed the others, standard Arctic practice. By then the three men were suffering from sunburn, snow-blindness, chapped lips and numerous small ice cuts. On their right they were close to the Transantarctic Mountains, which crossed the island continent to a similar ice barrier (Ronne Ice Shelf) on the other side. Icy cliffs tinged black and red rose to 14,000 feet and Scott named them the Britannia Range. They crossed a white world of ice and snow no man had travelled before.

For Christmas dinner, Shackleton produced a small plum pudding he'd hidden. The 28th was their provisional turn-back date, but a wide valley led into the mountains to their right. Scott named it Shackleton Inlet and the headland Cape Wilson. All agreed to push on to the southern headland, which revealed a new 'coastline' further south. Wilson sketched the view to 83 degrees south. They attempted to gather rock samples from the mountains but again could not cross the ice-joint.

On New Year's Day, 1903, the three men and eleven surviving dogs turned back. They were at latitude 82 degrees, 11 minutes south, the furthest south man had ever reached. They'd established that any journey to the South Pole must find a crossing of the ice-joint, ascend one of the glaciers tumbling down the Transantarctic Mountains, and then cross whatever lay on the other side.

The three men were within their safety margins with four days of emergency rations remaining, but the dogs were finished. From the 5th, the men were forced to do most of the sledge-hauling while the fittest dogs killed the weakest. At their stores depot they killed the last two dogs. Neither Scott, Wilson nor Shackleton was satisfied with the performance of the huskies.

Shackleton's health broke down, his lungs haemorrhaging on the 15th. It was all he could manage to ski as he struggled with a heart and lung problem which would one day kill him. On 25 January, they saw the smoke plume from Erebus volcano from a hundred miles away. By 3 February they were back at the original base. All three were exhausted and Shackleton went to bed in *Discovery* before dinner. Scott suggested: 'I say, Shackles, how would you fancy some sardines on toast?' There was no reply; 'Shackles' was asleep. The three men had travelled 960 miles through Antarctica.

The resupply ship *Morning* arrived and, regretfully, Scott sent Shackleton home. After a month's rest and good food he was still seriously ill, and winter in Antarctica was no place to recover. Some historians claim that Scott and Shackleton fell out during the Southern Exploration. There is no evidence for this. Both men's reports, diaries and letters record the greatest respect for each other, while other people's diaries, including Dr Wilson's, record no disagreement. Shackleton welcomed Scott home personally in 1904 and Scott hosted a dinner in Shackleton's honour in 1909. The allegation of a falling-out was written twenty-two years later – after Scott, Shackleton and Wilson were all dead and could not sue.

After a second winter in Antarctica, five more scientific expeditions were made into the interior. Scott led a three-man expedition over the Transantarctic Mountains at the Ross Sea end and onto the Polar Plateau, 9,000 feet high. Scott, Petty Officer 'Taff' Evans and Stoker Bill Lashly reached furthest west on 30 November and saw that the Plateau continued west and south as far as the eye could see. As Scott surmised, it continued to the South Pole. During their return, Scott discovered Antarctica's amazing Dry Valleys. Networks of bare rock valleys free of ice and snow with lakes, melt streams and floors of fertile alluvial mud, they are the driest places on earth – no rain has fallen there for more than two million years, and nothing grows.

In those 1903 journeys, Scott man-hauled 827 miles in eighty-one days, an average of 10¼ miles per day, including mountain ascents and descents totalling 19,800 feet. The Scott Polar Research Institute of Cambridge reports: 'Few dog parties, working under plateau conditions, have ever exceeded Scott's best, when on foot.' There was no doubt man-hauling was successful and versatile: it could cross any ice terrain, whereas dogs could not.

Scott's 1901–4 *Discovery* expedition collected such a wealth of scientific data and specimens that the final analyses were not completed until the 1960s. Of the other expeditions to Antarctica at that time, the Swedes had their ship crushed by ice and had to be rescued, the

Germans were trapped by ice and went nowhere, while a second British expedition under William Bruce collected valuable scientific data but did not penetrate inland.

Discovery left Hut Point to reach Portsmouth on 10 September 1904. At 36 years old, Robert Scott returned from commanding the most extensive and successful scientific and geographic Antarctic expedition ever mounted. He found himself a national hero and world-famous.

During his leave, Scott became good friends with author James Barrie (Peter Pan) and artist Aubrey Beardsley. Through Beardsley, he met and wooed sculptress Kathleen Bruce. The Admiralty, meanwhile, promoted Scott to captain and he returned to sea in command of the flagship and battleship HMS *Albermarle*. He was the youngest battleship commander in the navy. In September 1908, in the Chapel Royal at Hampton Court Palace, he and Kathleen Bruce were married.

Many from Scott's expedition had caught the polar itch. Scott, Barne and Shackleton all had Antarctic plans – initially unknown to each other. Barne joined Scott and together they pursued the vital development of motorised sledges. In 1907, Shackleton publicly announced his plans and agreed with Scott that he would make his base on King Edward VII Land, not Ross Island. Shackleton had stamps issued by the New Zealand Post Office with *King Edward VII Land* printed on them, but when he arrived there in 1908, he could find nowhere to land.

He inspected the Bay of Whales but discovered that since their balloon flights, massive slabs of the Ice Barrier had separated or 'calved' away. He considered it too unstable and dangerous to camp there. Reluctantly, he sailed west to Ross Island and erected his hut twenty miles north of Hut Point.

Using four ponies and no dogs, Shackleton headed south across the Ice Barrier at the end of 1908. He discovered a route over the ice-joint, ascended the Transantarctic Mountains by the Beardmore Glacier – losing his last pony in a crevasse there – and reached the Polar Plateau. Shackleton, Frank Wild (ex-*Discovery*), Eric Marshall and Jameson Adams man-hauled with no skis to reach ninety-seven miles from the South Pole before turning back. At the same time, a three-man party under Australian Edgeworth David man-hauled to the South Magnetic Pole and raised the British flag.

Scott officially announced his second scientific and geographic Antarctic expedition on 13 September 1909 – the day before Kathleen gave birth to their only child, Peter. The Royal Geographical Society, Nansen, the Admiralty, Barne, Shackleton and others had known of Scott's plans since 1907. Trials of the first motorised sledge were announced in January 1908, while newspaper reports of Scott's marriage confirmed his plans to go south again. Further motorised-sledge trials took place in Norway in March 1909 – with Nansen watching. There was no secret about Scott's plans; his second expedition was known about for years.

In 1907, meanwhile, Norwegian explorer Roald Amundsen had announced his plans for an Arctic voyage, an attempt to be first to the North Pole. However, on 15 September 1909, American Robert Peary announced he had reached the North Pole, while another American, Frederick Cook, claimed to have reached it in 1908. In secret, four days after Scott's official announcement, Amundsen changed his destination to the South Pole. Only a brother knew. Even his patron Nansen – who lent him his ship *Fram* for the Arctic expedition – was not told. Historians who claim that Amundsen did not know of Scott's expedition are clearly wrong. It was Scott who knew nothing of Amundsen's plans.

French explorer Jean Charcot, also eyeing the Antarctic, stated: 'There can be no doubt that the best way to the Pole is by way of the Great Ice Barrier, but this we regard as belonging to the English explorers, and I do not propose to trespass on other people's grounds.' When Peary proposed an attempt on the South Pole – from the other side of Antarctica – he actually asked Scott if he had any objections. They met in London and agreed on joint scientific programmes. Amundsen himself wrote to Nansen: 'It is not my intention to dog the Englishmen's footsteps. They have naturally the first right.' Yet that is exactly what he did.

Amundsen lied to Nansen, lied to the Norwegian government who part-financed him, lied to his sponsors, and lied to the press. Scott tried several times to contact Amundsen to arrange Antarctic-to-Arctic scientific programmes, so Scott's Norwegian skiing expert Tryggve Gran – recommended by Nansen – arranged a meeting. Scott and Gran travelled to Amundsen's home, but Amundsen did not show up. His secrecy reveals his chicanery.

It was not until Scott and his seventy-strong Scientific Expedition reached Melbourne in the *Terra Nova* in October 1910 that they received the truth from Amundsen. He telegrammed: 'Beg leave to inform you *Fram* proceeding Antarctic. Amundsen.' He had taken nineteen men, including a party of six champion skiers, and 120 dogs, and said he would be based on the opposite side of Antarctica.

When the news reached Norway, its people became hostile to Amundsen and Nansen remained ominously silent. Amundsen's sponsors asked the government to request more funds from Parliament; the government refused.

Scott reached Ross Island again in January 1911 and established a new camp at Cape Evans, ten miles north of Hut Point. A larger hut was erected and the huskies, ponies, the first motorised sledges in the world, scientific equipment and stores were transported ashore. Scott's plans for the next three years were many but simple.

Science was the major purpose of the expedition – the largest ever to Antarctica – and that is how it would continue. Scientific parties set out as planned that summer, including two more wintering-over parties to the north and east. Using dogs and ponies, depots were laid southward across the Ice Barrier for an exploration to the South Pole the following summer, while Hut Point hut was cleared of ice and used as a forward depot. Scott laid the first Antarctic telephone line between the two huts.

In February, during a voyage to deploy the eastern wintering-over party, *Terra Nova* discovered Amundsen camped just along the Ross Sea at the Bay of Whales. To his credit, Scott never condemned Amundsen for his subterfuge, even in his private letters. In fact, his instructions to his men were to lend assistance if the Norwegians needed it. Scott knew how unstable the Ice Barrier at the Bay of Whales was. Amundsen was taking a gamble making a base there.

A Norwegian sailor wrote of their discovery: 'Well, if they are planning something bad (we were constantly asking ourselves in what light the Englishmen would view our competition) the [120] dogs will manage to make them turn back ... I had better be armed for all eventualities.' The Norwegians apparently considered Amundsen's actions so bad they thought they might be attacked. Tryggve Gran wrote: 'I think Amundsen's enterprise falls far short of what a gentleman would permit: there is nothing like it in polar history.'

Even at Melbourne, it had been too late for Scott to make a race of it: he had only thirty-three dogs and seventeen Siberian ponies. Scott knew and admitted this. He wrote several times that if Amundsen found a route up the mountains suitable for dogs he would undoubtedly reach the Pole before him. Shackleton, though, had reported the Beardmore – the *only* known route – as unsuitable for dogs.

The irony is that American Frederick Cook had not reached the North Pole and it's probable that Peary hadn't either. After eighty years of doubt, Arctic and Antarctic explorer Wally Herbert, first to cross the whole Arctic via the North Pole, was given access to all Peary's records by the American National Geographic Society. He concluded Peary was probably thirty to sixty nautical miles west of the Pole and knew it. The North Pole had been there for Amundsen to conquer after all.

During the winter of 1911, a dangerous and bitter journey in twenty-four-hour darkness was made from Cape Evans to collect penguin eggs. Dr Wilson was attempting to establish the mutation of birds from marine- to land-life by examining penguin embryos. Wilson, Bowers and Cherry-Garrard completed this harrowing five-week journey. They used themselves as guinea pigs, experimenting with three different rations to find the best for extreme polar conditions, as well as testing improvements in polar equipment and clothing. It's from Scott that modern polar clothing derives, not from Amundsen's reindeer skins.

With the return of the sun in a cold September, Scott authorised three short scientific journeys. These included a twenty-mile run for airing the dogs to Hut Point and back under Cecil Meares and Demetri Gerof, British and Russian husky experts. Meanwhile, at the Bay of

Whales, Amundsen set out on the 8th for the South Pole with six men and his dogs.

A week later Amundsen returned. Five of his dogs had frozen to death, with the other dogs' paws cut and bleeding from the ice. His men were frostbitten and demoralised and there were accusations of cowardice, and near-mutiny by second in command Johansen. Through not learning from Scott and Shackleton's earlier expeditions, Amundsen had not understood the differences between Antarctic and Arctic weather and snow. He banished Johansen and one other from the polar party and on his later return to Norway, publicly humiliated him. Johansen later committed suicide. Amundsen then set out for the Pole a second time on 19 October with four men.

Tryggve Gran, who knew both Scott and Amundsen, was withering in his comparison of the two leaders. 'Scott was a man. He would always listen to you. Amundsen would listen to nobody. He was only interested in himself. So Amundsen, as a human being, was not worth much, but Scott was worth a lot as a human being.' Without doubt, Scott had charisma.

From Cape Evans in October, the two motorised sledges set out hauling supplies for the polar depots. Those sledges were the world's first tracked vehicles – forerunners of the tank as well as the modern polar sledge. They covered fifty-one miles across Ross Island and the Ice Barrier before breaking down, all that was expected at that first stage of their development. Photographer Herbert Ponting wrote: 'To the memory of Scott must therefore be given the honour due to a pioneer of motor traction in the Polar regions, for he used it with a certain measure of success.'

Scott's 883-mile polar journey started on 1 November with ten ponies and sledges. He had to reach Shackleton's furthest south earlier than Shackleton, with more food and more fuel, in order to reach the Pole and return safely. With Shackleton's willing permission, Scott used his Beardmore Glacier route to the Polar Plateau, the only known route across the ice-joint. In comparison, Amundsen took two huge gambles in that he hoped to find another crossing further east as well as a glacier suitable for dogs.

Despite soft snow, the Siberian ponies averaged twelve miles a day across the Ice Barrier, the men skiing or walking alongside. The dog teams were the last to leave, for they were the fastest. Closer to the Beardmore, the ponies were killed one by one with a bullet to the head. Their meat was buried for use on the return journey, a precaution against scurvy and food for the dogs. At the foot of the Beardmore, an unseasonal four-day blizzard delayed the expedition.

Further east and unknown to Scott, Amundsen's good fortune was remarkable. He'd reached the mountains and found a passage across the ice-joint. In addition, the glacier before him was not split by crevasses, ice-falls and chasms like the Beardmore – it was suitable for dogs. Near the top, Amundsen killed twenty-two dogs to feed the others.

Scott – nothing if not flexible – used his dogs two weeks longer than originally planned, hauling sledges a further forty-five miles up the Beardmore until it was too dangerous to use them further. Many of the roped men fell into hidden crevasses, but if a dog team had gone down it would have taken its sledge, stores and, possibly, the driver with it. Meares, Demetri and their dog sledges returned to Cape Evans.

From then on sledges had to be man-hauled, yet both Scott's and Shackleton's experiences of the Polar Plateau showed that a good speed could be maintained. Three depots were left up the 136-mile glacier and the Polar Plateau was reached on 21 December. This was a scientific exploration, so the men were surveying, recording, mapping and writing as they travelled because, in the future, others would follow. Robert Scott has a lot in common with James Cook. Both were Royal Navy, both were great explorers, both were scientists, neither would be unnecessarily rushed, and both looked after their men.

From the Plateau, four more men returned, with Scott's instruction to store dog food at One Ton Depot on the Ice Barrier. Eight men then continued towards the Pole. On Christmas Day 1911, they hauled sledges for fifteen miles. Bowers observed: 'One gets down to bedrock with everybody, sledging under trying conditions. The character of a man comes out and you see things that were never expected. I think more highly than ever of our leader...' Their average increased to twenty-three miles a day across the Plateau and soon they were ahead of Shackleton's time, mostly on skis but walking when it was faster. They were using the polar rations tested in the mid-winter journey and found them sufficient, while two more depots were left on the Plateau, at 3 degrees and 1½ degrees latitude from the Pole. The two teams celebrated New Year in their tents, drinking tea with chocolate rations and talking until 1 a.m.

On 4 January 1912, Scott announced the final polar party as Edward Wilson (doctor and scientist), Henry 'Birdie' Bowers (Royal Indian Marine, navigator and meteorologist), Edgar 'Taff' Evans (immensely powerful as well as their sledge and ski repairer) and Lawrence 'Titus' Oates (Royal Iniskillens, also powerfully built). The three returning men were second in command Lieutenant 'Teddy' Evans and Stoker Bill Lashly, who were the most tired of them all, and Tom Crean. Scott judged Oates only slightly stronger than Crean, his most difficult choice of all.

Much has been written about why Scott took five men rather than four, but there's no evidence that he had originally decided upon four. Four was often the sledging format employed, but not always: three men sledged south in the *Discovery* expedition. There is a sketch made by Wilson at Cape Evans of a five-man team and it's possible that is what Scott always planned. A five-man team from the last depot to the Pole and back makes a lot of sense. The sledge weight remained essentially the same but for fuel and a sleeping bag, yet there would be another man hauling. In addition, five men is safest for crossing crevasses.

Scott's last order to Teddy Evans was for the dog teams to meet the five returning men between 83 and 82 degrees south, between Southern Barrier and Middle Barrier depots. Fifty to ninety miles from the Beardmore.

Southward the five sledged. They passed Shackleton's furthest south on 6 January. At 10,500 feet, they had to cross a sea of difficult fish-hook ice waves, or 'sastrugi', and resorted to walking. They were back on skis by the 10th when the temperature plummeted. By noon of the 16th they were approaching the South Pole, a featureless white plain with a long downhill slope. They saw mock suns with long horizontal halos. At around 4 p.m. Bowers saw something ahead, a black speck, perhaps a cairn, perhaps a reflection from the sastrugi.

As they approached, the object grew into a black mark, then larger until they could see it was a flag and an abandoned campsite. In the disturbed snow they saw sledge, ski and paw marks. 'The Norwegians have forestalled us and are first at the Pole,' wrote Scott. 'It is a terrible disappointment, and I am very sorry for my loyal companions.'

Scott continued, navigating his own path to the southernmost point on earth and checking his position with sun-sights. They camped, and on the 17th marched outwards on different bearings – 'the coldest march I ever remembered,' wrote Wilson. With the sextants of the time, it was impossible to establish the exact location of the Pole. Even the best of them were accurate only to about a quarter of a mile. Compasses were completely useless and spun wildly.

With the final set of sun-sights, Scott and his men established their position at latitude 89 degrees 59 minutes 14 seconds South, within three-quarters of a mile of the most southerly point on earth. They planted the Union flag.

Amundsen had been less painstaking with his sun-sights. Wilson noted: 'From Amundsen's direction of tracks he has probably hit a point about 3 miles off ... but in any case we are all agreed that he can claim prior right to the Pole itself.' In the Norwegian tent were the details and a letter for Scott from Amundsen. He had arrived on 14 December 1911, four weeks and five days before. Scott's scientific exploration had taken twenty days longer to reach the Pole than Amundsen's racing expedition, which had left earlier.

'Great God, this is an awful place,' Scott famously wrote. It still is.

On the return journey, there was disappointment but no depression, observed Dr Wilson. However, Scott noted on 23 January that Taff Evans was not well – 'There is no doubt that Evans is a good deal run down ' – but no one knew what was wrong with the powerful man. Back across the sastrugi, some skied while others walked, but none slowed the others and they still covered twenty miles on such days. They found all their depots and reached the top of Beardmore with no trouble. They had food, fuel and were on schedule to return to Cape Evans before the end of March, the end of summer.

On 8 February Evans was unable to haul, yet that was not yet alarming. There were good and bad days for all of them, and at the same place in 1909, Shackleton had had to stop hauling. Evans skied behind to resume hauling the following day.

The scientific programme continued. While descending the mountains, Wilson and Bowers uncovered rocks containing fossilised leaves, coal and other minerals, with important discoveries at Mount Darwin and Mount Buckley Cliffs. They collected 35 lb of specimens. These discoveries established that Antarctica was once a warm-climate continent, and the Permian period leaf fossils led to the realisation that Antarctica was once part of the ancient supercontinent 'Gondwana', with Australasia, India, Africa and South America. Was carrying the 35 lb samples critical? No. Such a small weight did not make any difference. What caused their later problems was something else entirely.

By 16 February, the team was approaching the base of the Beardmore when Evans collapsed in the sledge harness. Dr Wilson described Evans as 'sick and giddy and unable to walk even by the sledge on ski, so we camped.' Scott recorded: 'Evans has nearly broken down in brain we think.' Something catastrophic had happened to Evans but no one knew what it was or how to treat it.

They were ten miles from the next depot. After a short rest, four men hauled the sledge while Evans skied behind as he'd done before. He had troubles with his ski bindings and stopped at least twice to adjust them – a slow and bitterly painful business with sore and frostbitten hands. Gradually, he fell behind the others. At the next halt, he was out of sight, so the four immediately went back to him.

Scott wrote: 'I was the first to reach the poor man and shocked at his appearance, he was on his knees with clothing disarranged, hands uncovered and frostbitten, and a wild look in his eyes. Asked what was the matter, he replied with a slow speech that he didn't know … He showed every sign of complete collapse.' By the time they got him into the tent he was comatose. He died quietly at 12.30 a.m. without regaining consciousness.

There is only guesswork still about Taff Evans's condition. Of the likely causes for his death, Dr Wilson thought it might have been a brain haemorrhage caused by a fall into a crevasse two weeks before. In his 'Message to the Public', Scott put his death as 'concussion to the brain'. Yet Scott actually recorded the beginning of Evans's deterioration on 23 January, before the fall. Wilson makes no mention of scurvy and he would know, being familiar with the disease. Scurvy takes three to four months to present itself and it was only two and a half months since Evans and the others had eaten fresh meat. A recent theory is that Evans was suffering from 'cerebral oedema'. This condition of fluid on the brain was unknown in 1912, but it can cause sudden clinical deterioration of the body. It can be caused by infection, a blockage, a fall, even a minor stroke, and can be exacerbated by altitude.

Anti-Scott biographers point to Petty Officer Evans being spiritually alone, cut off by his 'social superiors', which hastened his decline. There's no evidence for this; it's mere invention. In fact, Taff Evans was an extrovert. He swapped yarns with Scott, Wilson and Bowers. He'd sailed with Scott in the navy, sledged with Scott many times and cheerfully shared three-man sleeping bags with Scott and others. There was no class divide. Scott was the son of a Plymouth brewer, while Wilson and Bowers chatted with anyone.

A few hours later Scott, Wilson, Bowers and Oates reached the depot. The next day they crossed the ice-joint onto the Barrier and reached the first pony camp, where they dug fresh meat out of the ice. Ten thousand feet lower than the Plateau, the temperature was appreciably warmer. The dog teams should have been approaching from the north, and there was a line of depots all the way to Cape Evans. They had fresh meat, extra rations and fuel, a new sledge left for them, and only 400 miles of the 1,600-mile journey remained. They set out and reached the Southern Barrier Depot on the 22nd, to find some cooking fuel had evaporated from the sealed cans. Away from the mountains, though, their speed increased and they averaged fifteen miles per day.

Without warning, the weather changed. On the 25th, the temperature dropped to –20 degrees, on the 27th it was –30, by 2 March it had reached a vicious –40, which is the same in both Centigrade and Fahrenheit. Yet it wasn't the cold itself which threatened disaster, it was the change the temperature made to the ice and snow underfoot. The surface turned crystalline. This created immense friction, anchoring the sledges to the ice, dragging at the runners like thick mud.

Although Wilson and Bowers still recorded their scientific data, Scott was by then the only one keeping a diary. On the 2nd they reached the Middle Barrier Depot. Again they found fuel had evaporated from the sealed cans. The wind was blowing unseasonably into their faces, and Oates's feet were frostbitten: 'Titus Oates disclosed his feet, the toes showing very bad indeed, evidently bitten by the late temperatures.' He continued hauling with the others.

On the 3rd they travelled ten miles, on the 4th nine, on the 5th eight. On the 6th they made only six and a half miles and Scott recorded we 'feel the cold terribly. The surface ... is coated with a thin layer of woolly crystals ... These are too firmly fixed to be removed by the wind and cause impossible friction on the runners. Amongst ourselves we are unendingly cheerful, but what each man feels in his heart I can only guess.'

Elsewhere on the 6th, *Fram* arrived in Australia and Amundsen telegrammed the world that he was first to the South Pole. Publicly Nansen congratulated Amundsen; in his diary he recorded his disappointment.

In Scott's team, Bowers maintained his meteorological log until 19 March, and from this and subsequent weather records it's now understood what happened. Scott planned the polar journey with meteorologist George Simpson, later Director of the Meteorological Office of the UK. Simpson's weather predictions were based upon all known information. Yet 1912 was an abnormal year – a rogue year. In late February and March was the worst weather ever recorded on the Ice Barrier. Scott experienced temperatures 10 to 20 degrees colder than average. The conditions were ferocious, the ice under the sledges like glue. From going very well, suddenly they were in desperate trouble. Where were the dog teams?

Dog food had not been taken to One Ton Depot as ordered. There is no apparent explanation for this. Teddy Evans had passed Scott's second order to Meares and Demetri for the dog teams to meet Scott ninety to fifty miles from Beardmore. By then, though, Evans was near death. He hadn't eaten his meat rations and had contracted scurvy on top of severe exhaustion. Dr Atkinson assumed command and saved Evans's life, but Scott's orders were not carried out. Meares's father had died in Britain and he left Cape Evans in late February by the resupply voyage of *Terra Nova*, in which Evans also left.

Only then did Atkinson order Demetri, Cherry-Garrard and one dog sledge to One Ton Depot. They reached it, a quarter of the way across the Barrier, on 3 March. More food for the polar party was deposited but still no dog food, and they camped. 103 miles south, the exhausted polar party skied towards them.

On the 7th, Scott wrote: 'We are 16 miles from our depot [Lower Barrier]. We hope against hope that the dogs have been to Mt. Hooper

[Lower Barrier]; then we might pull through.' They reached the depot on the 9th. There is no diary entry that day.

On the 10th he wrote: 'Yesterday we marched up to the depot ... Cold comfort. Shortage on our allowance all round. I don't know that anyone is to blame. The dogs which would have been our salvation have evidently failed. Meares had a bad trip home I suppose.' As well as fuel evaporation, discovered later to be from faulty can manufacture, there was less food than ordered. Scott reported: 'Oates' foot worse. He has rare pluck and must know that he can never get through. He asked Wilson if he had a chance this morning, and of course Bill had to say he didn't know. In point of fact he has none. The weather conditions are awful...'

They left Hooper on the 10th, but a blizzard struck after only a few hundred yards and they were forced to camp again. On the 11th they sledged six miles. All were frostbitten by the extreme temperatures and Oates was near the end, unable by then to use his fingers. Although still hauling, he was slowing the others' progress through the time he took to prepare himself each day.

At One Ton Depot in the same freak weather, Cherry-Garrard was in anguish over what to do. Atkinson had said that if Scott had not arrived at One Ton Depot before him, he was to judge what action to take. On the 10th, Cherry-Garrard and Demetri returned to Hut Point and telephoned Atkinson at Cape Evans.

Scott made no entry for the 12th, but it was probably then that he distributed the opium tablets to Bowers, Oates and himself, leaving Wilson the morphine. Each man was thus able to make his own decision about his life. On the 13th they were blizzard-bound. On the 14th they pushed on. It took all morning to prepare Oates, the three cumbersomely dressing him. At noon, in −42 degrees, they sledged northwards a few more miles before the weather deteriorated and they were forced to camp again.

On the morning of the 16th, blizzard-bound in their tent, Oates awoke and dragged himself out of his sleeping bag. He said: 'I am just going outside and may be some time.' Scott wrote: 'He went out into the blizzard and we have not seen him since ... We knew that poor

Oates was walking to his death, but though we tried to dissuade him, we knew it was the act of a brave man and an English gentleman.'

Some biographers have belittled Oates's gesture as suicide. Dr Wilson, a devout Christian and in the tent, wrote to Mrs Oates: 'This is a sad ending to our undertaking. Your son died a very noble death, God knows. I have never seen or heard of such courage as he showed from the first to last with his feet both badly frostbitten – never a word of complaint or of the pain. He was a great example.' Oates knew his frostbite was destroying his companions' chances of survival, that through his slowness they might never reach the next depot. He also knew they would not leave him. Twice he asked and twice they refused. Suicide? The Bible states it more clearly: 'Greater love hath no man than this, that a man lay down his life for his friends.'

The blizzard eased, the three broke camp and sledged north, still carrying Oates's sleeping bag – in case. On the 17th they were blizzard-bound. On the 18th they reached fifteen and a half miles from One Ton Depot, just three days away at their improved speed since Oates's leaving. They were eleven miles from One Ton on the 19th when another blizzard hit. By then, all of them had severe frostbite, Scott the worst by his own admission. On the 21st Wilson and Bowers planned to ski to One Ton and return with fuel and food but the blizzard made it impossible. They lay inside the frozen tent, battered by the moaning wind.

Scott recorded: '22 and 23. Blizzard bad as ever – Wilson and Bowers unable to start – tomorrow last chance – no fuel and only one or two of food left – must be near the end. Have decided it shall be natural – we shall march for the depot with or without our effects and die in our tracks.'

Atkinson and Patrick Keohane reached the Barrier from Cape Evans on the 27th, searching for their companions. They lasted thirty-five miles in the desperate conditions before turning back.

Scott's last entry was dated 29 March. 'Since the 21st we have had a continuous gale from W.S.W. and S.W. Every day we have been ready to start for our depot 11 miles away, but outside the door of the tent it remains a scene of whirling drift. I do not think we can hope for any better things now. We shall stick it out to the end, but we are getting weaker, of course, and the end cannot be far. It seems a pity, but I do not think I can write more. R. Scott.'

On 12 November, a search party led by Atkinson including Gran, Cherry-Garrard, Demetri and his dogs reached them. Canadian Charles Wright first saw the tip of the tent poking above a snowdrift. They dug it out and looked inside.

It's probable that 43-year-old Scott died last, for the sleeping bags of Wilson and Bowers were tied from the outside while Scott's was not. Scott's right arm was resting across Wilson, his great friend. Dr Atkinson certified death from natural causes and recovered the opium and morphine. In their last letters, the three men's thoughts were not of themselves but of their families. Scott's final sentence reads 'For God's sake look after our people.'

There are always 'if onlys', but what killed Scott, Wilson, Bowers and Oates were not 'if onlys'. It was not because they failed to use dogs and ponies; they used them wherever they could. They also skied wherever they could. It was not because they failed to use accepted Antarctic practices; they established the accepted practices. It was not through missing depots, for they found them all. What killed them was the extraordinary weather.

Scott realised this and blamed no one except himself, for a leader is responsible for everything, even for events beyond his control – as Amundsen and Shackleton are responsible for the deaths in their various expeditions. Scott wrote: 'Subsidiary reasons for our failure to return are due to the sickness of different members of the party, but the real thing that has stopped us is the awful weather and unexpected cold towards the end of the journey. The traverse of the Barrier has been quite three times as severe as any experience we had on the summit. There is no accounting for it, but the result has thrown out my calculations.'

There is an accounting for it now. From subsequent records and the calculations of meteorologists George Simpson of Britain and Susan Solomon of the United States, it is established that 1912 was a freak weather year.

A cairn of snow was built over the tent and a cross of Tryggve Gran's skis erected on top. He wore Scott's skis back to Cape Evans to ensure they travelled all the way. Above Hut Point Scott's men erected a nine-foot-high wooden cross, the Ice Barrier behind. It's there today. On it is carved 'In memoriam', the five names, and the line 'To strive, to seek, to find, and not to yield.'

It is the last line from Tennyson's poem 'Ulysses'. They are apt because they are true: the five explorers strove, sought, found and would not yield, even to circumstances beyond their control.

Evans sledged and skied until he collapsed, struggled forward on his knees until he was unconscious and died never knowing where his strength had gone. Oates sledged and skied until he saw his frostbite would slow and kill his comrades, so left to slow them no longer. Scott, Wilson and Bowers pushed on until constant blizzards made further travel impossible, and died together naturally.

They did not yield.

Recommended
The Voyage of the Discovery *Vols I & II* by Robert Falcon Scott.
The Worst Journey in the World by Apsley Cherry-Garrard.
Diary of the 'Terra Nova' Expedition 1910–12 by Dr Edward Wilson.
Scott's Last Expedition (personal journals) by Robert Falcon Scott.
The Coldest March by Dr Susan Solomon.
Captain Scott by Sir Ranulph Fiennes.
Film: *Scott of the Antarctic*, Ealing Studios, 1948.
The Scott Polar Research Institute, Cambridge.
The Royal Geographical Society, London.
Antarctic Museum, Christchurch, New Zealand.

Men of Bristol and the
Discovery of North America

In fourteen hundred and ninety-two,
Columbus sailed the ocean blue.

Christopher Columbus did discover Central and South America but he didn't discover North America, and he wasn't the first to cross the Atlantic Ocean – the 'green sea of darkness'. Some of the earlier discoverers of America were British: certain men of Bristol.

In the 1400s, the Catholic Church taught that the earth was flat and this was the general belief in Europe. If you sailed east of Asia or west of Europe you'd fall off the edge of the world. A few courageous philosophers, scientists and navigators disagreed. Englishman Sir John Mandeville explained in his important 'Travels' of about 1357 how the earth must be round and therefore a circumnavigation should be possible. Scientists calculated the size of this round earth but, from using incorrect measurements, made it smaller than it is.

In 1492, Christopher Columbus calculated that on this smaller earth a western route straight across the Atlantic to the East Indies must be shorter than the eastern route around Africa. When he discovered the islands of San Salvador, Cuba and Haiti that October he called the area the West Indies, believing he'd arrived in the Indies by this western route. It's said that 'When Columbus left he didn't know where he was going; when he got there he didn't know where he was; and when he came back he didn't know where he'd been.' There is a certain truth to this but, without any doubt, his voyages rank among the great discoveries in mapping the world.

Five years later, in 1497, John Cabot departed Bristol in *Matthew* on 20 May. He sailed south around Ireland and then westward across the Atlantic to North America. He first sighted what is probably Cape

Breton Island about 24 June, turned south as far as Nova Scotia and landed near Cape Bauld or Cape Degrat. Cabot then sailed back north and east along the coast of Newfoundland, recording the amazing numbers of fish there. He lowered overboard a basket weighted with stones and pulled out basketful after basketful of cod. Having marked the position of Newfoundland, Cabot returned to Bristol. Yet if Cabot wasn't the first to North America, and Columbus not the first to cross the Atlantic, who were the first discoverers and just who were the earlier men of Bristol?

As far as is known, the Vikings were the first Europeans to reach America. From Norway and Denmark in their longships and sturdier halfships, they made numerous voyages west between AD 700 and 1066. They invaded and settled Scotland, England, the Faroes, Ireland, Freisland and Normandy, and Iceland around 870.

In AD 982, Eric the Red, son of a Norse chieftan, was banished from Iceland for three years for murder. He sailed westwards to discover and settle Greenland. Bjarni Herjolfsson sailed even further west in 986 and sighted more land, but it wasn't until the explorer Leif Ericsson, Eric the Red's son, sailed west in 1003 that a landing was made. Leif discovered Baffin Island, then sailed southwards along the coast of mainland Labrador to reach Newfoundland and Nova Scotia.

Leif Ericsson called Newfoundland 'Vinland', after the wild vines and grapes which then grew there. He stayed just one winter before returning to Greenland. There is a later voyage by Leif's brother, Thorvald, who wintered in the same houses built by Leif. He was attacked by native Canadians and was killed by an arrow in one of those skirmishes.

There are spurious claims for other discoverers of North America. St Brendan the Navigator is one. He may have reached Iceland (the Vikings found Celtic monks living in Iceland when they landed around 870) but Brendan's voyage times and distances make claims of a North American discovery impossible, even of Newfoundland. The great English explorers of 880 sailed north and east, not west. Ohthere sailed around the top of Scandinavia to reach Archangel in Russia while Wulfstan sailed through the Baltic to explore the Prussian and Estonian coasts. Another Atlantic myth concerns Madoc, a Welsh prince, reputed to have established a North American colony in about 1170. It's a good story based on no known facts.

Contact with Greenland ceased during the Great Plague which ravaged Europe in the 1300s, and the Viking settlements died out. It was then that the fabled islands of Antilia, the Seven Cities and Hy-Brasil appeared on charts of the Atlantic Ocean, as cartographers sought to record half-remembered fragments of past knowledge and myth.

Columbus believed in the existence of Antilia and the Seven Cities – placed in various positions west of the Canary Islands, Spain and Portugal. He hoped to find the Antilias on his way to the East Indies. The division of the West Indies into the Greater and Lesser Antilles derives from this myth. Columbus also believed in the existence of Hy-Brasil, which was usually placed somewhere to the west of the British Isles. It's probably a Celtic name meaning Isle of the Blest or Fortunate Isle. There's no connection with St Brendan and none with Brazil in South America, which the Portuguese named after a red dye tree.

It was Hy-Brasil that the men of Bristol thought they'd reached when they discovered land far west of Ireland in the 1400s – before Columbus sailed west. Its position was lost, searched for in many voyages from Bristol, then found again in John Cabot's voyage of 1497. It was North America.

In the 1400s, Bristol was the second seaport of England and its merchants and seamen had a taste for adventure. Their fishing boats sailed regularly to Iceland for the important cod fishery and their merchant ships traded with Flanders, France, the Basque country, Spain, Portugal and into the Mediterranean. As early as 1440, merchant Robert Sturmy sent two Bristol ships to the Middle East, to open a direct spice trade and circumvent the middlemen of Genoa. They were wrecked by storms, but he repeated the attempt in 1458. On that occasion they were destroyed by corsairs hired by Genoa. In response, King Henry VI arrested and fined every Genoese merchant in England.

The Bristol trade with the Basque country in Spain was particularly important. The Basques were then great seafarers, trading all over Europe from Bristol to the Canary Islands, from the Azores to Egypt. To Bristol, the Basques brought wine, iron and oil; from Bristol they shipped fish and English cloth.

Seamen from both Bristol and the Basque region took part in the discoveries of Madeira (1419), the Azores (1432–53) and the Cape Verde Islands (1459). Bristol seamen also took part in the Spanish conquest of the Canary Islands in 1451 and received grants of land there, while Basque seamen accompanied Columbus to the West Indies in 1492. Bristol seamen and merchants were common figures in Bilbao, Lisbon, Seville and Cadiz, the major Basque, Portuguese and Spanish ports.

It is recorded in Spanish documents of the 1400s that Bristol seamen were known for being interested in Atlantic voyaging. It's also recorded in Basque documents that Bristol seamen had made a transatlantic discovery, and for this discovery even a date is given – before 1465. Those documents support a Bristol oral tradition of the 1400s, where Bristol seamen discovered a land to the west of Ireland which they reported as Hy-Brasil.

British documents record voyages from Bristol specifically in search of Hy-Brasil in 1480 and in 1481. There may also have been a voyage in 1482, for the sailing licence issued in 1480 was for three years. A letter to the King of Spain from his envoy in London states that Bristol sent out ships in search of Hy-Brasil in 1491, 1492, 1493, 1494, 1495, 1496 and 1497. Accepting that the earlier Spanish and Basque documents are correct, supported by the Bristol tradition of a discovery, then these nine or more voyages from 1480 to 1497 must have been attempts to rediscover – not discover for the first time – this land west of Ireland.

The renewed Bristol interest in Hy-Brasil was almost certainly caused by a threat to its Icelandic fishery. Since 1470, the more than 100 cities of the continental Hanseatic League trading alliance had increasingly challenged England's interests in the Icelandic fishing grounds. English ships were forced to sail fully armed and clashes at sea with Hanseatic ships were frequent. There were undoubted economic and military pressures to find a new fishery.

If there had been no evidence of land in the 'green sea of darkness' west of Ireland, it's very unlikely Bristol merchants would have borne the expense and danger of even a single voyage of exploration, let alone nine or ten. Unlike its seamen, Bristol merchants had no tradition of exploration, only of fishing and trade. However, when that vital fishing trade was seriously threatened, if the merchants and seamen of Bristol had known that there was land with a *fishery* to the west of Ireland, then they would have been prepared to take the expense and danger of nine, ten, or any number of voyages to find it again.

The voyages of 1480 and 1481 also carried ice. Ships searching for new lands did not carry ice; ice was for preserving fish and was carried by ships expecting to find a fishery.

King Henry VII's response when John Cabot claimed the Newfoundland fishery for England is also significant. Cabot was immediately summoned to court, rewarded with ten pounds and granted a pension of twenty pounds a year. This was a very generous income in 1497, especially to a foreigner. Although his ship and crew were from Bristol, Cabot himself was from Venice.

Further, the envoy in London for the Republic of Milan reported in 1497 that this new Newfoundland fishery 'could bring in so many fish that this kingdom [England] would have no further need of Iceland'. Henry VII immediately announced a larger expedition of several ships to Newfoundland the following summer, led by Cabot.

It was the fishery that was important to Bristol, it was fish the Bristol ships were after, and it's evident that the merchants and seamen of Bristol knew of this fishery west of Ireland. It falls to Bristol merchant John Day to provide the confirming evidence.

John Day and the Lord Grand Admiral of Spain were in communication with each other, there being no war between Britain and Spain at that time. There survives a letter from Day written in Spain towards the end of 1497 replying to a letter from the Grand Admiral. There were then two Lord Grand Admirals of Spain; one was Don Fadrique Enriquez, the other was Christopher Columbus.

Enriquez was an administrative rather than a sailing admiral. There are no records of any interest in Atlantic voyaging and records suggest he was not in Spain at this time. Columbus on the other hand was a sailing admiral who was vitally interested in Atlantic voyaging. He was in Spain in 1497, and two documents that the Grand Admiral asked Day to provide are known to have had an important influence upon Columbus. One is Marco Polo's 'Travels', a copy of which Columbus passed to his son and is now in the Columbus Library in Seville. The other is 'Inventio Fortunata', a 1340 English manuscript in Latin about an imaginary journey to the North Pole. John Day sent 'Travels' to the admiral but did not have the other manuscript. It seems likely that the Grand Admiral was Columbus rather than Enriquez, though it is the detail in Day's reply to the Admiral that is most important.

John Day gave an amazingly accurate account of Cabot's Bristol voyage of 1497 to North America. As requested, he provided voyage times, distances, weather, compass variation, positions of the new lands relative to positions in Ireland and Bordeaux, its topography, Cabot's landings, details of the English claim, artefacts discovered, and information about the fish along the coast. He also sent with the letter a copy of a map of the discoveries, since lost.

John Day first referred to Cabot's discovery as 'the Seven Cities Island', but finished his account with: 'It is considered certain that the cape of the said land was found and discovered in the past by the men from Bristol who found Brasil as your Lordship well knows, it was called the Island of Brasil and it is presumed and believed to be the tierra firme that the men from Bristol found.'

This is a very clear statement, not an aside, or vague gossip with which to round off a letter. Day's letter also reveals that the Grand Admiral was aware of John Cabot's little-known and unsuccessful first voyage from Bristol in 1496.

Columbus almost certainly visited Bristol in 1477 during a voyage to Iceland. In his journal, he describes the high tides found at Bristol, the second highest in the world. If the Grand Admiral who wrote to Day is Columbus, then it's possible he heard of this earlier Bristol discovery while he was there.

Everything that Day wrote to the admiral about Cabot is confirmed by other surviving accounts of 1497. Day provides more exact detail because he himself was a Bristol merchant and shipowner. In fact, he was in Bristol when Cabot returned that summer and almost certainly spoke to the seamen who made that great voyage. Every merchant in Bristol would have talked to Cabot and his crew: they had returned with a position for Hy-Brasil.

It is illogical to disbelieve John Day's information and the Spanish Admiral's knowledge of the earlier Bristol discovery but at the same time believe and accept all Day's other statements – Cabot's discoveries, Cabot's first voyage, Marco Polo's book, his business in Spain, the rest of the letter, all confirmed by other sources. Day could not have invented his statement about the earlier discovery because it was already known to the admiral: 'as your lordship well knows'.

Day's letter confirms the earlier Bristol discovery, supported by the Spanish documents, the Basque document of a Bristol transatlantic discovery before 1465, and the nine or more Bristol voyages from 1480 to 1497 sent specifically to find Hy-Brasil. The question is not 'if' but 'when' did men of Bristol discover North America?

The Basque documents categorically give the discovery as before 1465. Day's statement in Spanish is written 'en otros tiempos' – literally 'in other times'. In fourteenth-century Spanish this phrase meant at least one generation or a quarter of a century in the past, as opposed to merely a few years ago. That puts the date at least to the 1470s. The surge of exploratory voyages from Bristol began in 1480, indicating that the discovery took place before then. The Bristol tradition of an Atlantic discovery does not specify a period, except that the tradition was in existence well before 1490 and, probably, before 1477 when Columbus visited Bristol.

Whichever date is correct, the important fact is that *all* are before Christopher Columbus's 1492 voyage to the West Indies. The sequence of European discoveries of the Americas is thus: Viking Bjarni Herjolfsson sights north America, Leif Ericsson lands in North America, Englishmen of Bristol rediscover North America, Christopher Columbus discovers and lands in the West Indies, Central and South America and claims them for Spain, and John Cabot lands in North America and claims it for England.

How did those men of Bristol discover and then *lose* Newfoundland? Although Bristol ships traded near and far, it was along established shipping routes. The original Newfoundland discovery was probably accidental, a fishing boat blown westward in a storm.

The passage between Bristol and the Icelandic fishery was made around the west of Ireland. Iceland itself is west of Ireland, and the English fishery of Snaefellsnes was further west of Iceland again. A boat returning from Snaefellsnes may easily have been blown further west by an Atlantic storm, sighted Newfoundland and returned to Bristol with a description of the new land and the amazing numbers of fish. There are records of these easterly storms, the last being 1962–3.

As for 'losing' the new land, while the Bristol crews of the 1400s were very capable seamen, their navigation was medieval, relying still upon primitive compasses and lead lines. The new scientific instruments of navigation – the quadrant, the astrolabe and the log line – were in use by Genoese and Venetian navigators, but it's extremely unlikely that a Bristol fishing boat or even a merchantman would have been able to afford them, or known how to use them. In 1497, it was John Cabot's navigation which determined the comparative latitudes of Newfoundland and Nova Scotia with Ireland and Bordeaux, not Bristol navigation.

Losing Newfoundland in that 'green sea of darkness' of the vast Atlantic was as easy for the men of Bristol as rediscovering it was difficult.

Recommended
The Principal Navigations, Voyages and Traffiques of the English Nation by Richard Hakluyt.
The Argument for the English discovery of America between 1480 and 1494 by David B. Quinn.
New Light on the 1497 Cabot Voyage to America by L.A. Vigneras, The Hispanic American Historical Review, Vol. 36, No. 4.

Lisa Potts

The unknown man ran along the fence dividing the nursery from the infants' areas, having taken the long way around to St Luke's School from his nearby flat. He was carrying a grey bag across his shoulder. In the bag, there was a sixteen-inch-long machete, a smaller knife, a bottle of petrol and two iron bars. As he came around the corner of the school building, he took the machete from the bag.

In front of him by the fence three mothers had come to collect their children: Reena's mother, Surinder; Wendy Willington; and Fatama's mother, Azra. On the other side of the fence, packing up their end-of-term teddy bears' picnic, were the children from the nursery, teacher Dorothy Hawes and young Lisa Potts. Lisa was the nursery nurse, as well as a popular 'Sunny Owl' at the nearby Merry Hill Brownies.

Without warning, the man lifted his arm and brought the machete down upon Wendy Willington's head. She dropped her carrier bag and fell to the ground.

'Quick, run inside!' ordered Dorothy Hawes, shepherding some of the children towards the nursery building.

Blood poured freely from Wendy's head. At the sight of it children and parents began to scream. Dorothy pushed some children inside while Lisa Potts gathered those around her and also made for the nursery. The man – tall, black and wearing a trilby with a chin strap –

lifted the machete again and smashed it upon Surinder's head. Surinder half-turned away before she, too, collapsed to the ground. Then he brought the blade down upon Azra. There were then three women lying by the fence with terrible, shocking wounds. The man leant over the fence and tried to grab one of the nursery children, but the child ran away.

Children clustered around 21-year-old Lisa Potts, screaming and crying her name, lifting her long skirt, trying to hide beneath the black pleats from the terror of the playground. As she ran, pushed and carried them towards the nursery door, the man leapt over the low fence.

It was 8 July 1996. Just four months after the Dunblane school massacre in Scotland, where sixteen children and their teacher had been murdered by a mad gunman.

'The man's lips were drawn back and there was the most frightening, angry grimace on his face,' Lisa recalled. 'It was as if he was laughing.'

Lisa shoved the children with her through the open doorway of the nursery and saw Dorothy Hawes with more children inside. She realised immediately from the numbers that there must still be several children outside, so she went back to the playground. The man saw her and rushed up to her, his right arm raised high, his face bent down against hers.

Lisa lifted both arms to protect her head from the descending knife. The machete struck along and into her left arm. Yet she didn't feel any pain, only wetness inside her red cardigan. Within the sleeve, though, her left arm and hand were cut half through, her ulna bone sticking through her skin, and the hand hanging from its tendons. She started to bleed, although her main artery was not severed.

Lisa turned away and grabbed and pushed more children through the doorway. The huge knife lifted again. It swung down towards the neck of Francesca, the little girl clutching Lisa's skirt. Potts threw out her injured left hand to divert the blow; the blade skimmed past her fingers and slashed across Francesca's face and jaw, opening the whole of her left cheek from ear to mouth. The child's eyes glazed over. Waving the machete in the air, the man wheeled away and ran across the playground while Francesca dazedly walked through the doorway and into the Reception classroom.

Children were running around the playground in complete panic. The man approached Philippa Parlor's daughter, Emma, but her mother threw her sideways, away from the flashing blade. Philippa grabbed her two children and another child and ran them into the toy shed, where she held the door against the man's attempts to force it open.

Meanwhile, Lisa gathered more children and pushed them into the nursery building. Only two children remained in the playground – Marium and her younger brother, Ahmed. Ahmed was only a visitor to St Luke's nursery school that day; his actual enrolment was after the summer holidays.

Lisa Potts then faced a very difficult decision. Should she go into the nursery, close and lock the door to ensure the safety of all the children sheltering there, or should she return again, herself severely injured, for Marium and Ahmed? It was one of those defining moments, a decision which can determine the rest of a life. She turned back into the playground.

The two little children came screaming and running towards her, with the man at their heels. Marium cannoned straight into Lisa's legs, crying: 'My brother! My brother!' There was blood spattered over the play-safe tiles of the playground. Ahmed tripped and fell and the man raised the machete.

Lisa swooped on Ahmed, scooped him into the crook of her damaged left arm and lifted him away. Down came the machete above Ahmed, across went Lisa's uninjured right hand to stop the blow. The blade sliced into Lisa's hand and cut open the top of Ahmed's head. She turned for the nursery, with Marium at her feet and Ahmed in her arm. She ran in but could not close the door behind her; the man had a foot in the jamb, wedging it open. Now there was blood running freely from Ahmed's head and from both of Lisa's hands. The young boy was conscious but very quiet in her arms.

To one side of the vestibule was the half-glass panelled door to the Reception classroom with twenty-five children, temporary teacher Linda, injured mother Wendy and Francesca with the terrible wound to her cheek. In the vestibule itself were cupboards and the children's dressing-up trolley, while on the other side was the passage to the nursery. Behind Lisa was the man, gradually forcing the outside door open. In that small vestibule with Lisa, Marium and Ahmed were another six or seven children, their frantic screams piercing into Lisa's brain. Among them was Surinder's daughter, Reena, with blood upon her face and her right cheek sliced open from another swipe of the machete in the playground.

Inside the Reception classroom Linda made the difficult decision to hold the door closed in order to protect the children inside. She yelled to the headmistress to telephone for the police and ambulance. At the same moment Lisa Potts also understood that she could not lead the man that way, not with all the children inside, and removed her hand from the door handle. She lay Ahmed on the floor at the side of the dressing-up trolley and covered him with clothes to hide him.

The man burst through the outside door and blocked the passage to the nursery. They were trapped. The machete in his hand lifted once more and the children screamed. Lisa bent over and gathered the children to her, protecting their huddled bodies with her body and her bloody arms. 'I shall die here,' she thought.

Down came the machete, once, twice, onto her back. 'Miss Potts! Miss Potts!' the children screamed. The man turned back to the outside door.

Somehow, Lisa was still alive. Her body flooded with adrenalin, so the pain she felt was minimal, mainly a deep throbbing from the wounds to her arms. She ordered, pushed, kicked and shoved the children into the passage to the nursery. From the corner of her eye she saw Ahmed's small feet sticking out from the clothes. The man had not noticed him. With Marium clinging to her skirt, with the wounded Reena under one arm and another child under the other, Lisa forced the children along the passage. The man saw the movement and turned back once more, racing after her.

Another blow from the machete cut Lisa Potts down the back of her head. That she did feel; a quick, sharp pain. She continued running, herding the children to the nursery. Square in the way was a large water tray. Severely wounded, carrying two children and with Marium hanging to her skirts, Lisa hurdled the tray and ran across the nursery to the far door which led to the main entrance of the school.

Blood began to pour from her head, changing the collar of her white linen blouse to crimson. She glanced behind. There were all the beautiful colours of the nursery – the decorations for the children's last day of school – and the extra red of her blood on the floor. Otherwise the room was empty. The man was gone.

Pushed by Lisa, the children went through the doorway and into the main entrance to the school. 'Where's the man?' people were crying. 'Where's the man?' Lisa took the children to the head teacher, where her secretary took charge of them.

'Oh no, Lisa!' the head teacher said at her wounds, and took her into the main building and through the dining hall, where parents and children cried in alarm at the sight of her. Her blonde hair was red and the trail of her blood spattered the floor. There, and in the three other classes at the infants' end of the school, teaching was still going on, no one realising what had happened in the nursery school. The attack had lasted for less than five minutes.

Lisa was taken into the activities area where towels were wrapped around her arms and her head and her back to try to stem the bleeding. The new Reception teacher for next term was there, like Ahmed attending the school just for the day. 'What a day to visit!' Lisa said to her brightly.

A mother ran through: 'This man's got a gun, he's going to kill us all!' she screamed. 'I don't think he has,' Lisa said calmly, 'I didn't see a gun,' but thought: 'If he has come back with a gun there's no way any of us are going to survive.'

Two policemen ran in. 'Are you all right?' one asked, the standard question for people in shock. 'Yes, I'm fine,' Lisa replied, nodding her bloody head. He looked at her closely. 'Is this his?' he asked, showing her a grey shoulder bag. 'Yes.' They passed through. Then an ambulance arrived.

'Do you need a stretcher?' asked an ambulance man. 'No, I can walk.' Lisa didn't want the children to see her lying on a stretcher; they might think she was dead. She walked to the white ambulance parked at the main entrance to St Luke's School.

Already inside the ambulance was Francesca. She lifted her head and looked at Lisa with huge eyes. 'Miss Potts,' she mouthed. Reena and her mother joined them, and a policeman drove the ambulance to Wolverhampton's New Cross Hospital while the ambulance men treated the wounded in the back. Ahmed was in a second ambulance with the other two wounded mothers. Lisa talked to the children all the way, telling them of the 'special plasters' the hospital had which would make all of them better.

Lisa Potts required four hours of surgery that evening to save her left arm and hand. In all she had five severed tendons, a multiple fracture requiring a metal plate, a chipped skull, deep cuts and two long lacerations down her back. Francesca had a metal plate inserted into her jaw and stitches, while Reena, Ahmed and the three mothers, Wendy, Surinder and Azra, required multiple stitches. Lisa was in hospital for nine days before being allowed home to convalesce.

The machete man was quickly found, arrested and charged. In his trial several months later, he was found guilty of the attempted murder of four adults and three children. He was sentenced to life imprisonment and ordered to be detained indefinitely in a secure hospital. During the year following the attacks, Francesca, Reena, Ahmed and Lisa received many local and national awards and commendations for their courage.

In June 1997, it was announced that Lisa Potts, 21-year-old nursery nurse of Wolverhampton, had been awarded the George Medal 'for absolute bravery' in 'saving the lives of three children'. In a ceremony on 13 November at Buckingham Palace, with her family watching, Lisa was presented with her George Medal by Her Majesty the Queen.

At the time, seventeen months after the attack, Lisa still suffered nightmares, flashbacks and chronic post-traumatic stress disorder. She'd also had a further three operations on her left hand. Since Lisa's award only four further George Medals have been awarded. All were posthumous.

Recommended
Behind the Smile by Lisa Potts, with Jill Worth.

The Men of Colditz

There were two qualifications for Allied soldiers to be sent to Colditz Castle as prisoners. They had to be officers and they had to have escaped before. Men who had tunnelled out of other prisons were sent there. Men who had walked out dressed as guards, labourers and even women were sent to Colditz. In that way, the Germans managed to assemble a group of the most imaginative, determined and experienced enemy officers *in one place*. In that context, it is perhaps not so surprising that when the prison was finally relieved by American soldiers in 1945, they found a fully working glider in the attic, ready to go.

The interned soldiers were all allies, whether from Poland, Canada, Holland, France, Belgium, Britain or, towards the end, American. However, there was always the chance of a 'stool pigeon', a man planted by the Germans to spy on the prisoners. Security had to be tight, even among their own men. It is astonishing now to consider that the Colditz prisoners constructed realistic identity papers, uniforms, disguises, a typewriter, keys and tunnel equipment from the few supplies they had or could steal. Their beds were straw mattresses over boards that found use in shoring up tunnels, false doors and cupboards and even as carved guns and glider wings. For tunnel lamps, they used candles made from cooking fat in a cigarette tin, with a pyjama cord wick.

Colditz, known to the Germans as 'Oflag IV-C', had been used in World War I to hold prisoners and is about a thousand years old. One side overlooks a cliff above the River Mulde. Situated in the heart of the German Reich, escapees had to cross four hundred miles of hostile territory in any direction. The walls were seven feet thick, but the first escape attempts involved Canadian officers just picking up buckets of whitewash and a long ladder and walking out, pretending to be painters. They were quickly recaptured, then kicked and battered with rifle butts. The stakes were always life and death for those who tried to escape and despite the schoolboy quality of some of the attempts, it was never a game. In the 'Great Escape' from Stalag Luft III in 1944, fifty out of the seventy-six escaping officers were caught and shot.

The garrison at Colditz always outnumbered the prisoners. The entire castle was floodlit at night and as well as a hundred-foot drop on one side, there was a nine-foot barbed-wire fence, a moat and a thirteen-foot-high outer wall. The Geneva Convention enforced the humane treatment of prisoners, at least in theory. German officers were interned in England and there was a joint benefit in avoiding brutal treatment. Food and Red Cross parcels were allowed in at irregular intervals and the prisoners could send carefully censored letters home. They could buy essential supplies, such as razor blades for shaving, toothpaste, soap and even musical instruments. They were allowed to cook for themselves on small stoves in the dormitories.

The day began at 7.30 a.m. and was organised into four daily roll calls in the main courtyard. At first, the largest contingents were Polish and British. From those, there were a variety of talents available to escape teams, from lock-pickers and forgers to civil engineers. There was a theatre in the castle and they put on elaborate productions and musicals while in Colditz. One of the posters for a performance was replaced by the following: 'For Sunshine Holidays, visit Sunny Colditz, Holiday Hotel. 500 beds, one bath. Cuisine by French chef. Large staff, always attentive and vigilant. Once visited, never left.'

The prisoners were allowed to exercise three times a week, from fencing to football and boxing. They were even allowed to keep a cat. When it vanished, the prisoners assumed it had gone to find a mate, until its body was discovered wrapped in a parcel in the camp bins. For all the surface gentility of their treatment, savagery was always close by. The last roll call was at 9 p.m., at which point the 'night shift' began – the escape committees of Colditz.

In January 1941, a British tunnel plan was put into action with the construction of a sliding box to go under floorboards. Even if the floorboards were taken up by investigating Germans, the theory was that the rubble-filled box would look solid enough and hide the tunnel below. It passed inspection shortly after construction and the guards saw nothing suspicious. However, the tunnel was abandoned as too easy to find. The men involved were locked into their room after some minor offence and in protest, unlocked and removed the door from its hinges, carried it around the camp in slow procession and presented it to the German officers.

Pat Reid, MBE (later MC and author of *The Colditz Story*), spent part of a night in the Colditz brick drains, working to break through a wall. Taking turns with Rupert Barry and Dick Howe, they spent several nights scraping with bits of steel and nails. The underground bricks and cement proved tougher than their improvised tools. Another manhole entrance to the sewers looked more promising and the men used the canteen as a base, having made a key for the door out of a piece of an iron bed. They made better progress, but found the way blocked by thick clay. Reid's next idea was to make a vertical tunnel from the first, so that it would be possible to go some way from the buildings underground before heading for the outer wall.

On a surprise night inspection, the absence of the working tunnellers was discovered and the commandant told the men in the dormitory they would all be shot. The Germans began tearing up the floor and summoned dogs to search. The dogs found nothing and Reid had to hang on to a manhole from underneath as guards tried to lift it. He and the others constructed a false wall in the tunnel, hiding their supplies behind it. After that, they returned in darkness to their beds. The

Germans were astonished to have them reappear at morning roll call and the commandant was criticised by his superiors for a false alarm.

After that, the Germans seemed to discover the tunnel location suspiciously quickly, though they did not breach the false wall. The presence of a German spy, or 'stooge', in their midst had to be considered and security grew tighter.

The camp population increased in 1941. Around two hundred and fifty French officers arrived, then sixty Dutch and two Yugoslavs. In addition to those, the escape committees now included Irishmen, Canadians, Australians, New Zealanders, Jews and an Indian doctor. They were united by a common enemy and had to keep each other informed so that one escape attempt did not ruin another.

Some of the British contingent found a guard who was amenable to a trade in contraband goods. They bribed him to look the other way for a crucial ten minutes of sentry duty. Eight Britons and four Poles prepared to use the still-undiscovered first tunnel they had dug in the drains. Cutting a square of earth from below, Reid was the first out into the courtyard, but a floodlight came on instantly. He was surrounded by armed Germans – tipped off by the guard they thought they had bribed to silence.

Other attempts followed. French labourers carried a British officer, Peter Allan, in a straw mattress being taken to soldiers' quarters in a local village. A fluent German speaker, Allan made it to Vienna and even spent part of the journey with an SS officer who gave him a lift. In Vienna, he was refused help by the American Consulate, at that point not in the war. Exhaustion and starvation saw him taken to a local hospital where he was arrested and sent back to Colditz for solitary confinement.

Around the same time, a French officer, Lebrun, made it to the local station before being apprehended. Lebrun was an athletic and determined escaper, however. In July 1941, during his exercise period, he leaped the outer wire with the help of a friend who made his hands into a stirrup. Lebrun then climbed the wire from the outside and used it to get over the outer wall. He stole a local bicycle and cycled between sixty and a hundred miles a day, posing as an Italian officer. He avoided capture and crossed to Switzerland seven days after his escape. From there he made it to the Pyrenees before he was taken prisoner by the Fascist Spanish and broke his back jumping from a window. Crippled, Lebrun survived the war. His belongings in Colditz were later received at his French home in the parcel he had made and addressed before his escape.

Two Polish officers tried the perilous climb down the outer cliff, but were discovered and captured by a German who heard the noise and opened a window right by their rope of tied sheets. In his excitement, he shouted for them to put their hands up, which they couldn't do without letting go of the rope.

Meanwhile, the British prisoners had begun another tunnel. They had home-made compasses, copied maps, rucksacks and some rare German money, smuggled in with new arrivals to the castle. They created civilian clothing by altering RAF uniforms. Twelve men were to escape, but that too failed when the Germans discovered them.

The Dutch contingent was more successful in 1941, managing to smuggle six men over the outer wall and wire in pairs on successive Sundays. Four out of six reached Switzerland safely. The other two were sent back to Colditz.

Winston Churchill's nephew, Giles Romilly, was sent to Colditz towards the end of 1941. He was closely guarded, though at one point he almost escaped, disguised as a French coal-worker unloading supplies. Towards the end of the war, when Germany was losing badly, the 'Prominente', or famous prisoners, were moved to a prison camp at Tittmoning, with the intention of using them as hostages. Romilly and two others escaped Tittmoning with the help of Dutchmen he had known in Colditz. One of the three was recaptured, but Romilly eventually made it back to England after the fall of Germany.

By December 1941, the inhabitants of Colditz had managed to get hold of some yeast and began brewing beer from anything organic, sitting on the jars and bottles for hours on end to promote fermentation. After that, they created a still and made 'firewater' that the Poles called vodka, of a sort. With Christmas on the way, they had quite a good collection of different vintages.

As a trained engineer, Pat Reid had become the official 'Escape Officer' for the British contingent. He noticed that the theatre stage overlapped a floor below that led to the German guardhouse. He approached Airey Neave and J. Hyde-Thompson to take part in a new plan. Neave said that only the Dutch could make realistic German uniforms, so two Dutch officers were brought in for the attempt. They made uniform buttons, eagles and swastikas by pouring molten lead into intricately carved moulds, then attached them to adapted Dutch greatcoats, which were similar to the German ones. Leather belts and holsters were cut from linoleum and they carried well-forged German identity documents.

Reid and a Canadian, Hank Wardle, cut through the ceiling of the room under the stage, camouflaging and repainting a removable hatch with great care. They were experienced lock-pickers and the doors beyond gave them no trouble. It went like a charm. Airey Neave and the Dutchman Tony Luteyn went first and Hyde-Thompson and the second Dutchman followed the next night. As Escape Officer, Reid could not go himself – his skills were too valuable. The Germans discovered they were missing four men and began to search the castle.

Neave and Luteyn crossed to Switzerland, making Neave the first Briton to escape from Colditz successfully. He went on to become a Conservative MP in 1953 and later served as a minister in Margaret Thatcher's opposition government. Tragically, after surviving so many perils, he was killed in a car bomb planted by Irish Republicans a few months before the 1979 election. His book describing the Colditz escape is a great read: *They Have Their Exits*. Hyde-Thompson and his companion were caught and returned to Colditz.

The Germans discovered the stage hatch with the help of a Polish informer whom they controlled by blackmail. The Poles discovered his identity and their senior officer gave the commandant a day to remove him before they hanged him themselves.

As 1942 crept by, the French contingent worked on a tunnel that had its entrance in the clock tower. They also sent out one Lieutenant Boulé, who was dressed as a beautiful blonde woman. The disguise was rumbled when 'she' dropped her watch and a guard returned it. The Dutch tried one large man sitting on the grass, hiding a smaller man beneath his coat while he dug a shallow grave. Dogs discovered him before he was missed.

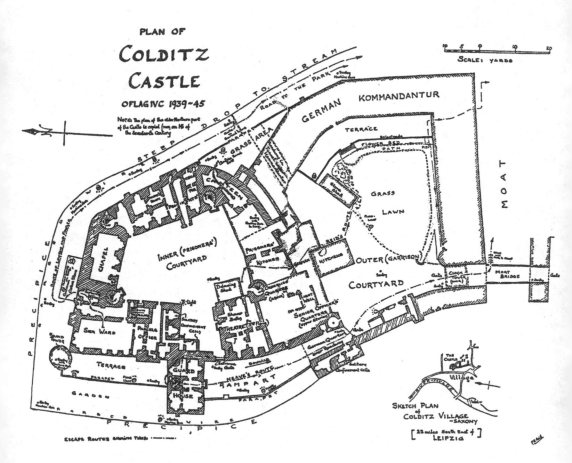

By that time, there were sixty British in Colditz. One of the best known, Douglas Bader, arrived during 1942. Morale was dropping with the number of failed attempts and so few successes. Two officers went insane and had to be restrained from committing suicide. Another feigned madness in an attempt to get himself sent to Switzerland. Bader's presence helped morale no end. For a man with artificial legs, he was irrepressible and announced he was ready to join an escape over the roof of the castle.

Squadron leader Brian Paddon was removed from Colditz around this time to be court-martialled at another prison camp. He escaped his guards and was the second Briton to reach England. Other attempts were less successful, but they went on continuously. Pat Reid planned an escape through the commandant's own office, with the help of a Dutch watchmaker who could get through the more complex locks. Reid began a tunnel under the commandant's desk, working at night. When the time came, eight men assembled in the office and six broke through to a storeroom, leaving Reid and Lieutenant Derek Gill to hide the route. They were all dressed as German soldiers and their 'sergeant' was saluted by the guards as they walked out the following morning. Of the six, four were recaptured, but two made it to Switzerland by September 1942.

Pat Reid's final escape plan came when Dick Howe took over as Escape Officer and he could make a try for himself. Reid joined Ronnie Littledale, William Stephens and Hank Wardle in a run over the roofs. Split-second timing was the key as they had only instants to cross a courtyard when the patrolling guard turned. The noise of their run was covered by an orchestra practice which Douglas Bader conducted. Bader could see the vital sentry and the plan was for him to stop the music whenever it was safe to run. However, the Germans became suspicious and stopped the practice halfway through. The escapers reached the outer buildings safely, but were then unable to go further when a prepared key failed to open a vital lock. Reid found an unused basement with a very narrow, barred chimney to the outside. To get up it, they had to strip naked, then pass up their kits and redress on the other side. They crossed the moat, barbed wire and outer wall with sheet ropes, then set off in pairs. Reid and Wardle covered the four hundred miles in four days of train journeys and walking. All four made it to Switzerland safely.

In the four years of its use as a prison camp, more than 300 escape plans were attempted and of those, thirty-one ended in a 'home run'. The German habit of returning escapers to the same place meant that as often as they lost a potential route out, they learned from the experience of those who made it furthest. Vitally, the repeated attempts also tied up German soldiers and resources which would otherwise have been used fighting the Allies.

After fierce fighting, the castle was relieved by American soldiers on 15 April 1945. One of the last British plans was revealed behind a false wall in the attic – a working wooden glider with a wingspan of thirty-three feet.

Recommended
The Colditz Story by P.R. Reid, as well as the sequel,
The Latter Days at Colditz.
Reach for the Sky by Paul Brickhill.
They Have Their Exits by Airey Neave.

The Unknown Warrior

It is evening on the Western Front. The year, 1916; halfway through the mud and carnage that is the Great War. An army padre serving in France returns to his billet.

'I came back from the line at dusk. We had just laid to rest the mortal remains of a comrade. I went to a billet in front of Erkingham, near Armentieres. At the back of the billet was a small garden, and in the garden, only six paces from the house, there was a grave. At the head of the grave there stood a rough cross of white wood. On the cross was written, in deep black-pencilled letters "An Unknown British Soldier" and in brackets underneath 'of the Black Watch'. It was dusk and no-one was near except some officers of the billet playing cards. I remember how still it was. Even the guns seemed to be resting. How that grave caused me to think.'

The Reverend David Railton wrote to the commanding officer of British Armies in France and Belgium, Sir Douglas Haig. He proposed that the body of a soldier should be removed from the western front to Britain for burial: one soldier to represent all the dead of the British Empire and Commonwealth, to help 'ease the pain of father, mother, brother, sister, sweetheart, wife and friend.' Understandably, in the middle of a four-year war, there was no reply, but the concept of the Unknown Warrior had begun.

Railton survived the war and in 1919 was appointed vicar of St. John the Baptist in Margate, Kent. He left the army with the Military Cross and the memory of that evening in France. He'd thought further that such an unknown soldier should be buried only inside Westminster Abbey, because that great abbey – first dedicated in 1065 – was the 'Parish Church of the Empire', of a third of the world. In August 1920, he resubmitted the idea to the Dean of Westminster, Dr. Herbert Ryle. He in turn approached the King, the Prime Minister and the British Army, writing: 'There are thousands of graves...of 'Tommies' who fell at the front – names not known. My idea is that one such body (name not known) should be exhumed and interred in Westminster Abbey, in the nave.'

King George V was at first doubtful, suggesting that almost two years after the end of the war such a funeral 'now might be regarded as belated'. However, he was persuaded the idea would work and, on the 18th October, the Dean received a letter informing him of His Majesty's approval and of the suggestion that the burial should indeed take place on the next Armistice Day, 11 November 1920. From that day BBC radio and newspapers throughout the Empire, Commonwealth and the world carried regular reports of the project.

How was an Unknown Warrior to be selected from the more than one and a-half million dead British and Empire soldiers, sailors and airmen? How would he reach Westminster Abbey?

The desperately sad process of locating, identifying, transporting to war cemeteries, and re-burying the British and Empire dead along all battle fronts is carried out by the Commonwealth War Graves Commission, then under the command of Brigadier-General L. J. Wyatt. He gave orders that on 7 November, 1920, the bodies of four servicemen should be exhumed from the four great British battlefields of the Western Front; one from the Somme, one from Ypres, one from Arras, and one from the Aisne. Each must be from a grave marked 'Unknown British Soldier', each must be wearing a British uniform, and each must be placed in identical bags.

Four unknown servicemen were brought that evening by field ambulances to the St. Pol headquarters and there taken into the chapel. Each of the ambulance parties left immediately and returned to their base. At midnight, Brigadier-General Wyatt and Colonel Gell entered the dim, lamp-lit chapel. Wyatt wrote later:

'The four soldiers lay on stretchers, each covered with a Union flag; in front of the altar was the shell of a coffin which had been sent from England to receive the remains. I selected one and, with the assistance of Col. Gell, placed it in the shell and screwed down the lid. The other bodies were removed and re-buried in the military cemetery outside my headquarters at St. Pol. I had no idea even of the area from which the body I had selected had come; and no-one else can know it.'

Thus the soldier or sailor or airman was selected at random. The name of the man, his age, his regiment, his rank, where he died – all was and shall remain forever unknown.

In Britain, meanwhile, a special coffin was commissioned. It was made of oak from a tree in the grounds of Henry VIII's Hampton Court Palace. Around the coffin were forged wrought-iron bands, secured to the lid was the sword of a knight of the Crusades, selected by the king from the Tower of London. Carved into the lid was the inscription:

'A British Warrior Who Fell In The Great War 1914-18
For King And Country'

In Westminster Abbey, the nave was prepared. Flagstones were raised and a grave dug in the centre of the aisle, in pride of place, directly inside the Great West Door.

A quiet service was held in the St. Pol chapel by chaplains from the Church of England, the Non-Conformist Churches and the Roman Catholic Church. On 9 November, the coffin shell of pine was carried by field ambulance and escort to the Chapel Ardente in Boulogne, where it was placed inside the oaken coffin brought from Britain. There the Unknown Warrior rested overnight with an honour guard of British and Dominion soldiers. Brigadier-General Wyatt also sent six barrels of earth from the Western Front with which to cover the coffin in its Westminster grave, so that the Unknown Warrior 'should rest in the soil on which so many of our troops gave up their lives.'

On the morning of the 10th, the coffin was carried to HMS *Verdun*, berthed at Gambetta Quay, for the Channel crossing. Lieutenant-

General Sir George MacDonogh represented the king; Marshall Foch represented the French government.

The procession following the coffin was more than a mile long, of French infantry, cavalry, disabled soldiers and children. More people lined the roadsides to the quay. The destroyer *Verdun*, launched in 1917, was chosen because she was named after the Battle of Verdun of 1916.

Halfway across the English Channel, as *Verdun* entered British waters, six Royal Navy destroyers met and escorted her into Dover. Unbidden, gathering slowly during the day and waiting in silence, thousands of people lined the quaysides of the ancient port. A 19-gun salute was fired – a field marshall's salute, the highest military honour – and a band played. The coffin was transferred into the same railway carriage that in 1919 had carried home the body of Edith Cavell, and borne to London.

During the war some 1¼ million wounded soldiers, sailors and airmen had passed that way, but the passage of that serviceman was particularly poignant. The *Daily Mail* wrote of the journey through Kent: 'The train thundered through the dark, wet, moonless night. At the platforms by which it rushed could be seen groups of women watching and silent, many dressed in deep mourning. Many an upper window was open and against the golden square of light was silhouetted clear cut and black the head and shoulders of some faithful watcher... In the London suburbs there were scores of homes with back doors flung wide, light flooding out and in the gardens figures of men, women and children gazing at the great lighted train rushing past.' This serviceman returning might just be their missing serviceman – their brother, father, son or friend.

The bridges over the line were also packed with silent watchers, the steam and smoke from the engine shrouding them as the marked carriage passed beneath. When the train drew in to Victoria Station, more people thronged the platforms and concourses. There the Unknown Warrior remained overnight with an honour guard of the King's Company, Grenadier Guards.

On the morning of 11 November, 1920, at 0915, the Unknown

Warrior was carried to a gun carriage pulled by six black horses. Draped over his coffin was a very special Union flag on which were placed a British helmet and side arms. The flag was the property of the Reverend Railton and it, too, had seen action. It was the flag which Railton had used as an altar cloth for makeshift services and for the celebration of Holy Communion along the Western Front.

From Hyde Park, the Royal Artillery fired a 19-gun salute. Twelve of the highest ranking officers – led by Admiral-of-the-Fleet Earl Beatty and Field Marshall Earl Haig – attended as pall bearers. Following the carriage were the mourners, including 400 ex-servicemen of all ranks. All that had been arranged.

What had not been arranged – like the men and women on the quayside at Dover and the silent watchers along the railway line – were the thousands and thousands of silent people standing along the kerbsides and pavements of London. From Victoria Station up to and along the Mall, through Admiralty Arch and down Whitehall, the mourners watched and paid tribute. One unknown soldier, sailor or airman returning home at last to represent the million and a half still lying in Belgium, France, Germany, the Middle East, Africa, the Pacific Islands, in all the seas; and, especially, the hundreds of thousands with no known grave.

At the newly-erected Cenotaph – created in the same vein of remembrance as the Unknown Warrior, and meaning literally 'empty tomb' – King George V stepped forward and laid his own wreath of roses and bay leaves on the coffin. His hand-written card read: 'In proud memory of those warriors who died unknown in the Great War. Unknown and yet well known, as dying and behold they lived. George RI'

There followed a hymn, a simple prayer, and then from Westminster the deep chimes of Big Ben proclaimed 11.00 hours; the eleventh hour of the eleventh day of the eleventh month, the moment the Armistice was effective in 1918 to end the Great War. On the eleventh chime, the King released the two Union flags covering the Cenotaph and the tomb was unveiled for the first time. There was a two-minute silence in Whitehall and all across the kingdom – from London to Belfast, Cardiff to Edinburgh, Land's End to John O'Groats. A lone bugler played the forlorn notes of The Last Post, 'calling to them from sad shires'.

The procession resumed along the crowded, silent streets of the capital, the King and the Prince of Wales walking behind the Unknown Warrior in his final journey through London and into Westminster Abbey. The congregation of that parish church that day was 1,000 widows and mothers of men killed in the war, the nave lined by 96 holders of the Victoria Cross. The oaken coffin entered the Abbey by the North Door. It was carried by the pall bearers through the Quire, along the length of the Nave, to the grave immediately inside the Great West Door. The choir sang 'I am the resurrection and the life, saith the Lord.' Dean Ryle conducted a simple service.

To the soft singing of the traditional 'Lead, Kindly Light' the Unknown Warrior was lowered into his grave, there to lie forever amidst the kings and queens, princes and poets, the writers and composers, and other saviours and preservers of freedom.

King George stepped to the grave. From a silver shell he scattered earth from the Flanders' battlefields on to the coffin: 'Earth to earth, ashes to ashes'. The service was completed by the Reveille: the Union flag from the Western Front was draped over the pall.

By the time the Abbey closed its doors at 11 that night more than 40,000 people had paid their respects to the Unknown Warrior, leaving wreaths, flowers and single poppies around him and around the four servicemen standing honour guard. Tens of thousands more visited the Cenotaph. There, silent lines of men, women and children wound throughout the misty November night, leaving a sea of wreaths. Two wounded soldiers walked sixty miles to lay wreaths to their comrades.

On the morning of the 12th – unrehearsed – the silent pilgrimage to the Warrior in the Abbey resumed.

It had been thought to close the grave after three days, but that had to be delayed. A chorister at the service, Reginald Wright, wrote: 'A feature that lives vividly in my mind was that, after the service was over, thousands upon thousands of people streamed into the Abbey hour after hour, day after day, and when they got to the grave they cast their red poppies onto it. Gradually, the area became a mass of red poppies.'

In the first week, more than 1¼ million people passed the grave of the Unknown Warrior, mourners from the Channel Islands, England, Ireland, the Isle of Man, Scotland, Wales, and from the countries abroad. A policeman recorded: 'One old lady came from the far north of Scotland. She carried a bunch of withered flowers, and told me with tears in her eyes that the flowers came from a little garden which her boy had planted when he was only six.'

On 18 November the grave was finally closed and filled with the earth from the battlefields of the Western Front. A temporary marble slab covered the opening, on which was inscribed 'A British Warrior Who Fell In The Great War 1914-18. For King And Country. Greater Love Hath No Man Than This.' Again, the Union flag covered the tomb. The mourners continued their pilgrimage for almost a year, leaving their flowers, poppies and tributes.

For the following Armistice Day, in 1921, David Railton's Union flag was removed from the tomb and dedicated at the High Altar to all those men and women of Great Britain, Ireland and the Dominions who had died in the Great War. It now hangs permanently in St. George's chapel, to the left of the Unknown Warrior. Its removal revealed the permanent tombstone, the stone that lies there today. It is of black marble from Belgium, inscribed with words composed by Dean Ryle set in an inlay of brass from melted down shell casings. It reads:

BENEATH THIS STONE RESTS THE BODY
OF A BRITISH WARRIOR
UNKNOWN BY NAME OR RANK
BROUGHT FROM FRANCE TO LIE AMONG
THE MOST ILLUSTRIOUS OF THE LAND
AND BURIED HERE ON ARMISTICE DAY
11 NOV: 1920, IN THE PRESENCE OF
HIS MAJESTY KING GEORGE V
HIS MINISTERS OF STATE
THE CHIEFS OF HIS FORCES
AND A VAST CONCOURSE OF THE NATION

THUS ARE COMMEMORATED THE MANY
MULTITUDES WHO DURING THE GREAT
WAR OF 1914-1918 GAVE THE MOST THAT
MAN CAN GIVE LIFE ITSELF

FOR GOD

FOR KING AND COUNTRY
FOR LOVED ONES HOME AND EMPIRE
FOR THE SACRED CAUSE OF JUSTICE AND
THE FREEDOM OF THE WORLD

THEY BURIED HIM AMONG THE KINGS BECAUSE HE
HAD DONE GOOD TOWARD GOD AND TOWARD
HIS HOUSE

The text at the end of the inscription is adapted from the Second Book of Chronicles, chapter 24, verse 16.

Within the borders of the tombstone are inlaid four other texts: across the top, 'The Lord Knoweth Them That Are His'; along the left 'Greater Love Hath No Man Than This'; across the bottom

'In Christ Shall All Be Made Alive'; and along the right, 'Unknown And Yet Well Known. Dying And Behold We Live'. Around the borders of the grave are banked poppies of red silk, the red poppies that grow in profusion over the British battlefields fought in the defence of Belgium, France and a free Europe.

Other nations have followed suit with their own Unknown Warrior or Unknown Soldier tombs. France, obviously the first country to be aware of the British intention, copied the concept the same year with a burial at the Arc de Triomphe in Paris.

The United States buried her Unknown Soldier at the Arlington Military Cemetery in 1921. That same year, the United States awarded the first Unknown Warrior the Congressional Medal of Honour while Great Britain awarded his American counterpart the Victoria Cross. On the northeast pillar of Westminster Abbey by the Unknown Warrior hangs the ship's bell of HMS *Verdun*; on the southeast pillar hangs the Congressional Medal of Honour. Australia, Canada and New Zealand recently have made their own commemorations so that their subjects, too, have in their country an unknown serviceman returned home to represent all those lost abroad.

The tomb of the Unknown Warrior lies in one of the most beautiful buildings in all the world. Above rises a fan tracery of vaulted stone, inspired soaring curves which flow throughout the building to link the intricate roofs of the many chapels into a single harmonious church. The tomb below is purposefully simple, unpretentious, humble, requiring no triumphal arch, no eternal flame, not even a railing.

Yet it is the only grave in the floors of Westminster Abbey that is never walked on – by anyone, at any time, in any service. Coronations, weddings, baptisms, funerals all proceed around it.

Today, the Unknown Warrior has come to represent the dead of all conflicts, of the 1914-1918 Great War, the 1939-1945 World War, those between and all those after; the men, the women; at home and abroad.

'And when we die,
All's over that is ours; and life burns on
Through other lovers, other lips.'

(Rupert Brooke, 1887–1915)

Recommended
The Story of the Unknown Warrior by Michael Gavaghan.
The Unknown Warrior and the Field of Remembrance
by James Wilkinson.
Westminster Abbey, City of Westminster, London.

Heroes

When someone rows across the Atlantic, conquers Everest, or runs seven marathons in seven days, they are admired across the world. Our lives are gladdened by the achievement and we feel that they have done something great. They are heroes because they inspire the rest of us, even if it's just for a moment.

Yet there is a second definition, that a hero is one who accomplishes something noble, risking it all in the process. Nelson may be the best example, as he lost his life defending against a tyranny that would have overrun the world. Most people can see the difference between Nelson and a cricket team winning the Ashes, or a football team winning the World Cup.

At no point do those definitions suggest a hero must be likeable. The heroism is in the life, in the achievement across just a short span of years, not in the man or woman themselves, and whether they were a good friend, father or mother. Good men sometimes do bad things and it is even possible that many great lives come about to atone for some sin, real or imagined, in the past.

When the word is overused, it does reduce its impact, but that is not necessarily a bad thing. We cannot all stand against tyranny, though perhaps more of us should when we encounter its cold hands on a daily basis. Yet if a man is described as a hero for saving a child on a frozen lake, most of us can see we could be that man. It is heroism within the bounds of possibility.

Being aware that courage is still admired is not a danger to society – far from it. A 'have-a-go hero' is a popular phrase for one who risks life and limb to stop a mugging or burglary, or even to have a word with a few kids causing trouble. It is an obvious truth to say there may be risk involved in such an action, but if every good man or woman turned away with eyes downcast, well, that would scorn the memories of Edith Cavell, Robert Scott and Douglas Bader, who would have waded in, metal legs or not.

However we abuse the word, heroism will never be common or easy. The peculiar truth about humanity is that we deal with fear on a daily basis and that it often conquers us. That does not matter as long as you recognise there are times when you must not 'step off the kerb' to let someone pass or something terrible happen.

It is true that only a coward can be brave, as a man who feels no fear has conquered nothing. It is also true that when one person speaks up to stop some wrong, others often join in, desperately relieved that, at last, someone said something. It is not easy to be the one to speak up, or the one to step in. If it were, we would not value and admire those who do. One final truth remains beyond the petty irritations of life in which we lose ourselves: all that is necessary for the triumph of evil is for good men to do nothing.

The men and women in this book were sometimes possessed of incredible self-confidence and personal belief. Others doubted their every action to the point where they could hardly act at all. For some, their heroism is contained in a single moment, while others seem to have lived a life that stands out like a thread of gold. It may not be possible to live like Nelson, but we can be inspired by his life and others like it. We can know that in our history is the blood of greatness, and in our culture, for all its flaws and dark misdeeds, there can also be light.

Index

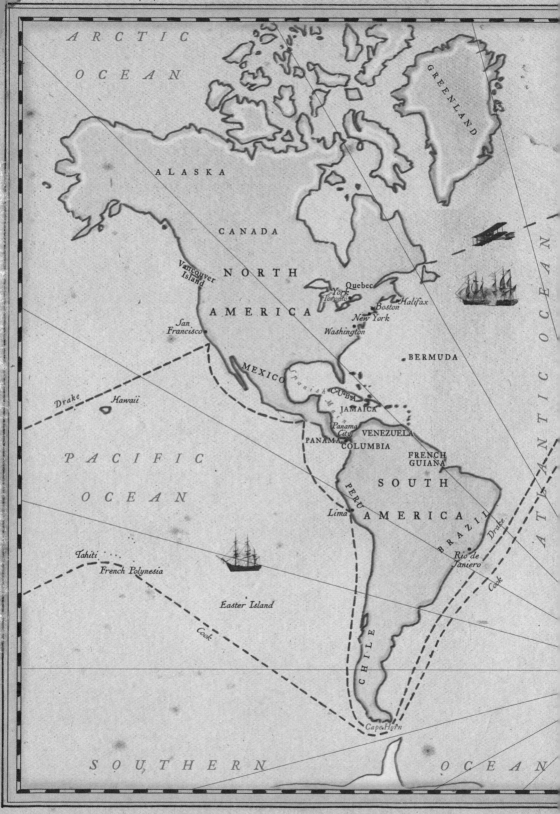

ARCTIC OCEAN

GREENLAND

ALASKA

CANADA

NORTH AMERICA

Vancouver Island

Quebec
York
Toronto
Boston
Halifax
New York
Washington

San Francisco

BERMUDA

Drake

Hawaii

MEXICO

Spanish Main

CUBA
JAMAICA

Panama City
PANAMA
COLUMBIA

VENEZUELA

FRENCH GUIANA

PACIFIC

OCEAN

SOUTH AMERICA

PERU

Lima

BRAZIL

Drake

Rio de Janiero

Tahiti
French Polynesia

Cook

Easter Island

CHILE

Cook

Cape Horn

SOUTHERN OCEAN

ATLANTIC OCEAN

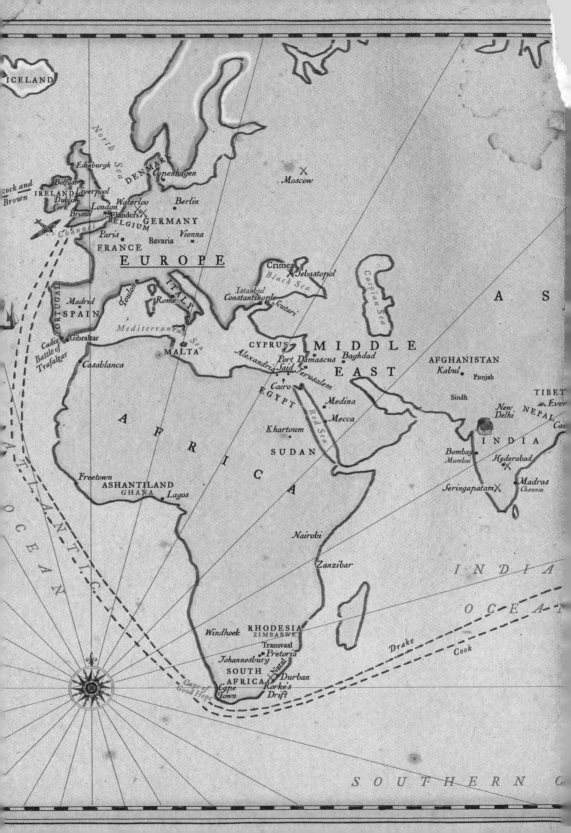